OTHER WORKS BY BROOKE MEDICINE EAGLE

Buffalo Woman Comes Singing:
The Spirit Song of a Rainbow Medicine Woman

THE LAST GHOST DANCE

A GUIDE FOR EARTH MAGES

BROOKE MEDICINE EAGLE

Daughter of the Rainbow of the Morning Star Clan
Whose Helpers Are the Sun and the Moon
and Whose Medicine Is the Eagle

Ballantine Wellspring
The Ballantine Publishing Group
New York

A Ballantine Wellspring Book
Published by The Ballantine Publishing Group

Ballantine is a registered trademark and Ballantine Wellspring
and the Ballantine Wellspring colophon are trademarks of Random House, Inc.

The Earth Mages Unlimited logo is a trademark of Brooke Medicine Eagle.

www.randomhouse.com/BB/

LIBRARY OF CONGRESS CATALOGING-IN-PUBLICATION DATA
Medicine Eagle, Brooke.
The last ghost dance : a guide for earth mages / Brooke Medicine Eagle.
p.   cm.
Includes bibliographical references.
ISBN 0-345-40031-3
1. New Age movement—United States.   2. Earth—Religious aspects.   3. Indians of North America—Religion.
4. Medicine Eagle, Brooke—Religion.   I. Title.
BP605.N48   M44   2000
299'.7—dc21   00-040380

Text design by Holly Johnson

Manufactured in the United States of America

These teachings are dedicated,
with much love and
continuing gratefulness,
to Stephen.

I also want to honor
the Dawn Star
of this new day on Earth,
Master of Love,
through whom this teaching comes,
and
Dawn Boy,
who dances
love and power into the world
along the shimmering edge of Spirit.

*Who would have thought
the dancing could make such trouble?
For the message I brought was peace.
And that message was given by the Father to all tribes.*
—*SHORT BULL*
Brulé Sioux Ghost Dance leader of the 1890s

CONTENTS

CONTENTS

LIST OF EXERCISES

CHAPTER 13

CHAPTER 14

CHAPTER 15

PREFACE

We are in the time of the New Ghost Dance.
—A Message from an Old Woman of the Earth
Brought through by Carol Aitchison

All of us alive on Lady Gaia at this time have the opportunity to be an active part of the Rainbow of Light that creates the bridge into a new and Golden Time for All Our Relations and us. At this point in human history, we have the opportunity to literally bring Heaven to Earth. Our ability to visualize and believe that it is possible for us to lift ourselves up, to pick up the profound work of our Earthly ancestors and move responsibly into our own piece of the action, and to fully embody Spirit is what will make this ascension possible. The exciting part is that we have the opportunity to complete something Mother Earth and humanity have been working on for aeons.

The Rainbow Bridge to a renewed Earth was first shown to me in a vision given me by White Buffalo Calf Pipe Woman, the mysterious holy woman who came many generations ago to a small group of Lakota people, bringing the Sacred Pipe that represents the Oneness and holiness of the Circle of Life. She, whose name is often shortened to White Buffalo Woman, has been an inner guide and teacher to me and to many others of this generation, as her wisdom invites us to walk in a sacred manner on Earth, honoring All Things, not only as our family, but literally as part of our wholeness.

This particular time, she took me to stand at the edge of an enormous chasm made of black, shiny stone and asked me to look around. Looking across the gap, I saw a sight that thrilled my heart. On the other side was a radiantly golden world. Everything had an iridescent aura, like we sometimes see on a spring morning after rain when the dew picks up the many-colored light. There were people and animals there on a broad, flowering plain under crystal snowcapped peaks—with no sound but a soft breeze and happy laughter. Out of the sacred groves of enormous trees on the hillsides came rushing pure, clear water. Children and young animals played there together, splashing and laughing and drinking the water without fear. Two-leggeds went about peacefully and joyfully, developing and exchanging their gifts and talents, taking in the radiant energy for nourishment and nibbling for their sweet taste the fruits and plants that grew about them in profusion. Happy songs of birds and people and the calls of contented animals echoed across. It was a glorious place—a golden dream for us and All Our Relations. I yearned to go there.

Then I turned to look behind me and was aghast at what I saw. There was smog on the horizon and acridness in the air, which I could see was harming all the living things upon which it settled, for everything had a dull, gray hue. There was arguing and fighting and warring, repression and prejudice, with everyone grasping what they could for themselves while snarling at others. Noise—screeching and pounding and roaring—filled the air. The scream of chain saws bespoke cutting the precious trees on the hills. Everything possible was being eaten, which made the people heavy yet did not nourish them. The lost, homeless, dispossessed, and sick lay all about, with many dying at the feet of those who hurried past. People wandered about, seeming alone and frightened even among their own kind. The deep hunger and need and grief of all filled the air.

I wanted desperately to get to the radiant life on the other side of the chasm. Yet as I leaned cautiously to peer over the edge, I could not see the bottom: the dark, slick rock dropped out of sight in the mist on both sides. The gap was much too wide to jump, and I had no other means to cross. A wailing cry erupted from my throat as I realized I could not get there.

All the while, White Buffalo Woman had stood beside me. Now she looked at me with compassion and said, "The bridge upon which you will cross into that beautiful life on a renewed and flowering Earth will be a bridge of light." Then she sent from within herself a rainbow of light that jumped across the chasm to rest on the other side. "To make a bridge, the light must become a rainbow. It is the only way!"

I looked at her, still in desperation, because I did not know how to make a rainbow.

"To make a rainbow, all colors of light must be included. None can be left out, or there will be no bridge." And she went on to help me understand the deeper meaning of this symbol she had given me: "When I say 'all colors,' I am referring to all things, all peoples, all beings. None can be left out. You must walk a sacred walk, acknowledging, honoring, respecting, communing, and cooperating with all things and beings in the Circle of Life. No one, nothing, can be left behind. You must live a life of inclusiveness, union, and sharing—letting the Light of Love flow freely among you. When all are included in a good way, the discordant song will become harmony and the light will automatically become a rainbow. Thus, all of you who are alive *become* the rainbow upon which the generations cross into this new and Golden Time.

"The rainbow also represents another aspect of our movement into this new time: lightening up! It reminds you that you will find joy and happiness by creating them through singing, dancing, and celebrating together in gratefulness for the beauty Creator has given. You must release your heaviness and those things that burden you—lifting your attitude, practice, and vibration to a higher level. You must let what you love and what brings joy call you forward from moment to moment, for in no way can you bring this radiant time by doing things that displease or de-energize you. Rather than working for it, *you must dance your lives as the old ones did.* Nurturing ceremony and joyful celebration will be not only the hallmarks but also the means into this wonderful future."

This vision, which affected me so poignantly then, still calls to me deeply. That iridescent scene of a renewed Earth beckons me every day of my life. I seek to unroll that dream before me as I walk, as one would lay out a beautiful carpet. Having stepped forward, I realize that the polluted scene lives within me as well as outside of me, and that, for me, awakening the dream into reality means cleansing myself of the attitudes, beliefs, and actions that comprise it, in order that I may invite others to do the same.

I also realize that the beautiful, iridescent place already exists on a certain plane of reality. It is the gift Creator has offered us from the beginning of time, if we will only cleanse the smog from our eyes and choose that sacred path.

Now, another vision has joined this one—a vision of another Rainbow, half of which has already been created and sent forth. During the time of European expansion and aggressive conquering of the Americas, Father Spirit sent a Messianic vision of this radiant land on "the other side" to a succession of tribal people, the most famous of whom was a Paiute named Wovoka, who shared it with the natives far and wide. They were shown a radiant life similar to that which White Buffalo Woman opened before me. Their visions came over a four-hundred-year period when subjugation, decimation, and finally genocide were taking place among American native peoples. The white man's greed for land and wealth was laying waste to the native tribes. Their lives were shattered, their homelands ravaged, the buffalo slaughtered and rotting in the sun, their families murdered, their dreams broken.

These radiant visions, and the Christ figure known as Dawn Star who brought them, gave the ravaged people renewed hope, offering them a way to re-create an even more beautiful life. Through the Spirit Dance they had been given, they would bring to life their golden dream. Their murdered relatives would walk again on green and flowering land; all that was destroyed would be made whole. It was to be a new world in which Earth and spirit are as one. So in the latter days, they made the shirts shown in Wovoka's vision, using what little leather was left or flour sacks from the meager rations given them on the new reservations; and they circled in the entrancing dance that was shown them. They called upon their loved ones, so many hundreds now on the side of Spirit, to lift them up into this radiant dream. They danced that golden dream into the ground, set it into the reality of the Earth plane, made their half of the Rainbow. Then even that dream was shattered. At Wounded Knee, innocent, peaceful people of the Ghost Dance were murdered by the cavalry because the fearful white nation did not see the peaceful, beautiful dream that could unfold from it.

Arapaho Ghost Shirt

Those dancers lifted into Spirit, to hold their half of the Rainbow until we of the present human generation could awaken and dance the other half into the ground of reality in this world. The vision White Buffalo Calf Pipe Woman gave me is the same vision; it has been given into the hearts and minds of many of this generation — it is alive and well. The Ancient Ones and native peoples have known and held these powerful dreams down through time. Although they seem to fade with our attention on other things, a fine, strong thread connects us to them. Our present task is to draw their essence forth and to weave a web of beauty upon which to dance our lives.

We can use our understanding of the past to move forward into our future. Whatever "facts" and knowledge I bring to you are meant as a way of grounding these prophetic principles in Earth clothing. Although you will undoubtedly learn from this book, it is not primarily instructional; instead, its purpose is inspiration and empowerment. It comes from the deep knowing that life is unfolding something marvelous and miraculous, and that the more quickly and completely we embrace this opening with our understanding, our trust and joy, and take our own personal action, the sooner the unfolding magnificence will spring full and bright into our everyday reality. Far greater energies are moving than what I can humbly describe in these words: *The ages and the aeons are coming around to fullness, to fulfillment of prophecies more ancient than time, as universal as the very Source of All Life.*

In the beautiful words of our modern prophet Ken Carey,

Listen, O humans of this present world: listen as the sparrow listens for her lover's call upon the breeze. We are speaking to you in your dreams, in snatches of song heard in passing, from the mouths of children, from these pages and words, but more than this, we are speaking to you from the center of your innermost being. Hear us, and remember yourselves.

We have come to initiate the most joyous age this Earth has ever known: a thousand year period of Earth healing and renewed harmony that will see the four-legged flourish, the two-legged awaken, the rivers run pure, and human-kind in conscious exchange with the stars.[1]

I chose the art for the cover, *Rainbow Sundancer,* as a metaphor that expresses the dance of life for we who choose to enter new levels of awareness for an awakening humanity. This artistic expression is a portrait that all of us are being invited to make our own. Vera Louise Drysdale[2] gave expression to her vision of an uplifted humanity through the traditional symbol from Native American culture; my approach is the same, yet the picture of a new world I paint in this book is one for all cultures, all peoples, each of us alive in this time on Mother Earth. The time has come for each of us, in our own personal and cultural way, to become an enlightened dancer of life: a fully awakened two-legged, creating and celebrating a renewed and flowering Earth!

This painting contains many levels of symbolism that I wish to share with you. First, it presents the interdimensional realms of the modern-day shaman: the *Earth mage* (magician) of whatever race, sex, or color.

It reflects our profound connection with all of things of Earth and demonstrates how Earth magic allows us to transcend the old image of Earthly life, thus bringing a radiant, spiritual presence into our Earth dance. In this way we become fully human—embodying *Spirit in balance with Earth* within ourselves.

The spirit dancer wears the horns of the shaman, who has the ability to dance in both worlds: the world of form and the world of the Shimmering Invisible. With the light of the Dawn Star in his heart, he offers that radiance out to the world through extended hands. Standing grounded in the pure and clear waters of the garden of Turtle Island, he brings down the Light of Spirit, and radiant wings are his gift. This spirit warrior stands poised on the Rainbow Bridge between Song and Light, at the point of power where we can dance beauty and abundance, unity, and joy into reality in the realms of Lady Gaia.

The sacred mountain rising in the background is red to symbolize the blood, the life force that lives in All Our Relations, and the moon brings in the sweetness of a clear night complementing a brilliantly sunny day. The dancer wears a skirt of red as a dedication to All Our Relations, and an apron of iridescent feathers to represent the Rainbow that contains all things, all beings, all realms. His evergreen head wreath represents the greening of a renewed Earth, and the flowers depict the flowering of life of Earth.

The *Rainbow Sundancer* painting reminds us that the Sun Dance is a dance done by men and women honoring the Light of Father Spirit, which gives us and our world the flowering of life from year to year; all primary cultures have such a dance of yearly renewal. By contrast, the Ghost Dance is the ecstatic dance that invites our ancestors' help in the new century's awakening of a renewed Earth, with the full flowering of Spirit in each individual. Here we see that to form the Rainbow Bridge, the Sun Dance must be blended with the Ghost Dance. These powerful rituals must now come together in one great ceremony, one eternal dance of renewal for Mother Earth and all her children.

Through this book, I am extending an invitation to you to step into the last Ghost Dance and the joy and beauty that will result from taking your part as a responsible creator, a partner in aliveness—*an Earth mage* who does positive Earth "magic" in service of All Our Relations. For it is as we bring these profound ways of being into our everyday Earthly life that we have enough magic to ascend to higher levels of functioning. It is a process, not of leaving Earth (rising above or beyond her) but of tuning in to Spirit alive, and thus rising *with* Earth and All Our Relations. Those who wish to remain with Earth on her journey into a higher level of being must choose to elevate their vibration to match hers. White Buffalo Woman and Dawn Star have told us that this vibration is one of harmonious resonance, of unity, peace, Love, and true Oneness. Those of us who choose this uplifting path of the heart will feel the richness, joy, and prospering that will be magnified through our actions.

Our time of awakening has come. It is the time for the *new* Ghost Dance, which in fact becomes the *last* Ghost Dance. This time we will be able to dance the vision fully into the ground of Earth and make it real. This book takes you with me on a journey toward that renewing dance of life, toward the bright new world that awaits us and All Our Relations.

—*BROOKE MEDICINE EAGLE*
Flathead Valley, Montana
Dawn of the new millennium

ACKNOWLEDGMENTS

I first of all want to thank Sparrow Hawk's family for allowing me to share his story, which is an intimate part of their lives as well as mine. It is a gift that speaks of their love for All Our Relations, which they express in their daily lives as well. Aria, thank you for holding the vision you have always held of Pavo and the shining model it will become in the world through your gifted voice and hands.

Most special thanks to my editor, Cheryl Woodruff, editorial assistant, Mindy Im, and the folks at Ballantine who had the courage and foresight to hang in there while this teaching came into form and who did such a fine job of creating a beautiful book from my pages of words.

My appreciation continues to grow for my agent, Wabun Wind, who has stood by my side as well—encouraging, advising, and coordinating in her usual loving and supportive manner. I am comforted in this remarkable and challenging process by her expertise.

Wonderful people have invited me to places of great beauty and have supported my life as I worked on this book over the years. To them, I owe very special thanks: Al Smith at our home ranch in Montana, Gail Elman and Dreaming Bear, Dayana Jon and Deep Bay Center, Mariah Wentworth and Richard Gerstner of Rainbow Hearth Sanctuary, and Gail Fitzhugh at the ancestor canyon in Arizona. *Aho, aho, aho!*

Much gratefulness goes to Rob Cox and James Redfield, for the work they have done that has elevated my understanding of this new dance of life on Earth—by sharing the ancient information that is now emerging to guide us. And to all the other teachers and leaders on the road sharing the news of a renewed and flowering world.

ACKNOWLEDGMENTS

For the cover artist, Vera Louise Drysdale, I have profound appreciation. Her expressions are filled with awareness and light, and *Rainbow Sundancer* seemed destined for this book. Her daughter, Linda Victoria, has worked with me to carry forward her mother's wishes for the uses of this beautiful art.

Thanks, too, to all my friends, family, teachers, and guides who supported me in this process—those in body as well as those in spirit: White Buffalo Calf Pipe Woman, Dawn Star, Stephen Lyman, Andrea Lyman, Tim Casady, Spotted Eagle, Grandfather Winston, Judith Star Medicine, Chief Joseph, Grandma Mary Allee, Karen McMullen, Heron Wind, my assistants Jan Myers and Pam Weivoda, Tek Nikerson, Co Carew, Hal and Shirley Jones, Mike Rubey, Carol Aitchison, Grandfather Fools Crow, Charla Hermann, John Tarwater, Falcon Von Karls, Jyoti Haney, Wendy Walsh, Ora June Big Back, James Buchanan, my loving ancestors, those who walk the peaceful way of FlowerSong, and all the Ghost Dancers who held the vision of a bright new day that we are now dancing into reality on this sweet Earth.

To the Ghost Dancers of the past, we are the seventh generation.
It is our joyful task to ground again in the Earth
their vision of renewal, to vitalize and nourish the seed
that was planted long ago.
As did the dancers of old, we vibrate the Mother Earth
with our dancing feet,
stepping to the rhythm of an ancient song to bring a radiant
and renewed Earth.

PART I

AWAKENING THE DREAM

We sometimes are awakened to our most profound lessons by the challenges Creator gives us. This is the story of such a summons in my life, and of the magnificent gifts it brought for me and All My Relations. I wish to share them with you, my two-legged family.

All of the names and places in this story have been changed to honor the privacy of Sparrow Hawk's family.

CHAPTER I

THE FALL

In taking each other as sisters, we were enacting
a deep and profoundly important truth:
that we are sisters to all things feminine.
And on a wider scale, it was a holy remembering
of our Oneness with all things.

"Are you sitting down?" Al asked me when I picked up the phone. It was a very strange thing for him to say, and I knew immediately that something was terribly wrong. I was surprised to hear his voice because I was about to fly out of Salt Lake City after doing a workshop in the area, and only ten minutes before, I'd checked in with him to confirm his picking me up when I arrived home. Everything had been fine then.

I immediately thought of my folks, who are both growing older and have health challenges. My heart was already pounding in the few seconds it took me to answer, "Yes, as a matter of fact, I am sitting down."

"Well, you'd better be," he said. "Sparrow is dead."

"*Who* is dead?" I asked in disbelief. I was sure that I had heard him wrong or that he, who sometimes doesn't hear well, had the wrong information.

"Your brother, Sparrow. Sparrow Hawk."

"That can't be," I countered. "Are you sure you heard right?" My mind could not accept this. *Anyone* but Sparrow Hawk. He's young and vital, and besides, he's the kind of person we need most of all on Earth right now. Can't be him . . .

Al said, "Brooke, *listen* to me. It is him. Your good friend Wendy called because Sparrow's wife can't handle everything right now. He died in a hiking accident in Zion National Park."

There was complete silence on my end. What was there to say? It evidently was Sparrow, and my world had just blown apart.

Sparrow Hawk is my spiritually adopted brother, and his wife is my sister in the same manner. In native ways, there is a ceremony for the making of relatives called *hunkapi*; it was given to us by White Buffalo Calf Pipe Woman, the mysterious holy woman who came to the Lakota people bringing the Sacred Pipe. This pipe is a holy reminder of the Oneness and sacredness of things and represents the interconnectedness of everything in the Circle of Life. When it was given to the people, seven sacred rites were also given, one of which was *hunkapi*.[1] This is a profound and formal ceremony whose intent is to honor and commit oneself to join in a sacred relationship with someone who is not your blood relative. For instance, marriage is a primary *hunkapi*. Native people use this ceremony to honor and confirm as family not only their mate but also spiritual sisters, brothers, uncles, aunts, mothers, fathers. The ceremony is not done lightly, for I was trained to understand that we have even more responsibility toward these new family members (perhaps because we consciously choose them) than we do our actual blood family. And of course, one also gets all of the new relative's family in the bargain!

Sparrow Hawk's wife, Aria, was the one with whom I had the deepest relationship. She had first been my student, then a participant in my Eagle Song wilderness camps, then a staff person there on occasion, who over the years became a best friend. We had talked for a long time about our special feeling as sisters, and I had frequently visited her home.

Sparrow (as we often shortened his name), initially shy, disappeared into his art studio often when I visited there, so it took me a long while to get to know him. Over the years of our connection, I grew to treasure him as I did Aria. He was such a fine human being, and the more I became acquainted with him and his work, the more I valued our growing friendship.

He was one of the most simply loving people I knew. His love was like soft, mossy ground upon which you walk in your moccasins and yet hardly notice until you realize how sweet it feels to be there and then think to look down. Sparrow's deep caring was a ground of being, not something showy or loud. And his love of the natural world brought us together, too: he was a most accomplished artist, who painted the natural world with a remarkable talent.

At the winter solstice in 1995, Aria and I had done our formal *hunkapi* ceremony. She and Sparrow Hawk were building a new home—more a temple, really. It was taking many years, but the living room was complete enough for us to do our ceremony there, looking out over the beautiful Idaho landscape and down at the lake far below beyond the meadows. This was such a special place to hold our ritual—a new home and land that were dedicated to being in harmony with All Our Relations. I sensed that White Buffalo Woman's work of Oneness was being made real there, and I was happy we could formally join our lives in such a place.

The ceremony was simple yet very powerful. We had asked another woman to conduct it, so we could just enjoy participating. (Aria and I are often the ones leading ceremonies, rather than receiving them.) We began by telling stories of our initial acquaintance, our growing connection—sweet, poignant, and humorous things, as well as those that helped those gathered as witnesses understand how we had come to this special moment. Then we followed White Buffalo Woman's ancient instructions by going behind a blanket and painting each other's faces for the occasion. This part was both fun and very intimate, as we whispered together about the symbols we were sharing. When this was complete, we stepped out to make our formal vows.

In Black Elk's rendering of the ceremony, he reminded us of White Buffalo Woman's words regarding *hunkapi*. In taking each other as sisters, we were enacting (and reminding our community of) a deeper, more profoundly important truth: that we are sisters to all things feminine. Each female two-legged is our sister, as are all things feminine in all the other kingdoms and realms. *Hunkapi* is, in fact, a holy remembering of our Oneness with All Things.

The word *holy* among primary peoples does not refer to an institution such as a church, or a being such as a god in long white robes with a long white beard. It refers to the true meaning of the word from the old Latin, meaning wholeness. It is also related to *heal*. *Holy* refers to the entire Circle of Life and the oneness that characterizes our true relationship. In an individual, "holiness" might be described as the ability to hold in one's attention at all times the welfare of All Our Relations. In the words of Black Elk:

> Through these rites [*hunkapi*: the making of relatives] a three-fold peace [is] established: the first peace, which is the most important, is that which comes within the souls of men when they realize their relationship, their oneness, with the universe and all its Powers, and when they realize that at the center of the universe dwells *Wakan-Tanka*, and that this center is really everywhere, it is within each of us. This is the real Peace, and the others are but reflections of this. The second peace is that which is made between two individuals, and the third is that which is made between two nations. But above all you should understand that there can never be peace until there is first known that true peace which . . . is within the souls of men.[2]

This understanding was shared with those present and acknowledged by each of us. We spoke our commitment to each other as sisters, as lifetime family, then exchanged tokens that symbolized it: cornmeal to represent being willing to nurture each other in body and spirit, water to symbolize the purity of love flowing between us and the importance of caring for the waters of the planet, crystals for clear communication, shawls for warmth and caring for each other, and songs to offer up the energy of our hearts.

All the while, Sparrow stood in the background and beamed. Suddenly my inner perception saw his face flooded with light (which happens only when Spirit is pointing out someone special to me). I realized that I should formally adopt him as well, which was unusual because he "came along with the package" anyway. And so I called him up to stand with us and acknowledged him ceremonially as my brother. After that, Aria and I exchanged personal gifts that we had made for each other, and the formal ritual was complete. We celebrated with a feast and party. Sparrow, as well as Aria, was now officially part of my family, and we would grow closer and closer as the months passed.

All these things and more flashed before my eyes in those moments after Al convinced me that he was truly speaking of my brother, Sparrow Hawk. When I stopped crying, I asked him what had happened. "He got caught in an intense spring snowstorm while out on a 'short' hike and had to stay out overnight in freezing temperatures. He fell trying to make his way back." My mind still didn't want to accept this. Sparrow had hiked and scrambled and climbed all over Zion for most of his life. It was his spiritual home, the primary inspiration for his work. He must have been hypothermic, and this must have made him clumsy. I couldn't even begin to understand.

"Aria is in Zion now, staying at the lodge. Get in touch with her there," Al said, giving me all the details.

"Yes, I'll do that. And don't expect me home. I'll call the airlines to change my reservation, rent a car, and be there with her in a few hours. I'll be back in touch then."

My suitcases were packed, so it wasn't long before I was headed across the greening hills, past blossoming orchards, and on into the red-rock country. It was a beautiful spring day, which made the loss even more poignant. I cried and cried. I wailed. I screamed out my lack of understanding.

"Why Sparrow, Great Spirit? He was a model of the kind of human being we need on Earth. A man who exhibited love, harmony, sharing, caring. A man who was making a positive difference at all levels of his life. These are the things we need here, so why Sparrow, of all people??????" The answer to that question would change my life forever and awaken my spirit in a way I could never have imagined.

Aria and I had stood together just three weeks earlier in front of the Mayan Temple of Inscriptions at Palenque—the magnificent ruins where the plains rise to become mountains in Chiapas, Mexico. We dedicated our lives to the Light as the Lacandone elders (Mayan elders of the area) prayed with us.

"Whatever it takes for us to bring this new, Golden Time into reality on this sweet Earth, we will do it," we had said. Had we known that the loss of our precious Sparrow Hawk was what it would take, would we have been able to utter those words, make that commitment? We spoke those words as the golden light of evening lit up the drops of rain glistening all around us. The drone of the elders' voices, the jungle sounds, the calls of exotic birds—all these sang of something new and wonderful coming. Yet our faith would have been sorely tested had we known our precious Sparrow would be taken from us.

While I drove, I mourned the loss for Aria. She and Sparrow had been so in love and in such total alignment about their lives and work. I had seldom seen a couple so right for each other and so happy day to day. They were working hand in hand with builders to create their dream home on new land: Pavo, the peaceful place. After four years of intensely focused work, this home/temple was soon to be ready for their family.

I thought, too, of how it would be for the boys—now nine and ten—losing their dad, their best pal, their constant companion, their playmate and inspiration. He and Aria had spent enormous energy, time, and money helping to create a Waldorf school in their area, just so the boys could have a good education. Because Sparrow worked in his studio at home, he and the boys were together more than most fathers and sons in today's society. I pictured the three of them, bouncing incredibly high on the big trampoline in the yard as he showed them how to do flip after flip. Nine in a row was Sparrow's record. The boys were screaming with delight.

I thought of all the people around the world whom Sparrow Hawk had touched with his art, slide shows, and magnificent photographs. The way he communicated his love of Mother Earth and all Her creatures left people everywhere feeling the same inspiration and exhilaration he did when he stood high on the canyon walls, looking out across the magnificent landscape of Zion. His loss would be a very personal one for them, too.

But mostly, in those moments, I thought of myself, my own loss, the shattering of my world. I was wrenched with grief when I contemplated the fact that I had been flying home to Montana in order to get my things together and go to be with them at Pavo. For many, many years, I had been looking for a place to ground my energy, to devote myself to the land, and Pavo was beginning to feel like that place. Aria and Sparrow were putting White Buffalo Woman's ways into action in the real world by walking a way of harmony, inclusiveness, communion, and Oneness more profound than I had ever seen. They initially picked the land so that they had first water rights to clear, pure springs bursting from the southeast-facing mountainside. They wanted their home to be independent and sustainable and so were off the electric grid, using solar power for their needs.

And most important, they checked *each and every step* they wanted to take with the spirits of the land. They worked in co creative harmony, determining what would work best, not only for them but for those who already lived upon the land and for the sweet Earth Herself: where the house was to sit, where the roads crossed the land, where the garden would be, if and where a pond would be created. All these were checked in minute detail with the spirit or devic presences of the plants, animals, and other beings with whom they shared the land.[3]

Moreover, Aria had done in-depth research to make sure that absolutely *nothing* toxic was used in building, decorating, or anything else that occurred there. Pavo and all beings there were honored as sacred and worthy of the best. Sparrow was planting a small orchard in the garden area, and tall, double stands of raspberry plants would soon eliminate the need for a garden fence to keep the deer and elk out. Much of the family's food could be grown there and in the greenhouse. The forest provided healing herbs and berries. The whole place was designed to be sustainable and beautiful, honoring and cooperating with All Our Relations.

All in all, in every detail, it was the kind of place where I would be proud to give my energy. And what was exciting was that they had recently formally invited me to be a part of that community as it developed. This was something they did not do lightly, because they wanted to involve only people who would support and continue their harmonious practices. I was the only one they had asked so far, and I was thrilled to think of adding my energy to theirs in that beautiful place. At last, after all those years of looking, I had found a place that felt right to devote my energy to. Pavo was a model of all the things I'd been teaching for years. It would be home, to both my heart and my teachings.

I felt that Sparrow's death had shattered everything! I was devastated, and my mind went through the worst possible scenarios. Perhaps we wouldn't even be able to keep the land, because he had provided the primary financial support. Maybe our dream of this being a model of how to live well and happily in the coming times was not to be.

I just couldn't understand how this had happened; why Creator and Sparrow had decided that this was his time to leave the Earth plane. Pavo was the finest thing I had seen happening throughout all my travels and inquiries. Why was it being threatened? And how could this be happening to me? It was only a few short months after I'd made my "final" decision and commitment. Now what? I felt as though I'd fallen off that cliff myself, betrayed by something I could not understand. What had I done wrong? Where had my thinking been off? Above all, what was the lesson in all this? It was too dramatic an event not to be something very important. But what? Why? I couldn't conceive of any answer that made any sense whatsoever.

Then I topped the last ridge and looked into the magnificence of Zion in the dazzling spring sunlight!

CHAPTER 2

SPRINGTIME

*Now I understand that even death is safe
and that Love always surrounds each of us.*

Sparrow loved us even more than we loved ourselves.

Something shifted in me as I looked into that beautiful valley, radiant with late-afternoon sun. My heart lifted as the sweet scents of spring flowers wafted to my nostrils and birdsong filled my ears. The grandeur I witnessed, the blossoming renewal all around me, awakened a sense of new life and filled me with an inexplicable hope. I could feel a kind of delight and joy almost dancing across the giant stone walls. My worst fears seemed instantly less real; the tears on my face were now more from joy than from loss.

What the scene brought to mind was a native verse I had long known and had even sent to others who experienced this kind of loss[1]:

> Don't stand at my grave and weep
> For I'm not there; I do not sleep.
> I am a thousand winds that blow.
> I am the diamond's glint on snow.
> I am the sunlight on ripened grain.
> I am the gentle autumn's rain.
>
> When you awaken in morning's hush,
> I am the swift, uplifting rush

Of quiet birds in circling flight.
I am the soft stars that shine at night.
Do not stand at my grave and cry.
I am not there; I did not die.
—*INDIAN PRAYER*

I got back in the car and drove down into that burgeoning valley to Aria.

She came into my arms as I opened the door, and we cried gently together for a short while. Then we sat and talked about all that had happened. How she had felt an actual tearing sensation that made her really sick to her stomach at a time she later realized had been the exact moment when Sparrow Hawk flew from this Earth plane. The agony of not knowing what had happened after the call that had reported him missing. Then the news that they had found his body and the excruciating trip to Zion to formally confirm his identity. She had sat with his body, thanking it for being such a beautiful temple for his spirit, appreciating the fifteen exquisite years that they had had together.

"More even than loss, I experienced total gratefulness," she told me. "Our love is so deep and so beautiful that I feel I've had ten times that many years with him. I thanked Creator for the unparalleled gift that had been."

It was somewhat difficult to understand how she could have been so clear in that seemingly devastating moment of their last good-bye, but I soon began to understand. We walked outside and stood talking under the blossoming trees, looking up at the radiant canyon walls. When Sparrow had been lost, the temperature had dropped down to the last winter cold and snow. Now it had warmed, and life was bursting forth from every sunny nook and cranny.

"I always said Sparrow would leave this life either in his beloved garden at home or in this valley. Can you feel that Sparrow is here, everywhere? It seems to me his spirit, rather than being contained in one small body, has burst open to fill every cell, every flower, every bird, every rock in this place he loved so much," Aria said, her eyes taking in the beauty all around us.

And I could feel it, too. All around us there was Life, ever-present and abundant, glorious. I sensed Sparrow in the same way she did—free, unlimited, dancing across the canyon walls, the waterfalls, the clouds drifting through the turquoise blue sky. He seemed to be singing out, "Come, join me. Let's celebrate! Let's dance! Let's walk barefoot in the new green grass, hike up the rocky trails, sing with the frogs at Emerald Pool, swirl and play in the water." And so we did.

We lifted our faces to the spray from waterfalls that leaped off high walls because of the recent rapid melting. The boys joined us, and we walked to Sparrow Hawk's favorite camping sites, tucked away where he had private views of the magnificent scenery. We hiked up steep trails to the high points where he used to cajole us when we were tiring: "Keep coming. You can make it. It is so, so beautiful up here." He would be dancing ahead of us, a mountain goat in his favorite territory. And of course, the view would be totally worth the climb. Standing there with him, we were able to feel the power of the place and the wisdom of his coming back again and again for the inspiration it offered. We had always sworn to do the same, and yet he was the only one who actually did, some thirty or forty times in his thirty-five years.

His memorial celebration was to be held in the valley in several days, so we had many hours to enjoy that "playground of the gods." Each day the leaves on bushes and trees seemed to grow an inch. New flowers popped out, and we were greeted shyly by a jay who had made her nest on an old light fixture near our door. There was nowhere we could turn without hearing from the life around us: "New life, new life; resurrection; blossoming; the old has become new; there is no death, only the sleep of winter; the sweetness grows; all is well."

And that was exactly what we felt. Those days were filled with ecstasy and joy and communion with Sparrow rather than feelings of grief or loss. We found ourselves playing and laughing and skipping and enjoying life to its fullest. The first few days, we would look at each other occasionally and comment on the remarkable nature of our experience, but soon we forgot to do even that. Our nights were filled with stars blazing and twinkling in the sky and moonlight making shadow dances all around us. Our days were ecstatic, our sense of Sparrow's presence total and complete. Aria, eating alone in the restaurant one morning, felt and "saw" him come in and sit down with her, grinning and happy. He was wearing a favorite hiking shirt. It was one that the rescuers had not even retrieved, because they hadn't yet found the place from which he'd fallen or collected his wet, heavy clothes and cameras.

Then we began getting calls from people all around the country—everyone from close family to those who had only heard the news on the radio. They told of messages, poems, songs, and dreams that Sparrow seemed to be sending them. Some contained information very personal to the recipient; others were meant for Aria and those close to Sparrow.

One of the messages confirmed our experience there in the valley. "I never hit the ground," Sparrow said. "From the moment I fell, I was flying, and it has not stopped. This is a totally ecstatic experience, and I am fine. I know you will be, too, because now I understand that even death is safe, and that Love always surrounds each of us. My love is stronger than ever, and I am with you always." What a joy it was to receive these messages!

More reports came of transformative gifts he had given, as we shared stories and insights at the memorial held alongside the stream that runs through the valley. Looking up and out at a beautiful vista, those who arrived sad and downhearted seemed to be lifted up in the same way we were. The gathering was, as we had hoped, not funereal but celebratory; the pervading energy became that of gratefulness for having had the opportunity to spend part of our lives with this extraordinary being.

Many people shared their remembrance of experiences with Sparrow—sweet, loving, humorous, unifying, sad, and all inspiring. Then a pair of wild mallards flew into a nearby eddy, and loudly even they gave their testimonials, to the delight of everyone. We quieted ourselves to listen to the waters speak, as Sparrow Hawk had so often done when camping beside this stream. Then I shared my favorite poem, by Mary Oliver:

White Owl Flies Into and Out of the Field

Coming down
out of the freezing sky
with its depths of light,
like an angel,
or a buddha with wings,

SPRINGTIME

it was beautiful
and accurate,
striking the snow and whatever was there
with a force that left the imprint
of the tips of its wings—
five feet apart—and the grabbing
thrust of its feet,
and the indentation of what had been running
through the white valleys
of the snow—

and then it rose, gracefully,
and flew back to the frozen marshes,
to lurk there,
like a little lighthouse,
in the blue shadows—
so I thought:
maybe death
isn't darkness, after all,
but so much light
wrapping itself around us—

as soft as feathers—
that we are instantly weary
of looking, and looking, and shut our eyes,
not without amazement,
and let ourselves be carried,
as through the translucence of mica,
to the river
that is without the least dapple or shadow—
that is nothing but light—scalding, aortal light—
in which we are washed and washed
out of our bones.[2]
—MARY OLIVER

Later we sang and ate and talked and shared until the afternoon light
waned into evening.

One of the most pervading inspirations we came away with that day was Sparrow's loving support for us to live our lives without fear—to be all that we could be and to let nothing stop us. He had always gone forward without fear toward his highest dream, and reflecting on that made many of us realize that we had let the daily challenges of life get in our way and let our petty fears keep us from manifesting the best and finest of who we could be. In the early days when Sparrow was just leaving art school, everyone thought he was foolish not to pursue a lucrative career in commercial art. "You will be assured financial security that way," they had told him. He just nodded appreciatively, left the city, put on his backpack, and headed for the canyons and mountains that inspired him. He had chosen the freedom and joy of a rich aliveness rather than the confines of a comfortable living. And in the end, he had done very well financially. Many of us went away from that sweet afternoon pledging to release our fears and live our lives more fully in each moment—to offer freely to the world the rare and beautiful gifts that Sparrow had seen inside us and that we could no longer deny.

As we packed to leave that lovely place and those magical days, we wondered if this feeling of lightness and joy would follow us. And most thankfully, it did. Arriving home, we found all the family affairs in order—insurance taken care of, work on the Pavo house still progressing well, and Sparrow's presence radiant in his old garden and filling the land at Pavo. His celebration continued.

As friends gathered to talk, and cards poured in from around the world, I learned more about this remarkable young man than I had known even while he was physically with us. People shared amazing stories of the ways he had touched their lives.

Jon, a young man who worked at the Waldorf school, helped put into words for me the kind of love Sparrow had for others. "Sparrow and I were talking one day, and his clear, shining blue eyes were looking directly into mine," he said. "And I found myself continually looking down, unable to meet his gaze for very long. I couldn't understand what was happening, why I couldn't look directly back at him. And then I realized that Sparrow loved me even more than I loved myself." Tears sprang into my eyes as he said this, because he had "hit the nail right on the head." I had experienced that same unconditional love and hadn't even realized what had happened until Jon's words made it clear to me.

Shortly after that, I was given a deeply moving dream. In it, I was looking out my window at a beautiful bluebird, singing on the limb of a tall tree. Then a rain and sleet storm moved in, and when I next looked, I saw the bird, wet and frozen, fall tumbling down through the high branches to hit the ground.

And I ran . . . as fast as I could get out the door and to the bird lying there at my feet. I grabbed him up and tucked him into my shirt to warm him. But then in my panic, I couldn't seem to find my way back to the warm heater inside the house. I had to save his life! Tears were streaming down my face as I ran.

While I was running wildly up and down stairs and through corridors, I could feel the bird coming to and struggling a bit. I finally got to the heater, and the struggling continued, even more intensely. Looking down, I realized that whatever was inside my shirt was too big to be a bird, and then a squirrel popped its head out of the neck opening and jumped out, somewhat damp but scampering around.

I blinked my eyes, and the squirrel transformed into a young, blue-eyed boy, who grew before my eyes into a young man with tangled, sandy hair and loose jeans. He reminded me of the young hippies I had known in San Francisco in the seventies

He began showing me his recent paintings. The first one was of an evening scene, where the golden light flooded a room. The next was of a midnight rainbow, whose colors were the aurora borealis over the high, red-rock country. Finally, he showed me a scene of dawn's light streaming into the very same room.

He was very shy about what he had done but smiled mysteriously up at me, looking out of the corner of his eyes. "They're a series, you know," he said, gazing back at the paintings as though giving me time to perceive it myself.

Not being sure I'd gotten it, he explained, "The last hours were so happy and golden. There is so much beautiful light in our Earthly days; the first painting expresses my gratefulness for that. The next one expresses something of the kind of light one encounters in the night, the passage through the darkness that is sometimes called death. There the light is brilliant in its own strange way and totally surprising: the way is shown by a full spectrum of exquisite colors! And then the dawning of a new day. The light continues, wherever we are. All the realms and planes of life are flooded with light. On the other side of whatever darkness we may encounter, there is illumined dawn welcoming us. Do you see?" He looked at me with his eyes shining, as the light faded and I awoke.

The dream images came flooding back to me, and my eyes opened wide in amazement. I realized that it was Sparrow Hawk, and he had left us paintings exactly like those he described. He was showing us another perspective on the passage called death and telling us that he awakened from that night to a new day filled with radiant light.

Sparrow loved to fly and was fascinated by all manner of flying, whether bird, kite, or airplane (from paper models to Cessnas). Whenever the weather was right on my visits, he drove me to the little airport in town and flew us over the beautiful mountains of his home area, excitedly pointing out the sources of rivers, the homes of friends, and as we zipped over the top of a mountain, Pavo itself. Any excuse—whether to simply relax and enjoy, to be inspired by the vistas, to deliver Christmas presents to his family downstate, or to take a vacation trip all the way to the islands off the coast of Washington or California—was enough to send him up in that small plane. While in high school, he and his brother had even made a home video of a series of paper airplane flights, entitled "The Hawk Brothers' Flights."

I, too, love to fly, although I don't have a pilot's license. I wanted my body itself to fly, and as a young child, I tried and tried to make it happen. When I was a year and a half old, I would slip away from my mother, who was busy in the kitchen, and run (I had started walking at ten months!) for the old cars outside. Then I'd climb as fast as I could, up and up until I was standing on top of them. Usually, by that time, Mom had missed me and was running for me out the door, so I had very little time to lift my wings, flap them, and dive off into the clear air.

I was sure I could fly! And time and time again, my little arms did not make good wings, and I crashed terribly hard onto the ground in a belly flop. I would be so hurt and angry, so enraged that this physical body could not fly, that I would hold my breath until I turned blue and passed out.

My panicked mother would sprint toward me with all her might every time it happened. I don't think she ever made it before I flew off those old cars. I just finally gave up trying to fly in this body. I was literally crushed that it didn't work. Besides, holding my breath to leave this body and return to my spirit wings didn't seem to work either!

Then one night, a month or so after Sparrow left us, I had a numinous dream. I had often dreamed of attempting to fly: trying new methods, jumping, or standing on a high place in the wind, sometimes getting off the ground a bit. But this time, I could really *fly*. I lifted my arms, which became wings, and I flew as I had never imagined possible. Up and up, over and around, flips and dips and swoops. Wowee!! What absolute joy! I was ecstatic. Then I somehow realized that I could move through time as well as space, so I journeyed back and forward in time briefly. Then I thought to myself, "I wonder if I really am in my body doing this." So I flew up through an enormous group of power lines. Zipped right through with no sparks or problems. "Well, I'm not in my body, I guess, but this is great anyway!"

I continued to play around and finally came to rest as my consciousness began to bring me to physical wakefulness. In that half-sleep, I said to myself, "Wow, that was fantastic! That is the best I have ever flown." I was basking in the joy of it when Sparrow's face came clearly before me, saying, "See what fun I'm having???"

Time and again, he would be present—lighthearted, joyful. Sparrow loved tricks, jokes, and surprises. One of his most amazing tricks was revealed when the climbers finally found his clothing on the ledge from which he had fallen. A message had come through to us from a psychic friend that helped explain Sparrow's seemingly strange behavior of leaving most of his clothing behind him. He communicated to our friend that before he began climbing that fateful day, he had taken off his soggy, wet, cumbersome clothing and heavy camera bags to make climbing easier.

Since the rescuers didn't find these things when they found his body, where he'd fallen from remained a mystery. Many of the climbers from the rescue party who were Sparrow's good friends therefore made it their special assignment to find his missing possessions. On the morning the search party had first been organized and sent out, each person was given an 8½-by-11-inch sheet of paper with a description of Sparrow, where his car had been left, what clothing he might be wearing, his climbing habits, a photo of him, and other information that might be helpful. When his body was found, the official search was over. Several weeks went by. We wanted so much to have the cameras back because he often took photos of himself against the background of the stones, and we wanted all the information and understanding we could gain about his last hours.

Finally, one of those dedicated climbers found his things. They were on a ledge, much higher than was expected, folded and neatly stacked, just as Sparrow would do. And inexplicably, amazingly—resting there, exactly on top of that small pile, was a *paper airplane* made from the folded sheet with his description that had been given to the search party many weeks before!

Unbelievable!! There was no logical explanation for it, but when I closed my eyes, I could see Sparrow grinning broadly, his eyes sparkling at the joke. It reminded me of a story that his high school friend had told about one time when a group of them were camping. They had roasted wieners over the fire and gobbled most of them up in their ravenous, hikers' hunger. One wiener was left, and everyone really wanted it, yet no one felt good about taking the last one when there wasn't one for everyone. There was some kidding around about it, and finally Sparrow got up, walked to the grill saying, "I think this one has my name on it," and held it up for all to see. It did, in fact, have boldly written across it in mustard "Hawk"! His eyes sparkled and gleamed, as the others yelled in delight, trying to figure out how he had done that. "Just magic," he said. When I heard about the paper airplane, those sparkling, laughing eyes smiled at me again. "Just magic." He grinned.

He made it very obvious, again and again, that he is alive and well in the dimension he now occupies. As Chief Seattle had said and our native people had always known, "There is no death, only a change of worlds."[3] He had given us the real experience of something we had known only as a concept: Life is eternal and ongoing, and death is safe. He had, in that radiant springtime, shown us *resurrection* in a most poignant and beautiful way. It was a gift more precious than I would ever have believed I could receive from what had seemed such a tragedy.

But that was not all. Sparrow Hawk had much more to teach us.

CHAPTER 3

TOUCHING IN

With impeccable devotion, we must listen
to the voices of the larger life around us
—learning, awakening, tuning in—
so that each step forward is one of harmony.

One of the messages sent to us through our friend Shirley spoke of Sparrow Hawk's having perfected and completed his experience of physical life: he was ready to move on to the next level of learning and work, to ascend to a different plateau. And truly, the more I heard of his full and rich life, his unconditional love and generous giving, the well-developed talents he shared with the world, the more sense it made to me that he had chosen to leave this life.

I have long understood that our soul chooses both when we are to be born and when we are to leave this Earth. Those decisions are based on the soul's intent for that lifetime: what is to be experienced and when that growth and learning are complete. It also makes sense to me that the deep self chooses the way in which we leave as well as how—whether through a lingering illness, a sudden heart attack, a murder, an accident— in order both to have a specific experience for ourselves and to create a lesson for those left on Earth. This was made clear to me by an experience I had years earlier.

Because it was felt that I could clear the negative energy, I was asked to caretake a ranch in Montana where a horrible double murder had taken place. The couple had moved out from California, and from what

I found in her diaries, they had loved the openness, the small community, and the wildlife but found the area too remote and the winters too harsh. Friends reported that they had been ready to leave.

Back in the Midwest, a young man had grown up in an abused and deprived situation. He was probably what we would call a sociopath. He headed west to the wildlands of Montana because he could not get along with people. He was angry and in despair. Taking a bus to this remote area, he started into the wilderness with only a knife and a few groceries. It wasn't as easy as he had thought, and in a few days, hungry and tired, he made his way out of the backcountry at night. A huge yard light drew him to the ranch, where he found a refrigerator full of food in the garage ... and a rifle in the pickup. When the male owner came out in the early morning, the fellow got the drop on him, and the rest is sorrowful history.

In doing the clearing that I was asked to do, I meditated a lot with Celia, the wife, trying to contact her and understand more of what had happened. Knowing that, at a deep soul level, we choose our time and way of leaving Earth, I asked her why they had chosen such a horrible death. The answer that came through was loud, clear, and struck a deep chord within me:

> We moved away from the big city to this small, remote community in order to get away from craziness and violence. We were ready to leave our Earthly lives, and the lesson we found to leave for others is this: "You can't run away. So long as we as a human family allow any child, anywhere, to be abused and damaged, we are not safe. We must create good lives for all the children!"

I have shared her message through my teaching for many years now. And I always remember the gift they gave by their choice in leaving this plane of existence.

Sparrow Hawk had obviously chosen when and where to leave, and I could feel the powerful impact those specific choices held for us. Yet I was still mystified about his leaving at a time when his kind of beingness was so desperately needed on Mother Earth and when their new home and the dream of Pavo had barely begun. It was marvelous to have received the knowing that he was absolutely fine in this new phase of his life, and I was deeply grateful for that. Yet it just didn't seem like him to abandon such a beautiful, meaningful project as we had begun at Pavo. Was there more to learn than we had yet been able to perceive? I was certain there must be.

I sensed that I could communicate more directly with Sparrow Hawk to learn the lessons that awaited me, if I made the space in my attention for it. I began to meditate consistently and deeply and to gently open my consciousness to Sparrow. I simply wanted to be available to learn more, and indeed there was much more. My perception of him was often of his standing slightly above me, almost as though on an upward-leading trail, grinning lovingly down at me and calling me forward.

"I'm glad you realized that there was more," he said mischievously, cocking his head a bit and raising his eyebrows. "What you must understand is that I didn't, haven't, won't ever abandon you, Aria, and the boys, and certainly not our beautiful Pavo, which is so intimately a part of who we all are.

"Your feeling that I have abandoned the project is due to your limited understanding of what we were truly about there. *I* didn't even consciously understand it until I had such a remarkable change of perspective!

"Let's look back at what we thought we were about. It is still tremendously vital, only limited. All of us realized that we two-leggeds have caused a tremendous amount of damage to our lovely Lady Gaia and thus to ourselves—that the ways of living now considered normal are very much less than workable in the long run. If we continue these ways of life, we will prove once and for all to ourselves—to our sleeping and ignorant human family—that they are terribly unworkable. These ways do not sustain life: ours or others of Mother Earth's family. They are totally bankrupting the legacy of the seven generations of our children to follow us. What a terrible thing! Aria and I were very aware of this, and so Pavo came about not just to create a workable, beautiful, sustainable, nourishing, harmonious, nontoxic environment for our own family but to create a model for others to see and hopefully follow. With impeccable devotion, we listened to the voices of the larger life around us—learning, awakening, tuning in—so that each step of the building process was done in harmony. Aria perfected this even more than I. She went on to research widely the materials and ways of construction that would not bring anything toxic to this lovely, wild, and pure land we have named Pavo and dedicated to continued peace.

"We even asked that our workmen come to understand the deeper level of what we were doing, so they could learn to work with that dedication to harmony, both in the way they built and in the way they related to each other. Anger, conflict, and unresolved issues created an energy that did not belong there; we required that these things be quickly worked out. The process was sometimes far from perfect, yet it has been quite beautiful to see their awakening to a different level of 'building.' They were building a dream, a model of harmony, in all that they did.

"So, as you see," Sparrow concluded, "we were beginning to pay attention to the energetic nature of things—to the quality of vibrational energy we release there as well as the actual physical materials and structure."

I responded by sharing with him something given me in meditation by a beautiful wolf named Silver Shadow:

I am not given too much to pondering or speculation, but I do wonder sometimes about these two-legged creatures whom Creator has placed upon Mother Gaia. What gift do they bring? I know that each unique being brings a gift, but I have seen nothing from the two-leggeds that enhances the life of all. They simply crowd into a place, as they are doing all around me here, and do with it as they will. What I have seen is that the energetic vibration—the song of the Earth, which I can actually see—is dulled, dimmed, and made somehow unharmonic. It is unpleasant to watch, yet their people seem not to notice or else thrive upon it in some way.

I do, however, like to recall one older male two-legged who is very different. He is elderly now and does not venture forth so much, yet we have been friends for many years. He moves more gently and gracefully than others I have seen. Although he does not necessarily walk slowly, there is a fluidity to his movement that does not disturb. Maybe it is that *his inner song matches the song of life around him* and that he has not dulled it in the same way that all the others have.

"Yes, that's exactly it!" Sparrow said, enthusiastically. "What Silver Shadow shared is so important. That exact awareness of the quality of energy we bring to our new home is vitally important."

"Yes," I continued, "I know that as I walk the land at Pavo, I have been saddened to realize that the places we picked for our homes—the only open meadows available, really—are the very places loved by the elk who have always lived there. Although they move away when we are present, I see where they have bedded down in the long grasses to catch the morning sun, just as I like to do. And our presence steals from them yet another place that has been theirs down through time. In creating our home, we are taking theirs."

Sparrow nodded in recognition and agreement.

"Oh, but I remember one lovely thing," I said, brightening a bit. "I had walked down the trail in the early evening light; when I came back up into the meadow, my energy was soft and quiet. I was humming a little tune and being grateful for the scent of flowers wafting in the cooling air. As I came over a small rise, a bull elk on the other side of the meadow lifted his great head and stared at me, with both curiosity and some malevolence.

"I spoke to him, keeping my voice soft, and sent a blue line of energy toward him indicating that I was peaceful and open to communication. He moved about nervously, stepping with high, slow steps—lifting one foot at a time and holding it poised—toward the aspen grove near him. So I began to sing. I sang anything I could think of, because that seemed to relax him somewhat. He turned toward me, shaking his mighty antlers, in a gesture that conveyed his aggravation with my being there, disturbing his evening grazing. And up surfaced my sadness that we two-leggeds have often been so cruel to animals that they have become afraid of us, choosing to hide when they see us anywhere near.

"With tears running down my face, I sang out my understanding of his feeling and my sadness for what we two-leggeds had done to his and other 'wild' peoples. With our long-reaching guns, we have driven them away from us, so their beauty and magnificence no longer grace our lives. I wailed out, in high, fluted tones that matched his autumn calls, my heartache for the enormous loss to all of us. The big fellow tossed his mighty head occasionally but remained attentive, interested."

Sparrow, too, was attentive, interested, his eyes bright with tears like mine.

"Then I sang my pledge to the big herd bull. I asked him to allow me to make a home for myself there, and in return, I would protect his people from harm. No hunters would ever come again if I could help it. I told him that I only needed a small amount of actual space and that I would love for him and his people to come and lie in the sun near me in the slanting meadow, eat the grasses, let their calves cavort and play on the hill across the draw. I sent him images of the small dam we would put in, to capture water so that they wouldn't have to go down into the valley to drink when the springs and streams dried up in the heat of autumn. And after I ran out of images, I simply sang pure love to him, in waves of golden light that rolled across the long grasses of the meadow on the evening air.

" 'I know we can do it,' I cried. 'I know we can live together in peace, that our lives can benefit each other. I give my heart to being the kind of person who would be acceptable in your eyes, with whom you and your cows would feel safe to share the beauty of your young calves in the springtime.' My throat was growing tired; I realized I had been singing out strongly for over half an hour. In a whispered voice and with powerful intention, I intoned my final prayer: 'Oh, Great Spirit, let it be so.'

"It was growing dark, and, bowing to him, I moved quietly on toward my camp on the high edge of the meadow. Shaking his magnificent rack one last time, the bull elk moved slowly toward the trees, grazing his way into the night. He had not given his agreement to my proposal; it was not that easy. I knew I would need to make real my part of the bargain, be the peaceful person I spoke of, before he would bring his family into my presence. That was good enough for me."

"That's wonderful. I know you can do it!" Sparrow chimed in. "That is exactly what Pavo is about—that kind of perception and understanding, that kind of energy. . . . And more . . . ," he said, enticingly.

"But before I go on to talk about the next level of our work at Pavo,

27

I want to hear more of what Silver Shadow and the animals have shared with you. You know how much I love all the wild ones. That was a large part of my lifework, to portray them in all their beauty and grace, so that humans might taste a bit of the 'Heaven on Earth' they are missing. I did this in hopes that it would help awaken them to caring for our wildlands and the remarkable beings there—to preserving and protecting the larger Circle of Life. I wished for them to realize the deep loss we humans have incurred by not having good relationships with the animals. I hoped that they would want more than just a good painting on their wall.

"It was certainly worth giving my life energy to ...," he said a bit wistfully. "It's so important."

"I know that what you did made a tremendous difference," I told him. "And I would love to share with you the messages I received from the animals in my meditations." I got up from where I was sitting in my meditation, pulled out the folder of writings, and began to read.

CHAPTER 4

LISTENING TO THE GREAT VOICES

We are all children of Mother Earth and Father Sun.
We are calling out to you to awaken and swim more consciously
in this exquisite pool of Life.

You are one with all things and all beings—
graced with life and abundance as we all are.
How could you have forgotten??

"I know that the beauty you created on canvas, Sparrow, was only a part of the tremendous impact you made in people's lives. Another special aspect of how you lived your life was your demonstration of the sensitivity we must all eventually rediscover in ourselves for the good of our own lives as well as for the children of the generations to follow. You showed us the true joy of that kind of life!"

"We really need the other life that exists around us, in deeper ways than we recognize in these modern times, don't we?" Sparrow Hawk mused.

"And more than we sometimes remember. Right, Brooke?" he queried mischievously.

The look in his eye prodded me until I finally asked, "Am I missing something here?"

"You bet you are! Where are the porcupine quills you gathered with your teacher Dawn Boy right near your home?"

"Oh, yes . . . now I remember. We found a dead porcupine and gathered the quills for some future shirt or other projects."

"Exactly!" Sparrow exploded. "Porcupine has always given your people holy gifts of beauty through your decorative quillwork. When you found the porcupine, this was in your mind and heart for the future, and it has not happened yet. That porcupine is waiting, Brooke, and soon you will need a new dance shirt.

"The quills you gathered and the shirt you are going to make. They speak of the relationship of giveaway to beauty and spirit that the porcupine nation has always portrayed."

This talk of animals reminded me of something David Abram said in his wonderful book *The Spell of the Sensuous*:

> Humans are tuned for relationships. The eyes, the skin, the tongue, the ears, and nostrils—all are gates where our body receives *the nourishment of otherness*. This landscape of shadowed voices, these feathered bodies and antlers and tumbling streams—these breathing shapes are our family, the beings with whom we are engaged, with whom we struggle and suffer and celebrate. For the largest part of our species' existence, humans have negotiated relationships with every aspect of the sensuous surroundings, exchanging possibilities with every flapping form, with each textured surface and shimmering entity that we happened to focus upon. All could speak, articulating in gesture and whistle and sign a shifting web of meanings that we felt on our skin or inhaled through our nostrils or focused with our listening ears, and to which we replied—whether through movements, or minute shifts of mood. The color of the sky, the rush of waves—every aspect of the earthly sensuous could draw us into a relationship fed with curiosity and spiced with danger. Every sound was a voice, every scrape or blunder was a meeting—with Thunder, with Oak, with Dragonfly. And from all of these relationships our collective sensibilities were nourished.
>
> Today we participate almost exclusively with other humans

and with our own human-made technologies. It is a precarious situation, given our age-old reciprocity with the many-voiced landscape. We still *need* that which is other than ourselves and our own creations. . . . We are human only in contact, in conviviality, with what is not human.[1]

After absorbing those beautiful words in silence for a while, Sparrow said, "To be truly human is so precious. I think most people miss so much joy, beauty, and real aliveness by limiting themselves to the man-made world."

He looked wistful again, and I knew he had loved being on Earth more than almost anyone I knew. Even though he is now in an amazing realm, there is nothing as sweet as this Earth in many ways.

"So let's hear from the wild ones," he said, brightening a bit.

"Okay. First, I'll read you all of Silver Shadow's message,"[2] I replied. "It is so lovely, and very important for us to not only listen to but truly hear."

Love Song

I am one who gently moves across this land, extending
my love for every small parcel of it across the whole, in a
protective energetic gesture much as a mother might
place around her wandering pup. Everyplace one of my
paws rests, there is beauty. I stand in forest; I stand in
marsh; I stand in meadow; I lap the water of streams; I
stand in sacred aspen groves; I stand on turquoise green
and red stones; I stand on moss; I follow tracks of elk,
bear, and deer; I stand on footprints of two-leggeds; I
stand on grass; I stand on snow; I slip through mud.
With each step, I feel the joy throbbing up from the
center of our Lady Gaia. All the violence and damage
that have been done to Her by two-leggeds have not yet
stilled Her bubbling, ecstatic heart.

My mate has gone, and I must be careful where I
move, for some who see even my tracks would want me

dead. What a strange feeling it is never to have harmed someone and yet have them want to make you dead with their long-reaching fire and with such a strange intensity. I am glad for my nose and my ears; in most circumstances, they keep me well away from any danger. (I do not include the name of my people because so many seem to fear us and wish us harm.)

I am not given too much to pondering or speculation, but I do wonder sometimes about these two-legged creatures whom Creator has placed upon Mother Gaia. What gift do they bring? I know that each unique being brings a gift, but I have seen nothing from the two-leggeds that enhances the life of all. They simply crowd into a place, as they are doing all around me here, and do with it as they will. What I have seen is that the energetic vibration—the song of the Earth, which I can actually see—is dulled, dimmed, and made somehow unharmonic. It is unpleasant to watch, yet their people seem not to notice or else thrive upon it in some way.

Yet I do like to recall one older male two-legged who is very different. He is elderly now and does not venture forth so much; yet we have been friends for many years. He moves more gently and gracefully than others I have seen. Although he does not necessarily walk slowly, there is a fluidity to his movement that does not disturb. Maybe it is that *his inner song matches the song of life around him* and that he has not dulled it in the same way that all the others do.

I have watched two-legged children, especially in the old days when they more often roamed the forests and meadows, who had that same kind of energy. They seemed not to be so aggressively "going somewhere" but rather let the life around them draw them in meandering paths of exploration and joy. They seemed more like my children, who are drawn to sniff the scent of anything that has moved across the nearby land; their paths are seldom straight but wriggle and cross over and go back around and wander off one way and the other. As the pups grow older, they move down game trails in a much more purposeful way, but it is still not harsh. Their paws are soft.

Thinking of the way my people move reminds me of my name. I am called by a sound that tells about the color of my coat certainly; yet more important, it tells of the energy I carry, the way I move, the light yet dark that I blend to perfection. *Silver Shadow* is as near as I can say it to you, although it is much more than that.

Maybe those are the human words he called me— that quiet one to whom I became so accustomed. It was almost as if we became each other's family, for when I was lonesome after my mate's death, I would go near to his cabin, and he would somehow feel me there. He would come out and sit resting against a huge old white pine in the sunlight, near me but never looking directly at me. Then he would sing: beautiful songs that I soon began to recognize as songs of love. In reality, perhaps they were songs of love lost—plaintive songs that made my heart yearn for my mate, her beauty, her grace, her kind and loving ways, her power, her caring for our pups.

Over time, I began to sense that he, too, had lost a loved one and that he, like me, would never take another mate. He would hold that loving place in his heart, cherishing her and talking with her in the Beyond Place. Maybe it was that I could see her spirit shimmering and dancing to his songs. I don't know. What I do know is that eventually I would let him see me, and he would greet me with golden energy streaming from him. It became a habit that first summer for us to lie about where we could see each other or sometimes go on long walks together. Although we never approached really close, just seeing each other occasionally would give a feeling of companionship.

We finally got so we could even exchange simple thoughts, although they came as images more than words. I would see that he was going to go to the spring to fill his water carrier and then go on up a certain trail. I would move off and be waiting for him along the way. He would nod in acknowledgment when he saw me, always sending that joyful energy toward me, and continue on his way. I would follow at my own pace or sometimes cut across so that he would find me in front of him. At this, he would be surprised and delighted, and soon I began to lead on our walks. I think he liked to see my huge footprints on the trail, for he would chuckle and talk to me then. He always seemed to be telling me how fine I was, how able, how agile, how intelligent, how cunning, how playful, how kind. I never remember a harsh word or feeling from him.

Ah, just speaking of him, I miss our times together. I realize, in thinking of him, that I am lonely. I am lonely, and I almost fear these days to sing that loneliness out. My howling call brings danger instead of solace.

So I share these things with you as a way of inviting you deeper into my life and understanding. What is important as we move forward in this time is the connection of our hearts in Oneness and joy. That will solve *all* our problems, no matter the sphere of life in which they rest.

I will dare to call out this day. I will dare to sing the song of my heart, my loneliness, my sadness at the separation I feel, in hopes that some one of you may hear it, recognize it as your own, and open your heart. Whatever small thing might come of it will be good.

Listen . . . You will hear my call echoing down from the high ridge where I stand in an opening that looks far out over valley, lake, and mountain ridge. You will hear

my song no matter how far away in space or time you
may think you are.

In the one heart,
Silver Shadow, *for Wolf*

"That was fabulous," Sparrow Hawk said passionately. "I know it
will touch the hearts of many." His voice softened with melancholy, and
I knew he was thinking of Aria. "Yes, it will touch the hearts of many."

After a while, when our thoughts came back together, he reminded
me that the Sufi teacher Hazrat Inayat Khan likens nature, in all its
forms, to the holiest scripture that one can study, and he encourages all
to attune to its messages. The wildlands and the animals are open chapters in this text, inviting us to observe and learn. To quote Murshid[3]
Khan, "From the moment man's eyes open and he begins to read the
book of nature he begins to live; and he continues to live forever."[4]

"True!" Sparrow exclaimed. "So what else have these beautiful creatures shared with you?"

"Here's another favorite," I offered.

Song of Life

We can feel you, sensing us and what we feel; that is our
way of knowing and communicating. It takes an intense
focus of attention to turn these experiences into a
language of words, which then you might understand.
Hopefully, you will *understand* as though you were having
our same experience—"standing under" these same
conditions.

It is the season where killing our kind is allowed, and
a hard winter has already set in. You might think of us as
being afraid; yet the thing you call fear, we feel more as a
kind of pressure, an urging. It moves us in certain
directions, calls upon our intelligence and our experience
to bring ourselves and our young calves through this wet
and deepening shoulder-high snow. I, Long Antlers, have
never seen snow before in this odd combination of

weight and slipperiness, of density and glide. This
unseasonable warmth makes us sweat in our growing
winter coats and then become cold as night falls, the
temperature drops a few degrees, and our movement
lessens.[5] Thoughts float across my mind of attempting
to feed at night in the coolness. I rest, standing with
my body relaxed, then lay myself down, sinking into
the snow.

One of our young cows floundered and fell the other
morning as the herd was attempting to move to new
grazing. The depth of the layers of snow meant she had
no purchase with which to pull herself back up. Her legs
simply flailed and stuck deeply into the snow's weight,
which packed around her closely, making it almost
impossible to rise from her side. She was beginning to
panic—struggling and losing precious energy—until an
old, wise cow called to her to still herself, to lie back for
a moment and rest. We instinctively moved in around
her; and she, then being able to press against our
shoulders and legs, righted herself and stood panting
and spent. The herd stood for a while, breathing with
her, letting our life force fill her. Then an older bull and
a young one moved off into the forest a short way.
Finding a more sheltered place, they called to us. We
moved into that protection and, resting close together,
spent the night.

I think the young cow is still weakened. With things
as they are, we get so little food—enough for
maintenance yet too little for replenishment of such
depletion. The old bull who leads us has been very wise
so far—keeping us out of danger and finding an
adequate supply of nourishment. I am relieved that the
harsh, deep, chilling cold did not come this time with
Mother Earth's beautiful, ermine[6] pelt of thick and
dazzling white. When the Sun shone yesterday, we were
deeply stirred. We stretched ourselves and opened to

every ray of the precious golden light as it peeked around the clouds. We sent love to Sun Above—singing His praises for staying with us there above the high floaters that have amassed to cut off His sight of us for many weeks. His constancy with us lets us know how loved and how lucky we are.

You must excuse me, for I have only been describing *our* situation and not truly addressing you. I turn my attention to you two-leggeds now, thinking about you as I might one of my calves who does not know his way in the world. You concern me because I do not see you maturing, becoming *fully* human as our young do who grow up to be full-functioning, majestic elk. I see such a gap between you and the world in which you live—a gap of ignorance more than stupidity. Something has caused you to ignore the larger pool of life in which you swim and breathe. It is very hard on you, and certainly much more difficult for us, since you choose to wield so much power with so little thought.

We are calling out to you to awaken and swim more consciously in this exquisite pool. We do this, not for ourselves alone, but because we love you as one of our family and wish for you a happy, abundant, radiant life. Radiance is an experience of natural light in all its forms, including that warm light that shines from the heart. You do not even know radiance as I speak of it, living as you do so enclosed in your caves called houses with your hearts closed down. The light in which you live is harsh and monotone and cold, whereas ours is full-spectrum and resplendent. I hope you someday get to see/feel it within and around you as I do.

The Great Ones who help move and mold this life of Creation are moving strongly now, with the same heartfelt, loving intent that I have in my great heart for you. Much, much light is coming[7]—a washing in "oracular" light,[8] as it were. This is truly a lightening up, for all that is required of you is letting go of your hard grip on the things you now think make your world secure. Release them and let the stream of Spirit Light move you into rhythm with the great song of life that is being sung. Thus, with one simple, yet profound intention (the right balance of body and spirit), you will have moved into position to make a difference in both of the areas that are so in need of attention at this time on Earth. First comes lifting your vibration to include more Spirit, and second comes creating good relationship with All Your Relations.

This may seem too simple to you who have been trained in convoluted and logical complexities, yet it is exactly what must be done. This correction is in alignment with what you know to be the theme of this coming age: to quiet yourselves, deepen your spirit, and listen to the Great Voices around you. It is absolutely *not* just about doing things in the material, three-dimensional world. The Old Ones have told you in very specific terms recently: *The third dimension is the source of nothing.* All things come from Spirit—the Unmanifest, the starry womb of Buffalo Woman. Your thoughts and intent, unadulterated with negativity or fear, are what create the positive things that then become your reality.

A sustainable, beautiful path where harmony reigns is what you have wanted from time immemorial. You simply have not known how to get it. Your schools have trained your intellect (the process of analyzing things separately from their connection to All Life), yet they have let go undeveloped your intelligence (that which gives you knowledge to sustain life in this interconnected web). The work you do now must be the work of *intelligence*, for intelligence is manifested (made real) through the heart. And the heart is more than an organ of the body: it is the functioning process that creates the bridge between the individual and All Things. The heart makes available the vital information from the larger picture that you must have to do anything well.

So lift up your hearts! Your energy is dirgelike: plodding and out of tune with the dance of Being around you. What delight you are missing! We animals are most joyful at the coming of more light! Our clarity will allow us to be lifted easily into the balance of body and spirit, the semietheric state that will give us access both to things manifest and to that which is Unmanifest. What a wonderful view we will have from there—as when standing high on a mountain range, being able to see fully into the life of either side—and what joy at being able to communicate between and among the worlds!

Those of you who have some feeling of connection with me and my magnificent people may want to slow yourselves down, allow your consciousness to drift here to where we are in the deep forest, to breathe with us, and to know life through our pores. It is such a good life, even with all the pressure and violence from your kind. Mother Earth is so very sweet; we are grateful to be here.

And we are grateful to be here with you as you come into your fullness during this time.[9] As you lift yourselves to an elevated plane, we will all share in that exciting energy. You will feel with us more and more as you become increasingly open and willing. You are invited now to feel the full, deep breaths of fresh air in our chests, sense our swinging gait as we trot across flower-filled meadows, as we adjust our necks and backs to hold the weight of enormous velvet antlers growing from our males' heads. Join us often, for we are your family, and you are ours. We are all children of Mother Earth and Father Sun. We will all receive the light!

In beauty,
Long Antlers, *for Elk*

Sparrow Hawk smiled and said, "I love the part about intelligence being connected with the heart and how to live well upon Mother Earth. Physical life is such an incredible gift, yet it seems that people often make the mistake of thinking that security is connected with their pocket-book, when it is really connected with their heart!"

"Yes," I said. "Part of my teaching has been that Love is the bonding between things. It is the cosmic glue that holds things in union, whether the cells of my body or Earth and all Her children. It's what I call 'practical spirituality' or sacred ecology. When we connect through the heart, our spiritual understandings inform our daily living and make it more beautiful and workable. It seems right to me that this should be so.

"So much joy is possible for us! I am continually amazed at the graciousness of the life around us. Even though we have done so much damage, they are willing to have us grow into a more and more beautiful life. There is never any violent or destructive energy sent our way, only an understanding of our Oneness on this sweet Earth and their bright hope for the future of all as we two-leggeds awaken to more wisdom."

"There is such wisdom among the others of our Earth family, isn't there?" Sparrow Hawk said thoughtfully. "It's simply a matter of tuning in. My father and grandfather are Christian ministers, and I remember a quote they gave me from the Bible, knowing how much I loved the natural world: 'Speak to the earth and it shall teach thee' (Job 12:8)."

"Yes," I said. "It's true that the same wisdom comes from almost all traditions. And some of the information that is given us when we ask can be quite specific. Wait 'til you hear what Whale has to say!"

"Okay, I'm ready," Sparrow urged.

Song of Oneness

I could not help overhearing the ongoing conversation about life on Lady Gaia at this present time. Although my physical body is no longer a part of that life, my heart's intention remains with Her—an intention for a joyous song of life on Her sphere.

One exquisite lifetime I especially remember. I can

close my eyes and feel the silken waters as they caressed my great body. It was given me at that time to be an extraordinarily magnificent creature, even among our fine and beautiful people. My physical abilities were awesome: I could dive deeper, leap higher, swim farther, live in colder water, send my song farther than any other whale in the oceans at that time. I was called World Singer because it was said that whenever I sang, it could be heard in all the waters of the world. What a wonderful thought . . .

Yet among my people, I received no special recognition or praise. The highest praise I could receive was to hear others, including sea creatures very different from us, murmur when I sang: "I feel so happy and so much at one with All Things when I hear this lovely song."

I understood, as is the deep knowing among all cetacean people, that we long ago accepted the charge of being stewards of Lady Gaia and all her children. Our work is that of attunement and balance through the waters: we keep a close sonic eye on the pulses of the planet and continually tune them with our song. Each one of us, when we sense any other's song, pass it along in a chain of harmony. When I would sing, often the whole of my people sang with me wherever they swam. The baby ones would wiggle with pleasure and cavort in the sweet water as we did this. It was a song filled with power and beauty and harmony and balance.

Our part of stewardship of Earth is to work through the waters. You two-leggeds are the second part of this great triangle with Lady Gaia, who is mother and partner to us all. Yet today it saddens me that I must speak to you about not doing your part. You have not only failed in your stewardship of Earth, but you have also turned to killing our cetacean peoples and polluting the waters in which we live—the very waters of life that flow through your veins as well.

In your path of development, you decided to learn to manipulate things and gave yourself those wonderful five-fingered hands with which to do it. Such a great gift and yet such a tremendous challenge. When you can manipulate things in that way, you must exercise great care, for you can as easily damage things as not! When you first began this exploration, it was simply that: a very obvious way to see the effect of your thoughts and actions. This was good, and you learned many things.

The challenge came when you began to feel that it was necessary to manipulate the things of your material world in order to be secure and happy. That became very dangerous, not only to you but to all others deeply affected by your actions. I cannot guess how it came about, but that feeling must have come from a sense that life would not continue to care for you naturally and simply as it had always done. Or perhaps after you had manipulated things long enough, the lack of balance you had created made it impossible for you to rely on the abundant flow of Life itself. One thing I do know is that for balance to come again to Lady Gaia and Her children, you must remember that you yourselves are part of Life, not separate from it. You are one with all things and all beings—graced with life and abundance as we all are. How could you have forgotten??

And how is it that you fail to remember your pledge to care for this great Lady and Her children? What fog rolled onto the shores of your being and obscured this primary pledge? It is incomprehensible to me! Yet whatever that fog might have been, I see it lifting like a veil from your eyes. Life, in its greatness and goodness, is seeing to that. Our cetacean songs are adding to the warm light that now lifts this concealing vapor. They are urgent songs from a diminished people, yet they are powerful songs. Will you listen to their call? Our remembering can be yours as well, if you but join your consciousness with ours.

Go, those of you who live near Mother Ocean, and sit beside Her mighty waters. Listen with rapt attention to the voices who speak from deep within Her. Come, those of you who are swimmers; come into the waters. Rest upon their swells and feel the ecstatic song that courses through your every cell. The song of life that is being sung, though urgent, is still a most beautiful song. It is filled with the colors of the tropical fishes, the nurturing of the waves kissing the shore, the peacefulness of anemones waving, the swiftness of fishes darting, the pulse of your own heart's blood, and the richness of the myriad life of the waters.

And it sings in the small waters that run in streams and rivulets through the land. Wherever they are not damaged, polluted, and changed, the song is still ringing. Sit by a stream and listen to its gurgling as it moves toward the sea. Look upon a still lake colored at sunset with pink and violet. Sense the power of a raging current. Do what you must to reclaim the naturally pure waters as well as the swamps and marshes that bridge water and land.

You will be able to tell when you are doing your work of stewardship well because the waters will again be pure. Will it not be worth the devotion required in order to see your children playing in clear streams and drinking pure waters wherever they roam? Does it not frighten you "awake" that the very waters you give your children are not clean and healthy? It concerns us greatly. And without you on land doing your part, no one's children will be able to have their natural birthright—that of a healthy and radiant and joyful planet.

Therefore, do your work of stewardship with joy and

high intent. What more wonderful thing to be doing than that which will make your world shine? Look inward to feel if what you do day to day—what you call work—pleases you, pleasures you, makes your life happy and full. This work of stewardship will. It will fulfill you in a way you cannot now imagine, especially as more and more of you join together to create and magnify the power you wield.

Soon there will be breakdowns in the complex means fashioned by you two-leggeds to separate and "protect" yourselves from the world of nature. Without a doubt, this will happen organically because too many resources are being used to support that unhealthy way of being. Those who are willing to design a life of simple beauty that receives the abundance freely given by a loving Mother and Father are those who will find joy in the coming times.

Please remember that whatever requires tremendous amounts of energy, whether from you personally or from a source you cannot control, will not be worth having in the coming times. Mother Earth is going to be very strict because She needs all Her energy to regain Her strength; that is the best thing She can do for you. What She is asking of you is to grow up a bit and make a partner of Earth rather than acting so much like suckling babies.[10] You can see well what is coming: every science and intuition you have tells you that the ways you live cannot continue. Why wait until the Great Changes force you to do things differently and thus make it very hard on you and your little ones? Why not begin to take responsibility now, making it a joyful task to find simple, powerful beauty in your ways of life? What joy and peace and plenty you will find as you do this! Nothing bad or negative or harsh awaits you—only clear air and pure water and a flowering world.

Turn your hearts and minds to listen to the Great Ones among you, the ones who can teach you about designing your living in a sustainable way. For truly, the only things that will last are those which, after they are up and functioning, can perpetuate themselves with a minimum of input from you. Seek this principle at every level of your life, so that you design things to work in a cooperative, interdependent circle that maintains itself.

Remember that your intent is the key. Come together, clear any personal obstacles, and focus your intent on one point. Feed that point of power with your attention, your love, your action, your joy, and your laughter. Thus will you be able to do magic, as my people do magic when we sing together to balance the world.

Ah, yes, even from where I now am, I remember so clearly the exquisite life I lived there in the waters of Lady Gaia. As time passed and I grew very, very old, I could feel that my powers were diminishing; I was then ready to leave that magnificent body. So I swam as fast and as far as any whale has ever swum, up north into colder and colder waters, and I dived deeper and longer than any whale has ever dived. Then I threw myself, flying high into the air, and burst my great heart! Yet never did I feel the heaviness of my physical body as it fell back into the water; I only felt myself flying, swimming in a light so beautiful that greater joy than I had ever known filled me, and it still does.

My love comes to you, streaming and flowing as a great song and a great river. Join me in this river song that flows into the Oneness of Mother Ocean.

In unity,
World Singer, *for Whale*

"That was amazing!" said Sparrow Hawk. "World Singer's experience sounds so much like mine. We are both flying and flowing in a new and beautiful light. And I honor my continuing life as dedicated to good stewardship. My physical life brought much joy and pleasure to me, as well as to others, because I did make that conscious choice to create a better world."

"It's true," I said. "You certainly did model for all your friends, family, and fans that doing what you love—dedicating yourself to the natural world—really worked in everyday terms. Your life was successful and rich, in all ways."

"Yes, it was a good life. So I hope others learn to listen deeply to the beautiful creatures around us, for they seem to have a knowing of something brighter coming than even you two-leggeds on Earth yet perceive!

"You will hear more of this later," said Sparrow Hawk enticingly. "There is beauty coming that you cannot yet even guess!

"The understandings that these wonderful beings are sharing with us were understood and practiced by native, primary peoples all around the globe," he continued. "As we two-leggeds begin to remember who we are and our true Oneness with all life, we will naturally awaken more fully again to our responsibility toward others. We will respond in harmonious ways to their needs and feelings and lifeways just as we would any other member of our family. It will make us very much happier and more content to do so; our lives will be made much richer and sweeter because of it.

"You and I both know this and devote our lives to it—and many others are doing the same," Sparrow reminded me, and I nodded.

Then he continued on in a way I had not expected: "Anyway, this practice of harmony is not real news; it has been done before, among many primary peoples around the world, even quite recently. It is only a step in our awakening and certainly necessary in our life practice.

"However, the most vital and important message I have for you is about something we two-leggeds have not done in remembered time. It concerns a leap 'forward and upward' in our evolution that most of our human family have not even thought of, let alone considered making," Sparrow said excitedly, his eyes sparkling and his energy starting to buzz. "This is the really exquisite part, and I can hardly wait to tell you!"

CHAPTER 5

RENEWING THE
VISION

*Dawn Star planted a seed
that was the understanding of our true nature as humans:
that we live in both the visible and Invisible realms
and that great beauty and harmony and flowering can come
to two-leggeds through the honoring and development
of our capacities in the Invisible.*

"When I left the Earth plane, you felt that I had abandoned our work at
Pavo," said Sparrow Hawk, grinning mischievously. "Nothing could be
further from the truth. I had to leave to help you and Aria and others to
move on to the deeper work that was as yet unrecognized. The intentions
we all held were high and beautiful yet, as I indicated before, too limited.
There is more, much more.

"Our work there had to do with living on the physical plane in a
highly conscious, cooperative, harmonious, loving way with All of Life.
We felt that living day to day in that way would not only be joyful and
sustaining for us but would also model something special for other people. In that way, we were attempting to make a difference in human life
on Earth. It was our intention to lift it to a better place, to create more
health, well-being, unity, and peace among All Things in the Circle of
Life. Yet even you, who have said this a hundred times, are not yet fully
cognizant of the level of work that is needed: 'We must work at the level
of Spirit; working solely at the physical level will not be enough.' Does
that sound familiar?"

"Yes, it does," I replied, knowing that I had said *exactly* that many more times than a hundred. "But I thought we were doing that in our communion with the nature spirits and the Spirit level of all beings who live at Pavo and all around us."

Sparrow explained: "At one level, you're correct. That is the Spirit level *within* the physical realm, and that way of doing things seems new because so few are presently actually practicing it. That work is vitally important in itself and as a baseline for the next level. It's obviously a profound part of our work and truly Aria's predilection and expertise.

"It's worth looking at that level of our experience before moving on to the next level. It is truly the beginning place for the transformation that we are all seeking. We are cut off from even our everyday reality in so many damaging ways: we no longer have a clear and innocent perception of the spirit-filled life moving in all things around us all the time. There are many examples. All our food is oversugared and oversalted, which cuts off our ability to taste the real sweetness of things and to distinguish healthy, nutritious food. Artificial light and staying inside most of the time cut us off from the health we find in being outside in the natural light of Sun, moon, and stars."

"You're so right," I replied. "My people remind me that natural light is deeply healing, even suggesting that we take a sunbath every day, letting the Sun nurture our entire body for half an hour. They also taught me that the light of the moon and stars is remarkably soothing and healing to our nervous systems. Because we live in the glare of artificial lights, we miss the healing our stressed and worn-out nervous systems really need!

"We live in a culture that no longer sees or listens to what is around us. Everything is pitched to the level of violence. It seems that we are so deadened in our senses that we need to be hit hard before we feel the impact of anything. This deadening means that we are very dense—and that is quite the opposite of being light and awake and open to the subtle realms of Spirit."

"It shows in our fear of death, doesn't it?" Sparrow reflected. "Because we have no sense of the ongoing, eternal nature of life, we selfishly keep people who are very ill trapped in their agony and pain through artificial means rather than freeing them to be born in Spirit and move on in a natural way."

I continued the thought: "It reminds me of the native teaching about the earliest days when two-leggeds were given the opportunity to decide whether to have Death as a part of their experience. They discussed it for a long time before deciding, and what finally made them choose to have Death was that without it, there would be no Birth. There would be no children, no youth, no newness. Without fall and winter, we would miss the burgeoning of spring. I think the Old Ones made a wise decision. Yet today we forget how these natural cycles work as a wholeness. A few people are actually recognizing this and taking steps to celebrate the fullness of the cycle of human life, which includes birthing into Spirit at its physical end. I am working with a new organization called the White Owl Center, whose purpose is to create conscious, joyful birthing into Spirit as we experience what is now called death."

"That is so important," Sparrow Hawk acknowledged. "One aspect of what is called karma—often thought of as the balancing of all our actions over our lifetime—is also created at our death. Whatever thoughts or feelings we have at the moment of our passing create a most powerful impact, which we must then deal with in lifetimes thereafter. This means that most of those passing into Spirit these days go with tremendous fears and negativity and isolation instead of understanding that death is simply a clearing of rigid structure in order to create true freedom. It would be good for everyone to read some of the literature from those who have died and been resuscitated. Their experience is universally about light and joy and awakening at a new and broader level."[1]

"Yes, and all that makes me think about how little we really experience the wonderful life we are given during our physical Earth days," I said. "We live more in our heads than we do in the real world. We have 'dates' with nature rather than a real relationship with the natural world living in beauty around us. Even ecologists, who pay attention to the larger life in many good ways, often do so because they know that better relationship is important for our ongoing human life, not necessarily because they love and care for the world around them.

"Take our trees, for instance. It is one thing to preserve them because they create the cycles of air we need to breathe and have much to do with our water as well. It is quite another to care for them, to love, honor, and respect them because they are part of our family and great inspirations to us. The latter is what I call sacred ecology. It is a deeper level of that caring relationship, and it brings even more joy and beauty into all our lives."

"It's very strange, too," Sparrow said thoughtfully, "that those who now have the financial resources to buy beautiful pieces of land usually have little time to be in relationship with it. Many people with fewer resources are being forced off the land by higher taxes, and these are the very people who most often had developed a deep relationship to the land over generations. They were committed to it in a way that does not happen without real dedication.

"Everything is very much out of balance. When we take a good look at our destruction of nature, it is almost unbelievable. Out of our fear of and separation from what is wild, we have waged an intensely destructive war on our own sweet Mother. What ignorance we live out!"

"Yes, and it brings up deep sadness for me," I said. "I'm reminded of a situation I encountered recently in a place I have learned to love very much. A wealthy young California man bought a piece of property that included a spectacular grove of old aspen trees at the lower end of a very wet and marshy meadow. Because that was the area with the most spectacular view, roads were built across the meadow for access to the house, and a pond was put in that threatens to cut off the water that the aspen grove requires for its life. If this man doesn't pay close attention to the amount of water that now gets through to the grove, the aspen could easily die during the drier months of summer, and he will have begun the process of killing off the beauty he thought he could simply buy with money. He becomes an invader, an enemy, albeit unconsciously. It takes more than money to live in good relationship with the life around us.

"In that same area, a noxious plant called Russian knapweed is overrunning all the meadows and thus taking away the natural feed for all the herd animals. Knapweed produces a kind of chemical that destroys all other plant life around it and spreads like wildfire. Through the ignorance of those who steward it, this beautiful old ranch is becoming a wasteland in the dry areas, where knapweed spreads uncontrollably.

Even worse, the knapweed can spread from there into the Bob Marshall Wilderness, where it will take away the food of all the wildlife there. Newcomers have sometimes looked down upon the ranchers who have used the land to run cattle, yet ranchers and farmers have kept the weeds in check and thus benefited all the life in those areas. Being good stewards to the land takes much more than many city people understand. There is more to loving the land than to simply be there enjoying it a few months a year. It takes an active intelligence and deep relationship."

"Our lack of awareness is astounding," Sparrow agreed. "Very few people show the kind of true caring that means taking the time to develop a meaningful relationship with the life around them before they act for their own short-term benefit."

"That lack of awareness is truly amazing," I said. "Here's a true story of a boy whose dad is a butcher in England. The boy's grandmother is a friend of mine, and she is a vegetarian. When the boy was asking her why she didn't have bacon for breakfast or hamburger for lunch, she told him it was because she didn't like to see animals killed in order for her to eat those things. Her grandson looked puzzled and asked what she meant. She patiently explained that bacon and ham are made from dead pigs, and hamburger and steak come from cows we have to kill. This little son of a butcher was stunned! At first, he wouldn't even believe her. It is shocking to realize that even a butcher's son does not know that meat comes from dead animals!

"Many children, and even adults raised in cities, don't have the slightest idea of the simplest facts of Earthly life. One of the things I saw at my wilderness camps was that most people had no idea how to make or fix or repair or create any of the essential things needed for simple daily living. I responded to that by having simple craft projects at each camp to help people come into some awareness of those things. It is easy enough to be insecure and anxious in the modern world, but not to have even the most basic skills must leave people with a deep feeling of insecurity and fearfulness. For instance, many of them could hardly use scissors and had never held a sewing needle in their hands. We cut out leather and made little medicine pouches, which allowed them to improve these elementary skills.

"Another of my responses was to produce a camp called 'Living in the Cradle of Mother Earth,' which focused on showing participants all the abundance around them and giving them the 'survival skills' of being able to take advantage of that abundance. It's surprising how empowering it is to actually be able to make fire yourself, to construct a simple shelter, to make a salad from the 'weeds' along the path, and to make cordage by twisting fibers from the stems of plants!"

I could see that Sparrow Hawk was anxious to tell me something more, so I finished with the story of a man who had lived in Japan for fifteen years studying with martial arts masters. When he stepped off the plane in the United States, he was shocked at the deadness and disease and heaviness of the American people. He saw a degenerating culture, a culture in its death throes in the midst of unbelievable plenty.

Now Sparrow happily continued with the most amazing part of his lesson. "These signs of the times are what Aria and I saw that impelled us to model something different at Pavo. We recognized that everything we need is provided by the natural world around us, if we can only overcome our ignorance of it. We knew that we must find more and more ways to open ourselves to receiving the abundance around us. If we keep building homes that simply use up resources and give back garbage, then we will eventually have nothing left. We two-leggeds must awaken to Spirit alive in everything Earthly. We must love, respect, and honor that life before we can expect to wake up to the larger life of Spirit in the realms around us.

"This waking up is the deeper and even more profound lesson." He smiled as a child does who hands you a very special gift. "I'm speaking of going beyond the merely physical! That's the reason I had to leave—not to abandon you and Pavo but so that I could help you understand that it's time to go 'beyond' the normal plane of reality. You have spoken about it and already know the importance of this in some ways. Yet even you did not understand the full implications of it!

"The time has come for those on Earth to lift our vibration beyond the manifest realm, beyond the visible spectrum. The vibrational spectrum resonates across the whole of creation, and is basic to it. Manifest life takes place in a certain portion of that spectrum which is visible to the human eye, yet it obviously does not represent all of creation which is possible to perceive as we fine-tune ourselves and our perception."

His voice had become more resonant, as though he were speaking in a large cave. I felt that a presence even greater than Sparrow was speaking through him. *"The time has come to ascend into the Invisible realms, to lift our vibrations to more subtle levels and become one with the Unmanifest realms as well as the manifest.* We must remember that as humans, we live (although unconsciously at this point) in the Invisible as well as the visible realms. Now it is imperative to become more familiar with the Invisible. Some call it 'moving to the fifth dimension.' It is a place where we are awake enough at the level of Spirit to be conscious and functional and thus able to work there in order to make a difference in what happens on Earth. It means stepping outside the limits of structure, which we now hold so strongly yet are not real in the deepest sense.

"This has been the sphere of the shaman. It is what shamans and certain highly developed medicine people have been doing down through time but the general populace has not been ready to take on themselves. Those masterful ones move their consciousness into the Invisible with clear intent and 'imprint' the energy there so that when it becomes manifest, it creates a totally different reality than existed before. This is magic, real magic!!"[2]

The enormous voice became Sparrow's familiar one again. "I had completed my work on the physical plane, so I was able to 'go up the mountain a little farther' and beckon you to join me. From this more ascended state, I can help lift your vibration so that you can stand on a new pinnacle and see the world differently. It *really* is beautiful up here, and you *can* make it!"

These last echoing words were ones that he had called out to us on our hikes in the mountains. It suddenly dawned on me: Sparrow was doing the same thing he had always done—focusing his energy on climbing higher, finding the beauty there, and beckoning us to join him. Tears sprang to my eyes . . . it all seemed so right. Everything was going to be all right!

I looked inward again to focus on Sparrow's presence, and he was looking right at the center of my body with utmost concentration. I could sense the energetic fibers of my body awakening and tingling.

"Reach out to me from your center," he encouraged me.

I didn't know exactly what that meant fully, yet I did it and felt luminous fibers reaching toward him to connect with his. As we connected, he seemed to recede and fade, become less visible, and to pull me with him. It scared me, and I broke the contact, my own fibers snapping back into my center so fast it made me rather sick to my stomach for a minute.

After a moment, Sparrow Hawk appeared more clearly again, with an inquisitive look on his face. He never could figure out why anyone would be afraid to scale the greatest heights.

"Will I die if I go with you?" I asked him in a nervous whisper. "I'm afraid I won't come back."

"No, no, that's not the idea. We have simply held structure as an artificial boundary. Either being in the physical body or leaving it entirely to be in other dimensions is the way of the past." His voice became huge and resonant again. "The new dance that two-leggeds are being asked to do now is to remain in their physical bodies and be able to move at will into the Invisible *and* out again. The possibilities are endless ... unlimited. We are coming to a time on this sweet Earth when these things will be possible for all people. They will not only be possible but will actually be a requirement for continuing life on Earth. It *is* a huge evolutionary leap.

"The Yuwipi men of the Lakotas have done this;[3] Toltec women seers have done this;[4] the Ascended Masters of the Himalayas have done this.[5] There have been some two-leggeds in every primary group who have done this *and* been recognized for that powerful service to the people. Yet modern American culture has not openly recognized as valuable and special those with the gift of walking between the worlds. We must now understand that respecting, honoring, and *making use of* their talents will allow us to follow their lead into another level of awareness. Now is the time for all of us to do it!"

The great voice continued: "We will lift ourselves up into what some call the realm of Spirit (although Spirit lives in every realm). That realm lies outside the territory of time and space, and so 'there' we have access to all time and all space.[6] Because we are able to be in touch with all and everything, we will have access to incredible wisdom and thus enormous power to become one with the world of harmony and peace for which we all yearn. The human family will then be able to join with our relatives who have gone beyond, in *all* kingdoms of life.

"Do you feel this in yourself?" Sparrow Hawk's voice returned again. He seemed to be nodding in affirmation even though it was a question. "Perhaps all you need to know is that *I feel it in you*. Know that when you acknowledge this realm of Spirit and set an intent to open your perception to it (for it is all around and within you always), you will step gracefully into that sweet and spacious territory. One of the fine ways of doing this is through consciously connecting to someone on the other side of the gateway you have called death—those called by many peoples the ancestors.

"Pick someone high and clear and invite that individual to show you around. I'd be glad to volunteer, and so would any and all of the masterful ones."

Here his jocularity came back to the surface. "Make a date, lighten up, and open up!

"Wouldn't you like to get together with a visionary leader like Crazy Horse[7] or a warrior and medicine man like Short Bull?"[8]

It was as if those words had knocked me off a cliff, and I was falling into a deeper understanding and connection. Stimulated by the images of this Lakota leader and Ghost Dance priest, I found myself dancing in a circle of Ghost Dancers. These were Lakota people in the backcountry on the long grass plains, imprisoned on small reservations. Crazy Horse, who had the spiritual power and charisma to draw together a mighty cross-tribal force to create a bloodbath among the whites, had been given a vision to make peace—to cut Native losses and look toward a distant future of renewal. I saw that these dancers had just experienced the loss of this great war, in which many people on both sides had "gone to the other side." It was toward the end of that war, which had become a genocide to open the way for white settlement and gold mining. Troops of the U.S. Cavalry, whipped into rage by their superiors, murdered Native men in battle and staged surprise attacks on worn and tired and hungry villages, running sabers through the aged, sharpened poles through the bellies of pregnant women, and smashing in children's heads.

What outsiders called the Ghost Dance came among those Native people then, giving them hope of a renewed Earth and inviting them to connect with their relatives in the Beyond World. Guided in vision by the Christ light (by the one some native peoples called Dawn Star[9] or Morning Star), they lifted themselves into the invisible and communed with the *hundreds* of friends and family members who had just made that passage.

Think of how strong the pull of the invisible realm was to them then! The Christ of the entire Piscean Age came to use that energetic pull—terrible as it was at one level—to take His great lesson for two-leggeds a step further. The "conquering of death"—His demonstration of resurrection—had been one of His most stunning and essential teachings. So He called to the people—many different ones from different tribes around the same time—and showed them in visions how to conquer death through the Spirit Dance.

The early work of Dawn Star came about at the dawn of our age, and He continues to be an elder brother to *all people* as the high shaman of the Piscean Age.[10] He appeared as a magical shaman, the one who first brought this understanding for everyone rather than just a select group. His mission was to "set in the ground" of the Earthly plane a vibration, a seed, of what was to come, so that it could soften and germinate and grow upward through the ground until such time when it burst forth from the Earth visible to all. That seed was the understanding of our true nature as humans: that we are spiritual beings, with the capability to be aware of both the visible and invisible realms, and that great beauty, harmony, and flowering can come to two-leggeds through the honoring and development of our capacities in the unmanifest realms—the timeless, spacious world that is, to our physical eyes, invisible. Working in this realm is modeled for us by those who exhibit extrasensory perception, by shamanic healers who journey into Spirit to effect their cures, and by our highest Earthly masters who are in contact with the timeless wisdom of Spirit as well as the details of Earthly life.

"What a powerful time to set this in the ground," I could almost hear Dawn Star saying in the early Ghost Dance days, "when so many loved ones have died, thus lifting to that Invisible realm where they can assist those who remained behind." When those early dancers went to the Beyond World, they continued to hold the dream of this spiritual dance strong, as did some of their remaining living relatives, until it could reemerge to be made real on Earth.

As humanity opens new vistas of Spirit, it often happens in this manner. Some extraordinary, masterful person or persons set a tone, do a practice, a teaching, show a way on Earth that is new. Then it jumps into flame and spreads like wildfire because it is so beautiful and powerful. Yet the people of that time do not have the energy needed to make the new way real for themselves without the presence of someone who lives in that brighter realm. Therefore, when the inspirational figure leaves, the wave of elevated energy soon wafts away on the breeze and dissipates. Yet the most vital piece of the puzzle has been put in place: *The seed of truth, which has been so carefully planted and watered with practice in the physical world, will grow and in its own time come forth upon the Earth. It is inevitable. It is the way of all things.*

At last, my mind understood the connection! I realized that those of us alive in the present time are standing on Earthly ground as the sprout unfolds into the light again after being set by Dawn Star 2000 years ago. We are the heirs of the Ghost Dancers from the 1600s to the 1800s. That seed's sprouting into the light was the Harmonic Convergence, which occurred on August 17, 1987.[11] *The seed was danced to life long ago, and those of us alive now are awakening to our role in watering the plant, in caring for it within ourselves and within all things in such a way that a flowering of Spirit is blossoming in the garden of Mother Earth.* We are the other half of the Rainbow, reaching high to catch a radiant ball of light thrown to us from generations past.

For them, *we are the seventh generation.* We are to catch that light and ground it again in the Earth, to revitalize and nourish the sprouting seed that was planted long ago. And to do this successfully, our consciousness must rise up and over the crushing of the Ghost Dance dream—leave below us the horror, the terror, the genocide that seemed to "end" that first dance—and join our people on high just as they did in the old days. Together we will vibrate the Mother Earth with our joyous song and dancing feet, stepping to the rhythm of an ancient song, to bring about a radiant and renewed Earth.

———

I could see that Sparrow Hawk was my most immediate connection to that Invisible realm and thus to all those who had gone Beyond. Behind him, I could sense a whole ancestral line stretching into the far distance, and they were all walking toward us. It was the Old Ones handing down and down into our generation the spirit song of the Ghost Dance along with its sacred altars, the physical objects that had held that resonance until we could pick it up.

"*Aho,*" I said, thanking Sparrow Hawk in the Native way and nodding to him. "You have opened a beautiful path before me.

"Hey ho," I shouted out, looking toward those beyond him in the realm of Spirit. "It's wonderful to see everyone!"

PART II

FINDING OUR PLACE
IN DEEP HISTORY

My startling experience with Sparrow Hawk set me on a pilgrimage, a sacred journey to connect our human ancestral past to the task before us in this generation. I walked forward, in order to find the bridge that would meaningfully close the gap in my understanding.

What I found is profound information—an ancient multicultural map created especially for those of us living in this time. It is alive and radiant with meaning and usefulness for each of us.

CHAPTER 6

SPIRIT DANCING

The basic elements of the vision are timeless:
a renewal of the devastated Earth;
a return to the old ways of harmony with the land;
health, vitality, and youthfulness for the people; awakening
their own traditional spirituality to a new level
of good relationship and caring for one another; and
reunion with loved ones who had gone through the gateway of death.

So is there hope? Should we dance again?
Shall we let our hearts rise on the vision we are being given?
Deep history—prophecy—given us by peoples all around the world
urges us to move toward that vision with all our hearts.

In order for us to join the ancestral line of Spirit Dancers and move forward with true understanding, I believe we must first go back in time to reconnect there. That is precisely what my vision of dancing with the Lakotas had given me and I hope to give to you.

To look back at the years of warring and immense suffering is not easy for those with ancestors on either side of the conflict between the Native Americans and the invaders. Sometimes we would rather leave behind things that have become painful. Yet true healing means we must go back and begin from where we left off, no matter which side of the conflict our people were on. This is how we integrate the lessons rather than deny them.

Now, happily, we are being offered the incredible power and intent that those powerfully dedicated Ghost Dancers set into the energetic pattern of Earth. We are being given this metaphor to awaken and attune our consciousness in a way that both heals the old wounds and opens us to new possibilities for the children of all races and peoples. It is a remarkable opportunity for many people who are conscious of the genocide wreaked by their land-hungry European ancestors. And it is also an opportunity for Native people to step out of victimization into empowerment. Crazy Horse had the visionary ability to see that all people would get the renewed life and world they sought only when cooperation, spiritual brotherhood, and unity reigned. By letting go of the outmoded "eye for an eye" kind of thinking and moving forward with White Buffalo Woman and Dawn Star in the ways of peace and unity, we can bring about something wonderful for ourselves and all the coming generations.

It is important, as we begin, to understand that *all* cultures receive spiritual light and guidance from Creator. The Bhagavad Gita, Bible of the Hindus, says that God sends teachers and prophets to every people when they need them. The Christian Bible speaks of those gifted with visions, along with healing, interpreting visions, and so forth. The Koran says basically the same thing—namely, that God has sent all men instruction and messengers as they needed them and in tune with their culture and specific conditions. There is a general truth about humankind: We receive light from Heaven in various ways, and some of it comes through teachers, prophets, visionaries, and others who serve Creator's purpose.

The red race, or Amerindians, of the Americas are no different from any other group of nations. The four thousand or so language and tribal nations have gotten a myriad of lessons and light over thousands of years in an almost unimaginable and nearly infinite variety of circumstances. The Natives were even warned of the coming of the white-colored ones en masse and the karma and problems that would be associated with this change. Indian people have received counsel and light all along during their history, but most often the white culture has denied, ignored, or even covered up these prophets and their messages. Ironically this includes destroying records of Jesus Himself having come to the Americas as the highest possible prophet.

Even though his story is only partly known, the prophet Degana-widah of the 1400s has influenced the entire human race by helping to bring the form of the U.S. democratic system to the world. It came through the Iroquois, to whom he taught the system straight out of a vision six hundred years ago. His vision of a new government of many tribes in a federation was a gift of peace and an answer to the problems of war, vengeance, and suffering that the Indians were experiencing among themselves. The power of that vision not only reformed the eastern Indians but also was given by them to the U.S. government to provide an example for the rest of the world. Based on this, peoples could modernize past whatever system they were in, to become a new, peaceful Earth, with small and large nations sitting down together. This is the vision of peace, given six hundred years ago, that is manifesting around us today.

Soon after the new government of the Iroquois league came into being, the white man began to arrive in great numbers, and Indians faced the problems that invasion brought. They naturally returned to Creator and their religious leaders to help deal with the challenges, including new diseases and wars. Very early on in the colonial period, Native priests and shamans began to notice that disease followed contact with the white people and their black-robed priests. The baptisms done were even considered to be witchcraft that brought death, and indeed, the groups of priests going out among the tribes did bring death, whether from measles, smallpox, or other new diseases.

As the situation rapidly deteriorated for the Indian nations one by one, Creator began to counsel them through prophets and visions appropriate to their time and situation, responding generation after generation. As the tribes faced defeat militarily, they were advised to live peacefully with the whites. When they were faced with outright extermination, God also blessed their fights for survival. However, Dawn Star was sent with many of the visions, one of which specifically directed them to build their own churches based in their tribal traditions as they moved forward into a more integrated way of living with the invading Europeans.

So now, as we continue our journey, let me tell you of the old days when the people danced and what their prophets saw. From these things, we can learn much about our own time.

What we will examine began in the late 1600s with Popé among the Pueblo peoples of the Southwest and continued on until its tragic ending as a major Native movement at Wounded Knee in the late 1800s. During this time, Native tribes were given visions through sometimes unlikely prophets of a happy ending to come after the devastation each tribal group had suffered at the hands of the European invaders. Since the guns and steel traps brought by the whites were wiping out the game animals, tribal wars broke out to gain more territory to hunt and trap. In each instance, the people's devastation was remarkably similar, as was their desperation to find a way to survive and live a good life once again. The visions given were clearly one vision. Although it was brought through each individual prophet in his own way, the basic elements of the vision were the same:

- A renewal of the devastated Earth
- A return to the old, sustainable ways of harmony with the Circle of Life
- An awakening of their own traditional spirituality to a new level of good relationship and caring for one another
- Health, vitality, and youthfulness for the people
- Lifting into the Invisible for reunion with loved ones who had gone through the gateway of death

In his classic research on the Ghost Dance, James Mooney traces the line of these visionary movements as they shifted and spread across the country.[1] In the early 1600s, the Spanish invaded the Southwest, bringing with them a missionizing subjugation of the native people. In 1680, Popé, a medicine man of the Tewa, was given a vision of renewed life among the peoples of the Rio Grande. His vision eventually inspired a unified Pueblo revolution, which led to the demise of all the missionaries living among them. Others fled until not a single Spaniard remained in all of New Mexico.

A century later, in the eastern part of the country, the Indian tribes there had allied with either the French or the British, who were battling to take possession of the "New World." The native people often hated the redcoats, who looked down upon them all as savages, and felt more connection with the French, who lived with them and learned their ways. Yet in the end, both white groups betrayed their trust and took away their lands. In 1762, among the Delaware came a man named Neolin, who envisioned a union of all native peoples of the Americas and preached a return to the old native way of life. "He advocated the restoration of aboriginal rituals, beliefs, and practices."[2] In the powerful vision he had been given, he was addressed thusly: "I am the Master of Life, whom you wish to see and with whom you wish to speak. Listen to what I shall tell you for yourself and for all the Indians."[3] The message was similar to those received eventually by many others, although in later times, the messages emphasized peace among all peoples and an end to the warring.

The Master of Life went on to tell the prophet:

> I know that [the French] supply your wants; but were you not as wicked as you are you would not need them. Before [the French] arrived, did not your bow and arrow maintain you? You needed neither gun powder, nor any other object. The flesh of animals was your food; their skins your raiment. But when I saw you inclined to evil, I removed the animals into the depths of the forest.... Again become good and do my will, and I will send animals for your sustenance.[4]

The prophet was sent back to the people to exhort them to use a special prayer he had been given for them and to mend their ways of relating to one another and of meeting their needs. This spread from tribe to tribe, until eventually the celebrated chief Pontiac shaped it into a movement of eastern tribes who unified to oppose the advance of the English.

Among the Shawano (Shawnee) in Ohio, another prophet brought forth a similar message in 1805. After seeming to fall lifeless until the very moment of his funeral, the prophet returned to consciousness with messages of hope for his people, exhorting them to give up the white man's whiskey and its drunkenness and leave behind their wicked practices of witchcraft against one another. In the past, he had been called Lalawethika (Noisemaker) because of his boasting and complaining. After his vision, he took the name Tenshwatawa (The Open Door), in honor of the new way open to his people. In return for this new life that was to come, he preached that the people needed to release their dependence upon the white man's things, to begin to love one another, stop warring, and be kind to their children.

This message spread among many, including the Cherokee, and soon generated elaborate rituals. For example, when the Ojibwa accepted the new revelation, they honored it by painting their faces black to acknowledge connection with the Beyond World and kept sacred fires continually burning.

Again, however, this religious fervor was used by another faction to create war. Tecumseh, a noble and powerful leader of the Shawnee, used the rising hope for the return of the old ways to unite all the tribes in the Southeast in a grand confederation to resist further advances of the whites. He understood the power of unity and made a desperate attempt to do something that would have worked had it come sooner. *Yet again, the spiritual power of his vision eventually became for others a war strategy. Thus, many times, the peaceful character of the doctrine itself was used to create secular, rather than spiritual, ways of dealing with the problems created by European encroachment. This has profound implications for us.*

In the early 1800s along the Mississippi, a Kickapoo man named Kanakuk received vision during his people's darkest hour, and he urged them to hold their ground, based on revelations of a way of peace he had been given by a Messianic Christ figure. George Catlin, who painted the Plains peoples of this time, wrote in his journal, "I was singularly struck with the noble efforts of this champion of the mere remnant of a poisoned race, so strenuously laboring to rescue the remainder of his people from the deadly bane that has been brought among them by enlightened Christians."[5] Many who heard Kanakuk turned away from dissipation and began to dance with the prayer arrows he had shown them how to make. They danced and sent prayers for peace and the renewal of their world.

In the 1870s, a man named Tavibo originated a Messianic lineage of prophecy among the Paiute tribe who lived in Nevada. In 1881, in southern Arizona, the Apache medicine man Nakai' Dolin'i preached a doctrine of supernatural powers and communing with the spirits. In his visions, he saw the whites being driven away very soon. At the same time, a new ceremonial dance that had similar elements was introduced among the Potawatomi and Kickapoo in Kansas. In Montana, in 1887, Cheez-tah-paezg (Wraps His Tail) of the Crow nation began to speak of invulnerability to the white man's bullets, as many others in the past had done.

Around this time, Smohalla, a Umatilla who had "died and come back to life again," began preaching a religion called Dreamers, in which he spoke of the red man's ruling his own country again. As Mooney wrote:

> Dreamers was a new and peculiar religion, by the doctrines of which they are taught that a new god is coming to their rescue; that all the Indians who have died heretofore, and who shall die hereafter, are to be resurrected; that as they will then be very numerous and powerful, they will be able to conquer the whites, recover their lands, and live as free and unrestrained as their fathers lived in olden times.[6]

This doctrine influenced Chief Joseph's Nez Percé people through the principal Dreamer priest in his band, Toohulhulsote. The primary ceremonial of this new religion was a dance.

This dancing religion was reawakened by a visionary revelation in Wovoka, son of the Paiute prophet Tavibo. It then began to spread at a tremendous rate through all the tribes.

It was said of Wovoka:

> On this occasion "the sun died" (was eclipsed) and he fell asleep in the daytime and was taken up to the other world. Here he saw

God, with all the people who had died long ago engaged in their old-time sports and occupations, all happy and forever young. It was a pleasant land and full of game. After showing him all, God told him he must go back and tell his people they must be good and love one another, have no quarreling, and live in peace with the whites; that they must work and not lie or steal; that they must put away all the old practices that savored of war; that if they faithfully obeyed his instructions they would at last be re-united with their friends in this other world, where there would be no more death or sickness or old age. He was then given the dance which he was commanded to bring back to his people. By performing this dance at intervals, for five consecutive days each time, they would secure His happiness to themselves and hasten the event.[7]

Tribal medicine men soon came from far and wide to hear Wovoka's message and to take the dance back to their own people, all of whom were in desperate straits, barely able to stay alive. Among them, in 1889, was a delegation from the Sioux nation. Into the dance, they then began to incorporate the Sacred Pipe, which had long been an integral part of their ceremonial life. New, special shirts were made, of leather when it was available (since they had been exhorted to return to aboriginal habits) or of simple trade cloth and flour sacks when that was all they had. Among them, and most other prairie tribes, this ceremonial was designated the "Spirit" or "Ghost" Dance because much emphasis was placed on the reunion with all their dead relatives so recently lost. It is by this name that we have come to know it.

The renowned warrior Red Cloud, the great Oglala chief Sitting Bull, and many other Lakota leaders felt they and their people should do as the Messianic visions had instructed. And so the Ghost Dance began among the Sioux. They had realized that the white man's promises meant nothing, for their people were starving.

The new dancing ceremony began at dawn with the cleansing and purifi-cation of the stone people lodge (sweat lodge).

Then the leader and his assistants prepared the people for the dance. The face of each was painted. Forehead, cheeks, and chin bore circles, crescents, and crosses that symbolized sun, moon, and morning star. Colors varied, but red, the color of Wi the Sun, became also the color of the Ghost Dance among all the western tribes.... No other part of the body was painted, for Ghost Dancers were fully clothed.

The central feature of the costume, worn above buckskin leggings, was the Ghost Shirt. It was a sack-like garment of cotton cloth or muslin ornamented, like the face, with painted circles, crescents and crosses, and with designs symbolizing the eagle, magpie, crow, sage hen, and other birds and animals having special significance in Sioux mythology. Many were fringed and adorned with feathers. The medicine man preached that the Ghost Shirt made its wearer invulnerable to rifle bullets. If soldiers fired at an Indian so protected, the bullets would fall harmlessly to the ground.

The dance began about noon. Dancers of all ages and both sexes sat in a large circle facing the center of the dance ring. Often, when several hundred participated, they ranged themselves in concentric circles. The dance leader, flanked by his assistants, took station at the foot of the prayer tree and gave detailed instructions to his followers. Then, raising his arms to heaven, he prayed, "Great Wakan Tanka: We are ready to begin the dance as you have commanded us. Our hearts are now good. We would do all that you ask, and in return for our efforts we beg that you give us back our old hunting grounds, and our game. Oh, transport such of the dancers as are really in earnest to the Spirit Land far away and let them there see their dead relatives. Show them what good things you have prepared for us and return the visitors safely to earth again. Hear us, we implore."

The people stood and clasped hands. Someone started a Ghost song. It was rhythmic but without rhyme and evoked misty images of the past. The song rose in intensity and took on emotion. The dancers bent their knees to produce a rise and fall of their bodies, and with a shuffling side step started the dance rings moving slowly and hypnotically to the left. Those rewarded with a journey to the Spirit Land told wondrous tales of their adventures, inspiring others to struggle yet harder to bring on a vision.[8]

Ghost Dance Inspiration

My Father, have pity on me!
I have nothing to eat,
I am dying of thirst—
Everything is gone!
—*ARAPAHO GHOST SONG*[9]

By praying, dancing the Ghost Dance, and singing the Ghost Dance songs, Indians could "die" and journey to this paradise for brief visits before it actually appeared.... Here they would find all Indians who had once lived on earth—friends, relatives and ancestors. Together they would enjoy eternal life, unmarred by pain, sickness, discomfort, want, or death. On every side, deer, antelope, and elk would roam in abundance, and herds of buffalo such as only the old people could recall would once more blacken the prairie.[10]

The Lakota Ghost Dancer Little Wound tells of his remarkable experiences:

When I fell in the trance a great and grand eagle came and carried me over a great hill, where there was a village such as we used to have before the whites came into the country. The tepees were all of buffalo hides, and we made use of the bow and arrow, there being nothing of white man's manufacture in the beautiful land. Nor were any whites permitted to live there. The broad and fertile lands stretched in every direction and were most pleasing to my eyes.

I was taken into the presence of the great Messiah, and he spoke to me in these words: "My child, I am glad to see you. Do you want to see your children and relations who are dead?" I replied that I would, then God called my friends to come up to where I was. They appeared, riding the finest horses I ever saw, dressed in superb and most brilliant garments, and seeming very happy. As they approached, I recognized the playmates of my childhood, and I ran forward to embrace them while the tears of joy ran down my cheeks. . . . We all went together to another village, where there were very large lodges of buffalo hide, and there held a long talk with the great Wakan Tanka. . . . After we had eaten, the Great Spirit prayed for our people upon the Earth and then we all took a smoke out of a fine pipe ornamented with the most beautiful feathers and porcupine quills.[11]

The people grew increasingly desperate, as it became obvious that the agents and white men were lying and cheating and had never planned to help them in their great distress. So they chose to disobey the orders to stop the dancing. People abandoned their farms and stock, withdrew their children from school, and flocked to the dance centers. They made sure the agents in charge knew that no violence was contemplated, that no arms were carried, and that the renewal was one to be created by spiritual, not physical, means. Short Bull, one of the Ghost Dance priests, urged a great gathering near Pine Ridge to dance even though the troops should surround them.

Government forces exerted more and more pressure, and some of the Native groups fled the agency areas. Tempers flared as fear was ignited. And this eventually led to attempts to arrest the leaders in which many of them were killed. It culminated in the desecration at Wounded Knee, where starving families of Sioux were massacred and thrown frozen into a common grave.[12]

> For the fires grow cold and the dances fail,
> and the songs in their echoes die;
> And what have we left but the graves beneath,
> And, above, the waiting sky?
> —*THE SONG OF THE ANCIENT PEOPLE*[13]

With Wounded Knee, the back of the Ghost Dance had been broken, although it has survived in guarded ways until the present day. Ghost Dances have been held through the ensuing years under such names as "Spirit Dance," "Giveaway Dance," "Naraya," and other disguises so as not to call down the reign of horror again. A breath of the great Messianic wind had come whispering itself among the faithful and carried the spirit of healing and renewal forward so that it was never completely lost among the living.

We will never know from the reports of whites exactly what the tribal people saw and understood. Yet it is clear that these visions, born of desperation, called for a renewed world, a world of Spirit. One of its most poignant aspects was reunion with loved ones so brutally slain in their fight to preserve their ancient lands and their ways of life. And in some ways, given the concerted governmental effort to exterminate them, they had little choice but to give themselves to dancing awake a new world through the visionary ceremonials.

My children, my children
Look! the earth is about to move.
Look! the earth is about to move.
My father tells me so.
My father tells me so.[14]

In this song, the dreamer tells his friends, on the authority of the
Messiah, that the predicted spiritual new earth is about to start to come
over and cover up this old world.

The spiritual challenge they had at that time was to keep the focus of the ceremonials on a
vision of beauty for all people. Yet in a period of such genocide, it was an almost superhuman task to hold that positive vision for even the invaders.
Again and again, what was added to the original vision by the Native
dancers, and understandably so, was the prayer that the demonic conquerors would be not only vanquished but totally destroyed in order to
bring about a world of peace and beauty.

Different dates have been assigned at various times for the fulfillment of the prophecy. Whatever the year, it has generally been
held, for very natural reasons, that the regeneration of the Earth
and the renewal of all life would occur in the early spring. . . . The
date universally recognized among all the tribes immediately prior
to the Sioux outbreak was the spring of 1891. As springtime came
and passed, and summer grew and waned, and autumn faded again
into winter without the realization of their hopes and longings,
the doctrine gradually assumed its present form—that some time
in the unknown future the Indian will be united with his friends,
who have gone before, to be forever supremely happy, and that this
happiness may be anticipated in dreams, if not actually hastened in
reality, by earnest and frequent attendance on the sacred dance.[15]

Only in retrospect can we see the importance of what the dedicated dancers have done to set this seed in the ground. For when nothing

happened with the flowering of spring in 1891, and the devastating vulnerability of the Ghost Shirts to the white man's bullets was so hideously demonstrated, the people who believed were ridiculed. For many, the dream was shattered; to them, it had been for naught. And yet some steadfastly held the vision and continued to dance, knowing it would come to pass at a time in the future they could not determine.

Even today, without an understanding of the great cycles of deep history, it might be easy to scoff again at any idea of an awakening of Spirit that will bring about a new world. Yet one of the things I've seen in my lifetime is that Spirit does not run by our small human clock. In the place beyond space and time where life is known to be eternal, our personal sense of the timing is of less concern. So often, predictions by us two-leggeds of when and where great transformations will take place fail to prove true. Yet the movement of Creation is much larger and grander than we can see with our physical eyes and understand with our limited brain. Only in numinous vision can we see the full scope of things, and it is difficult, if not impossible, to translate that into human language.

I'm personally joyful to be experiencing the time when the Aquarian Age comes to us around the great Wheel of Time. It's wonderful to me that, as in the time of the old Ghost Dances, there is an intangible yet very real sense of a renewed Earth coming. And this hopefulness arises in spite of the destruction of many things precious to us, our Earth, and our ways of life. I know there are traditional Native people on reservations, as well as métis leaders in the cities, dancing again the vision of the original Ghost Dance. These dances in which I have participated are being dedicated to upliftment and spiritual renewal. Some gatherings are open to all people of peace; the ceremonies send nourishment out in four directions to all people and Mother Earth. Perhaps again, we are awakened *because* of this dark time in which we find ourselves at many levels.

One major challenge we face in this time, as did the Ghost Dancers of old, is that of *holding a peaceful, inclusive, loving intent*. The key given to the prophets in their visions was that peace, love, and unity reign in the

Chief Joseph

hearts of those dancing. To pray earnestly for a renewed world of beauty and abundance was paramount; yet this did *not* include deciding how that would look—for example, that the white invaders would all be conquered, decimated, or pushed back. Holding this outcome as the intent nullified the spiritual agreement; the vision did not manifest. *The magic of the vision was its inclusive unity*; it did not, could not, include warring and hatred. The "best outcome for all beings" had to be held as the intent. Therefore, the fatal corruption of the vision by war leaders meant that the dream could not come true.

This is why we must now totally abandon fearful, separatist, and angry methods of moving forward. They will only magnetize more conflict and aggression. We must remember and take to heart White Buffalo Woman's message about the Rainbow that will build the Bridge to a new time: it must be inclusive of all. We must recall and practice Dawn Star's admonition to create a spiritual brother/sisterhood of all peoples.

So is there hope? Should we take our place in the circle of dancers? Shall we let our hearts rise on the vision we are being given? Should we take Sparrow Hawk's message to heart? Or should we ignore it and protect ourselves from too much hope? Deep history—prophecy given us by peoples all around the world—urges us to move toward that vision with all our hearts.

CHAPTER 7

THE DRINKING GOURD

Whenever the precise moment of this entrance into the Golden Light,
prophecies of many lands tell us it is imminent
for those of us on this sweet Earth.
We will have made the Rainbow Bridge;
the covenant of a unified Heaven and Earth
will have been fulfilled.

I realized that to truly understand the movement of Spirit in our time—
the renewed Earth that the Ghost Dance prophets had envisioned and
that is possible now at the dawn of a new millennium—I needed to go
even further back than our recent experience on Turtle Island (the Native name for North America). It made sense to me that if this great vision is to come true, all peoples would have seen it, each in their own
way, and be expecting it. Here is what I discovered from my own knowledge base and from the records of others.

In research concerning prophecies and information about this specific
modern time from Toltec, Aztec, Mayan, Egyptian, Hebrew, Japanese,
Chinese, and other peoples around the world,[1] I found what provided me
an even more solid foundation upon which to base my hope for a bright
new world in our lifetime.

We are on the cusp of a new age. That is, Earth is about to move
into the influence of another sign in the zodiac, an event that takes
place every 2,160 years. In cycles of many, many thousands of years, it is
challenging to specify an exact date for the change between the ages.

Some who are knowledgeable about the great movements of time say we began the transition from the Piscean Age into the Age of Aquarius on January 23, 1997, signaled by a special six-star alignment. The Aquarian Age is the time of a cosmic pouring of the water of Spirit onto Earth from the Great Drinking Gourd in the sky, the Big Dipper. Its astrological symbol shows us a robed person tipping a container that pours a stream of liquid down upon what lies below. This liquid is spiritual water, "the ambrosia of the gods, the nectar that confers immortality." This Aquarian urn or drinking gourd is said to pour forth its divine liquid at the beginning of each Golden Age.

Many of us have heard various things from the Mayas, the Aztecs, the Hindu scholars, and others referring to a Golden Age that is supposed to be happening even now at cosmic levels and will come into our Earthly sphere sometime in the near future. The idea of it is entrancing. Yet much of the information can be just so many esoteric words because it's difficult to make real sense of it. Most people have no concrete feeling of connection to it and don't know what to do or not do about it anyway. The pieces haven't quite fit together. Often in the past when I heard about it, I didn't give much credence to it because I didn't really know what to do with the information. Perhaps you have felt this way as well.

One major issue that always comes up is, how in Heaven's name are we going to get from this mess we're sinking deeper into now—this very dark and violent time—to a Golden Age? It just doesn't make sense that it would work this way, especially if this blissful time is soon to come. No one had ever made it clear to me.

However, I've recently focused my attention and prayers on this. I want to know both what is happening and how I, we, can participate in the process. In what we've heard, there is always something said about raising our consciousness so we can move with grace into this Golden Time. Many of us are doing that, to the best of our abilities ... but what does even that mean, really? White Buffalo Woman has some answers to this, which I have been sharing with people over the years. She speaks of raising our consciousness through wholeness and holiness, by coming together, sharing, and cooperating. It's basically about being in good relationship with All Our Relations.[2]

Yet what is important to us now is how it all fits together. In response to that, this chapter presents some of the important things I discovered. It offers you information about what's happening from a deep historical perspective, with the goal of helping this all make more sense. In Part III (see especially Chapter 10, "Ready or Not!"), I'll offer some thoughts about what it means for each of us personally and how it may affect us as a human family. Then I want to share with you some things about responding in a way that's beneficial and useful for you.

You must understand that this information I'll be giving you is all circles and whirlpools, going around and around again. It's not going to be very linear. Some of it will be simple scientific theories, because you'll need these few basic concepts to lay the groundwork for understanding the really juicy stuff coming after that. So hang in with me. My intention and my prayer are for each and all of us to awaken joyfully in the Golden Time. *Mitak oyasin* (Lakota words meaning "All My Relations" and implying that the prayer is for all).

As I begin telling you about this, I want to send deeply heartfelt gratefulness: first, to the Ancient Ones who passed this information down to us through their stories, writing, and calendars; second, to my teachers and elders; and last and most specifically to an amazing Vedic scientist/alchemist, Robert Cox, who made it all make sense. *Aho, aho, aho.*

The Toltec/Aztec and other ancient calendars give us metaphoric information about this time we are now in. (The great cylindrical stone calendar that is used in these prophecies came from the Toltec era and was later used by conquering Aztecs who discovered it.) The Toltecs tell us that we are at the bottom of the ninth hell and say that this is the very bottom of the barrel—the worst it can get. And if we look around us, we can understand how this might be. Not only is age-old warring continuing, but there is pollution at almost every level; degradation of Mother Earth and the nurturing She provides; species genocide that robs us of vital links to life; personal and national violence at every turn;

premature aging; and rampant disease. Things have become so bad that in wonderful, beautiful middle-class American communities, parents are *afraid* to let their kids walk to school; people are homeless and starving on our streets; big-money interests who want more of the Earth for themselves are spreading AIDS and killer flus; children are using automatic weapons and bombs to kill one another with no sense of remorse or wrongdoing; our government is becoming increasingly fascist; and TV spreads it all around like a bad cold that everyone gets accustomed to having. And it seems to be getting worse!! "For centuries, negativity on Earth has consumed all that glistens, until it runs like molten lava within the veins of the beautiful Terra."[3] So given all that, what's the likelihood of a Golden Age coming? Looks pretty far-fetched, doesn't it?

Yet the Toltec calendar tells us not only that we are at the bottom of the ninth hell but also that after a decade or so, we will begin an ascent, coming into the beginning of a Golden Solar Age by 2010, and moving in time through thirteen heavens. Supposedly we are in that chaotic period of transition right now, in the twenty-five years after the Harmonic Convergence. But how do we start up the ladder? In response to that question, we find some very clear ideas from ancient seers in primary cultures. Especially interesting are those from the Indian Vedic tradition. Those great seers actually wrote down their wisdom after the last Golden Age. Because they wrote in Sanskrit, a language that is still being used, these works remain available to modern scholars. (We'll get around to how they got into the last Golden Age after I give you some of the basic concepts.)

One way of thinking of a Golden Age is that it is a period of universal enlightenment and holiness. During these times, people are consciously aware of their connection with All Things and are thus "God-realized," as some traditions call it. What this means is that people in a Golden Age are able to perceive any and all levels of Creation. In other words, they see right down to the very Wave of Creation through which things move from the unseen, nonphysical realms to the physical, from the Unmanifest to the manifest world. (You'll notice that I use the term *Unmanifest* to describe what is sometimes referred to as the Spirit realm. I do this because my elders have reminded me that Spirit fills all of Creation, including the physical, so to say "subtle," or "Unmanifest," realm is more correct.) Luckily for us, the ancient seers have passed down this information to help awaken a re-cognition of the larger cycles of which we are a part.

All Creation myths and stories tell us that there exists—always and throughout everything—a potent, chaotic, rich soup of intense energy. Take, for example, the subtle realm of space/air around us: scientists tell us that there is more energy in the teeniest particle of that subtle space than exists in the entire physical, manifest world. This amazing life force is within everything; it is the Spirit life of all things and exists in manifest, physical objects as well as in this Unmanifest primordial soup. From Unmanifest to manifest, there is an incredible range of beingness, of vibration—from the infinitesimal to the infinite—and everything is in constant motion from one realm to the other: in/out, visible/invisible, alive/dead, dense/subtle, and so on. My friend Rob put it so beautifully: *"Creation moves across a Rainbow Bridge from Song into Light."*

At Unmanifest, subtle levels, the vibration is sonic: it is sound, song. And at manifest levels, the vibration becomes a play of light creating *Maya*, the illusory world we perceive around us. In all Creation myths, including the Christian Bible, we are told that in the beginning, nothing was manifest. Then Creator spoke a word or sang a great song, and the world became manifest. "Let there be light." And the play of light began.

The ancient seers could observe this interplay between realms and noticed that its configuration is that of a whirlpool, beginning with an enormous mouth and narrowing down and down like a funnel, until finally

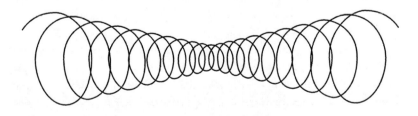

it comes to a still point, a point of nothingness. Then it whirls on into the other realm, growing larger and larger. Up and down, up and down, from infinitesimal to infinite, Unmanifest to manifest: in/out, physical/ nonphysical, alive/dead, material/subtle—an eternal play of light and sound.

The nonmaterial substance, the ground of being upon which all this plays, is a unitary Oneness through all things. It flows into physical exis-tence, giving vital life to all things manifest. I sometimes think of it as a golden elixir, nurturing the physical (for instance, our bodies) with everything that is needed both in body and in consciousness. This is what the Vedic seers refer to as *chitta*, or life force. In a Golden Age, there is an extraordinary abundance of it, creating high consciousness (omni-science, all-knowingness), radiant health and youthfulness, omnipotence (the state of being all-potent, all-powerful), and omnipresence (being in, conscious of, or having access to all time and space at once). However, in dark times—now, for instance—there is correspondingly less of it com-ing through into our beingness. We are more dense and dark, starved for this vital life.

One more property of this *chitta* is that it is a superfluid. Let me ex-plain what that is. In our world, things can exist in a solid, liquid, gaseous, or superfluid state. Superfluids are now part of modern scien-tific experimentation, so I can give you a simple interpretation of how they behave.[4] Superfluids (such as helium, which can be worked with in a superfluid state)[5] are so lacking in resistance that they don't have movement as we usually think of it. In other words, say you have a tall tomato-juice can of water and you whirl the can; the water inside will eventually turn, too. This is because there is a slight friction even in this very fluid liquid. But if you fill your tomato juice can with superfluid he-lium instead and whirl the can, the superfluid helium does not swirl. There is no friction, nothing to pull it around. It remains the same within the whole of it.

However—and this gets interesting—if you continue to whirl that container long enough, something begins to happen deep within this un-manifest, superfluid helium. Right at the very center, in a line only tiny particles wide down the middle of the tomato-juice can, a vortex begins to whirl. And there in that tiny line, subtle superfluid helium becomes manifest as helium gas. Continue to swirl the can and eventually all its contents turn to gas, manifest in the physical realm. Thus, this experiment demonstrates for us the swirling, whirlwind motion of the Wave of Creation that brings energy from the subtle realm into the manifest. That energy will at some time return to the subtle as well. This is the eternal way of the Wave of Creation.

Always interested in practical applications of such principles, I asked Rob if such activities as the movements of whirling dervishes and our Native dancing in circles for long periods of time actually bring through some of this *chitta*, or vital life force. He said, "Yes, definitely. Vedic teachers call this energy a *devita*." He reminded me that the heartfelt intent (intentionality, the focus of people's most profound attention) of those in the group guides what happens with the energy as it manifests. If a group dances for abundant crops, then the energy that manifests is guided by their intent to serve that purpose. Now that I understand this, I'm able to make better use of this potent process in ceremonies. As I gather people together in dance circles, I suggest the image of a genie we can create at the center—magical, whirling energy that says to us, "What is your wish, Masters?" This helps us focus on our intent for the dancing and on the command we have of our focused energy.

So back to the basic concepts. Do you get the general picture? Superfluid, vital life force cosmic soup whirlwinding down the funnel through a still point and becoming manifest: growing, evolving eventually into total solid, dense matter and then back down less and less dense until it reaches the still point, after which it becomes subtle, unmanifest. The process is unending.

Now before I go on, I want to mention a few more facts that are of profound relevance to us two-leggeds. Along the entire range of vibration—from infinitesimal to infinite, from microscopic to the enormity of the universe, from totally subtle superfluid to the densest possible matter—we two-leggeds stand at the center. And our hearts sit at the center of our selves, joining the realms in love and unity. Thus, the human heart stands at the very center of the Rainbow Bridge between Song and Light.

It is fascinating that the place of *power* is at exactly that same center spot. Nearing the still point of transformation is the place where subtle, Unmanifest energy can be acted upon the most powerfully—and what acts upon it is heartfelt intent. Until now, it has been the shamans' work to journey into the Unmanifest (sometimes called Spirit realms)—to go to those subtle realms and act with focused intention where they can potently influence what manifests as subsequent reality. Thus, we can see the benefit of all the work of shamanism, manifestation, spiritual healing, and so on. Here at this still point, the center of the Rainbow Bridge, is the place where the Ancient Ones have been telling us to focus our attention. "The heart is the center of all wisdom, for the heart is the connection to the Divine."[6] You are co-creators with the Great Creator. Your Sacred Heart (the place of connection to Source and to your own indigenous power) commands this place of power. Become conscious of how and what you create, so that you use your intent to bring forth a beautiful world.

Consider too, that the most potent force in the universe is Love— Love not as a romantic tryst but as unity, connectedness, harmony; as passionate, positive energy that creates, embraces, and includes. Here at the point of power is where the magnetic, inviting energy of the heart

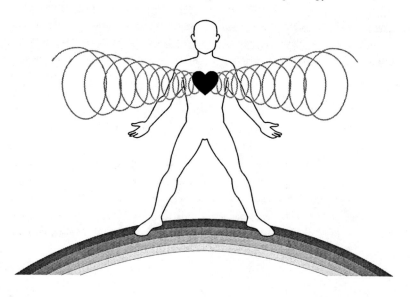

can be put to the best use. Intent that has this unifying, harmonizing purpose is mighty: *When you are acting in harmony with the Great Circle of Life, your intent is multiplied and magnified.*

And look as well at the potency of the nonmaterial aspect of things, as I mentioned earlier in the chapter. Our science and technology, up to this time, have focused on the material, structured side of existence. In the future, we will focus on the subtle spaces and the magnificent, unlimited energy available there.

Now, a quick review. There is vital life force that fills everything, everywhere. In subtle realms, it is a unitary superfluid of intense energy— whirlwinding into manifestation as physical matter and back out again as subtle energy. Standing in the center of that rainbow Wave of Creation, where the most powerful influence can be made, is the heart of us as two-legged family.

Allow these images to drift in your mind for a while, and let's look at another piece of the story, which concerns the turning of Mother Earth through Her great zodiacal year. If you like physical examples, get a glass or bowl and lay a straw or pencil across the top. The circle is the representation of the pathway of the Earth as it precesses in its orbit. In simpler terms, our Mother Earth moves around the heavens in a circuit, passing through the twelve houses of the zodiac[7] in a manner similar to the way we pass through the astrological signs in our yearly movement around the Sun.

In the age of the golden calf mentioned in the Christian Bible, Earth was in Taurus, then it moved into Aries, and now it is just passing the end of the Piscean Age into Aquarius (which corresponds to about 6:00 A.M. or dawn on an ordinary clock, early springtime of our seasonal year). For Mother Earth, each of these signs or ages lasts 2,160 years (very different from humanity's one month or so in each). This means that movement around the great circle, represented by the circular rim of your glass or bowl (the circle in the illustration), takes nearly 26,000 years! Over the aeons, our Earth goes around and around and around this great circle of Her grand year.

What the straw or pencil represents is a band of the *chitta,* or golden

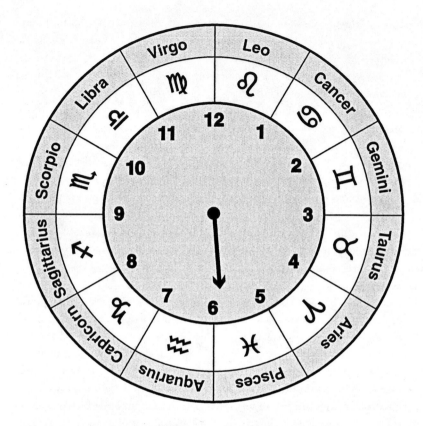

life force, that the Ancient Ones say lies across the Earth's path, cutting it twice in the great 26,000-year cycle. (It cuts through Aquarius on one side and Leo on the other.) This band is enclosed by an electromagnetic sheath that is wrapped fully around it, keeping the Golden Light/ life force concentrated and insulating it from its surroundings. (The *chitta* would move out into the rest of the universe and spread itself evenly without this unusual enclosure.) Vedic scientists tell us that it takes about two or three days for Earth to pass through the sheath itself, then . . . into the full radiance of Golden Light—concentrated *chitta*, intense, vital life force.

This life force then fills and enlivens everything Earthly, creating a

Golden Age. In a short time, all things and beings, including animals and everything physical, rise in consciousness, living in more and more subtle realms. All become aware of their connection with one another and All Our Relations through all of time, both unmanifest and physical, via this unitary vital life force that pervades everything. Humanity rises to incredible heights, given this omniscience and omnipresence. With two-leggeds totally loving, creative, and powerful—living in White Buffalo Woman's holiness—a Golden Age comes about quite naturally.

This lasts about one thousand exquisite years, and then Earth again passes out through the sheath. These high Golden Age beings—this advanced culture—persist for many centuries because the people are all-knowing and can continue the ways of Light. But gradually, as more and more generations of people are born who have not experienced the Light, the Golden Age and its ways drift away. It was at such a time about six to ten thousand years ago when the Vedic Indian seers and those from other cultures began to consciously realize they were losing it. They could no longer actually see the Wave of Creation; they were no longer unquestionably connected to all space, time, and beings. They knew that their knowledge must be set down before it was totally lost, and they did so in writing or in stories that soon became myth. Thanks to those who wrote in Sanskrit, Vedic scientists are interpreting for us now these ancient written records from their ancestors. Although these include information on every aspect of life, we will focus only on what is pertinent here.

So let's continue on the precession of the Earth around this great circle. Twelve to fifteen thousand years after the Golden Age, things have once again become about as dense, dark, and unholy as possible. There is comparatively little light and vital force within the dense, manifest realms. Since no light leaks through the covering of the band of light that the Earth approaches, and since it has been approximately twelve thousand years since the last time the Golden Light pervaded all, you can now understand how our dark, violent, polluted, crazy, unhealthy time came to exist. Until the moment the Earth passes through that sheath and into the band of Golden Light, *it will be the blackest it has ever been.*

So where is the Earth, where are we, right now? You've likely guessed

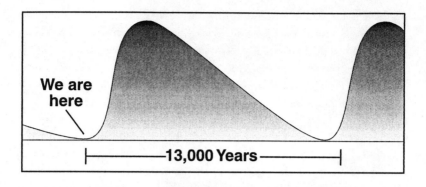

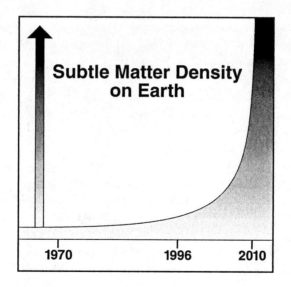

it. We're at the bottom of the ninth hell, in what seems the worst mess possible. Your straw or pencil cuts one edge of the circle at about where Pisces and Aquarius come together. Right about *now!* This information gives me the answer to how we can pop right out of the darkness into the light. As soon as I learned this, the whole process and all the predictions began to make sense.

———

What is the Golden Band? When is it coming? Give or take a bit in the 26,000-year cycle, of course, it is basically upon us *now*. The prediction is that we will enter into this belt or band anywhere from 2003 to 2012. The rise in available energy will be on a curve that moves through deep time and looks like what's shown in the accompanying illustrations.

Concerning the timing, the Maya people of what we now call Mexico still use their ancient calendars. For them, the 1995 spring equinox marked the completion of the dark period necessary for what they call the lost Solar Culture of the Americas to awaken again and flourish for the benefit of all humanity. This long-held teaching advises that the human race will have to enter on an awakened spiritual path if it is to remain a thinking species. Maya elders see 1995 as the end of the Age of Belief and the start of the Age of Knowledge. They say we are now in a time of transition leading to the new age in the year 2012.

People from all over the world gathered at Chichén Itzá and other sacred sites in the Yucatán on March 21, 1995, to reactivate the temples there and to initiate this solar destiny. Maya Daykeeper Hunbatz Men said at that time, "The waves of awakening and change have begun to roll. Nothing can stop it now."

Another image of the timing is the astrological one I mentioned before—the zodiacal sign of Aquarius, the light-bearer who pours the

water of Spirit down upon us from a beautiful jar. This water of vital life spirit from the spring at the Source of All Things is a metaphor for the Golden Light, concentrated *chitta*.[8] This is the pillar of celestial fire to which Robert Cox refers in the title of his book.[9]

This information from the ancient prophecies, which was written down many thousands of years ago to help us through this dark time, gives us a solid foundation for faith in the vision of a renewed and beautiful Earth, one that has been repeatedly given to humankind. It provides a sense of timing that the Ghost Dancers of earlier times did not pass on to us. *Whatever the exact moment we enter into the Golden Light, the prophecies of many lands and many times tell us it is now imminent for those of us on this sweet Earth.*

And it is even more exciting than that. We are coming to the end of a 200,000-year cycle as well as a millennium and an age. Because Creation moves in an upward spiral, this cycle of Golden Light will awaken us to *a whole new level of being in which we will be able to maintain that Light ourselves.* It is like the birth of a baby, who has been "alive and kicking" in the womb yet dependent on a source outside herself for her vital life support. But when this great wave of vital life force embraces us, we will have all the energy we need to move through the birth canal into a level of life in which we can be more consciously in charge of our own life force. At first, we may still be somewhat dependent, just as a child is, but soon we will stand on our own.

As always, we have our part to play in this unfolding drama. We must ready ourselves for the light that this great initiation will bring. It's wonderful to actually know that many among us are developing and reawakening technologies of spirit that will enable us to generate the vital life force we need in order to receive the incoming wave of light with ease and grace. Some of these are external and may be akin to the ancient chambers of light like that of the Great Pyramid, in which the pharaohs were initiated into enlightenment. The most powerful will be those internal means coded within our genetic makeup, to which we are reawakening.[10] These sacred alchemical processes will help us move into this whole new, illumined level of life.

This is an extraordinarily exciting time to be alive on this sweet Earth. Even in Her darkest hour, Lady Gaia is beautiful. Just think of what this epochal springtime will bring us! And then, the greening of summer!! Rob Cox says it beautifully:

The infusion of subtle matter at the time of Illumination will affect not only human life, but also will have a powerful evolutionary effect upon all the other beings on our planet. The plants will undergo such rapid evolution that new species will quickly emerge, more beautiful and fruitful than anything with which we are familiar. The herbs and minerals will become super-charged in their medicinal properties, and the atmosphere, which will be filled with subtle matter and thus endowed with conscious prop erties, will cause the seasons to be mild and come in time. The animals will also display more consciousness and will experience less misery, animosity, and fear. Human beings will treat each other, the Earth, and all of its creatures with honor and respect, and the very thought of war will seem incomprehensible. The Earth thus will be transformed into a Heavenly Paradise, a shining jewel in the sky, filled with wondrous forms of natural beauty and spiritual Light. This is not a fantasy. According to the ancient Seers, it is our collective destiny.[11]

We will have made a Rainbow Bridge. The covenant of a unified Heaven and Earth will have been fulfilled.

And the best news of all is that although there may be waves of darker and lighter times in the great cycles of the universe, we will never again have to be in the kind of darkness we are now experiencing. Our Mother Earth has moved through Her own initiation, choosing to become Lady Gaia, upon whom harmony and peace reign.

Of course, it is clearly possible for any or all of us to disregard this entire prospect of renewal—to live poorly and die sick even in this remarkable time. Yet I, for one, want to do everything I can to contribute to the full awakening of this bright new day and to stay around to experience it personally, in an illumined body.

We of this generation have already begun the work. Now let's take a deep breath, lift our gaze upward, and continue.

CHAPTER 8

WE STAND IN THE DAWN STAR'S LIGHT

*Through our action in the sixties, a powerful resonance
had been set in the reality of the physical Earth;
nothing would ever be the same.
Our generation was dancing the dream
of a renewed Earth into reality.
We had begun to make ourselves known.*

*We must understand ourselves as the vital link.
Our challenge is to keep the dream alive
and to dance it into the ground—
this time for good.*

So who in deep history are we? What of these present generations? Given the great sweep of history, it seems as though we are an afterthought, a small raft tossed on the swelling tides of consciousness, with no significant part in this process except to let the sea of transformation sweep over us, move us as it will.

It may seem that way, yet it is not so: each generation has its particular assignment. Although prophecy and the great cycles of time and change would seem to dictate what will happen, *it takes individual human beings to pick up the tune being sung at the center of Life and learn to sing it, then actually dance it, live it, into reality in the material world.* It has become clear to me that no one but those present on Earth can actually do that. And we are the generations present at this momentous time of transfiguration. We are the ones making it real in our everyday lives!

I realized that we *have* been doing our homework, to the best of our ability, so I want to review what we have accomplished. In order to do that meaningfully, I must again go back into our history, this time even further than the Ghost Dance.

Two thousand years ago, there came, walking across the water into Polynesia, an amazing being. He came from the Far East on the great ships that plied the waters, guided by natives who navigated on the great sweep of ocean currents by singing the songs that timed their turnings. These large boats would anchor in the ocean coves, and those aboard would take dinghies or other small craft through the reefs and shallow waters to the shore.

This master,[1] however, seized the attention of the people wherever He went by walking across the water onto land. From that startling beginning, He taught them about a new way of being that He had come to Earth to demonstrate. He was an itinerant preacher and prophet, a high shaman who moved from place to place sharing His message. From Polynesia, He journeyed to Central America and then moved in expanding circles throughout the Americas.

He spoke to the people of the appropriate and powerful use of the energies of life. He showed them how they could gather in the energy from Mother Earth and Father Spirit and, without restriction, send it out through their hearts into the world. In so doing, they expressed their fullest gifts, creating what seemed like magic.[2]

When they asked Him His name, He replied, "Call me what you will." And so they called Him by many names, including the Beautiful One. The Polynesians called Him Wakea, Fair God of the Waters. Some in Central America and Mexico acknowledged His spiritual stature and physical accomplishments by calling Him Ce Atl, Lord High One. There, in the tropics, He was also named Quetzalcoatl, the Feathered Serpent. This name, an Aztec combination of *quetzal* (an exquisite, long-tailed, iridescent bird of paradise) and *coatl* (serpent), honors His power within the Spirit world (air, the realm of birds) and upon the Earth (the serpent representing one who lives not only upon but within Mother Earth).

He held dominion over all the elements, for not only could He walk on the waters, He could also still or stir the winds. He seemed able to move through the air more easily than the finest bird that flies and demonstrated creating and extinguishing fire at will. He was named Hurukan, Great Wind Master, by those who witnessed Him dissolve to a breeze a great tornado in the Yucatán; and Wah-kea and Wah-ko, which mean Water Serpent (*wah* means "water"). In the northern Midwest, He was called Hea Wa Sah, He from Afar over the Waters.[3] His eyes, framed by long copper hair and beard (most American Native peoples have no facial hair, so this was quite remarkable!), changing from blue to green like the great ocean, looked down the vistas of the future. He wore a seamless robe embroidered with crosses at the hem and golden sandals on His feet.

They called Him Great Healer, for He healed the sick and raised the dead, bringing new life to all (the name Ila Acoma, Lord Miracle Worker, from a Central American tribe, acknowledges this). He touched the people with loving and restorative hands, in the palms of which were scars like crosses. Even the great jaguars loved His touch and rolled like kittens around Him. Whenever He spoke, all could understand His words, though they spoke many different tongues. He was truly a high shaman, demonstrating powers that awed even the finest of the medicine people in the lands He visited.

He came to model a way of life lived through the heart, speaking of a loving Father Creator and a beneficent Mother Earth. His teaching was of Oneness and unity among all realms, all peoples and things; as He moved among the peoples of the Americas, Quetzalcoatl created a spiral of light, a spiritual brother/sisterhood in which all people and beings were honored and respected as family. Love, found in the Sacred Heart, was the highest power, and awareness from Source, which channeled through the heart, the guiding principle. He asked the people to take responsibility for practicing this divine unity among themselves, not simply looking to Him in a worshipful way. Following His teaching, tribes began to trade and exchange and encourage one another and to respectfully allow and celebrate their differences. Given the energy and resources saved by relinquishing war, defense, and fighting, a flowering of life came among the people. Beauty, harmony, art, education, spiritual awakening, and enrichment at all levels created a new and exquisite life for everyone.

One of the keynotes of His way was that of forgiveness—the releasing of the old so that life energy was not held in thrall by past negativity and could be used for the magic of life in the moment.[4] It is said that He brought cedar from the great trees in Lebanon, whose pungent fragrance He used as a smudge (plant material burned as incense for sacred purposes) to promote this forgiveness and clearing. It is still used in this way today, including by some Dakota peoples who call Him Wakan Tah.

This amazing being was also a plant shaman, for He taught the people how to give loving attention and conscious energy to the food they grew, thereby increasing its size and, most important, its nutrient value at both physical and spiritual levels. This loving attention was shown to increase the health and vitality of all things, so that everything in the Circle of Life began to shine with a new radiance. He brought many of them, including the Hopi, seeds of melon, pumpkins, squashes, beans, and many other wonderful plants, teaching the desert peoples special ways of conserving water, including creating hidden underground cisterns. Cotton was grown in many colors and woven into gorgeous fabric, just as it is beginning to be again in our time. Beautiful birds sang in flowering trees beside clear streams that ran even through the cities.

Some, especially the powerful priesthoods that had controlled the life of the people, were not happy to see Him come. He preached a doctrine of individual relationship to God by teaching that the Great Spirit lives within each and every person and thing. Therefore, each person is able to contact the highest wisdom through his or her own Sacred Heart and need not pay the priests to communicate with or propitiate the gods. The Mayas thus called Him Itza Ma: the descending God sent by the Father to bring the ways of Spirit and Light to all the people of Mother Earth.

The priesthoods lost their power, and the people turned the heavy golden idols of their past into fine gold leaf to cover the temples, creating beauty and radiance for all who saw them even from a great distance.

Human and animal sacrifice, which had been practiced to propitiate the gods, was stopped. In its place, honoring all life and personally living the spiritual life oneself became the way. The society He stimulated was egalitarian, inviting and honoring the gifts and magnificence of each person.

As He moved north in the Americas, names He had been given in the south followed Him. In the Northwest, what we now call Mount Rainier stands out radiant above the land, seen for hundreds of miles around; it was given His name: Tla Acoma. As time passed and the name was slurred, it became Tlacoma, or Tacoma, and a city on the coast of Washington now carries that name. Nearby, the name Ce Atl was used among the people, eventually becoming the name Ce Alth (Se-alth), which was given to a great chief of the people there who spoke on behalf of the native people's love for the land in the 1880s. In our time, his name is written as "Seattle" and became the name of our modern city.

One of His names, which echoes most vividly into our modern times, is Dawn Star or Morning Star. This name was earned in several ways. Often He walked into a new tribe at dawn, with the light shining all around him like a halo that did not fade as the Sun passed away from Him. Also, during His time among them, early each morning, he took his twelve apprentices out to meditate on the dawn star. (Within each tribe He visited, He gave His discipline to a similar small group with whom He could leave His teachings—highly evolved individuals who could learn His ways and continue helping their people in His absence.)

These were reasons for His name, yet a more potent reason existed as well. *He was symbolically the dawn star of a new day on Earth.* His task was to model a way of love, unity, cooperation, compassion, and communion with All Things that would eventually become the way for all people to live. (In this way, He is Elder Brother to all those who follow and is called by this name as well.) However, He came to Earth long before the morning light of that epochal day had dawned upon the world. He was a single star, shining in the darkness. Yet that one small, powerful light set the tone for a whole new day to come in the future.

It is said that when He finished his teaching throughout the Americas, He returned to a radiant, burgeoning city in the south, where the temples shone golden in the sun. Golden Tula was a beautiful city where His ways had created a virtual flowering of all life. When the word went among the people far and wide that He would speak to them for the last time, they gathered for twenty miles around the temple on which He would stand. On that radiant day in Golden Tula when He spoke, every person who came to hear Him, no matter how far from the temple, heard and understood His words.

In my own mind I hear his words this way:

I have come among you to model a new way, a heartful and sacred way of being that brings about a flowering of all life. I have come singing FlowerSong. Together we have created great beauty in all the realms of life within and around us. But you must know that you are now at a great crossroads. Each moment of your life you make choices, and yet on this day, the choice you make is crucial to all life on Earth. You have a momentous opportunity: if you decide to continue in this sacred way of love and light and life through your hearts [He said, looking around Him at the exquisite beauty], what we have accomplished up to now will seem paltry and dull. Should you keep honoring the energy of life by pouring it forth unrestricted through your hearts, you will create a flowering never before seen on this sweet Mother Earth.

However, I say to you truly that if you take the other road—the road of fear, separation, conflict, greed, and dishonoring of the life of Spirit within all things—you will fall so far and so hard that, standing this day in Golden Tula, you cannot possibly even imagine how terrible it will be.

Thus spoke the one they called Kate-Zahl, the Prophet, because His spirit walked down the cycles of the future. His voice rolled out across the people, who shook their heads in disbelief that life could change and become that bad.

One way or another, far down the path of earthly life, the sacred and magical ways I have shown you will be the normal ways of

living. People will do these things I have done, and many even more magnificent. The human choice will be whether you get there with grace—by maintaining and building upon what we have already helped to blossom—or whether the entire garden will be left decimated, strangled and dying before you awake to rebuild this golden way.

This is now your cross: you must choose the way. But before I go, I will plant my heart—the heart of my teachings—under a banyan tree, which is the greatest tree in the southern lands,[5] that they might live there in the sweet soil, holding that energy for you. Your Sacred Heart, resting at the center of the cross within each of you, will be able to find them.

Being the seer that He was, Dawn Star was deeply sad on that day because He loved the people and the beauty they had built together. Sad, because He could see that the people would be unable to maintain the flowering He had brought among them—that they would fall very far and hard and the garden would be decimated before the people could maintain sufficient energy to hold the teachings and re-create the magic.

And as decades passed, Dawn Star's sad prediction came to be. The power of the Light seemed to fade. The priests insinuated their demands and rituals again. People turned from their hearts to their minds; material structure became more important than the flowing life of love and Spirit in all things. They began dishonoring one another and the life around them; separation and fear became the order of the day. Struggle for territory and possessions took the place of loving cooperation. The spiral of light descended into darkness.

Yet the Dawn Star's ways were remembered by some. Lines of "light" shamans, who worked the magic of love and union, were kept intact in a time of dark shamans, who did harm with their works. Their descendants kept the practices alive in small, isolated groups, and Spirit sparkled among them, weaving a tapestry of continuance. Female plant shamans in Peru created miraculous gardens on the stone temples there, generating new sources of food and nourishment for the people. Healers and others who carried the light gave restorative attention to the people.

As the centuries passed, and fewer and fewer kept the practices alive, the ways lived on in story. Each winter, when the snow was soft on the ground, the people gathered together to repeat the stories so that they might be remembered down through time. Thousands of years passed, and the stories among many tribal peoples became myth: few in modern times acknowledge a belief that they are true, and most seem to think of them only as metaphor. Too often, a bad feeling about Dawn Star/ Christ's message was created by missionizing Christians who brought oppression, cooperated with forcibly taking children away from their families, and frequently beat the tribal ways out of the children.

Yet Dawn Star came again in the time He had predicted—that of the great genocide and decimation of the tribal peoples of the Americas. He came to prophets of many tribes, giving them again the Messianic vision of a renewed Earth, which they could bring about by the very same principles He had taught two thousand years before. They were to put their hearts back at the center of their lives—to come together in peace and unity, dancing themselves into a spiritual upliftment that allowed them to see this vision themselves. But again in those recent times, the loving unity of the vision could not be held. The Ghost Dancers could not bring the dream into being. The time was not yet ripe for the seed to burst forth from the ground and become real.

Certain people remember Dawn Star even into modern times. When

I asked my Cheyenne mom about these old stories of our Elder Brother, she reminded me of the name of her people, the people of the Morning Star (Dawn Star). "Yes, He walked among us long ago," she told me. "We are His people. One of our names for Him was Wohogus, Light of the World." The Christ Light had been here among all the tribes of the Americas,[6] giving the message of love to all the people.

The great cylindrical Toltec calendar stone that the Prophet left the people[7] recorded the historic events of the Dawn Star's day and set out more things to come. There would be a return of the light-skinned ones, with their flowing beards. When the Spanish conquerors came in the 1400s, knowledge of Dawn Star and His ways was still alive among the people. His lineage of shamans continued to practice the ways of light and love.

On the exact day shown in the calendars of stone, the Spanish came. The Native people were tremendously excited, yet they had been told to look for a specific sign. If the cross the bearded ones brought was set within a circle, it meant that those carrying it remembered the ways of wholeness, love, and unity that Dawn Star had given. If, however, the cross stood alone, then those who carried it would have forgotten His true teachings, and great danger approached. History tells us that the cross stood alone and that the bearded ones wanted only to conquer the native peoples and claim the land as their own. These missionizing conquerors spoke of this same amazing teacher, calling him Jesus, but they only besmirched His name—killing and oppressing in the name of God.

Had these invaders been willing to recognize the Christ Light among the Natives, they would not have been able to subjugate them and label them as animals to be treated in any way they chose. Instead, the Spanish conquerors created a witch-hunt. Anyone possessing any knowledge or any writings of Dawn Star was killed instantly. As in all such terrible times, people pointed to anyone they disliked as one of His lineage of shamans, and that person was immediately murdered.

Terror reigned, and the sacred Dawn Star teachings went underground, often to be held in small family groups pledged to secrecy. Some of the lines let them fall away and turn to dust, feeling that they were useless against this onslaught. Other lineages whispered the secrets to new generation after generation, practiced the ways in secret, and passed the writings down from parents to children. Group ceremonies and celebrations had to be held in secret, far away from the conquerors' strongholds. This period is what I call the moonlight time of "Silverado," when the teachings could be practiced safely only under cover or "in the dark" rather than openly. Bringing Golden Light to the "House of Silverado" would come many generations later, as the Solar Age dawned upon the world.

The centuries passed. More Europeans came to the Americas, conquering the Native peoples with their firepower, their ordered regiments, their "gifts" of smallpox-infested blankets and alcohol, their lies, and their decimation of the great herds of buffalo that were the people's food supply. Different tribes, wanting to win territory from their neighbors, joined with the big guns to destroy the surrounding peoples. Native fought against Native; promises of land and riches were broken; the resistance to white settlement commenced too late; and genocide began. Hungry for land, for gold, for the extravagant beauty of the "untamed wilderness," the immigrants soon overran the tribal people. Some of the more peaceful, gentle peoples were simply crushed by the dark power of the invaders; but many others joined in the warring, glad to have bigger, deadlier weapons with which to wreak havoc on their tribal enemies.

The Native peoples had not stood together in love and unity, upholding the highest Light. In the end, their embracing of war, separation, and conflict brought what the Dawn Star had prophesied. No one could have believed that genocide would descend upon the people, yet it did. Their world was shattered and smeared in blood. Those who remained staggered under starvation and devastation.

Once the people of the Bird Tribes (Indians) lost touch with their eternal spirits, they were as responsible for what the Europeans brought as the invaders themselves. They were left with no choice but to blend with the invading warrior tribes, that in the end all might again become conscious and whole.[8]

Yet it was among these very people that the prophets arose and were given visions by the Christ Light of a renewed Earth. The Ghost Dance was spread among the tribes. The people danced; the killing intensified; and the spring of 1891 passed. They had not been able to stand unified to hold the peaceful circle intact, which was required for the vision to come true. Only a few continued the dance, holding the faith that the renewed world that had been prophesied would be hastened by their faithful practice. Even if it did not come in their time, they knew they must dance for the seven generations to come.

The blood of the Native people had been spilled, but their spirit still lived in the land. And that spirit came up out of the ground to be born again in the children of the oppressors. As 1960 rolled around the great wheel, other Native prophecies began to come true. The young descendants of the immigrants spontaneously began to emulate the ways of the Native peoples—braiding their hair, wearing leather, returning to the simple ways of the Earth, living in communal groups, talking of peaceful flowering.

The Dawn Star's FlowerSong teaching seemed to awaken in their hearts as they began to question the rampant oppression along lines of race and gender and to challenge the power of a government whose old, wealthy men sent the nation's young into battle to protect their moneyed interests. A new wave of consciousness swept over the land. Native people stood against great and dangerous odds to demand that they be given true religious freedom and honoring of their sacred sites,[9] and people around the world rose in support of them. Newly conscious groups concerned with civil rights, religious freedom, ecology, and peace began to come together in mutual support.

This growing unity threatened the powers in control. The government, military, big business, and international cartels all feared our new Oneness of thought and intent. Realizing that we could actually change the ways of things, and that their pocketbooks would surely suffer, they mounted a powerful campaign to divide and conquer. They turned Native against Native, Indian against "New Ager," rancher and forester against ecologist, effectively turning the tide of this emerging energy of peace, respect, and unity. Once again, as fear held sway, they were not above killing and devastation. Government troops killed American young people at Kent State. The second Wounded Knee came, with Bureau of Indian Affairs (BIA) officials and police colluding with some corrupt Natives to again take what belonged to the tribal people.[10] Once more, the conflict left bodies scattered across the reservation lands.

The dream of peace was not coming into reality. Once more, it had stimulated the opposite—anger, reprisal, death. Communes, with free love and often too many people crowded together, began to shatter—no one seemed to know how to actually create community life. The energy started to dwindle; civil and religious rights became a political football; hippies got jobs and blended back into the mainstream. Yet it is vitally important to understand that *once again, a powerful vibration had been "danced into" the reality of the physical Earth; nothing would ever be the same. We had begun to make ourselves known.*

The great circular stone calendar rolled along, marking important dates with regularity. Then on August 17, 1987, what became known as the Harmonic Convergence was celebrated. Looking deeply at the "Toltec/Aztec" calendar,[11] José Argüelles and those in concert with him awakened us to the need to acknowledge this important day. It was celebrated as a day of unity, sharing, global harmony, and peace. Many people around the world gathered to honor that day, often without knowing exactly why, except that it felt right and we knew the importance of joining together in prayerful ceremony. This was a new day on Earth.

My supporters gathered a group in the lovely mountains near McCall, Idaho, to "Dance Awake the Dream." I led them in ceremony through which we joined people around the globe in dancing all night to release the old. Then, dressed in white and rainbow colors, we greeted the dawn of a new day on Earth—a new era.

The deeper historical meaning of the Harmonic Convergence went unacknowledged by many, yet the prophetic date had been celebrated. What was actually being honored was this: The Dawn Star's heart—the light of His teachings—had been buried like a seed under the great banyan tree in Oaxaca (and in that deep knowing of the human family).

On this day in August of 1987, that heart burst forth from the ground, sending rays of Christ Light and His teachings into the hearts of all upon Mother Earth. The seed of the teachings, which had so long ago been buried under the ground of this continent, had opened and grown up through the soil of human consciousness until it burst out into the visible world to awaken our hearts. Our global circles formed and danced. Even though the Dawn Star had faded, this new day had now fully dawned. *Our generation was dancing the dream of a renewed Earth into reality.* We were doing our homework.

Another trigger of remembrance came on January 1, 1992, when a hundred thousand people around the world participated in gatherings to acknowledge the 11:11. My friend Solara, who focalized much of this energy, talked about it this way:

> [It] is a pre-encoded trigger placed . . . into our cellular memory banks prior to our descent into matter which, when activated, signifies that the completion of duality is near. . . . The purpose of this activation was to open the Doorway which is a transition zone between two very different spirals of evolution, those of duality and Oneness. . . . The overlapping of spirals remains in position until December 31, 2011; thus we have a twenty-year period to graduate from duality and make our ascension into Oneness.[12]

She suggests that we "physically embody the vastness of the Invisible on a daily basis until it becomes our new normal." According to Solara, "Ascension is a process, not an event."

In 1993, something very interesting happened, which bridged back to the days when the Spaniards drove the Dawn Star's teachings underground. A book in the form of a teaching story came out, telling of prophetic tablets that had come out of the lands of South America. It was said that a Native man brought a manuscript to a priest he trusted.

This manuscript outlines practices to help us clear and awaken ourselves to the ways of living spoken of so long ago—of coming into Oneness with one another and All Things. It includes an understanding of the process by which we raise our vibration into the Invisible realm. The story goes on to tell of the repression this priest experienced as he tried to share these teachings. The knowledge spread despite the fears of the Catholic Church, and the book tells the tale of intrigue and danger that led to the publication of these teachings.[13]

As it was expressed in the legendary "Song of Quetzalcoatl,"

Carry your great books into the jungles. Place your histories deeply in caverns where none of these [warring white men] can find them. Nor do you bring them back to the sunlight until the War-Cycle is over. For the children of War are these bearded strangers. They speak my precepts, but their ears do not listen.[14]

Some said the story is way too "far-out" to be believed and summarily dismissed it. With the historical perspective given me, I was keenly interested in what had been expressed, especially when I read that the insights were written in Aramaic, the language that Jesus the Christ[15] would have used in his time! Going through the book a second time, ignoring the story and outlining the principles, I found them to be in remarkable alignment with the historical teachings of Dawn Star. The Native man had brought the manuscript forward because it was time for all people to have the knowledge. And this originally self-published book, *The Celestine Prophecy*, became a bestseller all around the world.

Now, a second level of the teaching is out in *The Tenth Insight*.[16] Once again, behind the story line is a more penetrating insight. Its principles of living deepen our understanding of moving across the Rainbow Bridge into the Invisible to do the unified work that can make a profound difference in our manifest world and in the critical issues that fear places before us. "Leave a light at night burning for the time I will return through the Dawn Light, and lead you to My Father's Kingdom."[17]

The Dawn Star's light is coming to us in our time, just as it has for peoples before us. It has come in another remarkable way through an artist named Glenda Green. In 1991, Jesus appeared before her to sit for a portrait. While the painting was being done, He gave Glenda a new and empowered look at teachings and information that hold vital keys for our transformation and the renewal of Earth in this time. At the beginning of the Piscean Age, He came as an awakening star, teaching the ways of the heart. Now, through the book Glenda wrote in the early 1990s, He has deepened that teaching to help us complete the heart work of the Piscean Age and move gracefully into the Aquarian Age. *Love without End* contains such amazing and empowering material that you will want to read it and work with the transformative principles contained there.[18]

As the eve of the millennium approached, more and more people were awakened to our global interdependence by the Y2K challenge. Sustainable living began to make sense to a wider range of people. And an unprecedented number of people around the world joined in prayer and meditation on New Year's eve to hold the image of peace for humanity. People around the world were able to observe one another's rituals and ceremonies on television. This wove us more closely together in a conscious, global network of Earth's people. From all reports that reached us, the celebration of the new millennium was peaceful and joyful: the power of unity was moving in our hearts and minds.

The wheel of time has turned again, and new support for a whole and holy way of being on Earth has emerged! This gives me incredible hope for us and our sweet Lady Gaia. The dream of a Golden Time is still alive among those who held it in the sixties and seventies, and many others are awakening to it as human consciousness evolves to a new level. We are preparing to manifest a whole new heartful way of being on Earth, and as always, there is a backlash of fear, anger, repression, confusion, ridicule, and violence. *In the face of this, we must understand ourselves as the vital link.*

We have available the information we need. It is our work to *practice* these new ways. It takes discipline for us to stay focused on our task and to be willing to do the work. Yet such effort is not required forever—only for the short time it takes until it becomes easy and natural for us.

Our challenge is to keep the dream alive and to dance it into the ground—this time for good. We stand at the door of the House of Silverado. It is our heroic task not just to throw wide the door and let the Light in but to *take down the walls* and let the golden solar Light flow into our home forevermore! It is for *us* to bring gold to the House of Silverado.

CHAPTER 9

THE END OF TIME

"The true shaman is one
who holds the golden dream in [his or her] heart . . .
until it comes true on Mother Earth."

We two-leggeds surely face a challenge, yes. We face the despair of the darkest of times, before the coming of the Light. We are also confronted with those who have given up hope in the face of our current situation. And to make it even more challenging, we have prophets of doom telling us that the End Times are here—that everything will be destroyed! Given this, it becomes easy for people to be cynical and frightened, to grab any small bit of physical pleasure and security, at whatever cost.

I can understand people's response, and that is why this book has come: to give us the information and support we need to look beyond these next few years of darkness, to have hope and faith in the bright future we can create for ourselves and all beings.

So what about this "end of time" news? It can seem pretty scary, especially when all the horrible things that actually are happening around us seem to back it up. Certainly most of the media focus on the negativity more than on any positive stories.

Here's one wonderful way I have been shown to look at it. Can you imagine not having to look at a watch or answer to a clock? Wouldn't it be lovely to live life at your own, personal, intimate natural rhythm? To be called from sleep by the sweet chirping of birds and the sunshine pouring into your window from a horizon over sacred groves of blossoming trees? To get out of Time, in its regimented and linear aspect, and move into Time in harmony with the organic flow of things— Mother Earth's time?

Think of that. Truly think about it—and what it will actually mean in your life when there is no need to fear and bow to Time. When we understand that we are taking care of everything that's necessary by paying exquisite attention to Life within and around us, we will not lack for anything. There will be abundance and plenty, simply through a natural, pleasing exchange of the things we do well: our talents and the unique gifts each of us came to bring this time on Earth.

An ancient Mayan vase was recently decoded upon which were depicted the Seven Lords of Time. It says that the Lords of Time meet at the end of every age to determine the kind of time that will be experienced in the next age. It is important for us to cast our vote for a heart-based, flowing sense of time that transcends our current limits: no alarm clocks, no appointments to keep, no time clocks to punch; only flowing, synchronistic time that puts us exactly where we need to be exactly when we need to be there. I can feel my body start to relax just *thinking* about it! To me, this "end of time" stuff sounds fabulous!

It will be most interesting and amazing for humans to experience being outside Time, and therefore outside our current restrictions of Space, in a realm in which everything flows without restriction (superconductivity, superfluidity). It's a place of grace, really, where the flow moves back and forth with such great ease that it expansively extends its breadth— reaches into and beyond past and future. Thus, everyone will be able to interact with loved ones who have gone into the Invisible before them— our lineages, our history—as well as what may come to be. *We become the Children of Immortality.*

Realizing that, I understand fully for the first time what the Ghost Dancers of old were shown. It makes such good sense when I see it this way. As they lifted themselves up through prayer and ecstatic dance, they saw that it was possible to step beyond Time and Space and thus were able to have the experience of something poignantly important to them in that time of genocide—being reunited with their loved ones. At that time, however, they couldn't bring the renewed Earth of their vision into their daily reality. Perhaps it just wasn't time for it to happen.

It is important for us in this time to look at the positive nature of what is possible—what the "End Times" mean when we look at them through the higher perspective of love and timeless unity rather than through fear and separation. The eyes of love are looking in very different directions than the eyes of fear and limiting structure. With the tremendous in-pouring of light and energy onto the manifest plane, we will move with utmost speed in the direction in which we are looking. Thus, we will quickly reap the fruits of our thoughts and beliefs. This should be a strong motivation to wake up and begin taking responsibility for choosing our future!

It's also important to realize what supports our faith in moving forward. What can help us to feel that it's all worth the effort? It seems to me that Creator encoded the deep truth of all these great changes in our souls and our DNA, but our minds and hearts need some real encouragement right now.

In every people's ancient knowing, there has been a graphic image of the separation that will now occur. Love and fear are two completely different realms: they do not blend gradually into each other. At any moment, you exist either in the realm of love, unity, and wholeness or in the realm of fear, structure, and separation; they will now diverge at a most amazing, almost alarming, rate. There is a very real possibility of the darkest of futures; the wonderful news is that *we do not have to choose that reality*. We can step up to a different level, into dimensions in which an entirely different scenario unfolds.

Images of this from the Hopi tribe have been in front of our consciousness for many years. As you can see in the accompanying illustration, the smooth path of harmony will divide from the jagged path of

Prophecy Rock (Wutatakyawvi) near Oraibi

conflict, and they will spread far apart. Yet at one point, there is a ladder. At this time, we can climb up or down that ladder, no matter who we are.

"In my Father's land you will all have lodges,"[1] Dawn Star reminds us. We can move onto the upper path by focusing our attention on a light, clear, sweet, and flowering time. Or we can go down the path that leads to more and more disharmony. There the vibration will eventually become shaking so heavy that a great destructuring of things will happen on the third-dimensional physical plane.

Does this ring a bell for those of you who know the Book of Matthew in the Christian Bible? Is the image given there not the accompanying image? Is it strikingly similar to the Hopi image shown earlier? The sheep will be divided from the goats? Those who will be lifted up and those who will fall down? (Matthew 25:32) In Chapter 4 of the Book of Revelations, there is clear imagery of a rainbow that bridges the chasm between the two worlds. Do you recall White Buffalo Woman's message that the Rainbow is the connection between Heaven and Earth? It is called the *covenant*—a promise, a guarantee given us long, long ago and now being made real in its own time.

One of my students recently shared a similar vision she was given when I led a group on a shamanic journey (an ancient ritual way of drumming at a certain rhythm that stimulates movement into nonordinary realms).[2] She saw life moving down a great river in a most peculiar way. There was a large fish swimming at the surface, upon whose back was a white bird. These two had traveled this way together so long that the bird was no longer accustomed to flying. However, they could hear far ahead of them an enormous waterfall and could soon see the spray from it rising into the air.

Thus awakened, the bird started flapping her wings to renew her flying skills. And as the fish plummeted over the falls, she spread her wings and flew up and away, gradually lifting with the wind under her wings. The feeling of flying was ecstatic, and she soon found she could simply float there in her natural surroundings. (As I write this, a bald eagle flies across the bay in front of me and is lifted in circles on the thermal there—a demonstration of the joy and freedom we will find in flying!)

This image so clearly illustrates our coming experience: Our wings, though created for flying on the winds of Spirit, have not been used and are weak. As we see this time coming, we must do the work of exercising our abilities to fly or choose to sit still and be washed over the falls—the seemingly easy path involving competition, warring, conflict, and struggle. These thunderous waters will go down rapidly, tumble, and turn into mist. Their raging will break them apart, destroy them. The upward path, because it is one of harmony and unity with All Things, will connect to the Great Power that flows through All Life and be magnified to lift higher and higher, becoming more graceful and easier to maintain.

To me, these images from diverse origins are intuitively pointing to the golden dream that is possible for all—available to those who raise their energetic vibration to become light, loving, and easily lifted by the winds of time.

HOW TO FLY

It sounds to me as if we are being given a remarkably wonderful opportunity. So the only question is, "How do we get there?"

In order to proceed, we need three things:

1. We must gain an awareness of what is happening and what is possible, so we can make good choices.
2. We need not only to hold but to practice our faith in the perfection and magnificence that Creator holds for us.
3. We have to clear the way for the new by releasing the old with joy and gratefulness.

If you've come this far in this book, you do have knowledge of the coming changes. My old master Moshe Feldenkrais, an Israeli healer and learning expert,[3] taught us that "awareness is 50 percent of the process." Once our consciousness understands what is happening, it opens to possibilities of change that would never have been perceived in ignorance. Therefore, it is important that all people have this information and thus be able to make an informed decision about how they will use their energy to prepare for the coming times.

Once we make a choice, once we actively ask for assistance, we must

THE END OF TIME

keep our most sensitive perception open for what comes. In taking advantage of what unfolds before us, we begin to move quickly into the new. Change is the natural order of life, and once we set a direction, it takes much less energy to move forward than to hold ourselves frozen in an old, outdated position. Our choosing is our freedom. Our consciousness celebrates the chance to flow in greater harmony with what is happening around us.

We must practice our faith in the perfection that is possible. Because we have been steadily progressing toward the bottom of the ninth hell, it has been difficult—for most of us, nigh onto impossible—to hold any faith and trust in the natural unfoldment of perfection, beauty, harmony, and grace. These days to find even a bit of any of these positive qualities present in the life around us we have to search very hard. Yet our task regarding this negative past is simply to acknowledge that it *has* been true . . . and release it. In *Fireflies*, Rabindranath Tagore tells us, "Faith is the bird that feels the light and sings when the dawn is still dark."[4]

I was told once by one of my finest teachers, Master Kaskafayet,[5] that we must *personally* make this choice. It came about this way. A group of us were talking about physical health and vitality. Our master teacher jokingly said, "You should realize what has been the pattern lately on Earth: just 'blow through' one body—abuse it, undernourish it, drain it of vitality—and then trade it in for another one!" We were rather shocked at the idea, then realized that this is often what happens.

"Actually, I shouldn't suggest that 'trade-in' mentality to you, even in kidding. It won't be so easy to get a human body before long."

"Why?" we wanted to know.

"Because there won't be so many of them," he answered.

"But why?" we asked, even more curious.

"Because the human population will be much smaller than it is now."

Again, "Why?" We insisted on understanding.

"*Because in the near future, in order to remain in an Earthly human body, you will have to sign a contract with Mother Earth and Father Spirit.* That contract," he continued, and we all held our breath, imagining what difficult thing we might be asked to do, "*—that contract will require you to be willing to have it all.*"

We were stunned into silence. We had to think deeply about it to begin to understand. Seeing our wrinkled foreheads, the master added,

"You must be willing to live harmony, peace, beauty, grace, light, and prosperity fully into your own life. This is because [and his voice took on an enormous, numinous quality] that is what Mother Earth and Father Spirit have chosen for future Earthly experience to be. You must actively choose to be part of this, to accept it, to add your creative energy to it, or it will be inappropriate for you to be here on this transformed Earth. To hold expectation of anything less than perfection would simply drag everyone's energy down. In order for this grace and ease to happen, *all* of our energies must be unified in that direction—no one pulling the other way."

What had been said was so profound, and at the same time, it was such common sense! Yet in the past, that choice hasn't been as easy for us as it might at first appear. I personally had another lesson in this after being told by my guides that my *only* assignment was *joy*. I was strutting around, thinking about what an easy assignment I had received and very happy with it. Then a few hours later, something "went wrong." I got upset; I was angry and a little scared. Right in the middle of my righteous consternation and negativity, a sweet little voice whispered in my ear, "Where is the joy *now?*"

And I was shocked into realizing that I must *choose* joy in every moment, no matter what the circumstances. I have found that very difficult. Thus, it is a continuing *practice* to make that choice. I personally sought out Barry Neil Kaufman's "Happiness Is a Choice" work[6] to help support this practice. Through the books and classes he offers, you can learn to release all the excuses you have for not living in joy and move forward in a healthful, creative way to meet your challenges.

So let's continue our look at what supports our faith.

First of all, there is the tremendous wave of energy coming in for our use. Not a single person I've talked with says that things are slowing down, getting mellower, just drifting along cool and calm. When I speak of the intensity of the time, I see people's eyes widen and their nostrils flare. "*Yes,*" they say, "I'm really feeling that in my life!"

Dayana, another cosmic teacher of mine, expressed it this way in early 1996 through the group AMAG she channels: "What you are experiencing is a shift in the wind, a dramatic change in the terrain of consciousness. You who have been working to awaken—attempting to raise your consciousness, your vibration, to become lighter in every way— have been walking uphill against the wind. There is such a small amount of radiant life force [*chitta*] available that you have struggled just to maintain the plateau, let alone push yourself upward into the wind. Now you have reached the top! [Again, the voice speaking took on that enormous, almost echoing, numinous quality.] As of this time you call 1996, you are now walking downhill with the wind at your back. That is the shift you feel."

It was an amazing image, yet each of us had our "but still . . ." "But I still don't see things *really* changing. I mean, it seems to be getting worse. There are glimmers of radiance in the midst of clouds of darkness, but my life is still tremendously challenging, not gliding downhill easily."

"Let me shift to a slightly different metaphor," she said. "When you shoot an arrow at a distant target, you never shoot straight across. The arrow would never make it. Instead, you shoot the arrow into the sky, in an arc, climbing and climbing, until it hits a still point, and then it falls, coming swiftly to Earth. If you have aimed well, you will hit the target.

"On January 1, 1996, you let loose the arrow. For a few months more, it will continue to use energy in climbing. Now, sometime after equinox, the still point will be reached. The arrow will rise to the top of the arc, then fall, very fast. I hope you aimed your arrow well."

That statement made all our hearts pound. There was immediate silence as we quickly thought back to what our intention had been at that critical time a few weeks earlier. Brows wrinkled in concentration attested to inward searches. Then, one by one, faces began to brighten. When we spoke again, hesitatingly at first, and then with joy and celebration, we expressed our realization that we *had* been holding the golden dream, that we had been projecting a positive future, that we had been holding Love and radiance in our hearts as "where" we wanted to go.

She again dramatically switched metaphors: "Those of you who have been in a powerful motorboat may be able to imagine what it would be like to have your craft firmly secured to the dock and then put your engine in gear and give it the gas. The boat struggles and swings itself back and forth in the turbulent water. This might be likened to the time before

this equinox: it can be very challenging, given all that intensity and turbulence, to hold your focus exactly where you want to be going. Then, "tzu-
uuu," the rope is cut, and the boat jumps forward, heading full speed
toward wherever it may be pointed.

"*Keep your attention on the positive, on the golden dream, unwavering. In so doing,
you will arrive there . . . very quickly.*"

This poignantly reminded me of the words of a wonderful Christian
cactus shaman from Peru, Don Eduardo Calderón. He said—and it
echoes in my heart today as strongly as the day I heard him speak these
words years ago—"*The true shaman is one who holds the golden dream in [his or
her] heart, without condition or wavering, . . . until it comes true on Mother Earth.*"

There are specific practices I will give you in the following chapters that
will assist you in feeling assured of the positive possibilities in the midst
of our present chaos. However, in the meantime, I want to tell you of
one thing I do to help me unplug from any negative images of the future,
from the old patterns I carry, and from the consensus reality that we all
play a part in creating. I first heard of this in a book by Tony Stubbs[7]
and then added my own variations as I practiced it.

Take a moment to remember what an old-time telephone switchboard looked like. It consisted of a big board with lots of round holes in
it. And there were many, many black wires with plugs that could be
placed in any of the waiting receptacles. The operator knew which one
was which and chose the appropriate one. Think of your old ideas, beliefs, habits, outdated ways, negativity, fear, and resistance as the holes on
the lower part of the board. And think of the new possibilities of awakening, joy, beauty, abundance, cooperation, upliftment, and creativity as
the holes at the top of the board. *You* are the operator, so whenever you
run into any of the lower, negative ways of thinking and being, take a
moment to stop and imagine unplugging the wires from the lower level
and putting them into the upper one.

I have begun to see the upper level more like violet crystals with appropriate holes. Violet is a very healing, cleansing color, and the energy
around the wires begins to sparkle. I sometimes even see it as having a
silver glint that adds grace to the whole process. Then, because I know

that whatever old "holes" we leave open are an invitation to "plug in" again, I bring new wires of sparkling violet from the upper level and insert them into the empty black holes, thus filling them with the violet healing and cleansing energy, too.

To review:

1. Remember the many plugs on an old-fashioned telephone switchboard with two levels. You are now its operator.
2. Assign any negativity, fear, or resistance to the bottom level, with black plugs in those holes meaning you are connected to them.
3. Assign to the upper level positive, uplifting, loving, creative possibilities, represented by sparkling violet crystal connections.
4. Any time negativity comes up, imagine yourself unplugging these dark connections from the lower level and plugging them into the upper level of positivity.
5. Bring new violet crystal plugs from the upper level to fill the old black holes with healing and cleansing energy.

I like this quick meditation, because it reminds me that I am in control, and it feels great once I have unplugged from the negativity. Too often in the past, most of us have waited for someone else or some miracle cure to change our attitudes, our habits, our ways of being. Now is the time to change ourselves!

Another support we can find for our mind's understanding comes from the natural movements of the seasons, the cycles, and the epochs of Earth as well as our own bodily transformations. We have become divorced from these natural knowings, and it would serve us well to reawaken to them. Inasmuch as this current process is a quite cosmic one, we will find ourselves moving through it most easily as we truly embody ourselves in the reality we now occupy—that of our physical bodies within nature. Miracles abide here as surely as in some future world; we have just forgotten about the magic that lives in every passing day.

A never-ending miracle to me—one that has direct correlation to this epochal process—is the magic of springtime. To see a "dead," dried-up, stark world begin to come alive is resurrection playing itself out before our eyes. If it can be done in all the rest of the natural world, how can we be an exception? Our challenge in this remembering may be that we are tucked away inside our solid boxes called houses. We seldom step out into the freshening air except to dash wildly between buildings when necessary. To truly be in this world, we must get back into contact with All Our Relations around us.

Thinking of the human body itself, a prime example is that of a young girl changing into a woman. From a tiny, wiry, somewhat androgynous being, a girl enters puberty and develops into a young woman whose body suddenly has the miraculous ability to become a womb for the creation of new life. Similarly, a boy at puberty develops the sexual ability to populate the world!

Remember the beautiful quote from David Abram in Chapter 4 (pages 30–31), in which he reminds us so eloquently about our human need for "the others" of the natural world. Recall, as well, Long Antlers speaking (in Chapter 4) for the Elk people, who understand profoundly the coming of the Light. All the life around us, whether the elk or the bear or the stars or the grass, feels and knows what is taking place much more fully than we two-leggeds do, because they are naturally in harmony with the flow of life. They have no mental and emotional set that restricts them from full knowing. Given what you have now learned, you may find it very enlightening to reread all of what the "other voices" shared with you in Chapter 4. There are great lessons there for this coming time, which you may not have fully received upon first reading.

Being in contact with the natural life will help trigger these deeper knowings in you. I highly recommend that you spend at least one hour a day outside, even if it is just walking around your neighborhood observing the essential and instinctive life there. If there is no natural life around you and no means to reach it easily, then you might want to take a serious look at where you are living. It has not been designed to help you live a good life. Most cities and towns have some parkland or green-belt that is also accessible. These areas, as well as the country and wild-lands, are wonderful places to go for walks.

Watching the moon go through its cycles is also useful. Even in the deepest, darkest night of the waning moon, a sliver of light is waiting to wax into fullness. And a full-moon night! Even in what some think of as the dark of night, there is a silver brilliance that lights everything up with magic! Of course, in order to experience this fully, you must be away from the enormous lights that have been put on every corner to "keep the dark away."

There are less beautiful cycles you can see portrayed in the land as well. Everywhere from Africa to Arizona, we see the results of human exploitation of the land by observing the deserts that are present and increasing. I learned much about this in my classes with Bill Mollison, Australian founder of a way to design sustainable living called Permaculture. It was astounding to me when Mollison told us that some of Arizona's stark desert (which I thought had always been there) developed during the Second World War, when farming was attempted in inappropriate areas and failed, leaving the land barren. We saw photographs of dead tree roots, which showed that the topsoil had once been a foot or more deep over what was now only sand. Even though naturally very dry, those deserts had once been grasslands! In response to this, Permaculture workers influenced by Mollison's thinking came up with a remarkable process using a small land imprinter (a tractor-pulled roller that makes many, many fist-sized imprints in the desert). Into these small impressions, both seed and compost blow, and tiny pools of water collect. Voilà! Hardy grasses come back onto the land without further human intervention! Soon the desert experiences a miraculous recovery. Trees planted in six-foot depressions filled with mulch thrive in much the same way.[8] As we apply our ingenuity to the challenges around us, we can make a great and positive difference.

In our continuing search to find support for our hope in this time, we can also look at cultural cycles and epochal changes of the past. When enormous sheets of thick ice covered this land I look out upon, it would have been hard to imagine the beauty of forest and lake I see now; yet it is right here in front of my eyes. The great flourishing that happened in the Renaissance would have been impossible to imagine in the Dark Ages. During the days of slavery in the American South, it would have been difficult to picture the civil rights movement.

Yet somewhere in those dark years, a seed had been planted in the human psyche that burst into flower as time moved forward. Even now, at the bottom of the ninth hell, we are making amazing technological breakthroughs in global information processing and accessing (computers, the World Wide Web, cell phones, and much more), plus space travel and other areas that were only fantasies even a hundred years ago. From the perspective of people before these developments became manifest, they would have seemed to be miracles, and perhaps they are! Modern science vindicates these remarkable changes in emerging theories of change and growth. For a quantum leap into a new level to take place, perturbations in the status quo first create a seeming chaos before a jump to the higher level of functioning is made. We certainly have enough perturbation in our world right now to make a magnificent leap!

Some truly amazing things are already happening to give us just a small taste of what is coming. In the political arena, the dismantling of the Berlin Wall surprised us all. The cold war ended. The Soviet Union shattered. And now the end of the old European nations is in sight, with their Common Market and common currency. In their Oneness, enormous energy will be released to serve the people. The realization that the true enemies are toxins/pollutants and ethnic conflict is dawning on everyone. Dawn Boy has taught me how powerful it would be for nations to begin to call ourselves "God's Children of Earth" and for all countries to acknowledge their common roots in Spirit and Earth.

In another realm, material products that may eventually be used for awakening our spirit are appearing. David Hudson, a cotton farmer from Arizona, was unexpectedly drawn into a long and intense scientific research project that eventually led him on a remarkable journey of many years. Through it, he rediscovered ancient knowledge that helped him see that a white, powdery residue of gold mining may actually be "manna"— a substance that feeds the spirit body of humans and moves them rapidly toward enlightenment. The way it accomplishes this is still somewhat a mystery to him, even after years of study. He is now building a large complex where he can continue to develop means through which he hopes to produce this powder in quantity and research its effects for the good of all humankind.[9]

It may certainly be a part of the way we move toward the Golden Age with more grace and ease. This substance has been around as long as gold mining, and yet—bingo!—here is a total breakthrough in knowledge about its amazing characteristics and uses, which echo understandings from the ancient past. Much of what has happened to Hudson was spelled out in the Christian Bible and Hebrew history, in prophecies of Nostradamus, and in alchemical texts, yet he could not have conceived of such a thing before he was moved by some great force to pursue his research![10]

In *The Pillar of Celestial Fire*, Rob Cox tells some of the ancient story of this "manna" and speaks of using it in new technologies that will be revealed through spiritual researchers over the next few years. He tells us:

The most important of these scientific discoveries will concern . . . an inexhaustible source of subtle matter-energy. . . . Now is the time for these technologies to be rediscovered and utilized for the rapid spiritual regeneration of the human race. The new subtle matter technologies will enable us to develop methods for spiritual rejuvenation and healing that are far beyond anything imagined by modern science. Through such fundamental healing methods, otherwise incurable mental and physical diseases, as well as congenital diseases, may be completely reversed, and the body filled with spiritual Light and elevated to a state of perfect health . . . enabling virtually anyone to heal themselves and prepare their subtle bodies for the coming global illumination in a relatively short period of time.[11]

Recently an acquaintance in Idaho has brought forth another material that may prove to be quite amazing. Kim Dandurand was meditating in an area of pink/red rocks in southern Utah, when a great kachina (Native American archetypal spirit figure) came to him and gave him the formula for "Aulterra," a mineral combination that has been reported to produce miracles of healing both in people and in polluted substances.

Its basic energy is that of creating balance and of supporting the intent that is present. Kim says that experiments with humans show that it is helping to heal people with cancer, AIDS, and other diseases as well as improving vital energy in the land and in food grown where it has been used. When we listen, Creator gives us powerful information about how to use what is available around and within us.

Another interesting point that Kim brings us is that guides in this process continue to work with him to enhance his ability to hold perfection for himself, Mother Earth, and All Things. Without this kind of intent, it will be much harder to achieve the many miracles that are indeed possible in the next few years. A part of this process is to understand that what is happening to us and in the world moment to moment, day to day, is perfect. It is perfect from the viewpoint of the soul, for *the challenges we call to ourselves are grist in the mill of our continuing evolution.* Yet we can make the process easier and lighter and more joyful. That is the aspect of the process we are now creating.

When you take a look at the fact that what you hold in mind and pay attention to is what you are creating for yourself, you may be motivated enough to put some really good, concentrated energy into cleaning up the vibration you are maintaining and sending forth. What helps me have the heart to continue the work is to have the information, the assurance, the global prophecy about the beauty that is to come—to realize that we are all going to be okay and that we are learning and doing the best we can. Instead of struggling at the back end of what we have created with our mixture of negative and positive energy, we will begin to find it much easier, and tremendously more sensible, to use our energy to shift our focus toward the golden dream. And in this way, we can let the great forces sweep us there rather than struggle in the dense material world after our energy has solidified into form. We will understand the power of standing at the heart center of the Rainbow, where a short step into the Invisible with pure intent for ultimate perfection can create amazing transformation in the visible world.

———

As I look around me, I am amazed at all that is happening in support of our intention to move forward in a good way! It is true that we are in quite remarkable times: one might easily even call them extreme! The thing to remember in making your choices right now is that there is no in-between. So what have you got to lose? You can continue to image the coming end of time as violent, destructive, frightening, and wholly negative. Or you can pay the "money" of your attention to a different vision—that of a renewed and joyous Earth. Alice Bailey channeled the wisdom of a high master named Kuthumi, whose words are a definite encouragement, when he tells us that the Ascended Masters refer to this as a birthing process for the planet that is a part of Earth's evolutionary path. It is "the birthing of a planet into a star in the heavens[;] . . . it has been written since Babylon that the Earth would journey into the Age of Aquarius and become a Garden of Eden in the universe."[12] He states that entry into this new dimension is scheduled for the year 2012.

The epochal night is over. Rather than squeezing your eyes shut in foolish fear (of course it looks dark then!), open them to the dawning light. Come awake with joy and the expectation of perfection. Have the courage to hold that dream all day, every day. Step into the Invisible with your prayers. Know that you can create the "end of time" as something radiantly wonderful in your life. Then you will be part of bringing into reality, for you and All Your Relations, the golden dream of all humanity.

PART III

WALKING
OUR TALK

Whether we are ready or not, great changes are coming to our plane of existence. Our only choice is in how each of us responds. Will your personal transformation be to an uplifted plane of living on Lady Gaia? Or will you find yourself still in the same old school of conflict (wherever its new location!)??

Our next step is to walk into the reality of our daily lives the vision we have been given.

CHAPTER 10

READY OR NOT!

Who will be awake in the Golden Age
and dancing with joy?
It will be those who have lived in the Light,
who have done their meditative work to transcend the material plane,
who have done their emotional work of resolving old issues
and traumas, who have begun walking in sacred Oneness
with All Our Relations.

The great spiral of our evolving has been spinning and turning upward over the aeons. In doing so, it offers us challenges as well as enormous gifts for our continued growth. The level of our conscious evolvement is our personal choice in response to what is happening around us. Even as we must continue to listen intently for more knowledge of what is happening as it unfolds, we must also consider doing our part in the present. It is only right that we should be personally called upon, because human existence is an experiment in freedom. We can choose to do our part to move forward or stay behind; we can decide to be at one with All Life or at odds with it.

Even the challenges themselves are actually gifts. They enable us to grow into new ways of being. We have already taken our first step: becoming aware of the intensified movement of our Earthly evolution. Our path can be made easier if we hold a positive outlook on how to prepare for and work with these new energies.

Dawn Star puts it this way:

THE LAST GHOST DANCE

Humankind is standing precariously on the edge of destiny. It will either rise to a paradigm change or experience decline and possible destruction. This is an unavoidable confrontation. The options will be presented and the choices will be made.[1]

Giving you one metaphor for how it might look can help you focus on what you may need to do for yourselves. This view offers us many challenges and hurdles, yet each of us meeting them in our own way is exactly what we must do in preparation for the initiation to come. These challenges and hurdles are the test of our growth into readiness for this new phase of being: as such, they are a natural part of the progression of evolving. I believe that we two-leggeds have the ability to move forward in a good way; I also believe that Great Spirit has available what we need to meet these tests.

The baseline of our test is surely the manner in which we approach it. As the revered holy man of the Teton Sioux, Fools Crow, reminds us, "The important thing is to let Wakan Tanka and the Helpers[2] lead, and then to wait patiently for the answers."[3] We must follow the lead of the holy ones before us and immerse ourselves in Spirit, even as we face the seemingly tedious tasks of making the new real in our everyday lives.

Something helpful to remember is the wave progression that all growth and learning follow. This book will move you through it as well. First, we may seem to be floating on a plateau. Then something inspires us, illumines our darkness, lifts us up—we see the next level. We feel it. *Yes!* We are in fact coming to shore, and the waves begin to lift us up. At the crest of the wave, we are high and clear: we see the new shoreline. "Of course!" we say. "This is easy." Then, to our dismay, we seem to fall backward and down, tumbling into the trough of the wave. We get water up our nose; we splutter; we are confused and annoyed, to say the least. We are dismayed that the exquisite beach is no longer in sight. Difficult as it may be in those moments, we must remember that this trough is a natural part of the movement onto the next wave and the next and the next, and finally onto the shore. The trough represents going back into our daily lives with the new visionary information and doing the work there.

———

Whenever the exact moment of this entrance into the time of Golden Light, it is imminent for those living on this sweet Earth! When this great pillar of golden fire comes to us, how will we experience it happening? Is there something we need to do to prepare? What is our part in this? The challenging metaphor I now offer from the ancient Vedic sense of this coming time will perhaps of necessity put us into a trough. Once we are shown the shore, we must be willing to go back into our lives and do the work of putting this vision into practice. This can feel like going down and backward, yet this wave motion is the only way of moving forward and up. After I outline this possible scenario, ways of dealing with the challenges we may face will be presented in the remainder of the book.

When Earth hits the outer electromagnetic sheath that surrounds the concentrated light (this information is based on what was covered in Chapter 7, so you may want to do a quick review), several things may take place. First, everything electromagnetic may be radically changed or erased by the intense amount of energy coming in. This surely warns us not to be totally dependent on anything electromagnetic. The poles of Mother Earth will respond with their electromagnetics. Telephones, cars, engines of many kinds, thermostats that switch on most heaters—all these things have vital electromagnetic aspects. Certainly, your own body has a basic electromagnetic aspect, so having it fine-tuned, light, and open to positive change is very important. Gregg Braden suggests that the only materials that may survive the disruption of planetary magnetics and the base resonant frequency are those that are Earth-resonant.[4] All these things mean that we must pay a different kind of attention than the old programs tell us. *A secure future may have more to do with our inner ability to resonate with the larger life around us than with bank accounts and material goods.*

Passing through this sheath surrounding the light will supposedly take only a few of our days. Perhaps many affected things, such as engines, will work again when the energy settles down. However, electromagnetic records, such as those of computers, would most likely be permanently erased. Computer buffs, be sure to have hard copy! If you have money in a bank that keeps its records only on computer, those funds may just be blown away, and so on. You may want to start asking around to find out what things are in some way electromagnetically connected. Only then will you realize how much may be affected.

1. Ask knowledgeable people in many fields what things function electromagnetically and make a list of these things.
2. Then sit down and trace the implications of possible break-downs. For instance, if cars couldn't be started, this means I would have to travel to work and shopping another way. It also means the trucks that bring food and supplies could not run. This certainly implies that getting necessities might be difficult.
3. Meet with others in your community to talk about these things and make contingency plans. Only by working together can you truly prepare.

The way the world dealt with the Y2K problem gives me hope that we can gracefully handle other similar kinds of challenges coming our way.

Lee Carroll has brought through some very interesting material from a presence named Kryon, who is focused on being "of magnetic service to the Earth." His material approaches these challenges from another enlightening perspective. In *The End Times*, Kryon awakens us to the enormous ball of electromagnetic energy upon which we live (Mother Earth) and says that we will soon use this free and abundant energy for all our needs:

> You have absolutely enormous raw power resources that become available through the understanding and regulated use of the magnetic fields of your planet. All the energy you will ever need is there, not to mention the secret of passive flight [flight without mechanical means] using the magnetic grids.[5]

This gives us a positive inspiration from which to work. Perhaps we can begin to look at these challenges as an impetus to awaken to whole new ways of living, which could be much more beneficial than what we now experience. To choose a more sustainable energy source is, from all global ecological reports, absolutely necessary for our planetary survival.

In Glenda Green's informative book *Love without End*, the master Jesus speaks of the free and sustainable magnetic energy we have waiting at our fingertips. He reminds us of the magnetic quality and centrality of the heart in the process of awakening to these new technologies of spirit:

> Energy is a crucial survival commodity, and therefore its management has a profound impact upon consciousness. From the moment it was discovered that fire could be ignited by rubbing two sticks together, mankind has been building cultures upon friction-generated energy. Nuclear power plants are no exception to this. These "sticks" are more sophisticated, although the energy generated is still the result of a polar, resistive, friction-generated process.... Science is on the threshold of moving into a new era of energy that will base its performance on the principles of primal magnetism.... Now contemplate a civilization in which energy is not a commodity over which to fight or hoard. Can you see how that would change everything?[6]

The main idea is to be open, connected, and ready for change, holding an intent for that change to be positive. Another positive thought is that we may begin using photon (light) energy instead of our usual electricity. There is a sense that we could be assisted to change over very quickly to the use of this kind of energy. According to scientists, we entered the photon belt near the end of 1996; this belt is a large mass composed of light particles where our solar system will remain for approximately two thousand years.[7]

What seems vital is to open our minds to new possibilities and release our dependence on what has worked in the past. I believe that the universe is moving forward in a beneficent way and that if we actively invite new and better ways of living, they will be given to us.

I know radical scientists who have been working for decades on free energy and perpetual-motion machines.[8] They are stepping forward and taking responsibility for this change, as we all must in our own areas of expertise, before some terrible crisis forces our hand. For example, in the late eighties at the World Balance Conference, sponsored by the Swannanoa Institute,[9] Dr. Edwin Land, the man who invented the Polaroid Land process for cameras, spoke of his new invention. It consisted of two simple wires that are fastened onto the roof of a house and run to the ground to generate all the electricity one could need! He told us he learned how to do it by paying attention to how plants photosynthesize their food. And wouldn't you know, he was starving and scrambling for grant money to move his discovery into domestic use. The only ones interested were big electric companies that wanted to buy him out and suppress the information because they were afraid they would eventually be put out of business by it. Finally, a Chinese delegation picked up on his idea and offered him a million-dollar grant to use it in their country.[10]

We must, as an American culture, stop suppressing all this new technology and find a way instead to integrate it into our lives in a way that works for everyone. One thing this means is reworking our patenting system so that it is not so easy to buy up and suppress brilliant new discoveries and inventions. James Redfield addresses this in a very helpful way in the ninth insight in his book *The Celestine Prophecy*.[11] He talks about where the human race is headed in the next thousand years and suggests that the more we can connect with the beauty and energy around us, the more we will evolve.

> The core change will be the understanding that we are here to evolve spiritually. As a result of this understanding, there will be changes in our vibrational frequency. As we reach a critical mass in this upliftment, information will come in on a global scale. We will not tolerate any economic activity that threatens the life and aliveness of us and All Our Relations.[12]

Astrologically, 1997 was a year specifically indicated for the burgeoning acceptance of new and alternative technologies—many of which spring from ancient knowledge awakened again in our time. In whatever niche you find yourself—science, medicine, home building, communications, or any other occupation—the best thing you can do for yourself and the seven generations to follow is to embrace and include these new ways, making the transition voluntary and gradual rather than abrupt and forced. Actively ask to bring through what is useful and appropriate for our times; it will be much easier to do now than it has been in our recent past.

Back to our scenario: After those few days of electromagnetic disturbance, we move directly into the flood of Golden Light. My guess is that it will be like shifting from having a fifteen-watt bulb beside you to having a full 2,200 volts of electricity running right through you. A tiny example would be waking up from total darkness when someone shines a high-powered flashlight right into your eyes. *It will be intense.* If you are dense and blocked, *if* you are *not* accustomed to transcending the material plane, *if* you have not done your spiritual homework, it will be a tremendous jolt to the system.

In other words, if you are receptive, clear, open, and thus prepared for the shift, the current can move through you, lighting you up with a radiance unknown to us now. If, however, you are unclear, focused only in the material world, toxic, and resistant—emotionally or physically—the current could be blocked within you and literally burn its way through, ending your life. Yet reports from spiritual sources remind us that when a person can allow in and "hold" this much Golden Light, we see a halo, which is simply this Golden Light/life force filling up and swirling above an enlightened being.

Another way to think about the challenge of this inpouring of light is this. Have you ever been around a very awake and developed person who calls you on all your negativity, poor habits, unworkable ways, hidden darkness, and unconsciousness? Pretty soon, all your "buttons are pushed" by this person, and you are in a crazed emotional state, ready to explode! And still the pressure is there from this other person. If you have never been around a teacher like this, just imagine it for a bit.

Now, realize that this amazing Golden Light, vital life force, could be ten thousand, ten million, times stronger than this. In such powerful light, all darkness shows up. So all that has ever been denied, consciously or unconsciously; all unworkable habits and patterns; all emotional issues unresolved—*everything*—will come right up to the surface. (For those who know about Kundalini awakening, it will be an intense magnification of this.) *Raw, deep truth—unprotected by social norms and filters—will not only be staring you in the face; it will be (as I am wont to say) UP YOUR NOSE.*

Those who have focused only on the material plane and have put all their eggs in that basket will likely be in real trouble. It may be difficult for them to function: they will probably be totally out of commission as their own devils dance around them, or they will just be blown off this Earth plane.

Who will be awake in the Golden Age? Who will be dancing with joy? Who will be functioning and clear? Who will be in charge? It will be those who have lived in the Light, who have done their meditative work to transcend the material plane, who have done their emotional work of resolving old issues and traumas, who have begun walking in sacred Oneness with All Our Relations. Obvious examples are the highest masters and holy people on Earth—high spiritual people from all cultures who have attained enlightenment. Does this ring any bells for those who read the Christian Bible, about where one is laying up one's treasures? (Matthew 6:19)

Another admonition from many spiritual disciplines comes to mind: "Be as the little children." As Rabindranath Tagore says in *Fireflies,* "The child ever dwells in the mystery of ageless time, unobscured by the dust of history."[13] Members of the generation now maturing are well equipped to deal with this coming intensity. They are said to have a special violet band of light in their energetic spectrum that helps activate this new and different way of being. "The ancient texts emphasized that there would be a powerful generation born just before the Shift of the Ages. This generation would have a 'force' living within them. Within this force there would be a power beyond their knowing."[14]

The hazard is that many children have an expectation of a different world and are shocked and dismayed at what they actually find. I know of many young people who are terribly disillusioned. They are not seeing the beautiful world they expected, nor does anyone even speak of its coming. As a matter of fact, most of what they see and feel is about the "End Times" in a negative way: nuclear holocaust, wars and bloodshed, adults numb and hardened and seemingly heartless, jobs that have no meaning. These kids are in trouble if we do not give them an understanding of what is possible and of ways they can actively be a part of it. The other alternative seems to be alienation and suicide. Our young people need to be shown the way. They must understand that it is the sages and the children who will be leading us.

Now if you're like me, these possible scenarios are certainly motivation to begin assessing where you put the energy in your life. We two-leggeds are at a stage in our evolution when we are being given infinitely more responsibility individually. The old paradigm of having someone else— whether religious figure, master teacher, elder, or anyone else—"tell us how to do it" or "do it for us" has definitely changed.

The ancient seers give us a brief outline of three ways we can prepare ourselves for this awakening. They correspond to teachings I have given for years about the *three attentions*: the ways we can focus and give our energy to the world. Some of them may be simply commonsense approaches to our own growth and healing; others are perhaps less obvious and a bit more esoteric. Yet all are important.

1. *Lifeways and work of service:* The first approach suggested by the ancient Vedic prophets involves the way we live our lives—specifically, our work of service. This is akin to the first attention, which is attuned to our physical body experience, in all its forms.

2. *Contemplation:* This is the mental aspect of things, which may also include much of our emotional experience. (As you know, these are only divisions to satisfy the mind. Human experience is a wholeness and not so easy to divide in actual living.) In Native ways, this is called the second attention and includes an almost endless array of ways we can focus our minds other than our own actual bodily experience.

3. *Transcendence:* This approach involves touching into the transcendent world of Oneness through inner practices. Here is certainly the place of the third attention: our ability to focus on the wholeness of All Our Relations and All That Is. This is where much of the new work lies. Many of us have at least begun the work of the first two categories and

must surely continue it. Now it is vital to move into a profound inner practice that helps us become familiar with the realm of the transcendent, what I call the "Shimmering Invisible." The more we are able to touch into that realm, the better we will all function in the Golden Time.

The work of the Earth Mage involves all of these. With feet firmly planted on the living Earth and heart awake to the Spirit alive in All Things, this new human being walks forward in balance with self and All Our Relations.

FIRST ATTENTION:
LIFEWAYS AND WORK OF SERVICE

The first of the ways suggested by the ancient Indian prophets is how we have lived our life, with special attention to our work of service. It means learning to practice the ways that lead us to, and are the essence of, the new time. If we have been walking White Buffalo Woman's holy way of love and respect for All Things, if we have been doing the work of wholeness, if we have been awake to and fulfilling our own purpose, if we have truly been contributing to the vital life and health of All Our Relations, then we have been developing our capacity to embrace this Light.

So a vital first step is for us to take a look at this in our own lives. It's not too late to start making other choices, even now. The critical point for our well-being and integrity is that we become aware that there is a better way for ourselves and All Our Relations. For example, until I experienced how Aria and Sparrow approached their new land and building, I had not even considered some of the guidelines of harmony, purity, and wholeness they followed. Now that I know about these, it is important that I follow them.

We can walk with wholeness, respect, and love in any of our undertakings, and it's important that we in fact do that in all of them. Lightworkers are needed in all walks of life, not just in some special, groovy occupations. You know stories yourself of those people who have given that extra love and caring and energy to make an almost miraculous difference through whatever job they may be doing. It's time for us all to find ways to do that.

One thing we must be aware of in our work of service is that many of us have in the past done these things as duty, out of a fearful sense that we *should* do them in order to be good people rather than out of a heart overflowing with love for those around us. Mayan people have a wonderful greeting that is helpful here. When they acknowledge another person, they say, "You are another one of me." So rather than doing service from a place of needing "spiritual points," you may have to find a sense of connectedness with your own special gifts and to realize the joy of a true giveaway to "another you."

The following things are perhaps more obvious, yet I see this first aspect of preparation as encompassing the entire spectrum of how we've been using the life energy given us through our bodies.

PHYSICAL BODY

According to my tradition, the first (but certainly not the only) attention we must pay is to the physical body. We are here to *embody* Spirit. There are many other planes of existence where we can play without a body, but our purpose here on Earth is to experience having one.

When I think of our bodies, the first thing that comes to my mind is birth. This is because birth is very much what is happening to us now in a cosmic manner. When we're babies in the womb, we're aware of how to be born: we ready for movement through the birth canal in cooperation with forces greater than ourselves, according to a plan that has long before been set in motion. We humans are now those babies again, approaching birth into a much more expanded and amazing place than the womb of growth we currently occupy. This process of ascension and moving into a Golden Time is occurring now on this plane of existence. We have a choice. We either cooperate and move forward, or we die and are enfolded back into the Oneness.

If we plan to move forward, the most vital step is to truly embody our fullest selves right where we are. It is our aliveness and innocent, childlike perception[15] that will receive the knowings from the greater life, so we must move out of the deadening and dumbing habits we have learned. The problem is that many of us have come to a place of denying our bodies in ways both subtle and gross. Certainly, one kind of denial is lack of love and care for our physical bodies that leads to heaviness and poor health. This is quite obvious and ubiquitous in the United States today. We'd all do well to lighten up in every way.

A classic way to do this is through fasting and cleansing. This not only clears and tones the organs for health but also opens each cell to receive more light, thus awakening Spirit in the body. This kind of purification helps to raise our vibratory level, a key in awakening our higher consciousness. At this very moment, I am in a cleansing and healing process that I highly recommend. It is offered by Dr. Richard Schultze, a radical medical herbalist. It focuses on cleansing and support for digestive and eliminative systems, liver/gallbladder, kidneys, lymph and blood, and reproductive organs, plus parasite removal. The instructions that come with the herbs are well laid out, and the process can be done by anyone simply to improve health and clarity or to heal very serious diseases.[16]

I have always found fasting to be useful in releasing mental and emotional attachments as well. While you are doing this physical work, focus your attention on releasing what you no longer need at all levels of being. Releasing outmoded structures, ideas, and habits is a very healthy thing to do. A daily practice of forgiveness is very useful as a means of letting go of the debts you think others owe you. This strengthens your heart and opens you to the gifts waiting to come into that once-clogged space.

NOURISHMENT

After the cleansing, become acutely aware of what you put into your body to nourish and care for it. "The food we eat becomes a part of every one of our cells and is woven into the very fabric of our being."[17] Most of our bodies are programmed by our genetics to eat some meat protein, which is quite heavy and poses major health challenges, both from its fatty makeup and from the unhealthful foods and chemicals sometimes used to stimulate growth.[18] It is clear that you can do very well without animal protein if you learn to get what you need from other sources. The lighter we eat, the higher our vibration can become. We really need only a small amount of protein *if* we combine our food well. An amazing book about how our body processes food, plus suggestions for truly nourishing ourselves, is Dr. Jack Tip's *The Pro-Vita Plan*, the best dietary and health book I have ever found.[19] Following his commonsense recommendations, you will find that you can eat very lightly, consuming mostly vegetables and grains, which also helps elevate your consciousness. The suggestions offered in *Eat Right for Your Type*[20] are also useful because they are attuned to your own bodily makeup and genetics.

Another thing I am paying close attention to is the Spirit life, or lack of it, in the food I eat. Most foods commonly available today are grown in mineral-depleted soils and are also remarkably lacking in the vital life force that feeds our Spirit. They are grown unconsciously, picked before they are ripe, left too long before we eat them, and often contain pollutants that are damaging to our life force rather than nourishing to it. This creates the continual challenge of finding healthy, nourishing food to eat. First of all, we must awaken to growing healthy, vitally alive food and consuming it in a conscious manner. James Redfield speaks of this in the third insight of his *Celestine Prophecy*,[21] and biodynamic[22] and organic farmers have long been working toward this goal. Yet until we consistently grow this kind of food, we must find alternative nutritional support. In the meantime, buying from local organic farmers and cooperatives is the best alternative. I like to be sure that I take an excellent colloidal mineral supplement regularly. Three concentrated "superfoods" that I use every day I'm away from a garden come from very dedicated people who understand the needs of the human body for nourishment that goes beyond just physical matter: I take Pure Synergy, produced by healer Mitchell May;[23] Four Plus foods, produced by nutritional expert David Sanborn;[24] and The Ultimate Meal,[25] formulated with vegan diets in mind. I'm sure you can find others as well.

On the completely opposite side of things, we need to pay special attention to what is happening with genetically engineered foods. Often these unhealthy foods are not even labeled, and they affect us all.

> U.S. Food and Drug Administration (FDA) records reveal that it declared genetically engineered foods to be safe in the face of disagreement from its own experts—all the while claiming [that] a broad scientific consensus supported its stance. . . . Besides contradicting the FDA's claim that its policy is science-based, this evidence shows [that] the agency violated the U.S. Food, Drug and Cosmetic Act in allowing genetically engineered foods to be marketed without testing on the premise that they are generally recognized as safe by qualified experts. . . . Consequently every genetically engineered food in the U.S. is on the market illegally and should be recalled for rigorous safety testing. The FDA has deliberately unleashed a host of potentially harmful foods onto American dinner tables in blatant violation of U.S. law.[26]

It is important for the well-being of those you love to join eminent scientists and other concerned consumers in making sure that these foods are taken off the market and that proper testing is conducted. We must act together on issues like this and make our voices heard![27]

Dawn Star speaks about a remarkable solution to our dietary needs:

> [Many dietary and energy issues] will take care of themselves when your energy frequency is high enough to manufacture what you need. Your body's energy level [may be] too low right now to provide everything for you without support and compensation. Directly receiving sunlight at sunrise or sunset will actually help increase your frequency levels. Whenever you do this, your body chemically responds, helping to manufacture certain nutrients your energy level is otherwise too low to produce. Actually, much of the value of hard mineral traces in your bodies is the energetic matrix generated by them. The sun can provide this directly, for it contains both the substance and the fire of every mineral available in your solar system.[28]

BODY-ORIENTED THERAPIES

Focusing on your body in other ways is vital as well. Any work that clears, opens, vitalizes, and enhances your bodily life will lift your vibration and bring you more into line with the incoming light. Many people are now taking advantage of the fine massage practitioners in their area. Simply getting in touch more deeply with your body produces remarkable results. The powerful work of Moshe Feldenkrais is excellent for freeing the body to become fully functioning.[29] Craniosacral therapy does wonders as well.[30] Applied or educational kinesiology, which I discuss in Chapter 11, is also very useful.

Another approach that would be powerful for everyone is called "freeing the natural voice,"[31] which opens the throat chakra (energy center in the throat, concerned with manifestation and creation of the golden dream). This approach is not about being a great singer (although that could be a joyful result); rather, it's about being able to pour your energy forth without restriction. Practices such as Qi Gong and Tantra also awaken the life force within us and connect us with the larger Life.

Another approach that would benefit everyone is to consult with a traditional *constitutional* homeopathic doctor, who will help your body heal and become more whole and functional by clearing the issues that have arisen for you at present. The next step is to work backward through your whole life, since homeopathy can clear trauma, disease, vaccinations, and inherited predispositions to poor health (called miasms) from the tissues.

A wonderfully revolutionary kind of body approach is that of Emilie Conrad.

Her love of primitive movement helped her to discover the essential, primary movements common to all life forms that lie beneath the influence of culture. These primary movements are a "cosmology" of life, where form is resilient, dissolves, and shapes itself anew. She is interested in our biological anthropology as an unfolding of our "humanness," not as creatures upright and apart, but belonging to the swell of life in which all life forms are a subtle biomorphic play.[32]

Conrad's students tell me that her Continuum process moves them deeper into their biology than anything they have ever known, awakening their very cells through micromovements and flows.

Those who have experienced this deep inner awakening report that there is a kind of bodily aliveness that they had never imagined possible. This kind of wakefulness from our cells upward will be very helpful to us in feeling our way into the new way of being. Too often our current bodily images are dictated by television and magazine ads. But in looking toward some outside ideal, we deaden our sense of ourselves and our love of and appreciation for the true wonder of our physical body because it does not match up. Rather than exploring ourselves more deeply, we shut down and take a pill, attempting to find what we can only discover with exquisite attention to ourselves. The story of Life lives inside us as well as in the natural world around us. Our task as Earth Mages is to be willing to study it!

There are also some very specific things we can do to prepare through the physical/bodily realm. Researchers now tell us that it is necessary to have truly fine, cold-pressed polyunsaturated fats (specifically the essential omega-3-6-9 fatty acids) in order to absorb the light from the Sun, photon belt, and other sources.

Dr. Johanna Budwig, a seven-time Nobel Prize nominee from Europe, is considered by many to be *the* foremost authority on fats and healing.[33] She worked as a biochemist for decades and did much to help unravel the different kinds of fats and how they affect the body. She helped prove that the essential fatty acids (EFAs) found in fish oil, hemp, some seeds and grains like flax, sunflower seed, sesame seed, and so on, are a key part of human health. Their properties enable them to help move oxygen all over the body and in this way affect basic metabolism and health in myriad ways. Essential fatty acids help stop the rest of the fats and oils from clogging the system. They lower cholesterol and help the metabolism of the other fats. Dr. Budwig found that flax oil, high in essential fatty acids, could reverse some types of cancer and was highly preventative in other types, like lung cancer. Processing oils—especially with high heat, as we have been doing in the United States—is what destroys the essential fatty acid omega parts.

Thankfully there are plenty of good cold-pressed and refrigerated flax and other oils available.[34] It is relatively simple to add some of this oil to salad oil, pour it over rice or potatoes, or even spread it with garlic on bread like butter or olive oil. Olive oil itself has a fair amount of EFA if it is cold-pressed and virgin. Take a tablespoon a day with sulfur-containing protein like cottage cheese or the supplement MSM[35] to meet the requirement. Herbalist friends of mine are finding that ingestible hemp oil is a wonderful supplement because it has a nearly perfect balance of the omegas.

As one faces the entire fats and oils issue, it becomes clear that some knowledge of essential fatty acids and care in one's diet with regard to EFAs is a major revolution in human health. It may dramatically reduce cancer, heart attacks, and many other degenerative diseases.

Another physical focus is to change our bodies from carbon-based to the silica-based structures that carry and transmit light. I'm now working with spirulina algae, oat straw tea, and other forms of nutrition to help create this.

I've already mentioned that fascinating work is being done now on technologies and materials that involve manna—the literal spiritual food of our awakening that Creator is revealing to us.[36] This manna is an unusual white powder of gold with a superconductivity that enhances our Spirit. An Indian woman in California has discovered a natural white powder, perhaps created from a meteorite strike, that gives remarkable healing properties to the herbs she uses in her practice. She and others who now work with it call it "chamae."

I, and many Lightworkers with whom I converse, see the universe, the Mother Life, as incredibly beneficent and believe that we will be able to manifest what is required as we need it. And we are definitely in need of the things that will help us as much as possible before we actually enter the Golden Time—technologies of Spirit that speed the process of absorbing Light.

A final offering for your bodily clearing is very simple. Old-time healers as well as modern physicians are recommending this as one of the most healthful and purifying things we can do: drink *pure* water and plenty of it.[37] Remember that this means water, not other fluids: eight to twelve glasses per day, every day. Ask your local health department to have your home water analyzed for purity as well as bottled waters you might use. Check the water sources of your children's schools and your workplace. Also remember that well water or springwater is often polluted by industrial and agricultural runoff, so it is not guaranteed to be pure. Hopefully, this will start you on a journey to clean up the environment around your home area so that pure water will once again be readily available from natural sources.

SUSTAINABLE LIVING

An additional way to think about the life energy we are given is to assess how well we have used the resources Creator has provided to us—to consider how sustainably we are living. Have we been good stewards of every precious bit of energy and every resource? Have we been respectful of all life, even as we have made use of it for our own sustenance? As great changes come about on Mother Earth, you will be able to greet them with joy if you are also prepared by living in ways that are balanced and harmonious with the life around you. Consider whether your way of living is natural and easily maintained within your community or needs to be supported far and wide, with technologies over which you have no control. Living in moderation and voluntary simplicity could be the keys to our survival. The challenges offered by the Y2K computer glitch at the turn of the millennium served us in that they awakened many people to their need for more sustainable lifeways.

A Hopi elder recently said:

This is the hour! And there are things to consider:
1. Where are you living?
2. Where and how is your life energy being spent?

3. What have you created in your relationships?
4. Are you in right relationship?
5. What is your access to pure water?
6. In what state is your garden?
7. Are you now willing to speak your truth?
8. Have you created, or are you participating in, community?
9. Are you being good to each other and all things?
10. Are you remembering *not* to look outside yourself for leadership?

There is a river flowing now very fast. It is so great and swift that there are those who will be afraid. They will try to hold on to the shore. They will feel they are being torn apart and will suffer greatly. Know [that] the river has its destination. The elders say we must let go of the shore, push off into the middle of the river, keep our eyes open and our heads above the water. And I say, see who is in there with you and celebrate.

At this time in history, we are to take nothing personally—least of all, ourselves. For the moment that we do, our spiritual growth and journey come to a halt.

The time of the lone wolf is over. Gather yourselves! Banish the word *struggle* from your attitude and your vocabulary. All that we do now must be done in a sacred manner and in celebration. *We are the ones we've been waiting for.*

Here the elder is reminding us of the many ways we can awaken, pay attention, and create a beautiful world now.

I'm reminded of several examples of people putting these things into practice. Friends of mine in Texas at our Whole Works Permaculture Institute realized that although they live near a lake, they would not have water for themselves or their garden in the event of an extended power outage. They have recently put in two five-thousand-gallon holding tanks for pure water. You can personally keep a good supply of bottled water in your home for any emergency.

All our everyday acts are important, too. Recycling is something we are all aware of as a way to help the Earth. I like actor and ecologist Dennis Weaver's reminder: *"Reduce, reuse, and recycle."* Buying our foods in bulk to reduce the amount of packaging, keeping lights off in our home when not needed, replacing with motion-activated lights all the huge, unnecessary yard lights left on all night around homes in the country, carpooling to save petroleum resources, making a practice of planting trees—these kinds of simple actions add up when we all participate. The important thing is to do them!

Many people I know are taking a hard look at their relationships and letting go of those people who do not hold a positive and empowered image of the future. They are opening the space for relationships that match the future they wish to create. A group in Chicago that gathered around a powerful elder had to decide whether to break up when that person moved on. They chose instead to continue doing the rituals and gatherings that had become so important to their community, realizing that they did not need to look outside themselves for leadership.

SECOND ATTENTION: CONTEMPLATION

The second way the ancient seers suggest is contemplation—the mental and perhaps even emotional aspect of our work. Contemplative monks, who spend their lives dedicated to this spiritual pursuit through the use of their minds, demonstrate one very obvious path. Yet for those of us who do not live in cloistered situations, there are alternatives. For the majority of us, our current challenge is to awaken our spirits while living in the world rather than retreating from it.

The telephone switchboard exercise I gave you in Chapter 9 certainly fits into this category of how we can begin to take command of the direction in which our thoughts and emotions pull us. Working with prayer, affirmations, and mantras also falls in this category.

The simple, profound contemplation of nature is also vital. This is dealt with extensively in later chapters.

Also important are the global meditations many of us have been doing over the last decade. Whenever we hold an image with great intensity, we are practicing this aspect of preparation. Holding an image of the beautiful world that is possible is a ritual that we can do every day.

The mental and emotional releasing possible through fasting and forgiveness, which was mentioned earlier in the chapter, actually fits in this category. Whether or not you are fasting, find something to forgive and let go of every day, in order to stay in tune with the ever-changing flow of life. As you learn to release the outmoded structures of your life, you will find less fear present, because fear is generated when we cling to the structure rather than the heart/spirit of things. Structures always change and decay, so finding more lasting values can eliminate much of the baseline fear we experience.

As we continue our exploration, there will be even more things that fit in this category.

THIRD ATTENTION:
TRANSCENDENCE

Transcendence involves touching into that transcendent, holy, and whole world through meditative, inner practices. The more you are able to touch into that realm, the better you will function in the Golden Time. Holy ones down through time have reached their elevated state through this avenue and given us ways of living in the world that come from that inspired place. The goal is to achieve total communion with the Great Source of Life: Creator, God, Wakan Tanka, or whichever name you use.

Thomas Mails, in working with the Lakota holy man Fools Crow, pondered this concept, which Fools Crow called immersion:

The amount of time spent in immersion is never wasted, and it reverses the usual procedure we follow when we are faced with time-consuming and critical chores. Ordinarily, we think we must rush and organize to get at the work because there is so little time. If we pray at all regarding the situation, it is only briefly, because we have so much to do. Then we spend the entire day working on the chores and end up frustrated and drained. With immersion, you spend a lot of time in prayer, obtain from the Higher Powers the strength and guidance you need, and then finish those same chores in a fraction of the time, ending up fulfilled and fresh.[38]

Native people of different tribes talk about this same thing. I have been taught to call it "becoming a hollow bone." Others say "a hollow reed." This is a wonderfully useful image and practice. Living in holiness is living as a hollow bone, through which Creator can pour information and guidance into the world. You become a conduit for the highest and finest.

The practice is basically simple. It is a matter of doing it deeply and often.

1. Find a place to do this regularly. It could be a meditation corner in your home or a special tree outside.

2. Go there and assume a pose of humbleness and supplication. Some people find that getting on their knees is surprisingly effective. You may want to try this (use a pillow to make it more comfortable if necessary).

3. Pray in your own way to be made a clean and open vessel—ask that any resistance, obstacles, or stumbling blocks be removed. You will find that making yourself new, childlike, fresh, and receptive in this way feels wonderful. Use ritual movements as much as possible to help bring the process alive in you: use exploding breaths, "pull things out" with your hands, or do whatever you are moved to do.

4. Having attained this clarity as much as possible, open totally to receiving what Great Spirit has to offer. This may come in many forms, yet opening your arms in a receptive gesture is always helpful. And feel yourself receiving what is given; again, pat it into your chest or whatever action helps it feel real to you.

5. Stay with the receiving process as long as you need to. Soak yourself in these energies; absorb as much as you can. Imagine yourself filled to overflowing from an unlimited source.

6. The overflowing will trigger your remembering to begin the giveaway. Start sending this energy outward to All Your Relations. Let it

stream, throw it out in handfuls, and so forth. Do this knowing that the more you give away, the more you are filled, and the more good energy you channel onto Earth.

The master Jesus has always represented the power of the heart in connecting to Source. This goes beyond our normal perception of the heart as only an organ.

In the depth of your being is your own sacred center. It is the still, quiet chamber deep within where you are one with the Father. Through this connection is your own indigenous power. . . . The Sacred Heart has an exact location in the body which can vary slightly in every person. . . . It is located in the space between the spine and the physical heart, anywhere from an inch above the physical heart to three inches below it.[39]

Adding this understanding to your meditations can deepen your practice in a beautiful way. Focus your attention on this actual physical area as you quiet and ask for connection with Source.

Some of you have been doing your homework in this way for years via various meditative practices from spiritual traditions around the world. Others may want to begin the simple practice above or connect with the transcendental and other teachers who work with the process of ascension in your area. I have personally always found it challenging to sit in meditation, so I now supplement my practice with a series of fantastically empowering cassette tapes from Centerpointe Research Institute, which sonically move you into the deep yogic states of meditation and whole-brain functioning.[40]

Many teachings and books are available by those who address our ascension directly, including Joshua David Stone, Barbara Hand Clow, Sheldon Nidle, Bob Frissel, and Drunvalo Melchizedek.[41] Oughten House Publications in Livermore, California, specializes in books on ascension.

A book I find especially inspiring is the classic entitled *The Door of Everything*, by Ruby Nelson, through which Creator says to us:

I stand at the Door of your consciousness, knocking. If you will only turn toward me, emptying yourself out to receive my Spirit, I will pour so much Light into the reservoir of your heart that it will run over with goodness all the days of your eternal life.[42]

Native cultures have used sacred plant medicines to help them experience the transcendent. Psychoactive plants have been used in respectful and responsible rituals by all primary peoples to awaken them in the world of Spirit and to commune with All That Is. My teacher, who is a plant shaman, introduced me to the cactus medicine peyote in order to teach me how to stay "awake and functioning" in nonphysical, dreamer states. Sacred mushrooms used worldwide, fermented plant drinks (like *balché* among the Lacondones of the Yucatán), the cactus San Pedro used in Peru, and a multitude of other plants and plant concoctions give us a valid and powerful way to ritually touch into nonordinary realms of transcendent experience.

Looking toward the unknown is always a bit frightening, yet there is so much that is wonderful and miraculous happening in the midst of the seeming chaos. Great guides like Fools Crow help us to see that everything we need to make this a smooth and graceful transition will come to us if we can just tune in sufficiently. Assessing what we have been doing, as well as looking at basic things we can begin to do now, helps us feel empowered, rather than frightened, by what is coming. All the previous suggestions are examples to give you a start in thinking about how to respond to the newly incoming energies.

In facing any fear that comes up, it helps to remember something I have taught for years: *Fear is simply a response to the unknown.* Its real function is to bring us fully awake to what is happening, not to make us hide our heads. It can be a way of getting us to dance on our toes and be ready for the adventure rather than standing around flat-footed and unaware. Statistics in a recent survey are a hopeful sign: 96 percent of respondents believed in the soul, 91 percent in miracles, 85 percent in angels and spirits, 82 percent in heaven, and only 65 percent believed in hell or the devil.[43]

Another important thing to understand in considering fear and the unknown is that our human focus has been primarily on the material world, on structure. Structure, by its very nature, is a passing thing. The material world shifts, decays, changes, and crumbles. If we know ourselves and life as something more than bodies and material things, it allows us to be aware and less fearful as we watch the unknown unfold. This is why transcendent practice is so vital.

I sense that all of our evolution and unfoldment is couched in something beautiful and whole that is larger than we can see with our current limited vision. I think the universe is a beneficent place. A useful question to ask yourself in every situation is "How does this serve?" There is always a learning to be gained, something new to experience, something trying to awaken or be birthed into our reality.

Sparrow Hawk had always reminded me of this, and I had been thinking of him. At this point, it seemed he could not help but come through to up the ante. "Even the ninth hell is total perfection!" said Sparrow, grinning.

"The ninth hell is perfection? Are you kidding? I have a hard time seeing that!" I retorted.

"Of course, it's perfect. Our human objective was one of freedom— even to do something as seemingly silly as to believe we were separate from the great Oneness, to bind ourselves in darkness and heaviness, to lose touch with the Light. And we did a magnificent job of it!! We proved to ourselves that even something that radical was part of our freedom.

"The exciting part is that now we have proved it, so we don't need to do it anymore. We can let go of that. We have stretched the rubber band as far as it needs to go—no problem. When we release the tension and stop doing all this work of pulling away from what is real, then we will pop back into harmony with the speed of a rubber band contracting. It will take much less time going Home than struggling to go away!" he said, cocking his head and looking at me with shining eyes.

"I really like thinking of it that way!" I said excitedly. The rubber band metaphor made it easy to understand. Often we think that we have strayed so far from our own heart's path or our spirit or our connection to Source that it will take forever to work our way back into integrity and unity. What's true is that we are always just a breath away. In changing our viewpoint, we find our way Home much faster. I'm reminded of my *Confluence* gathering copresenter, Irish philosopher and poet John O'Donohue, speaking about Heidegger's sense of the spiritual journey. He reminds us that it doesn't have to be a long uphill struggle involving years of dedicated suffering; the journey is really about a quarter of an inch long! Most of you know from your own experience that going toward an unknown destination always seems to take longer than the journey home. And we as a human family have made the turnaround— we are headed Home.

So now we have gained some understanding about coming into this Golden Age. We two-leggeds stand at an amazing point of power. We must do our spiritual homework. It is our task as Earth Mages to become conscious co-creators by using our intent on both sides of this Rainbow Bridge on which we stand—in the Unmanifest realms as well as here on the Earth plane. Thus, we do our part to create a time of unity, beauty, peace, and light. The knowledge lives deep within us. And it is by our personal clearing and openness, by our intent and our practice, that we will bring our knowing forward.

The words of our contemporary Ken Carey connect to our deepest knowings and help us co-create the Golden Time from within us as well as receiving it from all around us. He is one of our modern prophets, and his words can help us move joyfully and fearlessly into this new time.[44]

The following traditional Din'e (Navajo) expression is used in many forms, including in ceremony. The Beauty Way ceremony is attributed to Dawn Star when He was alive in Din'etah.

We will again walk in White Buffalo Woman's sacred way, in holy Oneness with all realms of life. And all will be beautiful. We will truly be able to say, with our Navajo relatives: "We walk in beauty. We walk in beauty. Beauty before us and beauty behind us. Beauty to our left and beauty to our right. Beauty above us and beauty below. Walking a beautiful path."

SINGING A SONG
OF BEAUTY

Leave room in your consciousness for the mystery of Life.

*The most important lesson in the entire process
is that the method you use to transform yourself
must have the energetic quality of the end you seek.*

Now that I had a base of information to contemplate and an awareness of transformation asking me to respond, what next? How could I best proceed? Not being enlightened, I couldn't decide exactly how and where to begin. So it made sense to call on brother Sparrow Hawk and others among my guides in the Shimmering Invisible. When I took time to open the door of silence, Sparrow Hawk came through with his usual sparkle, excited to continue our dialogue.

"I've been thinking about co-creation," I told Sparrow Hawk. "And it makes me think about when the Great Creator formed this Earthly plane. Our native myths tell us that in the beginning, everything was a total Oneness. Then that Oneness, whom we call Creator, got lonesome for someone with whom to enjoy life. So Creator sang a great and poignant song, describing all the beauty and myriad forms, and the world as we know it was born in all its diversity. To make it interesting, freedom was given to us two-leggeds so new ways could emerge. We were given all possibilities to play with; yet set within us, because we are all part of the great Oneness, is the yearning to be consciously connected again with All That Is. Now we are the ones who are lonesome!"

"And now people on Earth have the conscious opportunity to sing the song of Creation in harmony with All That Is," Sparrow replied from the perspective of his level of being. "Humans have always been co-creating—that's one of the special gifts Creator gave to the human family. The fun of being Earthly and physical is that you can see what you're thinking and feeling actually take form in the material world. Now we are becoming conscious of our choice and realizing that harmony feels and works better than anything!

"Working with Spirit, alive and conscious in all things—the four-leggeds, the wingeds, the green growing ones, the microbes in the land itself—is a vital and important beginning. Yet, as you already know, it is just a beginning. The fun has only begun at that level. Creator means for us to know how to do magic. It is part of the gift of true life and aliveness.

"This is an exciting time in the realms of Earth and star," Sparrow continued, his blue eyes sparkling. "It is the moment of the first flower of spring, which presages the burgeoning warmth and light of this great cosmic year. And we—you and I and all our friends and relations—get to be present for it. We are weary of the dreariness of late winter and the cold rains of early spring. Yet they have prepared the way for the flowering that is now under way. So lift up your heart and be glad! Take off the heavy clothing that protected you from the cold winds. Open your windows. Take a brisk walk in this new air. You cannot help but smell the wafting fragrance of beauty bursting forth all around you. The beauty will transform you as your attention turns toward it!"

"I can't wait, especially since you make it sound so easy," I replied. "But I know there is still work for me to do personally. You know, I don't even think work is the right word anymore. Yet I'm certain that being passive and remaining exactly the same as I have been is not it either."

"You're right," Sparrow agreed. "Our old pattern of language does not work very well for this new way of thinking and being. That will be one of the first things we change so that we can speak easily and clearly with one another of our blossoming experience. Since speaking is literally creating vibration, our choosing words that are clear, loving, empowering, and expressive of our spiritual experience is an important ritual action for our transformation. Speakers of the East Indian language of

Sanskrit have long held an advantage. In Sanskrit, which is the finest language for expressing the ways of Spirit, the Invisible, Unmanifest aspect of things is indicated by simply adding an *a* at the beginning of the word: "tree" is the visible; "*atree*" would be the Invisible or spiritual aspect. An "*abody*" would be the spiritual or energetic aspect of the body. It's very convenient.

"You're also correct that what we're being asked to do now is not 'work' as we normally think of it. Rather, it is an inward turning of attention that requires diligence and discipline yet not much actual expenditure of energy. It is rather about garnering our energy to give it to beauty and positive things—not wasting it on negativity, past issues, or fearful expectations. And even this is more a matter of simply letting something go than of trying to make something different happen. When we release the old patterning, the past expectations, the outmoded beliefs, when we take off the heavy clothing of negativity and lighten up at all levels, then the truth can touch our skin and nurture us. It can call us to warm ourselves in its light.

"This clearing and releasing can take place in many ways, at many different levels. You yourself have been doing this quite intensely for the last year or so in the time you have taken for your own personal renewal."

He was right. I have shifted from focusing my full attention on teaching others and making a positive difference in the unfolding world *outside* myself to focusing more attention on my own experience—body, mind, and spirit. The decision, the intent, to bring myself up to a level more closely resembling the level I wanted for the outer world was my inspiration. Once I made it, many pathways opened before me to help me accomplish this. Each of our circumstances is different, so there is no exact prescription for the means of our transformation. However, since what I have done may serve as a stimulus to your own process, I will share it with you.

First of all, I realized that my soul is just fine. It is eternal and wise—no problem there. It is my true life, with each incarnation being a day in that life. My spirit, too, is perfect, although perhaps I haven't yet given it enough energy to fully develop and be of greatest benefit to my life. On the other hand, my physical body and emotions, my mind—now *there* is where some work could be done to release energy for the benefit of my spirit. This is pretty much true of us all. It's the patterning of our physical bodies, formed as they were in the vibration of the ninth hell, that so needs transformative attention.

No sooner do we think about choosing this pathway of clearing than we come to realize that it will take our attention and energy away from other things going on in our lives. And, bottom line, it may cost time, effort, and money. It means we're going to face all our beliefs about security and about what we need to do to have life truly work for us. What a contrast with the prevailing notion, which looks perfectly reasonable since we've all bought into it and play that game—that we dash about, work hard, make money, invest it for the future, and so forth. To take time for silence, to focus attention on clearing our outmoded habits and patterns, to change our diet, to perhaps pay others for help in clearing our emotions and restoring our physical health and energy, to spend time in nature regularly—these things mean a major shift in our priorities. We can't just take a pill and have all these things change automatically.

QUALITY OF ENERGY

The most important lesson in the entire process is that the method you use to transform yourself must have the energetic quality of the end you seek. In other words, you can't dash wildly about to create peace in your life, although we've all tried that: "If I can just get this and this and this and this done, then I can sit down and have some quiet time." You know as well as I do that it doesn't work that way. Instead, try stopping for a moment, taking a few deep breaths, intoning softly to yourself, "I am a peaceful person with plenty of time to accomplish all that needs to be done." This will create much more peace in the long run than frantic hurrying to complete all your tasks. *Becoming* what we want to create for the future is the challenge we have in every moment.

What we wish to accomplish is to create *quality in the process* rather than thinking of it only as an end product. This is what the *I Ching*[1] means when it tells us not to lust after outcomes. We must break the fearful cycle that pushes us to try to make things okay. Emmanuel once said something that has been most helpful to me: "Fear says, 'Come to me, I will make you safe,' while love says, 'You *are* safe.' "[2] We must learn to proceed from trust rather than anxiety.

A good exercise is to examine any moment in your life and get down to what is motivating you. Simply notice how much you base your every decision on some fear, logical as it may seem. "I need to go to work, because I'm afraid I'll lose my job if I don't. If I lose my job, I'm afraid I won't get another easily. Good jobs are hard to come by. If I can't find another job, how will I take care of my family? I hear stories every day of middle-class people who have lost their homes and end up living in their cars . . ." On and on it goes.

Even if you can't suddenly leave your job and find your true calling, then change the way you think about your job. Question the fear motivations and practice transforming them in the moment. "I'm going to work because I like to support my family. I can make a difference right where I am. As I bring my knowledge and skills and truth more fully into my everyday life, I am moving toward more and more appropriate work. Opportunities to do what I would most like to do are opening up each day. I intend to have a fabulous day today—to feel good and do something good for others."

Is that kind of thinking too much of a stretch? It's certainly a different way to approach your day, isn't it? It's an example of making the difference in your life right now rather than waiting until "someday" when everything is finally just right externally and then you can be just right within yourself. *The news is that the inner experience comes first. This, in turn, is what eventually creates what happens externally.*

INTENT

Recall that we stand at the heart center of the bridge between the energetic Invisible and what manifests as real on the physical plane. When we do our positive mantra about our day, we need to take a brief moment to imagine ourselves stepping across that line into the Invisible, as though whispering our positive intent to a genie we can see only with our inner eyes. That energetic genie can make more difference in what manifests for us than trying to push and shove the material world around.

Intent, placed in the Invisible, in shamanic time, is extraordinarily powerful. Stop using your energy to pout and complain about what is. Shift your attention and do something positive and powerful about your life!

The throat chakra is seen by both Native Americans and East Indians to be the energetic place of Creation because of its relationship to the essence of all life: vibration. This is the place of manifestation, of making the golden dream real on Earth, of becoming co-creators with the Great Creator. Dawn Star's teachings remind us of the power of resonance to set in motion patterns of cosmic song. Music transports the soul directly in spiritual communion. This is a native teaching I have been sharing for a long, long time. Apaches, among others, use the metaphoric symbol that we are in the time of the nine-pointed star, which sits energetically at the throat chakra. To learn to use the song of our life in positive ways is to walk a powerfully shamanic way. Make your entire energy, including what you speak, what you want to magnify into your world.

Conscious co-creation is the practice of this new time, the Aquarian Age. As each of us Earth Mages turns our attention to creating a more beautiful personal reality, not only does that help us individually, but it also begins to shift the quality of intent held in the world, which is a determining factor in what happens in the larger world around us.

Beauty represents a special harmony and synchronicity within the oneness of spirit. Beauty is a landmark along the pathway of spirit ... a message to you that you are walking in harmony as you follow the guidance of spirit through life.[3]

The ancient Chinese art/science of Feng Shui (fung shway) is something I am using to help people literally bring home to themselves this manifestation of beauty and harmony. It is a wonderful way to practice the magic of attracting what we need and want into our lives through environmental affirmations. Recognizing that the vibrational energy in our surroundings affects us tremendously, Feng Shui teaches us to manipulate our environment to enhance and empower our lives. The basic principle is that we do something in the physical realm to portray what we are holding in the Invisible realm of ideas, dreams, fantasies, and wishes.

Here are several examples:

- I help a young single woman who wants a lasting love relationship to make that clear in the energetic area of her home that represents love and marriage. The positive symbols she places there act as a magnet to manifest her dreams.
- A cluttered store with dingy windows is made orderly and bright, with welcoming banners flying outside to attract customers, and business picks up remarkably. People are drawn to the lively energy.
- A man with financial challenges is shown that the area representing wealth for him is a junky and unconscious backyard. He makes it into a beautiful garden and brings prosperity into his life.
- A developer uses the sound energetic principles of Feng Shui to plan his housing. The development is beautiful and conscious; the houses are lovely to be in and sell very quickly.

These ritual actions in the physical world attract and magnify energy from the Invisible. We can do our "home work" by beginning right where we live and work: creating richness, beauty, harmony, and magical results![4]

As we become willing to do our homework even more fully, we can begin to join with others to magnify our good intentions, as James Redfield has so beautifully laid out for us in *The Tenth Insight*.[5] When we begin to work at that level, things start to move quickly, and we see some major shifts in the reality we experience outside ourselves. White Buffalo Woman has said to us again and again that *we must work together*: it is the only way to magnify our energy enough to build the Rainbow Bridge. We will talk more about ways to work together in the next chapter. And you may also want to make use of the other resources that are abundantly available.[6]

EMOTION

I have learned from my master teachers, like Moshe Feldenkrais,[7] that the traumatic and unworkable patterns we hold in our bodies—the emotional charges that tie up our energy and pull it into negative configurations— are simply a matter of nervous system patterning. They are electromagnetic hookups that we fashioned as we learned about our world. Those that were the result of high emotion (either positive or negative) have the strongest connections and are the ones on which our system relies in times of stress or uncertainty. This means that it is especially vital to become aware of the patterns set in us through trauma. They will be the ones our brain accesses in stressful times and may be absolutely the opposite of what we consciously want to be doing.

Working with our emotions is definitely a priority in our process. As recent research is showing us:

Emotion is the switch that triggers specific DNA codes within your body, . . . the same codes that allow you the freedom to live without illness, disease and deterioration as you progress through the linear time of your life. Researchers have now demonstrated to the Western world that human emotion determines the actual out-patterning of DNA within our bodies, . . . discovering that the arrangement of matter (atoms, bacteria, viruses, climate, even other people) surrounding your body, is directly linked to the feeling and emotion from within your body.[8]

The work we now have to do to clear ourselves has thus become easier because of the availability of new therapies for releasing our unwanted nervous system patterns. Aspects of what we have thought of as our true personality (which is merely our ingrained habits) can be shifted in a heartbeat. With the right methods, there is often no need for most of us to undergo the expensive, ingraining work of going over and over our traumas in extended analysis, of digging deep into the unconscious over years of time, to deal with our simple, neurotic patterns. New methods are available that very quickly track the connection patterning that we wish to release—whether in the present or the past, in emotions, body organs, meridians (energy pathways that have been used in Chinese healing for five thousand years), or chakras (swirling vortices of energy in the human body, shown us by East Indian systems)—and then, with energetic intent, blow the connections. "Poof," and another layer is gone.

You do, however, have to pursue these methods diligently, because negative patterning has many layers. If you have a therapist who is helping you achieve fabulous results now, you may simply want to add some of these sessions for the different beneficial outcomes they may produce.

Sometimes, one does not even need to consciously track all the events that created the negative, outdated, or otherwise unuseful pattern. Many people, including me, are finding great transformative power in the new work called EMDR (Eye Movement Desensitizing and Reprocessing, or more commonly, eye movement therapy). Using therapeutic head and eye movements in conjunction with traumatic events is extraordinarily helpful in allowing the release of the deep negative or unworkable patterns and allows people to get on with their lives in a good way.[9] I have found remarkable results in each session, which show themselves immediately in my life. I've recently become a practitioner of another, amazingly powerful therapy: Thought Field Therapy, which quickly cures phobias, reduces trauma, pain, grief, and anger, and transforms many other unworkable patterns. If we each took advantage of these new spiritual and emotional technologies immediately after trauma, it would never have a chance to build up and cause us so many consequent problems.

Early work of this sort was in applied kinesiology, which has spread to many other treatment modalities. All are based on using the body's electromagnetic response to receive "yes" or "no" answers about what is happening within us. The technique offers a way to communicate directly with the body tissue and consciousness that lie below our usual awareness. Research has shown that whatever is positive for the being[10] at the present moment *strengthens*; that which is not useful or beneficial at the moment weakens and drains. This is immediately obvious through a method called "muscle testing." In this method, the "neutral" strength of a muscle (say, your raised arm or your closed fingers) is checked; then a substance or an idea is introduced, and the muscle is rechecked for continuing strength or weakness. The body's responses of strength or weakness are remarkably clear.[11]

In a few places around the country, you can find practitioners of the emotional release work called Bioenergy Balancing, which helps to overcome the diminishment we feel from emotional blocks and to release and restore the body's right to exultation. It has been most helpful to me in clearing old patterns and uplifting my daily energy, and I find it very useful in addition to other kinds of growth work. My practitioner Jyoti talks about it as learning to master the emotional body and can refer you to practitioners in Colorado, California, and other places.[12]

In order to investigate these new therapies, ask around to determine who is doing this kind of work near you and who is getting the kinds of results you would like for yourself. If you do not have any of these magical practitioners in your area, become one yourself. What a wonderful way to create right livelihood for yourself!

Some of you may be interested in the Southern Seers' ways of working with this kind of clearing. Don Juan Matus spent years teaching Carlos Castaneda just exactly these techniques, and Carlos shares those ways through a series of books that started in 1969 with *The Teachings of Don Juan* and has continued through *The Wheel of Time*, published in 1998. To read the series is a remarkable learning experience, especially the books in which he talks about Don Juan's teaching methods and he himself understands more of what was being taught. The Seers' system centers on ways of garnering energy from its usual tie-ups in thinking and emotions, so it can then be given to the spirit body—what they call "the dreamer"—and thus increase our personal power. Once we have more energy and awareness given to the invisible, spiritual aspect of ourselves, we have the possibility of increasingly deep perception through the illusory veils of everyday life, which leads to innocent, deep perception and a very magical way of being in the world. A series of videos and a recent book, *Magical Passes: Practical Wisdom of the Shamans of Ancient Mexico*, show you the powerful physical movements the shamans used to do just this.[13]

Now Castaneda and the next generation of his apprentices, plus others who have studied his work, are offering us fabulous material on that

Yaqui and Toltec way of knowledge. Taisha Abelar, in *The Sorcerer's Crossing*,[14] tells the story of her learning to cross the Rainbow Bridge and awaken her dreamer in the Invisible. Her comadre Florinda Donner does the same from a slightly different perspective in *Being in Dreaming*.[15] Victor Sanchez has recently given us his very useful and easily understood rendering of these ways, in exercises that are very forthright for the use of modern people.[16]

Caroline Myss has received these same understandings from her own intuitive work. She shares them with us now through workshops and through a very special series of cassette tapes called Energy Anatomy.[17] In these, she helps us recognize how we have our energy tied up in a debilitating manner and gives us very concrete ways to release the old patterns and begin consciously managing our energetic lives so that manifestation and magic become possible in our own lives.

We are awaking to the usefulness of the system known as mirroring and find it in many forms. Gregg Braden offers a fundamental and very complete way of mirroring, based in the Essene texts of old. I highly recommend this process with inner awareness that he calls "The Seven Essene Mirrors of Relationship."[18] They provide a useful and important means, through observing our relationships, to clear ourselves of the "buttons" or "charges" that our beliefs about certain experiences have for us, thus eliminating the need to draw these kinds of experiences to us in the future. They make us aware of the lessons reflected in our daily interactions, our judgments, our sense of loss, the forgotten things we love most, our relationship to parents, our dark nights of the soul, and our sense of perfection.

And of course, many Native American ways of cleansing and clearing are extremely powerful. Working through purification (sweat) lodge and ceremony are primary ways. In almost every area of the country, there are native teachings available to help you learn about the ritual and spiritual ways. Ask around for who is working with integrity on this path.

Remember, always, that you have tools to work with on your own. Do fasts from negative thoughts; concentrate on appreciation and gratitude for everything in your life; consciously let go and forgive. It also helps to let go of past suffering by embracing the lesson it brought. Glenda Green tells the story of a woman whose husband had a brain tumor, from which he then experienced an instant and total remission. Glenda suggested to the wife that instead of constantly complaining about the brain tumor, they might offer thanks for the tumor, because it gave them a chance to experience a miracle! Our soul chooses these challenges to teach us what we came to Earth to learn. The sooner we can embrace the lesson, the more quickly the suffering will abate.

At so many levels, the information is already there. What is needed now is our commitment to use and practice it. Lakota elder, medicine man, and teacher Wallace Black Elk[19] once said that many people around him are really "into" the groovy Native path until he brings up the "c" word—*commitment*. Then they aren't quite as interested. So it's time to really get down to doing the homework before us.

The surprise here is that if you are truly committed, you will find that much of the work and growth you have already done applies. What you're gaining now is simply a deeper understanding of what is possible with the clarity you are achieving. Some of you do have very competent and wonderful therapists. Others have different ways of doing this same clearing of the emotional body. Whatever method is right for you, *use* it!

SILENCE OF MIND

The Southern Seers' way focuses on the mind as well as the emotions. Thinking and emotions, they remind us, are where we tie up the majority of our energy. The works mentioned earlier in the chapter are good places to go for clearing practices. Buddhist and Vedic practice and many other approaches are focused on giving us ways to touch into the Invisible rather than continue the mind chatter that keeps our old ways in place.

Fasts with a spiritual intent such as vision quests are excellent practices. Let me explain why they can be so powerful. My mentor Dawn Boy taught me that human consciousness likes to be busy: it can be occupied with high-level awareness, openness to new experience, and positive intent as readily as with low-level entertainment, rerunning old patterns, and negativity. Fasting—whether it be from food, TV, our usual daily routine, physical activity, or our old habits—uses this aspect of our makeup to our advantage.

Traditional vision quests are comprised of several useful parts:

1. *The groundwork laid before the quest begins:* This would include cleansing the body by eating lightly, practicing the quieting of meditation, and getting our purpose or intent clear.

2. *The fasting itself:* This includes leaving behind everything but vital necessities like the minimal clothes we wear and what is needed for protection from the elements. Among the things left behind are family and friends, daily routines and employment, familiar surroundings, food, sometimes water, and even physical movement (we are asked to sit, unless doing very specifically prescribed actions such as prayer).

3. *The vacuum created by leaving all this usual activity behind:* As questers, we soon find that the real challenge is to create a vacuum *in the mind,* for in the face of our inactivity in all other areas, the mind often goes wild with thoughts, chatter, fear, imaginings, memories, expectations, and the like. We discover that we've brought our usual life with us via our mind, even though we have done all the outer work of leaving it behind! This is why a previous meditation practice in which we have learned to still the mind is so helpful. Yet it's worth a few days of our time even to discover the remarkable strength of our mind's tendency to carry the old and outmoded!

Even if our meditative practice has not been developed, moments arise during a vision fast when the mind slips into stillness, into the deeper quiet of the heart. Dawn Boy reminds me that then comes the gift—the real reason for the quest. For into the vacuum we have created, something must come! Our consciousness calls out for something to engage it. And what engages it but Spirit! The Invisible—that more subtle realm that we usually override with our preoccupation with what is "real" and visible—has a chance to come forward and present itself. Voilà!! Vision! We see beyond the veil and perceive the deeper and more universal truths at the heart of things that go far beyond the mind's dualistic thinking. We begin to understand the potent usefulness of the heart as a deeper, finer, more visionary and intelligent guide than our usual mind, whose function is simply to categorize, store, and retrieve past experience. These heartful moments are invaluable and can change the course of our lives.[20]

If we are aware of its true process, this kind of questing reinforces how invaluable it is to learn to still our minds and to focus our intent on opening to the Invisible in our daily lives. "Leave room for the mystery," my teacher Dawn Boy would exhort me. "Don't fill your life up with all your petty knowing." Leave space for something more mysterious, more beautiful, more magical, more profound than you can presently comprehend. The Great Creator has more beauty in store for you than you can possibly imagine at this point in your life!

The basic skill is that of silencing the mind and opening the spiritual heart. If there is any one thing I would recommend for you, it is to find a practice that assists you in this.[21] It not only helps you receive information; it helps you receive information from Source that is individual and meaningful to you personally. Although everyone is going through this transformation, each of us has our own needs and our own path. Listening deeply is our personal responsibility. It will serve us profoundly.

One of the important aspects of the silencing is to stop the inner chatter through which we continually create our world. We think and keep concepts together through language. We do our thinking in words, and a large part of our emotional experience most often takes place through words. Seldom do we have pure bodily emotion or a kind of thinking that goes beyond languaging. So our internal dialogue is how we put our world together and how we create the images through which we determine our reality. In order for the new to become available to us, we need to stop this languaging.

Here's the silencing technique I use. It is based on the Southern Seers' ways and works because it is grounded in our physiology. The focus is on your physical ears—specifically, the entire ear canal—so that you can begin by awakening that part of your body.

1. Turning your hands backward, place your palms over your ears. Do this in such a way that you create by gentle pressure a "vacuum seal," so that when you speak, you hear it from inside your head, not outside. Now you have effectively sealed your ears.

2. Keeping up this gentle pressure, massage your ears and ear canals by rotating your hands around in circles, forward and back. Also press in gently so the air pushes against your ear drums. Wake up the entire inner and outer ear!

3. The next step may take a little practice so that you can accomplish it and keep the seal on your ears. Putting your middle finger over your index finger and pressing, you can pull it off with a snapping motion. Your middle finger should snap down, popping against whatever your hand rests on. Try tapping on one of your knees or on a table first, if you need to. Notice that you can give whatever is under your fingers a good strong tap that way.

Once you have this down, then go back to the position with your hands sealed over your ears and tap the back of your head with this method—eighteen times.

4. When you take your palms down from your ears, you may notice a sense of more acute physical hearing. A friend tells me that in Taoist practice, this is called "beating the heavenly drum."

The idea of this first part of the technique is to awaken your actual sensing of your physical ears and ear canals—to create more awareness there—because this is where your attention must be for the actual silencing part of it.

5. You can even lower your jaw dramatically, as I do, to open the area around the inner ear from the inside.

Now you can create an even greater awareness by adding your imagination.

6. I suggest closing your eyes as you continue awakening your ears, because it cuts down on distractions.

7. Sitting upright where you can breathe fully and easily, begin drawing in full natural breaths through your nose, and as you release your breath, imagine that you can send the air out through your ears! Continue this until you have a more awakened sensation in your ear canals.

Relax a few moments and enjoy the clarity of your hearing. When you actually do this exercise, you may just continue right on through, but while you are learning, you can take a brief rest here.

Now for the actual "silencing" practice:

1. Place the tip of your tongue gently on the roof of your mouth on the ridge of palate behind your teeth.

2. The final and most crucial step is to put all of your attention on the openings of your ears, listening intently. (Remember that you want to be able to really feel your ears and ear canals, so if you can't, it might be helpful to actually put your little fingers into your ears and give a little massage there to get more in touch with exactly where to put your attention.)

3. When you are focusing your attention there, you will not be hearing words inside your head. *If you are hearing words, you are not focused on your ears, so return to focusing on them.* Put all your attention there. Let any word that comes up be a signal to draw your focus back to your ears.

Practicing this technique, even in conjunction with other meditative practices, can be very useful.

4. In time, you can open your eyes and look around you yet still not be naming things and talking to yourself about what you see.

5. The idea is to eventually move about through your day without constantly languaging—without naming and categorizing things in your old ways.

As Dawn Boy urged me, "Leave space for the Great Mystery to offer something new and wonderful!"

Everything is unfolding in beauty; we need only stop holding on to the historically and personally familiar.

MANIFESTING THE HIGHEST

Once you find that you can maintain the inner silence, then another step is possible. To best understand this, you will want to remember the Wave of Creation and how our vibratory intent is what determines how the potent energy of the Invisible manifests in our world. In other words, what we "hold up in front of" that energy as it comes into physical reality is like a mold or a "cutout pattern" for the light to come through. Everything that we are and everything that we are running inside our minds is what creates the pattern.

When we come to true silence, what appears is what Creator is sending through, unrestricted, and it is of very high quality. We are becoming the hollow bone. As a matter of fact, the definition of the Christ energy is the ability to allow the energy of Creation to move through the heart, unrestricted. It means letting go of our control and manipulation to a large extent and settling into the silence of the Sacred Heart, the place of connection to Source and to our own indigenous power.

Yet when we become clear about something that we choose to manifest, that silence is potent. When there is nothing else in the pattern, when the space is open and clear of all our usual images and beliefs, then we can manifest exactly what we hold in our hearts. In that instance, what we place into the silence is singular and receives all the energy that is coming through; in this way, it manifests immediately!

Although an enormous amount of energy is available, we normally have it tied up in many other ways. We must learn from what the great masters are doing when they literally manifest things before our eyes! They place a seed of intent into the silence, which then has the total energy available to make it become real. Nothing clouds the picture—no old ideas, no limitations, no past history, no negativity. It truly is *magic*, and this is the science of it!

What we are doing is stepping into shaman's time, stepping into the Invisible, just "across the line" where our personal energy impacts the incoming energy most profoundly. If we were able to focus our intent far out in the Invisible, in the most subtle realms of the infinitesimal, it would still have to "travel" a long way before it became manifest, and many things could influence or change it on the way. In contrast, if we act on the manifest side—in the world as we usually know it—the density there requires tremendous amounts of our human energy. And this is how we have been attempting to make progress throughout most of our history. We have tried to make a difference in our world by pushing and shoving around material things. This has drained not only our personal vitality but also the resources of our Earth. As I have said before, the only way we will truly make a difference at this point is through working in a spiritual way.

It is our challenge to ourselves to learn this new, magical, graceful, and easy way of doing things—by *being* in a different way. And the key— the basic skill—is *silence* within the heart, whose magnetic energy attracts what we need without force or effort.

> The world is the ever-changing form that floats
> on the surface of the sea of silence.[22]

All the external practices we do come to naught if we can't find that place of silence within us. Our connection to our own deep and larger Self lies in the stillness, as does our bond with the great Source of All Things, from which comes true wisdom and unerring direction in our lives.

> In the mountain, stillness surges up to explore its own height;
> in the lake, movement stands still to contemplate its own depth.[23]

That direction toward our highest, finest, and most direct development of who we are and what we came to do reminds me of an airplane guidance system. It is invisible. The pilot hears "beeps" when right on the directional beam and must use certain special equipment to hear them. Our ability to pay attention in a certain way is our special equipment. The information that comes through certainly cannot be seen in the usual way. And it may not seem like much until we integrate it with our own actual physical experience. Even though the airplane is, and we are, usually off beam more than on, we can keep moving toward our goal in a good way by checking in often, so we don't stray too far off the beam. I'm sure what our higher selves are telling us is, "Tune in often!"

Elder Sara Smith of the Mohawk tribe, Iroquois Confederacy, reminds us of her good way:

> Meditation is much a part of my being ... which I now understand as allowing what is so to pour forth from within oneself. It's not from you but for you. I sit and still myself, to allow the

answers to come from within rather than me dictating what I want and what I think I need.[24]

Remember, too, what I said about emotion earlier in this chapter. The practices and resources given there can be profoundly useful in freeing up your energy to do the life-changing magic that is possible for us. Since negative thinking and old emotional patterns tie up so much of our energy, these are primary places to focus in freeing up the gift of energy Creator gives us each day. In doing so, we can more easily become a hollow bone, which allows present-moment power and inspiration to come through so that we may become conscious co-creators of a beautiful, whole, and holy life for ourselves and All Our Relations.

LIGHTENING UP!

To clear ourselves of old patterns, Creator has given us an especially wonderful tool, although most of us have forgotten to use it. In the Lakota way, it is said that there are four Great Powers: The first is the power that created All That Is. The second is the power or Spirit that lives in everything. The third is a mysterious power in the West that has to do with awareness. And the fourth is *heyoka*, the power of laughter, humor, and stepping outside the usual ways of doing things.

The magic and mystery of laughter is an amazing capacity that Creator placed within our own bodies as two-leggeds, available at a moment's notice. Laughter is Creator's way of helping us lighten up and release the old. It is a vital aspect of our everyday life and ultimately important as we approach these new times. In the words of Indian poet Rabindranath Tagore, "The burden of self is lightened when I laugh at myself."[25]

This fourth Great Power is one that we can use and practice with wonderful results, because it is Creator's gift of clearing. Recall a time when you were totally consumed by laughter and take a moment to realize that there were no thoughts, no images, nothing except the bubbling mirth of true laughter in your mind. Laughter's function is to cast loose all our moorings to the past and open our minds totally.

In the few moments after we have laughed like this, we are able to program our consciousness with new information that goes deep and hooks up powerfully. It is a bodily metaphor for our own personal power that resides within our bodies in the everyday world. Perhaps you and your friends can make a game of creating really deep, joyful laughter, knowing that the first words you speak will be what you are wishing to create in your life.

One of our most useful tools is that of humor and of being able to spin ourselves out of depression and frustration by creating laughter. Sometimes we need our friends to help us with this. I have a set of warm, witty, humorous stories by Garrison Keillor from the *Prairie Home Companion* series on Minnesota Public Radio entitled *News from Lake Woebegon* that lighten my spirits immensely. In *Lake Wobegon Days* (page 39, note), Garrison describes "Woebegon" as derived from an Ojibwa word meaning "the place where [we] waited all day in the rain." You may have a favorite funny movie. It's great to keep these things on hand for emergency upliftment!

In the midst of all our focused "work" on ourselves, it is refreshing to know that Creator has given us a happy way of doing the clearing we want and of creating an energy that is one we want to magnify. It is a constant challenge for us to "lighten up" in the midst of the process of lightening up! We often get terribly serious about the process, forgetting that we must continue to create the energetic quality we wish to have in the end. As I often tell my students (and myself): "Remember that the Great Spirit is *not* the Great Serious!"

Letting go of what we don't want is only one side of the process; creating what we *do* want is just as important. So find ways to spend time laughing and remember to bring images of beauty and radiance and a golden world into your mind after that good belly laugh!

NATURE AND SOLITUDE

Mother Nature can be a helpful partner in our process, too. Although we two-leggeds have interfered with and influenced much of what surrounds us, there is still a Web of Being, beyond what we can control or manipulate, that moves All of Life forward. This numinous web is evident to our deeper awareness whenever we take time to quiet ourselves in nature. By quieting ourselves, I don't mean just not talking. I'm referring to that inner stillness mentioned earlier in the chapter that allows us to really see and hear what is happening around us.

An image I often use is that of a spiderweb. Although its fibers are tremendously strong, it is very delicate. The slightest breath of breeze or the movement of a tiny insect caught in its elastic fibers communicates information to the spider resting upon it. So when you're in nature, let your mind be as open and flexible as a delicate web in the sunlight. Then the subtle, the simple, and the magical can play upon its fibers like the strings of a harp.

I learned this from a spider who had made her web very near the head of my bed, weaving together some special objects there. In order to call my attention to them in a different way, she danced on the web in such a way that my still mind heard an actual tune, a vibrating of the strings. It was a tremendous gift.

I like John O'Donohue's way of speaking of nature: "The great divinity called nature is not matter but a luminous and numinous presence which has depth and possibility and beauty within it."[26]

Taking time for solitude in the natural world is a vitally important practice for us as humans. In that solitude, we seldom find isolation or outward silence. Instead, we find a great, buzzing family of life all around us. The wind whispers, the trees dance in the breeze, the birds fly by or sit to sing a song of beauty, insects busy themselves in every nook and cranny, flowers nod and turn toward the Sun, and the rain blesses it all.

In such a setting, it is easier for us to understand ourselves as part of a numinous kinship that offers gifts of wisdom at every turn. When we come to a sense of outer belonging and the rightness of all the unity, then it may be easier to come to a sense of inner belonging—to accept all aspects of ourselves as parts of an evolving wholeness. In this way, both inner and outer solitude can bring us to a sense of the holy in all things.

VIBRATION

Speaking of tuning in to our larger kinship brings me to some thoughts on the vibrational nature of our reality. In Chapter 7, I spoke of the whole of Creation's being on a vibrational spectrum. The principle of vibration is the key to the upliftment we are seeking. Those who would create and step into a new and radiant Earth

> must have a vibrational frequency, earned through raised consciousness, which will match the vibrational frequency of the New Age. This phenomenon is absolute and will be measured by individuals' abilities to be open-minded, loving, centered, tranquil, peaceful and devoted. These individuals will command the vibrational frequency closer to the speed of Light which will be in alignment with the Age of Aquarius.[27]

There are some vibrations we can see, there are some we hear, and there are many levels beyond our normal ability to perceive, extending through both ends of the spectrum to infinity! When we step across into the Invisible, we are working with a different level of vibration, and a very powerful one. When we hold an image before our eyes of something we want to manifest, we are using vibration in a useful way. When we sing or speak out what we desire, we are using it again. And when we allow our passionate emotions to arise in support of what we seek, we are adding a final and tremendously powerful vibrational boost to our request.

When we wish to "lift our vibration," as I have said many times in this book, we are working in the same realm. Rather than getting frenetic and moving faster, this is actually telling us to do two paradoxical things: s-l-o-w down the body and its energy into peacefulness and stillness, ease and grace, and at the same time elevate the frequency of our energetic being. That difference might be seen as the contrast in quality between a big hunk of raw, bleeding cow (steak) and a delicate, sweet berry on the tip of a branch. It is like feeding ourselves with the energy of *inspiration* rather than relying simply on dense victuals. My Mayan friend David Burgos says, "My people do not call out the name of God. We do a deep inhalation, and that is God."

SINGING A SONG OF BEAUTY

"Yet what we 'call out' is also important," Sparrow Hawk chimed in out of the blue. "The actual capacity of our language to address our spiritual experience is important. Even more crucial is the way we use our voice, our vibrational center. You must remember that *every word counts*: every vibration sent out continues on and on, gathering energy around it. Add up the words you speak each day and see what energy you are magnifying for yourself to walk forward into."

His words reminded me of how much I love to listen to people who don't just talk about, but actually *speak*, the language of empowerment and upliftment. A classic example of this is my friend Caroline Casey, whose quarterly seasonal celebration tapes are a treasure. She is a visionary activist and astrologer who uses the large cycles of the stars and planets to address, very incisively, the concerns of our daily lives and political situation. Yet her words are always uplifting, energizing, humorous, and inspiring.[28]

GRATEFULNESS

The final thing I would have you remember to practice is gratitude. When you are focusing on things for which you are grateful, you are investing your energy in what you would like to see more of in your life. It is also true that an appreciative and grateful heart is more peaceful, thus setting a healthy tone for the entire body with its rhythm. This kind of strengthening of your heart is one of the best things you can do for yourself every day.

Be grateful for the gift of life you receive every day. Be grateful for the opportunity to be alive in this amazing time. Give thanks for the difficult issues that are in your face, for soon you will be clear of them and moving toward the Light more smoothly. Be grateful for friends, for grace, for the great Light that Creator is sending our way to uplift us into a time of exquisite beauty on Lady Gaia.

"This talk of vibration and gratefulness brings me back full circle," I told Sparrow. "Our Native peoples' Creation myths say that Creator sang a great song and the Earthly world came into being. That great song continues, and we now join in its tune with more awareness. Our singing and chanting in harmony and gratefulness can be added to that song of Creation."

As Sparrow Hawk replied, I remembered what a beautiful singer he was—singing four-part jazz harmony as well as many other things. "Literally singing in harmony is one powerful way to practice getting the idea of true harmony into the cells of your body, where it can be useful in your daily life," he said. "Primary peoples have a song for almost everything and sing together in their work. We would do well to become more conscious of the sounds we put forth and make them sweet songs of beauty and harmony rather than curses or exasperation."

"Yes," I said, "and through our songs, we can give joyful thanks that we are on our way Home!"

These words, which I gathered from meditations on the Aramaic words of Jesus in the Lord's Prayer, remind us of the power of the song of life and are a wonderful way to use our life breath:

O Breathing Life of all, Creator of the Shimmering Sound that touches us.
O Birther! Mother-Father of the Cosmos, you create all that moves in light.

Focus your light within us—make it useful, as rays of a beacon show the way.
Your name, your sound, moves us as we tune our hearts as instruments for its tone.
Create your reign of unity now through our fiery hearts and willing hands.
Desire with and through us the rule of universal fruitfulness onto the Earth.

As we find your love in ours, let Heaven and nature form a new creation.
Your one desire then acts with ours—as in all light, so in all forms.

Grant us nurturance each day of bread and insight.
Let the measure of our need be earthiness: give all things simple,
    verdant, passionate.
Produce in us, for us, the possible: each only-human step toward
    Home lit up.

Loose the cords of mistakes binding us,
As we release the strands we hold of others' guilt.
Lighten our load of secret debts as we relieve others of their
    need to pay.
Untangle the knots within so that we can mend our hearts'
    simple ties to others.

Let surface things not delude us,
Free us from that which holds us back from our true purpose.
Keep us from hoarding false wealth, and for the inner shame of
    help not given in time.
Deceived neither by the outer or the inner, free us to walk your
    path with joy.

From you is born all ruling will, the power and the life to do,
    the song that beautifies all: from age to age it renews.
Out of your astonishing fire, the birthing glory: returning light
    and sound to the cosmos.

Truly, power to these statements;
May they be the ground from which all my actions grow.
Ho!

CHAPTER 12

A SHAMAN'S WAY

Spirit is alive and powerful within all things,
ready to be awakened through our conscious intent and communion.

Shamanic practice is based in a stance that recognizes
that fully human beings have one foot on the ground of Earth
and one foot firmly planted in the Shimmering Invisible,
and that Spirit fills both realms.

There came a time when Sparrow Hawk suggested that we take a break from our intense communications. It became my goal to more fully walk his words into experience and wisdom. I realized that while all the things we had talked about were wonderful, I needed to focus on myself again in order to make these things real for me.

I began to hone my awareness of the truth of all things within and around myself. I focused on walking a shaman's path, dropping away from the intellectual thoughts that sought to capture my attention and keep me in my old patterns, into the shamanic way, which models the energetic pathway I wish to manifest for myself and All My Relations.

Shamanic practice recognizes that *fully* human beings have one foot on the ground of Earth and one foot firmly planted in the Shimmering Invisible, and that Spirit fills *both* realms. This is the Earth Mage's way. It is a way that can reopen pathways between these worlds and reactivate our connection with the living Spirit, making our communications with both realms rich and vital. This is a time in which we must apprentice ourselves to Spirit. We are past the stage of learning from others. Now we must continue our growth by doing, by putting into practice what we have already learned so we can ascend into our fully human state. This is what will make Spirit's gifts real in our everyday world.

In the remainder of the chapter, I share some of the things I learned through my practice.

HONORING THE SELF

A primary step is to begin honoring ourselves. We are a part of the Great Creation, evolving in perfection. Loving ourselves and dropping into a deeper trust of the unfolding process is an appropriate first step. It is crucial for us to understand that we are creatures who awe the angels, who are stepping out into the most challenging level of evolution. Too often we put ourselves down and are harsh with our bodies and ourselves. We must instead develop a gentle, supportive humor as our way of being with ourselves. It is not necessary to bathe and scrub ourselves with a wire brush, bruising and lacerating ourselves and our psyches, to awaken Spirit alive within us. It's much more joyful to soak and play in the water, softening ourselves into a gentle receptivity so our shy spirit can feel comfortable coming to splash and play with us. While our attitude can be softer, it does not mean that we should not use our bodies intensely. Sometimes a strenuous workout, an extremely hot sweat lodge, or an exhilarating run will awaken Spirit and vision within us. Pushing beyond our usual physical limits is often very powerful and is very different from damaging ourselves with extremes.

Ancient wisdom lives within us, not only in our DNA but also in the Golden Seed Atom. This tiny seed is the memory of our perfection, innocence, purity, Oneness, and all the lessons we have learned throughout the eternal life of our soul. Lying in the left ventricle of the heart, it is a memory outside of time. My sense is that this ancient memory was the part of us stimulated at the time of Harmonic Convergence, when Dawn Star radiated the essence of His teaching into the hearts of all. It would be good to take a moment right now to close your eyes and meditate on this tiny Golden Seed Atom in your heart. Take a deep breath and allow yourself to imagine it as you will. (I often see it as a tiny golden figure with an infant's rounded form.) Breathe and be with this image, making a connection with this ancient and everlasting part of yourself.

We must realize that Divine wisdom lives within us, readily available if we only make a practice of listening and moving with it. Here is part of a David Whyte poem I love, which reminds us of this:

What to Remember When Waking

In that first
hardly noticed
moment in which you wake,
coming back to this life
from the other
more secret, moveable
and frighteningly
honest world
where everything began,
there is a small opening
into the new day
which closes
the moment
you begin your plans.

What you can live
wholeheartedly
will make plans
enough
for the vitality
hidden in your sleep.

To be human
is to become visible
while carrying

what is hidden
as a gift to others.

To remember
the other world
in this world
is to live your
true inheritance.[1]
—*DAVID WHYTE*

A great place to begin any steps you take is with the acknowledgment of what Creator has already given us. Too often we think something outside ourselves must come to make things right, whether a savior instantly fixing everything or spaceships from an advanced culture beyond the stars showing us new technologies. This takes us away from the truth that everything we need has already been given to us. If we would simply apply Light to what we already have, we would reflect more Light to the world.

HONORING THE BODY

Our bodies are the instruments through which we experience life on this sweet Earth and manifest Spirit into matter. They are natural and innocent and connected to the clay of Earth from which they are formed. They love to move and play and feel and dance. Too often our bodies have taken a "bad rap" that actually belongs more to the part of our mind that creates judgment, distance, and separation.

Being fully alive in our bodies is to awaken the Divine on Earth, which is exactly what we came to do. But we must really *be on* Earth and fully embodied before we can raise Lady Gaia and ourselves up, so we mustn't take our bodies for granted. Mastering the art of living does not involve learning to control the body/self but learning to have a good and conscious relationship with ourselves, discerning with awareness, then respectfully commanding what we choose.

For example, at one time, I realized that my body was starting to feel deeply weary. In becoming more aware of myself, I discovered several things:

- I have lived out a stressful, work-hard model of life, so I am taking time to find relaxation and joy in my days.
- My body tells me it is depleted of many kinds of nourishment—from minerals to massage. So I am now paying closer attention to giving my body what it needs to feel and function better.
- My thinking has been shaped by the consensus reality around me, which expects aging and decline. I have now substituted "aliveness" for "aging" in my mind, realizing that I can be vitally alive and energetic until my body chooses to leave this physical plane.
- I realize that in our recent human past, people oftentimes lived only into their forties or fifties due to such factors as poor diet, harsh environment, and extremely hard work. This may have created a limiting attitude about our possibilities. Yet we know of others, like the Hunzas (people from the mountains of Pakistan), who live long, happy, and productive lives past a hundred years of age. Therefore, I have respectfully asked my pituitary gland (situated behind the bridge of the nose) to produce *growth hormone* rather than death hormone. The former is the hormone that keeps young bodies energetic, flexible, lean, and well toned. The latter moves us into the decline toward our eventual passing.

So rather than being angry with, dismissing, or rejecting my body, I am focusing my awareness lovingly upon it, listening deeply to the wisdom it gives me, then acting on that knowledge. I do this not just to return to "normal" functioning but to move toward the ascension and renewal that is possible. We will ascend only to the degree that we are fully alive and present in this body.

Another illuminating experience I have recently witnessed concerns a friend of mine who has for years been an inspiring model of our human ability to connect directly with universal wisdom. She has been able to open up to that Source and bring into our consciousness the richness of the information available when we function at those higher levels of communion. Yet she has often had problems with her body, her own sense of self-worth, and her ability to apply the outpouring of wisdom to her own day-to-day life.

Recently, her guides have cut off her universal connection as a loving way to push her to learn to be in her body and take care of it—to live through it rather than above it. This has caused her great inner struggle, yet as she comes through this challenging descent into matter, she is becoming a radiant example of integrating the two realms so vital to us today.

Because she was such a model of that higher and deeper connection, the challenge of full embodiment may be more obvious in her case. Yet I believe that all of us are being asked to become Earth Mages in the same way to fully embody ourselves. Then we can be the grounded beings needed to channel Light and Love for the creation of a renewed Earth for us and All Our Relations.

Our body's deepest desire is to express our soul's purpose in the physical world. Our physical presence is the temple of our soul, enlivened by our spirit. It was magnetically created through the principle of Love, which is the universal bonding agent, the connecting element of Creation. Through it, individual atoms choose to come together in Oneness to give shape to our expression on Earth. A sacrament is a "visible sign of an invisible grace." Therefore, the body can be thought of as a sacrament, a sacred part of ourselves.

Sparrow Hawk dropped a thought in at this point, saying, "Humans are star and stone become clay and bone. Yet that clay and bone must not forget the sparkle of Spirit, which is their heritage as well!"

The body loves to learn through ritual action and metaphor. Ritual actions are physical actions that, combined with focused consciousness, create living metaphors. Seemingly simple practices can be very powerful and empowering.[2] For example, when you are in the process of cleansing in your morning shower, consciously wash away any burdens you are carrying, anything you no longer need or want. When you're rinsing the toothpaste off your toothbrush, acknowledge that you are giving away all the words that do not serve to empower yourself and others.

A good way to release burdens is to find a stone that weighs approximately one to five pounds. Place it in a backpack or bag that you can carry for most of a day, consciously putting into the stone every bit of heaviness you experience in any and every realm of your life.

Then, do a little ceremony:

1. Take the stone in your hands and acknowledge that all your burdens and heaviness rest in this stone—both those things that you have brought to mind and those that are still unconscious.

2. Acknowledge that you are now willing to let them go.

3. Then, do either of two things: put the stone in a place where it will remind you to unburden yourself whenever you see it, or throw it into a river or a ravine and be totally done with it.

4. Afterward, smudge yourself, take a shower, and do some bodily activity you love that helps you feel and celebrate your new freedom and lightness. Put on a lively record and dance, take a walk in the fresh air, or do whatever pleases you.[3]

Become fluent in the language of your body and all the languages of life. Begin to use your body's intelligence more often than you have done before. For instance, you might say, "Body, I have a problem at work. Guide me to the part of you that will help me." Then feel/listen to the wisdom there.

It may take time and practice to listen deeply enough to be cognizant of the wisdom of your body, but it is well worth it. Your body never lies. I have found Eugene Gendlin's wonderful book *Focusing*[4] a simple yet profound guide to working with your body and the "felt senses" that are keys to it.

Another bodily aspect we do not honor as sacred is our sensuality and sexuality. We often come to it with our mind's judgment, the mores of consensual reality, or the hungers of not nourishing ourselves fully with true communication and loving touch. Once, in conversation with my guides, I was being instructed about these things, and I said somewhat stiffly, "Well, all this is well and good, but I don't want to engage in any sexual activity unless it's with someone with whom I have a committed relationship."

The wonderful old Lakota grandfather who is my guide just burst into laughter and began kidding me about my tight, preconceived ideas of sexuality. "Relax and allow yourself to play with these energies," he said. "Sexuality is a natural and enjoyable thing, not a mind game! You must trust yourself to do what is respectful and honoring of yourself and others and let go of your limiting ideas. *Stop living from your mind and allow the innocence and aliveness of your body to move you forward in all realms of your life.*"

This was a really important lesson for me. I had not realized how much my mind and thoughts were preforming my life and preventing the natural flow of energy from moving through me at many different levels.

HONORING OUR DREAMS

Let us begin with the dreams of our waking lives. An image comes to mind of Sparrow Hawk playing in Zion, dancing across logs over streams, capturing the beauty with his camera. This was an important part of his work, yet it looked like a vacation!

Sparrow Hawk came in to say, "I wanted to remind you that it was my body's wisdom that drew me back again and again to Zion. My body found an almost indescribable joy there. And I allowed that to draw me back again and again. I was following my body's highest dream, rather than ignoring it, when I journeyed there repeatedly. Yes, it was *always* a vacation, and it was what inspired and choreographed the gifts I subsequently gave."

"One of the greatest gifts you gave all of us," I said, "is that you followed your love, your bliss, your dream. You're the model for us that someone can become very happy and fulfilled, as well as wealthy and famous, even though that person is willing to give those very things up to follow his or her dream. Aria has told me that your contemporaries were blown away when you chose not to use your amazing talent to become a very well paid graphic artist in L.A. They thought you were crazy to follow your dream into the mountains! Yet by following your joy, you became truly wealthy, which is about being well, joyful, and radiantly healthy rather than just pursuing money."

"Yes," Sparrow said with more than his usual twinkle. "And notice that this is a very different approach to following your dreams than the usual one of working hard, making money, and *then* planning to spend time pursuing your dream when you can afford it. *We must realize that the rare and precious gem we came to give is found in what brings us greatest joy.*"

Our conversation reminded me of a favorite part of Mary Oliver's wonderful poem "Wild Geese":

> You do not have to be good.
> You do not have to walk on your knees
> for a hundred miles through the desert, repenting.
> You only have to let the soft animal of your body
> love what it loves.[5]

What a wonderful expression of this awareness and an encouragement to follow the dream of our bodies!

I realized also that Sparrow had not succumbed to another kind of pressure that often keeps us from our dreams—our family's ideas of what we should do with our lives. Sparrow's father and grandfather, whom he admired enormously, were both ministers. In a letter to his grandfather, he answered their questions about his following a different path from theirs. He pointed out that his own personal way of honoring and expressing Creator's life in all things was through his paintings rather than the pulpit.

So please remember that your special gift is unique and its expression must be in the form that brings you happiness. As my friend Robert Ghost Wolf summed it up, "Learn to listen to your own heart. If you learn that, you will come to know the wisdom of the ages."[6] Remember not to kill your dreams with rational or fearful thinking. That is killing of a most dangerous kind, whether you do it to yourself or others.

Our "night" dreams are also important. Often we wake up with scattered memories of dreams that fade quickly. These are likely our psyche working with images and feelings from our daily life and are well worth recording and reviewing. When I do this over time, I frequently find images, patterns, and lessons in the longer view that I hadn't recognized in isolated, individual dreams. Keeping a dream journal or small tape recorder beside your bed is a wonderful way to become more aware of this bridge between your inner and outer worlds. One useful technique for remembering dreams is this: drink a large glass of water just before bedtime, suggesting to yourself that when you need to get up in the night to go to the bathroom, you will remember your dreams and be able to record them. A variation is to omit the water and simply make the suggestion to remember upon waking not to move until you have rerun what you can recall of your dreams. Then sit up and record them on paper or cassette.

You can also "program" your dreams. Just as you are falling asleep, remind yourself of the issue or problem you would like help with and ask for a dream to guide you. It is also possible to do this during the day when you lie down for a brief nap. Give yourself twenty minutes to drop into dreamtime and come back with a solution.

Another aspect of the "dreaming" world is imagery. The images of our dreams, fantasies, and inner journeys are potent metaphors that arise from a deep well within us of which we are usually not conscious. Eligio Stephen Gallegos, in his book *Animals of the Four Windows*, expresses it very beautifully:

> Deep imagery is the primary mode of knowing totalities[; it] . . . is the primary domain of the shaman, who recognizes imagery as foundational, preceding and transcending knowing through thinking and sensing. . . . Knowing through sensing is a knowing of the outer . . . concerned with adaptation and survival. Knowing through imagery is a knowing of the inner, and its concern is growth, healing, and wholeness. . . . What thinking *can* do is to support and nurture imagery, learn from it, and be willing to enter into relationship with it.[7]

I spoke in Chapter 6 about awareness of the aspect of ourselves I call the Dreamer, which "lives" in the Shimmering Invisible. Meditating in silence, fasting and vision questing, and use of sacred plant medicines are a few of the ways we can bring our Dreamer into consciousness. Being awake beyond Space and Time is a powerful intent to unfold in our lives.

All levels of dreaming and imagery are natural bridges between your daily world and that of your deepest wisdom. The more you consciously walk across these bridges, the more ease you will find in bringing that wisdom into usable form for your own upliftment and that of All Your Relations.[8] And the more comfortable you will be in those transcendent realms that the ascended state encompasses!

HONORING OUR ANCESTORS

Another characteristic of shamanic ways is the honoring of those who have gone before us. It has been mistakenly seen as ancestor "worship," when, in reality, it is simply an honoring of the continuing connection we have with the lineages that produced us. As I come to know myself better, I realize that I am an outgrowth of the experience and physical expression of my ancestors. And it makes sense to me that from their "broader" viewpoint in Spirit, they have much to offer us on our path.

Love is eternal. My grandmothers used to remind me that our grandparents *always*, whether in this world or beyond, are thinking lovingly of the children of the generations following them. They are very much willing to communicate from their level in the Beyond World to assist us in this ascension process, just as those who had gone before helped the old-time Ghost Dancers. And through our subsequent awakening, we help them as well. When you clean up your act, you make an impact on all your ancestors who went before you. They aid us from their side, but our good acts also help them.

I was shown this when I connected more fully with each of my special guides: my grandmother Mary of the Teton Sioux, who stands behind me on my left, and my "uncle," Chief Joseph of the Nez Percé, who stands behind me on my right. Both of them experienced much trauma and tragedy in their physical lives and bore a sad, stern demeanor. During one meditation with Grandma Mary, I was feeling sad that she had been orphaned from her people and abused, never having experienced the joy of her native family life. I suggested to her that she was no longer limited by that past Earthly experience, that she could be exactly as she wanted to be now. It was a thrill to me that she immediately turned into a young woman with long black braids, dancing and twirling in a creamy white buckskin dress with long, beautiful fringes. The radiant look on her face was worth a million dollars! Since then, she has continued to appear to me in that happier, more relaxed, and lighter form, more integrated with the truth of her own ancestry.

Then I realized I could do the same with Chief Joseph, who suffered such deep sadness for his people, so I asked Grandmother's help. She went to him and dragged him out into the circle of lively dancers, and he, too, took on a younger and more joyful demeanor. These experiences help establish a different kind of connection with my ancestral lines. My ancestors' reconnection to a more harmonious tribal life is mine as well.

I have been told in vision by Chief Joseph that the ancestors have been waiting for those who will step forward to bring high and clear vision to the people again. I sense his energy always supporting anything I do that brings a better and more harmonious life to the people of Earth. It's clear to me that each of our ancestors is asking the same thing of us—that we awaken to and use our potential for creating a better world for the children of all people.

Recently I've been focalizing a series of gatherings under the title Song of the Nations, whose purpose is to continue providing my students and me with learning from the rainbow of nations. At a recent *Confluence* gathering, we heard from Celtic, Basque, and African teachers about the importance of our ancestors. Malidoma and Sobonfu Somé, Dagara African shamans, gave us a wonderful way of thinking about it: The ancestors have a broader point of view as they step into Spirit. In their former human form, they had unique and special gifts to give and most often did not accomplish this giveaway totally and completely. Perhaps the ancestors even did negative things during their lives that they wish to rectify. Awareness of this makes them sad. Therefore, they are eager to send their energy into their families still active on Earth so that their own unfinished tasks can be completed and they can help those on Earth they love to accomplish *their* unique tasks. Our ancestors are waiting for our call for assistance, and they wait and wait. As Malidoma put it so humorously and well, "There is enormous unemployment in the realm of the ancestors. We must make better use of their loving energy!" The Dagara tradition encourages this communion and working together as central to our lives.[9]

Although we have often been ignorant of it, African and other peoples around the world have danced "spirit" dances with their ancestors down through time. The wisdom and power that come through from these "ghosts" have routinely been used for healing, divination, and guidance in daily affairs. Our history books certainly don't remind us of the Spiritist movement in the 1800s here in America. The most famous Spiritist was William Harrison, a young boy of modest education who stunned the world. Sometime around his eighteenth year, the ghost of Emanuel Swedenborg, the great European psychic who had just recently died, came into the young man, possessed him, and began to deliver lengthy messages from "the other side." Harrison went on to write quite a number of books and was used by Harvard and Yale because he could apparently read several dialects of ancient Hebrew (which he had never studied) and could lecture on various subjects by becoming possessed by one of Swedenborg's friends on the other side. This man wrote very passionately about the liberation of women and the need for a new spiritual balance in society and new systems of healing. He also did some nature biology writing way ahead of his time. In his later years, he was famous all over Europe, but we have lost touch with this kind of practice and its usefulness.

If there is any such thing as "original sin" that we carry, it may be thought of as the cumulative tendencies of humankind down through time. Thinking of it that way, each of us has a responsibility to transmute what has been unworkable in our mutual human past. Working in unity with our ancestors, we can transform what has gone before as well as the future for the children of the generations to come.

There are many ways we can approach this honoring and communion; I offer you some of my favorites here.

I get together with others to do what I call the Grandmother Dance in order to honor my ancestors and touch into their knowledge:

1. We gather arm in arm in a circle and get comfortable stepping left together to an entrancing drum rhythm.
2. Then I ask each person to dance her or his mother and to honor her by bringing her consciously into the circle through the person's own body and its movement.
3. Then, moving back a generation, each person brings in his or her mother's mother, dancing that energy for a few minutes.
4. Then we continue on back through their lineage, dancing each grandmother in turn, back and back, far beyond those we knew, to the beginnings of Earth.
5. This journey continues past the human ancestors as we begin to honor our relatives the mammals.
6. Then we dance back through birds and reptiles and amphibians and water creatures until we reach the one-celled beings.
7. I continue by asking each person to allow one special individual from that long line of Earthly ancestors to come into his or her consciousness—one who has an important message for that person.
8. We dance this energy for a few more minutes, offer thanks, and then come to completion.
9. Each person has time to make notes or meditate a bit with this information; then there is sharing in pairs.

This form can be danced again and again, following the *father's* mother and her lineage, as well as honoring the male side, the grandfathers of both sides of the family. Often, in this process, wonderful information comes forth. An important benefit the dance always creates is an awareness of our unity with all our ancestors. We can use our connection with their larger view to gather information about the great cycles as well as the immediate issues facing us.

Another exercise I offer my students is about deep awareness:

1. Begin by standing and bringing your awareness to the front of your body.
2. Once you connect with those sensations, then extend your awareness outward in front of you for a short distance, then a longer distance, perhaps even into the future.
3. After a few minutes, take a deep breath and release that focus.
4. Turn your attention to your back and then to the area behind your back, and on further and further behind you.

Although this is a relatively simple exercise, it often brings up profound feelings and awareness. First of all, most people realize that they seldom focus their attention behind them—that sometimes fear is what initially comes up from their lack of awareness. As they get more comfortable with this space, I suggest they go far behind them in many ways, including into their own past and that of their ancestors.

To me, this offers an important kind of grounding that many of us in modern society do not have. Because we live separate from our parents, grandparents, our tribal villages, our racial lineages, we neglect to honor those things, and thus we lose the tremendous resources and cultural riches that were available there.

One way to ground yourself and honor your ancestors is to create an ancestor altar. In many cultural traditions, this is done by keeping a safely lighted candle burning in memory of those who have gone Beyond. Often photographs of those in our lineages are placed there or objects that come from those people. This honoring is a delight to our ancestors, who then reward us with lost knowledge, ancient traditions, and healing. As Caitlin Matthews and John Matthews remind us in *The Encyclopedia of Celtic Wisdom*, "We inherit everything from the ancestors. They have gone before us and remain the repositories of the wisdom and knowledge of our traditions."[10] In this time, we are opening to seek wisdom from all the lineages and traditions of our past, not just those of Native Americans. We will do well to honor all our ancestors. We can visit them through shamanic journeying to the sphere they now occupy and also in the lands where they used to live by journeying across the Earth.

Malidoma and Sobonfu urged us to call upon the ancestors often and passionately. We can cry for help, honestly tell them we are angry for any negative behaviors and patterns they displayed while on Earth, and ask for their assistance with the good things we desire to do. Dancing and singing with great energy are helpful in making this connection. Malidoma and I are planning Long Dances in which all participants can call upon and use these energies for personal and global transformation.

Many people communicate with me about losing touch with their native ancestry a couple of generations back. Others talk of losing their African, Celtic, or Oriental lineages when their ancestors came into the melting pot of America. Often people feel that they do not know all their ancestors, or in the case of adopted children, they may not know any of them! Trying to trace their ancestry back and connect to "long-lost" relatives on the physical plane does not always bring a positive and welcoming reception. Especially on Indian reservations, where people already feel overwhelmed by the non-Indian world, there is a likelihood of a closed or angry attitude when inquiries are made about a distant relative.

I personally have great sadness at the loss of the wisdom teachings from the grandparents in my background. Whether it was the Orkney Scots men who were tied up and thrown on boats to America in the "clearings" or the native tribes who suffered in the wars here, there was much shattering and loss of culture and so much that was not passed on to our generations. I, like many of you, have reached back for those connections, often without success. For instance, when my mom tried to establish legal connection to our Teton Sioux people to help fund our schooling, she met with failure. Several old, old Teton people remembered our family and what had happened in the past, yet they would not sign any legal papers because they said they had gotten cheated every time they put their X on paper! Since we lacked the means to travel and maintain personal connection over time, those ties were lost.

Malidoma made an especially important point about this physical search for ancestry. He reminded people that they do not need to know their ancestors or their names. Those physical things are no longer important. *What is vital and reassuring is that your ancestors do know you and are waiting for your call.* They love you and are ready to assist you. Sobonfu says that a good strategy if you know even one family member in the Beyond World is to use that person as the "employment agent"—to invite all the other ancestors to help.

An interesting thing to consider as well is that each of us likely has ancestry from more groups of people and races than we might at first think. Dawn Boy speaks about it this way:

> Recently revised ideas of contact between the Americas and the rest of the world have made it clear that Native Americans have received generous helpings of fresh blood from both West and East. Blood DNA markers and many material objects have revealed layers of Arabic, Roman, Phoenician, Egyptian, and even Hebrew from the Mediterranean. Traces of many Asian cultures—including Chinese, Japanese, Filipino, and Hawaiian—have been identified. This gives us an idea of America as an ancient melting pot; natives here may have been welcoming strangers with their stories and ideas for seven thousand years. On the other side of the coin, as many as one hundred thousand Indian slaves were taken to Spain and Portugal in the 1500s, where they inevitably mixed with local populations wherever they ended up. By the 1600s, many Indians had joined various navies and merchant marines as expert sailors, often specializing in working the highest sails, much like later native workers who specialized in skyscraper work. These Indians made ports of call worldwide and settled [in] many places, so their blood has spread to many places around the world, especially Spain and Portugal. Historians, anthropologists, and other scientists are finding similar mixings in Australia and Africa, with various waves of visitors adding strands to the local people.[11]

Even my own Scotch-Irish heritage is mixed because the Norse who came to Scotland and Ireland were bringing the Sami-Lapland blood. Long ago, before they started marrying Swedes and Finns, the Samis were red-skinned people with slightly slanted eyes. The Spanish and Portuguese came to Ireland during many different periods, including Jewish refugees from social turmoil. The actual trail of who is back a few generations in your family tree can lead from red to white and back to red again before you know it. And the Indian sides of the lightning-split tree that is my own ancestry are also mixed. The Nez Percé lived near Indians who were mixed with Mongolians perhaps eight hundred years ago, and the Sioux have various marks of having adopted a few Vikings. Light-skinned Crazy Horse seems to have been part French and maybe Viking. So being a "pure" Indian seldom means much about race. We are all holding mixed cards with ancient heritages and surprising hands. Erasing these borders of race is a wonderful challenge of truth to all of us. The recognition of this beautiful rainbow mix allows us to broaden our sense of lineages and, most important, to invite all the ancestors to help us!

I sense the ancestors' happiness when any two-legged children call upon them. They honor with their wisdom anyone who is interested enough to make that connection, and there is great joy in the sharing. At my camps in the "valley of the ancients" in Montana, wonderful energy surrounds our contact with the spirits there, regardless of their racial history or the students' bloodlines. It is the same in a magical Arizona canyon where I spend winter months. My friend Gail and I sat in meditation calling the ancestors at the site of ancient stone enclosures where we find many pottery shards. Their response was instant and very sweet. They urged us to spend time in that beautiful and spirit-filled canyon. "All the answers you need for living on this land you will find by being here with your hearts open." So my experience has been that wherever and whenever we are willing to connect, the ancestors are available and pleased.

In our modern American life, in which many people feel rootless and alone, it is a wonderful thing to feel this connection with our ancestors. For each of us, it's like having a great army of loving helpers behind us in everything we do.

HONORING THE ANIMAL NATIONS

As I went back into my deeper truth, I connected with my animal nature and thus with all animals in the Earthly realm. (By animals, I mean all the living creatures on Earth: four-legged, winged, creepers and crawlers, swimmers, and so forth.) The animal part of ourselves (you *do* remember that we are part of the mammalian group!) has an innate intelligence that can guide us unerringly if we don't override it with intellect/mind. I remembered sister Aria telling me that one of the first kinds of literature that is presented to Waldorf schoolchildren is animal tales. Animals are very close to us genetically; therefore, contact with their images can be very meaningful to us. This is especially true now, when we have pushed the natural world so far from us. Since animals live a life more harmonious with nature, they have much to teach us as we move toward that way of living with All Our Relations.

Through what is called "shape-shifting," shamans have allowed themselves to transform into other shapes and beings in order to gain the wisdom and intelligence they find there. Even if our shape-shifting is simply in meditations in which we honor and become of one mind with other life-forms, it will be profoundly useful to us. *Medicine Cards*, by Jamie Sams and David Carson,[12] have become very popular as a way of connecting to the animal powers. They offer a beginning place for our understanding that every form on Earth has intelligence that can enhance ours.

Domestic animals are often our teachers—for instance, the love and devotion of our canine companions, the independence and agility of our feline friends. The "wild" animals are also great teachers, but we have pushed them away from us by encroaching on their habitats and by using our long-range guns to make them fear our approach. If you are fortunate enough to have contact with animals in the wild, you know what a thrill it is to see and be with them. If not, you can ask them to come to you in meditation. The voices I shared with you in Chapter 4 came from a combination of those kinds of contact, and their wisdom has enriched my life immensely.

I highly recommend Eligio Stephen Gallegos's book *Animals of the Four Windows* here as well. Through it, he leads us on a wonderful journey of understanding. He shows us how to more fully integrate our "windows on the world"—our thinking, sensing, feeling, and imagery—by connecting with the animals who represent these functions. It is a modern shamanic approach, rich in possibilities. He tells us:

> Experience with the [inner] animals lets us know that mythology is something brilliantly alive, in the moment, and if we will relate to it directly then our growth, our healing, and our aliveness are its concern. . . . [Because we are mythologically illiterate,] we fail to see that mythology is potentially alive in each of us, and that its true source is something intimately personal and fundamentally essential to the fulfillment of who we are individually. . . . The mythological dimension is a much more adequate description of the foundation of one's being than those overworked frozen memories of what once had been.[13]

Paying attention to the animals around me as teachers, I learned something interesting not long ago. I have always had a more intense reaction to insect bites and other such skin irritations than most folks. Watching horses and deer stand grazing in a swampy area filled with mosquitoes, I began wondering how their systems could stand so many hundreds of insect bites. Why weren't they driven crazy by this? Then I realized that my own reaction to such bites had decreased markedly since I'd begun taking a supplement called MSM,[14] an organic sulphine nutrient that binds the foreign protein of venomous bites so the body can quickly expel it. Over the months, it has completely changed my reaction to toxins. I realized that humans get little of it in their diet because it is destroyed by the handling and heating of our foods, but animals get it from their natural feeding. Thus, once again, I see how the natural life of animals has more benefits than we can ever guess just by looking at the surface of things.

These kinds of awareness can come to us as we spend actual time with the animal nations. Last winter I spent early mornings observing a pack of coyotes who came to feed on a dead cow nearby. They had interesting ways of sharing and caring for each other. Although they came in to eat in order of their dominance, those not eating spaced themselves out at various distances from the feeding one and blended quietly into the background. It was obvious from the way they positioned themselves that they were not only waiting but also standing guard to guarantee the safety of the one absorbed in feeding. There was no fighting or conflict; they gracefully changed places as each ate for about the same amount of time. And when it became too light and busy on the ranch for the coyotes to be comfortable, the eagles came, sometimes eating together and sometimes watching, as the coyotes had done, from fence posts. Between them, they cleaned up the carrion until only white bones were left.

This indirect learning is available to us as well as the kind of learning I gained in meditating with the animals. The voices I shared with you in Chapter 4 came to me that way, stimulated by my being daily in their habitat. I believe we can easily contact those animals with whom we have a loving bond because of a special interest in them or because they are our allies. You may even find one of the animal nations spontaneously speaking to you in your meditations. I think they want to teach us the ways of harmony they know, because we are harming them with our ignorant ways—and because they have great love for us.

Another very deep issue to which to pay attention in our honoring of the animal nations is the fact that we are rapidly and systematically destroying them at the same time that we romanticize them, watch them with fascination on TV specials, and seek their spiritual guidance. We will soon find ourselves in the same position as many tribal peoples of the past whose myths tell of gods punishing them for their wrongful living by taking away all the animals. There are stories of this in many groups, including those involving Black God among the Din'e and the story of the Sacred Buffalo Hat among the Cheyenne. What we are doing to our relations in the Circle of Life around us will surely turn the great forces of Spirit-alive-in-nature against us! It is of primary importance that we not destroy the life Creator made around us, for in doing so, we shatter the ladder on which we stand.

One way to begin taking responsibility is to realize that when you have a special animal guide, you are then closely related in spirit to those beings. For instance, if I have Elk for an ally, I would never kill elks or eat elk meat. I would learn everything I could about them and support their life in any way possible. If Snowy Owl is my inner guide, then I should learn about the day-to-day life of snowy owls and the challenges they face in the modern world and determine whether there is anything I can do to make a positive difference in their quality of life. What this means is that you need to take responsibility for the *real* lives of your animal relatives—be aware of issues regarding their habitat, how pollution or encroachment is affecting them, and so on.

Then, perhaps this will awaken you to the plight of all the natural life around us. We sit in our "secure" boxes called houses, consuming enormous amounts and throwing out pollution and garbage. It is certainly a false security. We are not alone here.

The final tally of humanity's damage to the environment can be measured most tangibly by our devastating effect on other species on the planet. The world may be on the brink of a sixth great wave of extinction, comparable to the "Big Five" mass extinctions evident in the earth's fossil record. The difference is that this episode would be the result, not of natural environmental changes, but of the actions of the human species. Our domination of the planet has taken an enormous toll on the habitat of other species. Current extinction rates are believed to be 100 to 1000 times higher than pre-human levels and are projected to rise higher still as we continue to alter the natural world to meet our growing wants and needs. . . . In the end, our own survival will rest on our ability to preserve the resources that serve us by saving our dwindling forests, restoring fish in our water, and keeping harmful pollutants out of the environment. We may very well find that by protecting and nurturing the Earth for all living creatures, we can save ourselves.[15]

HONORING THE GREEN NATIONS

Shamanic peoples have always prized the landscape and the green nations upon it. These green-growing ones have made the way for us to be on

Earth by helping to create the cycle that produces the oxygen by which we live and breathe.

A wonderful experience is to exchange breath with the green life around you:

1. Stand near a bush or tree or flower and begin to breathe with it. You are fed by the oxygen it is putting out, and it, in turn, is nourished by the carbon dioxide you exhale.
2. Keep these conscious breaths going until you begin to feel yourself part of the circle of the green nations around you.
3. Then remember this as you walk through your days; remember upon whom the very breath of your life depends.

The plant realm also provides us, and the creatures we use for food, with most of our sustenance and nourishment, most of our healing medicines, and most of our tonics and extracts for well-being and longevity. There is a deep symbiosis between us. Eagle Song camper Gail Edwards shares beautifully about this and encourages us with her book, *Opening Our Wild Hearts to the Healing Herbs*.[16] You can deepen your sense of the healing and power of the green world at Rosemary Gladstar's Women's Herbal Gathering and the International Herbal Symposium,[17] as well as Pam Montgomery's Green Nations.[18]

In my Permaculture class on graceful and sustainable living, this was brought home to me through a discussion concerning raising cattle. In their pastures, you plant shade trees just far enough apart so that they will form avenues of shade for the animals. Cattle love shade, so you must protect the trees from cattle tromping the ground around the roots and rubbing against the trunks. Do this by planting spiny bushes around the base of the trees. Around that, add a ring of healing herbs such as peppermint and chamomile. Not only do these keep the cows from damaging the trees; they provide medicine for them, which the cows readily use.

I think it would be good for everyone to experience being in a true desert, one that is devoid of green life, in order to really appreciate the gift of the green ones. Primary cultures have always understood that trees are especially sacred. They have often tended sacred groves, which became natural cathedrals. According to my elders, trees can teach us the laws of life. So spend time with them and work to protect them. Learn about their qualities from being with them and from Celtic/Druidic texts[19] that provide a whole spiritual system based on the tree people. Take time to lie among aspen trees, listening to the secrets their heart-shaped leaves whisper with the wind. Sit with your back against a great oak and feel its wisdom and strength course through you. Lie down in fields of flowers, letting their exquisite scent transport you.

One exercise I did with the cooperation of a huge evergreen tree with long, sloping lower limbs. I had my students lie on those branches with their eyes closed, allowing themselves as much as possible to become one with the tree, its movement in the wind, its fragrance, its immense root system. Then they would open their eyes a slit and see the rest of their "tree self" climbing to the sky above them. Some who were more agile climbed high up in the tree and sat looking out through the top branches—feeling the sway and the energy there. Try this yourself, asking permission of the tree first. Spend time noticing the branching pattern of the tree and realize that this pattern lives in your own body as well—in blood vessels and capillaries, in your nervous system, in your limbs.

Another enjoyable and illuminating exercise is to get a small ten-power (10×) magnifying glass like those used in botany classes (often available through university bookstores) and take a walk, using it to look closely at grasses and flowers and bark. You will find there a different world than you usually observe—an extravagantly beautiful world. This kind of perspective is a good lesson: it is the difference between distant appearance and what truly exists. We look at life, at the level of reality we usually see, and think that's all there is, when there is so much more if we can only shift our perspective to illumine the beauty and variety of the life-forms all around us. Our possibilities in ascension are like this: we cannot see the subtler dimensions with our everyday eyes, yet they begin to appear to us as we do our homework to lift our vibration and open a new perspective.

Plants teach us about Spirit through their medicine ways. In his wonderful book on plant spirit medicine, Eliot Cowan offers an ancient system of using the spiritual or energetic vibration of plants for healing rather than using even their essences or herbal tinctures.[20] This kind of work, as well as therapy with homeopathic preparations, teaches us that there is more to life than simply the physical aspect. Spirit is alive and powerful within All Things, ready to be awakened through our conscious intent and communion.

Another profound aspect of the green nations is the fact that cultures down through time have used special "medicine" plants to alter their consciousness in ways that have served them well—to create a deep connection with nature and the Divine. Plants are our elder brothers and sisters and have developed ways of living and being that precede, complement, and enhance ours. Creator put us in partnership with them in more ways than just giving us food to eat and medicines to heal ourselves. My friend Terence McKenna was a mushroom shaman who felt that simian ingestion of psychoactive mushrooms from the manure of large herd animals was what stimulated the awakening of consciousness that led to human experience. There certainly seems to be evidence that plants open vistas in our brain by adding or replacing certain neural chemicals that allow us to experience new levels of perception.

There has been much negative propaganda about the use of mind-altering plants. Yet we need to face the fact that *everything* we ingest has a major effect on our consciousness, whether it be the stimulation of coffee, the sedation of chamomile, the effect on our heart of a glass of wine before dinner, the high-altitude oxygenation enhancement of coca leaves, or the debilitating effect of sugar. The thing we lack in the larger culture, which is present in tribal and primary societies, is a ritual process of using mind-altering plant substances in a good and life-enhancing way. Instead, we have chosen to make them illegal, creating a black market of enormous proportions. Thus, our people put themselves at great risk to obtain these substances and then use them poorly—to numb themselves, rebel, or get a sense of upliftment they are missing in their lives. Yet all the while, we find it very natural that people damage their health and become potential killers in automobiles using societally approved alcohol.

It's time to get out of denial and take a deeper look at mind-altering plants and how we can use them well, especially since plant sacraments are one very effective way to heal the split between the natural and the sacred.

As our modern materialist society obsessively seeks new technologies designed to control and exploit nature ... it becomes progressively dissociated from a spiritual awareness of nature. During the past several centuries, Western civilization's efforts to dominate and control nature ... have led to the gradual desacralization and exploitation of all non-human life forms. In contrast, shamanic people have always devoted considerable attention to cultivating a direct perceptual and spiritual relationship with animals, plants, and the Earth herself.[21]

The psychoactive medicines used are regarded as embodiments of conscious intelligent beings who become visible under the influence of the plants and who function as spiritual teachers and sources of healing power and knowledge. They are seen as mystical healing powers or energies that can manifest within a plant. In the Native American Church, peyote is ingested as a sacrament. Peyote is a teacher to many of my generation and certainly to me. There have long been sacred mushroom cults in Mexico, and now modern people often use psychedelic mushrooms in a less formal way. In South America, the cactus called San Pedro is used as a sacrament.

Anthropologists and experimenters have done extensive research on the beneficial uses of psychoactive plants. One receiving much attention right now is *ayahuasca* and the highly original forms of religious ceremony being developed in Brazil. It is a plant concoction that has been used since ancient times in the jungles there and is considered essential to the success of the healing or divinatory process. It provides visionary access to the realm of spirits and the souls of the ancestors as well as otherworldly realms and beings. The spirits who are invoked through shamanic song then heal the patient. The new churches have brought *ayahuasca* into mainstream urban culture and also focus on group worship with singing and prayer. A recent journey to Brazil allowed me to experience many levels of the powerful plant and ancestor spirits moving there.

There is certainly symbiosis and exchange with plants and plant teachers. It is obvious what we gain but perhaps less obvious what the plants receive in return. Ralph Metzner says it well:

> Based on this principle of symbiotic exchange, it is reasonable to assume that the "plant teachers" may be getting something beneficial in exchange for the remarkable knowledge, insight, and psychic or physical healing they provide. Certainly, one of the common experiences associated with ingesting *ayahuasca* is that people become aware of the interdependence of all life. Could it be that the profound consciousness-raising and compassion-deepening effects of the visionary plant brews are nature's prescription for the healing of the planet and the restoration of a healthy environment?[22]

We often see that those who work with sacred plants at the very least find themselves awed by the mysterious powers of nature and strive to live in a simpler way that minimizes environmental harm. In many instances, they awaken to preserving the Earth's sacred plant life and the indigenous peoples who teach us about them.

To truly honor the green nations, we must begin to protect them, care for them, and nurture them in the face of the devastation of plants taking place as we poison the life around us and decimate the landscape in many areas. Whether in our lawns or in agricultural fields, the chemical industry's war on what are termed "weeds" has devastated the microbes that keep the soil viable and productive. Modern marketing forces farmers to grow only a few hundred easily storable and transportable foods, when we have had thousands in our gardens until very recently. These and many more challenges face the plants and thus the human family, since our very lives depend on them.

And we are just beginning to awaken to the healing power of the plants to restore the soil. The use of fungi and bio-microbes as fertilizer, the saving of our heritage seeds and the sustainable diversity of food crops they represent, as well as many amazing solutions to the challenges we face ecologically are being gathered by a wonderful group called Bioneers (biological pioneers). Their publications, seed-saving, videos, and yearly conference are wonderful resources to help awaken you to honor and make use of the healing possibilities of the green nations.[23]

Without green-growing ones, without animals and other "wild" natural beings, without our ancestors, we would not, could not, be here. We are one part of an eternal lineage of life, and this time around, we have the privilege of living on this sweet Earth. We must slow down   stand still, even—and let the small flame of our deepest presence light up our daily selves.

The wisdom that lies in this shamanic sense of the world is profound. And we are now in great need of profound wisdom to guide us out of the forest in which we have lost ourselves.

Lost

Stand still. The trees ahead and bushes behind you
Are not lost. Wherever you are is called Here,
And you must treat it as a powerful stranger,
Must ask permission to know it and be known.
The forest breathes. Listen. It answers,
I have made this place around you.
If you leave it, you may come back again, saying Here.

No trees are the same to Raven.
No two branches are the same to Wren.
If what a tree or a bush does is lost on you,
You are surely lost. Stand still. The forest knows
Where you are. You must let it find you.[24]

—*DAVID WAGONER*

If we can but put on the magnificent shamanic antlers of the Rainbow Sundancer, the Earth Mage, we will have access, joyful access, to the Book of Life and its deep, gentle guidance. This is our task, we who have the good fortune to be alive in the sweetest, greenest place in a galaxy or two. And such beauty, such radiant beauty, within and around us, will be the ample reward for our commitment to Lady Gaia's star and stone, clay and bone. Without that deep and lasting connection of caring and communion with Earth, it only makes sense that we might falter and fall. With Her, we will rise up into a Golden Time. Each of us in our own unique way will become the Rainbow Sundancer.

CHAPTER 13

HONORING EARTH
AND SPIRIT

*The gift of a connection with nature
is the ability to communicate with and benefit from
the great wisdom that awaits you there
and to awaken yourself through that communion
to a new level of being.*

*Spirit magic creates
the highest good for the greatest number
with the least energy.*

I continued walking this shamanic pathway, letting it open to reveal the magic of the world around me. As I let myself relate more fully to all things Earthly, their radiant Spirit began to reveal itself more and more, informing and awakening me to the Spirit and magic within myself.

As you descend into the heart and substance of the Earth, you will find Spirit alive and shining, waiting to assist you in your conscious upliftment. The gift of a connection with nature is the ability to communicate with and benefit from the great wisdom that awaits you there and to awaken yourself through that communion to a new level of being. This process is a vital one if we are to truly embody Spirit in the way that's necessary in renewing our world.

209

HONORING THE EARTH

*The ground on which we stand is sacred ground.
It is the dust and blood of our ancestors.*
—CROW CHIEF PLENTY COUPS[1]

We often take Mother Earth and our life here for granted. Rather than reading the Book of Life and studying its mystery, we generally live our lives thinking we can *manage* everything, feeling we *need* to manage it. This leads to continuing ignorance of the beauty and possibilities around us. And it also prevents us from seeing that we're living lives that are unnecessarily stressful. We ignore the gifts and the alchemy that Creator has placed before us rather than using our free will to explore the presents/presence we have been given. When we realize that through its own alchemy, the Earth produces from its womb this dazzling array of ongoing life around us, it becomes easier to realize that magic is truly afoot and possible. It also makes it clear that ascending into a different level of co-creation ourselves is not only probable but quite an obvious unfoldment.

One thing I often have my students do is take time to relate to the actual soil of the Earth. Go to a place where the soil has not been recently disturbed by machines or to a happy garden. Take a small hand spade and dig gently into the soil, opening its fragrant richness to your senses. Run it through your fingers and enjoy being in contact with the Earth in such an intimate way. You can also do this with sand. Remember that each crystalline grain of sand was very likely a part of a mountain or cliff at one time and that each minute particle is unique and special. Cure yourself of thinking of the dirt as something dirty or unclean. The clay is your body. The soil is the source of your life. Give thanks.

As our elder brothers and sisters, the stones and crystals from the Earth have much healing to offer us as well. They help us clarify and magnify our intent and reclaim the power to transform our lives. Cindy Watlington, in the introduction to her useful and magical *Crystal Deva Cards*, expresses it this way:

The New Millennium holds the potential for an entirely different existence for Planet Earth and all its family. The space/time continuum is opening to release the old and accept the new. Like no other time in history, change will affect every aspect of our lives and our world. It has been prophesied for thousands of years that this would be the time of the Great Awakening. . . . You will, in actuality, step from one reality to another, from the dark into the light. In the process, you will shed layer upon layer of excess baggage you have been carrying. This is also a time when old, inaccurate belief systems are crumbling and giving way to the Truth. . . . Collectively, we are beginning to shift our focus from fear, uncertainty, hatred, and separation to faith, confidence, love, and cooperation.

The Crystal Devas bring messages of self-empowerment and hope for all of humanity. They offer an evolution of consciousness and an escape from the entrapment of emotional entanglements. . . . [They wish to] ease our emotional and spiritual suffering, and re-establish communication and cooperation among all the Kingdoms—Human, Animal, Plant, Mineral—reminding us that all living entities are part of the same Universal Essence. Differences in physical composition are designed as a test to determine if we can see beyond the less significant exterior to the more important interior.[2]

Spirit alive within Mother Earth can obviously be helpful to us in many ways, including nourishing and enriching us. Many people find themselves drained of energy in the rush of modern life. You can make a shift in this by consciously connecting with Mother Earth and nourishing yourself, body and spirit, at Her breast. You are connected to the heart of Mother Earth through an energetic cord that originates just below your navel. Through this cord, and through the soles of your feet as well, you can draw up power and energy from the Earth. Practice this first with your feet and later expand to the cord.

1. Standing with feet as far apart as your shoulders, knees slightly bent, assume a relaxed and balanced position. It's wonderful and easiest to do this with bare feet on the sweet Earth, but it can be done anywhere,

even with shoes on. Wiggle your feet a bit to become acutely aware of your soles and their connection to the Earth.

2. Place your tongue on the ridge of palate behind your teeth. Now begin paying attention to your breath. With each inbreath, start to draw energy up from Mother Earth into your feet. You may feel it as tingling or "see" it as flowing light or sense it as radiant vitality. Just enjoy whatever sensations arise and let the energy continue up through your legs, torso, and head.

3. When the flow feels clear, then use your outbreaths to store this energy in your belly, like filling up a pool at the center of yourself. Keep filling until you feel nourished, revitalized, and empowered.

4. To complete this process, use a final intense outbreath with the intent to "seal" the pool within you for your use. If you do this on a regular basis, you will not become depleted.[3]

The more deeply you know the life around you, the more easily you can do magic. You will find it enlightening to consider the intrinsic patterns of the physical plane within which we live our lives. The first pattern is *branching*, a most common one we see in trees, rivers, crystals, and our own veins. It reminds us that our progress in the world comes from the base we lay down, both physically and spiritually, because we naturally grow in many directions. Our branching limbs reach skyward toward Father Spirit, light, and sky. Our branching roots spread through Mother Earth, clay, and stone to find nourishment and water and to stand in our place of belonging. In the words of an Aztec descendant, upon burying the placenta of his child:

We are planted here.
Man is a plant that grows and branches and flowers on Earth.

Next comes a pattern we often forget even though it is present all around us: the *meander*. City life gives us a false impression of straight lines in our world, yet in reality, they are nonexistent. The natural way of things is based on curves and natural changes of direction, no matter how slight. One of my favorite kinds of meandering lines is the one that creates the sutures in our own and animal skulls. You would also find it most interesting to look at videos of fractals, in which you can see the holographic images of the whole, reflected in even the smallest parts. For instance, a huge wave has "edges," which also have a wave pattern that has edges, which repeat the same wave pattern, on and on. This naturally changing pattern urges us to release our mind-set of straight lines and boxes. It invites us to find time to meander ourselves to see what Spirit has to offer when we have not preprogrammed our lives in straight lines between appointments.

This reminds me of the true function of the Sabbath. Creator invites us to take one day a week off, so that we have a chance to meander, instead of work at our lives. It is meant to be a day without structure, in which the heart and spirit reign supreme. We think we have outsmarted God by brashly deciding that we can work on Sunday if we want. Yes, that is our freedom, although by doing so, we deprive ourselves of a powerful opportunity for immersion into the wholeness, for connection with Source that nurtures, guides, and heals us. I highly recommend taking a Sabbath day and allowing everyone else to do the same. It is a practice that will enrich your life tremendously.

During my Lodge of the Wisdom Women camp at Blacktail Ranch in Montana, the grandmother spirits suggested to us that we add a day of required meandering before the women sat still for their visioning time. The instructions were that anytime they found themselves looking ahead, "going somewhere," or with a set direction in mind, they were to release it and focus back on where they stood at the moment. Then they could more easily feel what the next immediate step was from there. Afterward, many of the women talked about how difficult and rewarding this was, when at first they had balked at doing it because it seemed too frivolous. In the end, they realized the power of this ability to live more in the moment and be moved by their inner spirit step-by-step. Many of them discovered magical places to do the sitting portion of their quest that they never would have found otherwise and sensed how much this process could apply to their daily lives.

Straight lines seem to mean "tear here." Clean edges do not hook up and hold together the way a wandering edge does. Perhaps we need more wandering experience in our days in order to connect with the life around us more fully. Even an amoebic shape is simply a circular meander that continues to change form. It counsels us to allow constant fluidity and change so we may move organically through our lives and our world.

The next form is the *star burst*, demonstrated best in explosions—in the big bang through which Creation opened from Oneness into myriad forms. The star burst is also reflected in the scattering of seeds from pods when they burst. This pattern validates our need to occasionally burst forth, to rid ourselves of outmoded strictures and structures— even in appropriate emotional releases. Nothing is more refreshing at certain moments than bursting out in tears or stomping up and down in a harmless expression of rage. There is often a clarity that opens up within us when we allow those momentary, dazzling personal explosions, whose energy we send to Source for transformation. It is also important to remember that we can let the light of our true nature shine out in all directions as a gift to All Our Relations. In this way, we *are* the star.

The final pattern is the *spiral*—winding growth advancing forward around an ever-evolving upward circle. We see the spiral if we closely investigate the growth form of celery, of roses, of chambered seashells. Spirals inform us of the pattern of our own growth process: we often come around and around again to the same issue each time, touching it repeatedly at a higher level, bringing more wisdom to the process. It eventually becomes a whirling dance that moves us gracefully onward.

My elder gave me an exercise that involved working in a spiral manner with an issue that troubled me:

1. Begin by getting this issue firmly in mind.
2. Then go back through time noticing how you have faced it in various forms as you evolved. (Thinking of a stalk of celery helps me get this imagery clear. If you do not have a clear sense of its spiral, buy a bunch and take it apart, stalk by stalk, noting how it circles and circles down to the center. Roses also do this same thing, and of course, spiral seashells give a clear picture of it.) You will eventually come to the tender center of the issue, where the hurt or damaging belief first made an impact.
3. Once you come to the roots, go down through the roots of the issue until you are back to Mother Earth.

4. Disperse the energy of that issue into Her nurturing soil as you would spread fertilizer needed to grow an entirely new plant.

5. Imagine putting the roots of a new plant in this soil—seeing in your mind's eye what you wish to grow instead of the old way of being. Perhaps a beautiful rose can spiral up from this place.

The basic idea here is for us to make an openhearted relationship with the land and life around us as part of our real and continuing spiritual practice. Here are several questions you may want to answer for yourself and exercises to do as you assess your relationship with the landscape. There are many more.

1. Where is the nearest free-flowing water, and how clean is it?

2. If it is not clean, what can you do to return the water to purity?

3. What kinds of trees grow around you? Which one calls to you most strongly?

4. Gather as many individual leaves from different trees as you can. Lay them out, and compare the large and small differences among them. Did you ever guess they could be so different?

5. Use a tree identification guide to learn how the leaves help you identify different trees and their families. Did you know before who these tree people were that lived all around you?

6. When did you last plant a tree? Where can you do that now?

7. Pick out a one-yard-square place near you that you can observe daily or weekly through all the seasons. Do you begin to notice the minute changes and natural cycles of the forms there that you missed before?

8. Using a ten-power (10X) magnifying glass, look closely at the life-forms that occupy this square yard or any other place you care to look. What have you missed?

9. Is all grass the same? Pick a blade in various places on lawns and in natural grassy areas. Do you see how there is often a shade of pink somewhere on the stems? Had you known that would be so?

10. Examine a topographical map of your area or one in which

you like to hike. Did you realize how it was actually shaped, or hadn't you ever thought of it?

11. Pick up and examine stones from various areas. What can you see in them? Get a guide to the geology of your area and explore back in time the movement of the landscape and the great masses of stone.

Appreciating the exquisite beauty of Lady Gaia is an important aspect of our communion with Her. Last year, I was doing a writing retreat in a place that was cloudy almost every day. I would look out the window and groan, not feeling much like venturing outside into what looked so dreary. Yet when I took my two-hour hike every day, I found beauty and light radiating from everything around me.

As I paid close attention to both small and large things, their colors, textures, and smells lifted my spirits and increased my vital life energy—literally lifted me up. I was able to come back to my work with increased spirit and renewed aliveness. On the most joyful days, I felt myself at one with all the life there; on those days, deep insights emerged, and the animals spoke their wisdom to and through me.

This kind of fulfillment is possible only when you take the time to participate fully in the life around you. I love to do simple things like examine the uniqueness of a leaf, magnify the sensuous interior of a flower, or listen to a stream's changing language as I move along beside it. Such things will teach you as well.

A wonderful practice that helps you pay attention in this way is to write a haiku every day. Haiku is an elegant Japanese form of poetry that requires an expanded sense of presence in the world.

There are two basic elements of these simple three-line poems: (1) The form is five syllables in the first line, seven in the second, and five in the final line. (2) It requires you to take careful note of the gifts and messages of the natural world and the changing seasons and to use these images as metaphors to set a tone and mood for your observation/poem. The beauty of this form is that you must strip the image down to its essence—for in doing so, you make it much more profound and universal.

These are some classic examples:

Solitary crow
Companioning my progress
Over snowy fields.

—*SENNA*[4]

Here is mine for today. Although simple, it will reflect back to me my feelings of this day.

Sun finally came
through winter windows today
warming cats and me.

Not only are these seemingly simple poems wonderful to write, but a small book or journal of your haiku can bring the wisdom of nature's experience to you at any time, anywhere you are. You can bring to mind and heart the beauty that enhances the vital spirit life within you and helps you cross the border into the Shimmering Invisible.

HONORING WATER

As Earth was born of fire, so life is born of rain, of water. Although we think of ourselves as solid, we could more truly be characterized as liquid. Just as paying attention to getting the nourishment and minerals we need for our inner earth structure is important, giving honor to our inner water nature is vital, too. Drinking pure water supports this part of ourselves, as does paying attention to those parts of ourselves that are fluid, flexible, nonformed—sometimes thought of as our more feminine aspects.

Movement and change are the essence of our nature. When we are in our natural high state, things are flowing rather than static. Even lakes that seem to stand still have many currents moving within them. As water trusts itself to move freely in whatever pathways and drainage it finds, so, too, we must allow ourselves fluidity, trusting our natural movement between the visible and Invisible realms as well as in the arenas of thought and emotion.

The growing sense of everything's being fluid—nothing solid and therefore nothing *seeming* secure—will be coming up more acutely as we move into this new time. As Neva Howell sees it:

> There begins to be an inability to plan anything at all! This frustrating period, when every plan shifts and changes beyond your control or expectation, is the result of continuing to favor the logical mind over the intuitive mind. *Freeze nothing, but remain fluid and open to a better idea or a different direction.*[5]

Neva is telling us, rather than making plans and "setting them in stone," stay present in your moments and flow with the wisdom that presents itself until this flow feels more normal than solidity. I encourage you to be more trusting of Creator's flowing, changing life stream. This very fluidity is what helps wash away outmoded structures within and outside ourselves and makes the new more easily available. Begin now to honor the flowing water of your nature, which is willing to be present and awake to what is happening in the moment and able to trust the natural unfoldment of life. Also remember to give deep thanks each time you take fluid into your body and be sure that often it is pure, clear, sweet water you drink.

This brings up how little we have actually honored water and cared for it—how difficult it is simply to find pure water. In our ignorance, we have polluted almost every body of water around us as well as the deep pools beneath us. We have drained the aquifers with poor agricultural practices and by filling thousands of home swimming pools in desert climates. We have felt that weed-free lawns were more important than pure water for our children. Agricultural chemical runoffs of all kinds rival the polluting of large manufacturing companies. We are killing our oceans with trash and chemicals. And we are so out of touch that we refuse to recognize the importance of issues surrounding water; we stay too often in denial and apathy. Yet I sense that unless we awaken and take action *now*, we as a human family will be fighting tooth and nail over water in the very near future. Someone told me just the other day that big chemical companies, which are creating monopolies of seeds and food growing, are now moving to control water. If anyone hears more news on this, please pass the information along so we can all respond appropriately.

We have thought of water as a simple, blank, neutral thing, when, in fact, it is a crystal with many complex properties. Europeans have paid more attention to water's true qualities over the years. I highly recommend a book called *Living Water*, written about an amazingly perceptive Swedish forester, Viktor Schauberger.[6] It is a blessed eye-opener to read of what he discovered in the early 1900s about the qualities of living water and how our poor handling of water kills its most magical and healing nature. Rudolf Steiner spoke at length about water and the necessity of swirling and stirring it, much like what happens in natural streams. He has many formulas and methods, both for personal use and for use in agriculture, to improve our lives by treating water differently.[7]

Many of the challenges we have created around water have to do with disease being carried in it. As a solution, we have added more poison to it. Thankfully, Europe is outlawing chlorine for water and using ozone to kill bacteria. In the near future, I sense there will be an explosion of treating water with light through crystals.

One small way to bring home the vital importance of water is to do a vision quest without water for several days, as I have done and as other primary peoples have done down through time.[8] Until we experience deep thirst and the body's powerful response to the lack of water, I wonder if we will ever truly comprehend the centrality of it in our lives. What a beautiful, magical, essential gift from Creator and Mother Earth! We are ignorant children having poisoned the water with chemicals that interact for years, yet we have only just discovered the true potential of water to cleanse and energize life. It's time to truly honor our sacred waters: in both ritual and daily tasks, we must work to clear and purify the waters of life.

HONORING WIND

The wind lives within us and enlivens us as our breath. Down through time, wind and air have been metaphors for Spirit, and we take in this Spirit with our breath—inspiration. Make time often to slow down and consciously bring this breath of life within you, from the soles of your feet up, and to give thanks for it. Fill yourself with Spirit's life this way, thinking of it as silver flow that can fill and enliven each cell of your body. Hold the image of that enlightenment as a gift of Spirit to your body.

We received a powerful lesson in this with the passing of our Eagle Song[9] friend Jordan. I had given her the name "Sings the Beauty Dawn" after her first vision quest at these spiritual wilderness camps and knew how much the breath of life meant to her. We had sung together the beautiful song she received while sitting on the mountain during her second quest, "FlowerSong, Sweet Spirit Song," and the Cree morning song, "Over the Horizon," she taught us, which was sung in the meadow each morning at camp as a wake-up call.[10] As she lay dying of lung cancer, her breath slowed down to eight times a minute, then six, then four, then two. It was several minutes before we realized she had taken her last precious breath. That process made all of us acutely aware of the power and sacredness of each simple, yet profound breath we take.

We must also pay attention to how we use the inspiration we gain. Our breath is sacred, and we must use it well to speak the sounds of empowerment, communion, and caring. We can also use this wind as prayer, aligning our intent with that of Creator for the good of all. Here the work you have done to allow the flow of your natural voice will pay off. When you can open to an unedited version of Spirit's voice speaking through you in your day-to-day life, you will find a startling clarity in your communications. What is true for you personally, and the truth of things in general, will be expressed much more naturally.

If this is difficult for you, or if you find yourself wanting to blurt out really hurtful things, find a counselor or class to help improve your skills in communicating clearly, truthfully, powerfully, and respectfully. This truth does not necessarily follow convention or social programming, yet it moves our lives forward with grace and ease. It helps us express the profound feedback we have for others and put forward the Divine inspirations that can guide our mutual lives.[11]

Too often we think of the wind as something bothersome and dismiss it. A wonderful exercise is to go out on a breezy day with a friend. Play a game of walking beside or behind your friend in such a way that you are always out of the wind. Play "hide-and-seek" with the wind. You will learn much about this invisible aspect of life through this kind of play. You will feel how variable it is and how much the direction changes and swirls. These things will help your body move in less rigid patterns.

Another experiment with wind is to sit out on days when the wind is changing to blow from different directions. Close your eyes and allow yourself to feel the differences in each direction. What do these different winds seem to say, to stimulate, or bring to mind?

Scents waft to us on the breeze; they are one of our most primal connections to the world. Notice how the scent of something you remember from your past can bring that whole experience, including emotions, flooding into your consciousness. The direct brain link to smells is being used in a good way through *aromatherapy*, a science that employs different scents for the profound transforming and healing effects they have upon the human psyche and bodily functioning.

It's fun to experiment with blindfolding yourself and taking a slow "scent" walk—best supervised by someone who is not blindfolded:

1. Notice how much you can perceive simply by smelling. Can you smell the water flowing in a stream a short distance away? Is it the moss or the different grasses or ferns that give you a clue? Do you notice the fragrance of flowers more? Can you describe the scent of tree bark? What scents surprise and please you?

2. It's also fun to take a scent walk without a blindfold and simply smell everything that you would normally perceive only by looking at it. Open to the scent of the Shimmering Invisible. Does it have a special fragrance? Like the wind, it is unseen, yet its effects are powerful.

Sounds also come to us on the wind. Letting outer sound move through us without comment or restriction, as in the silencing technique described in Chapter 11, takes us to another whole level of perception, in which we can listen more easily to the voice of Spirit. For instance, the drum has lent us its sound across all of human time—unifying us with the heartbeat at the center of our circles and communities and creating enthralling rhythms that allow our brains to change lanes onto the inner pathway.

Down through time, the sounds of bells or chimes have been used to travel into the Invisible. We can follow their vibrating sound from the physical into the Invisible as it diminishes yet never dies. In this new time that is coming, the ear—which receives a much wider spectrum of vibration than does the eye—will replace the eye as the receptive symbol of a new way of being together. We will awaken to listening and truly hearing, honoring our ears for the incredible powers that they are.

Taking a "sound walk," similar to the scent walk, is quite fascinating. Once again, this is best done with a blindfold and someone guiding you to ensure safety. Let yourself notice *every* sound and realize how few sounds you have really paid attention to during your busy days. Does it amaze you how much sound "pollution" your nervous system must deal with every day?

One interesting metaphor I was given for shape-shifting is to let the wind blow through our form and change it. First, we must be secure enough to let our sense of self disperse in order to bring in another form. But then, as we let the wind blow through us in many different ways, we find ourselves clearer, freer, and more inspired. As we let ourselves be filled with inspiration, like a balloon with helium, we will find ourselves lifting up on the winds of Spirit.

We must also take a look at how our lives have affected and changed the wind. Prophets have long told us that this was to be a time of "great winds of change." We are feeling the truth of that in many ways, including the increasing frequency and power of tornadoes, cyclones, and hurricanes. Because of the warming effect of gaseous pollutants we emit into the atmosphere, the swirling and movement of the winds around the globe are being changed and strengthened. As they sweep destructively down on us, we often whine and blame Mother Earth for Her capriciousness. Yet, in truth, we must look to ourselves and how our daily choices—using automobiles excessively and allowing noxious industrial wastes, for example—lead to negative environmental changes. There are many choices we must make differently if we are to truly honor the wind.

A final, yet primary, thought about wind as air and space is that the particles that make up our bodies and all physical things are mostly space. We have given too much emphasis and power to the solid aspect of our lives and too little to the enormous empty and open spaces within and all around us. When we can pay more attention to these spaces, we will find technologies that astound us with their purity, beauty, and power.

Fire is the last of the four elements of our Earthly lives. It is given full consideration and honoring in the next chapter.

HONORING MAGIC

This brings me to thoughts of Spirit magic, which *creates the highest good for the greatest number with the least energy.* Magic is in disrepute today, yet in truth, it is sacred ecology at its best. When we use the power of clear intent, moving into the Shimmering Invisible to do our work, we are using a sustainable, nonpolluting, harmonizing magnetism—rather than wastefully expending enormous amounts of effort and energy to ineffectively push things around physically. In our past, doing it the "easy" way sometimes meant cutting corners, doing things poorly, or acting without integrity. That is a misuse of the word *easy,* whose actual meaning is "posing no difficulty; requiring or exhibiting little effort; free from worry, anxiety, trouble, or pain; affording comfort or relief; soothing; prosperous; well off; causing little hardship or distress (relaxed in attitude, not strict or severe)." Letting go of our need to expend effort brings up our fear that we are not doing enough. This is a confused and invalid measure for true accomplishment and good works. In the new time, creating a world of beauty through ease and grace will be the supreme act of service to our world and ourselves.

We must remember that this magic, at its best, is done through ourselves, not outside ourselves. It is less valid if we create something wonderful for others while leaving ourselves out. Magic comes through the wellspring of radical trust within us—a kind of perpetual surrender to our own truth that makes us available for joy at all levels.

I recently came up with an affirmation that helps me remember this every day:

> I give authority to magic, Love, and infinite grace
> in all realms of my life.

Part of the magic is to be open to revelation as a daily experience, not as something that was given only at the end of the Bible. In the Japanese practice of Mahikari, there is a profound saying: "Everything is the voice of God." This is very different from a consentient reality that believes only authorities or experts have the answer. It urges us to listen fully, both within ourselves and to the great voices outside ourselves, for the gifts that come from Creator in many forms.

I'm reminded of a time on my first vision quest when I received a great, magical lesson. Being young and impatient, I expected to receive immediate and major pronouncements from the animal spirits when a series of birds came near me at my site on the mountain. First, one magpie; next, two eagles; and then, three chickadees. None of them "spoke" directly to me, but each confirmed something: the magpie is friend to the buffalo, and I was questing under the blessing of the Sacred Buffalo Hat Lodge; besides, magpies had always been my favorite bird. The pair of eagles represented my major winged allies and good lifelong relationship. The chickadees brought remembrance of one of my Crow heroes, Chief Plenty Coups, who, as a young man, had a major vision in this same place that involved the chickadee people. Yet I was still impatient—no major message yet (I had been there only six short hours). Then five pigeons, birds I think of as representing filthy city streets, came winging in; disgusted, I turned my back on them. They lit on an enormous flat boulder about twenty feet above me and pecked around. I had been waiting for the magic number four and a significant message, and here were *five* of these silly birds clucking about. Something caused me to turn around and look at them again, when one of the birds on the edge of the stone opened its wings and dropped off the boulder, flying right straight at me. *It disappeared into thin air before it ever got there!* Four pigeons remained above me. I was stunned and my mind tried to explain it, until I realized the lesson and burst out laughing. I had been impatient and filled with expectations of just how this event should happen, when something more magical and amazing was shown me. It was a wonderful, unforgettable lesson.

We must also learn to honor magic and grace when they happen rather than explaining them away. Remember to accept these gifts for what they are before the ego appropriates them and convinces the mind it was actually responsible. Celebrate them rather than attempting to explain them away.

Magic happens when we step away from the strictures of the mind and the structures of the world. When we remove the walls and barriers of structure, we can collapse Time. This means bringing things into existence or transforming them in a moment, and communing without considerations of time or distance—what are now called miracles. Earth Mages learn to do this through the loving command of the heart's intent. This is why our heart-centered practices are so essential as we move forward into this new and amazing time.

HONORING THE GREAT CYCLES

Our schooling and modern culture have given us no appreciation of the great cycles of time that are continually breaking on the shores of our Earthly experience. We no longer gather together for twenty nights in the winter and tell the stories that begin with the Creation of the world and direct us into the future. This leads to ignorance of ourselves, our world, and the subtle realms. It leaves us unable to tune in to and harmonize with the great rivers of energy moving around us. At this point in human history, each of us is paddling our own canoe upstream in frustration and exhaustion when we could be joyously bathing, splashing, and floating downstream together. All it takes is a little attention to which way the current is headed, and we're in great shape.

The uplifting evolutionary pattern is set in the universe; we simply have to know how to hook up with it. This connection comes as we become consciously aware and set our intent: then everything from our DNA to Spirit moving in great cycles comes in to support us.

We must look around ourselves to learn the Story of Life and join in with our part. We can't continue to pout and ask Creator to make everything fit our human rationale. When we dance with the energy rather than fighting it, we will walk in beauty.

A relatively simple yet profound way to honor the cycles is by celebrating those that we can easily perceive in human time. We can join back into the lineage of our ancestors by celebrating the seasonal cycles. People down through time have ceremonially acknowledged the solstices and equinoxes, and often the cross-quarter days that fall between them, creating eight seasonal ceremonies. This practice is wonderful for us, our children, and our communities. It is a basic and easy way to connect our human time to the evolving circles of our lives and the great cycles that move around us.[12]

MASTERING TIME

At this time, many people are frenetically rushing, hurrying to make their lives work. It is true that there is a frequency acceleration that is giving us the energy to make the qualitative leap we are facing. But we think that the way to ascend higher and higher is to move faster and faster, given our American tendencies. (And the tension of our shoulders matches it!)

What we need to realize is that there is also an accompanying deepening of resonance—a mellowing out, getting down, stopping the old world. As Gregg Braden suggests in his dynamically illuminating book *Awakening to Zero Point*,[13] Earth is slowly spinning to a stop, likely to reverse its rotational spin. Scientific reports tell us that Greenwich clock keepers need to continually reset their master clocks to match the slower speed of Earth's rotation. These deeper resonances more truly reflect Earth's spirituality, telling us to ease up and deepen into ourselves as a prelude to ascending.

One of the most interesting ideas about dealing with time comes from Kim Dandurand's kachina guides. They are teaching him the art of *living backward*. The idea is based on the spiritual principle that the end of time is a point at which we blend again into the Oneness and perfection of All That Is. So that Oneness and perfection can be used as a beginning place rather than an ending.

Allow yourself to play with this idea, even though it doesn't necessarily make sense to your logical mind.

1. Start every day by recognizing and honoring perfection.
2. Then move forward from that point rather than slipping back into your old patterns and your history of imperfection. This means that everything is new and bright each day.
3. Since you have no history with anyone, you can see each person with fresh eyes.
4. Since you have no old habits or patterns, you are awake to consciously choose in the moment.

My sense is that although we don't quite know or remember how to do all these things, our willingness and intent will work miracles. Beginning to do them is good practice for much of what will be unfolding.

We don't know how to live this new life because we've never done it in this lifetime. Yet the deep perfection and Oneness that live in us as well are calling us forward with ease and joy toward a radiantly beautiful time on Earth. As we step beyond the artificial boundaries within which we have lived and walk the path with heart, we will ascend to the heights that Creator has created as our joyful heritage.

CHAPTER 14

LIGHT IN THE
DARKNESS

*We must recognize the nurturance and grace of our soul, which
have always been and will eternally be present.
This, too, is an honoring of fire and light, within and around us.*

*This sacred body we inhabit is not only clay and bone;
it is star and stone.*

HONORING FIRE

*Behold, my brothers, the spring has come: the Earth has received the embraces of
the sun and we shall soon see the results of that love!*
—*SITTING BULL*
Hunkpapa, Teton Sioux

The fiery light of the Sun is what gives life to all of Earth's children.
The Sun represents the infinite energy of Creation that pours upon us,
one and all. Fire has been acknowledged as First Grandfather by tribal
peoples, because it is the Sun's energy present on Earth.

As Okute or Shooter, a Teton Sioux, said, "All living creatures and
all plants derive their life from the sun. If it were not for the sun, there
would be darkness and nothing could grow—the Earth would be without life."[1]

Native peoples continue to honor fire as holy and have kept aware-

228

ness of right relationship with it alive in their ceremonies. It is the heart of connecting to Creator. The Sun Dance, an annual renewal dance among American Native peoples, is an honoring of the fire of the Sun and a supplication for its continuing support of life. Native women reverence their hearth fires as central to the well-being of their families. The transformative power of fire is central to purification lodges like the sweat lodge. The moon-shaped bed of embers, which is central to the altar in Native American Church peyote ceremonies, is a profound veneration of fire. In the center of the tepee during these ceremonies, tireless firemen transform this moon to eagles and suns made of burning coals.

Hawaiian people have the opportunity to observe the primal building of Earth from the molten flows of volcanic lava. Their goddess Pele reminds us that Earth is born of fire. I have stood beneath the earth there in a cave where an enormous vagina had been formed of molten lava. Its whereabouts had been secret until shortly before I was able to go there. I felt an intimacy with the body of Earth that I had never experienced before, and I sang songs from my womb to Mother Earth. Now that place is closed to visitors, yet it is still as vivid in my memory as the molten lava pouring into the hissing sea.

In modern culture, we have not honored fire in a good way. Instead, we have more often used its power for destruction. The hearth fire is gone from the center of our homes. The meditative magic of looking into a fire is almost a thing of the past. We have removed ourselves from the warmth of fire by installing central heating, which is taken for granted rather than honored. We have created the terrible fire of atomic bombs, and we have polluted our environment until global warming, which affects all of life on Earth, is a given.

We must make changes in our everyday lives that put Creator's fire back into a holy arena. We can no longer burn fossil fuel; we must find other means. Connecting directly to the Sun via solar energy is one obvious way. A Hindu fire ritual, *Agnihotra*,[2] is traditionally done at the moment of sunrise and sunset to purify one's own energy and the atmosphere. I have made it a part of my practice to work with such a fire ceremony, using buffalo dung, quinoa, and elements from the American earth. It is time for us all to return to recognition of the holiness of fire and to a re-cognition of the heart-fire of Creator, which gives us life.

There are many ways to use the transformative power of ritual fire. Fire ritual is a powerful tool for emotional and spiritual purification. One of our questing ceremonies is to gather wood during the day and keep a small fire burning all night with just what was gathered. Being with this fire brings great pleasure through the dark hours and clears depression, anger, and hate. It is a way to melt away any of the negativity of our most fiery emotions. Another powerful healing is to be with a fire for six hours at one sitting, wherever it is safe to have such a fire.

A common ritual is to offer food into the fire—a giveaway in thanks for its many healing gifts. At our wilderness camps, we also use fire ritual to help clear old things we are releasing and to send our prayers up as smoke. To do this, we invite people to write their positive prayer or what they wish to release on a small slip of paper or put its energy into a special piece of wood. This is then ritually offered to the fire for transformation or upliftment.

The breath of life drawn into our lungs fires our physical bodies. Love fires our emotional lives, giving warmth and passion to our days. To honor the fire within is to honor passion, a kind of aliveness that is often seen as unacceptable in our modern world of coolness and detachment. We are told it is too messy, too unbridled, too spontaneous, too danger-ous. We often act more like well-trained robots than the lively, curious creatures that are our true selves. This comes from having been con-vinced that conforming, doing what we are told, and causing no prob-lems is the "right" way, the "cool" way.

We are led to believe that fire is too risky, too unpredictable, too transforming. Yet the impassioned person is an alive and spirit-filled per-son, and it will do us well to find that part of ourselves, perhaps for the first time since we were small children. Fire's milder but wonderful cousin is enthusiasm (*en-theos* = "God within"). Although in its unbri-dled form, it may seem too contagious and revolutionary for our staid lives, we need more of *it* as well. Those who walk into the new world will be filled with fire and with light.

This way of living is portrayed by Mary Oliver's powerful words:

When Death Comes

When death comes
like the hungry bear in autumn;
when death comes and takes all the bright coins from his purse

to buy me, and snaps the purse shut;
when death comes
like the measle-pox;

when death comes
like an iceberg between the shoulder blades,

I want to step through the door full of curiosity, wondering:
what is it going to be like, that cottage of darkness?

And therefore I look upon everything
as a brotherhood and a sisterhood,
and I look upon time as no more than an idea,
and I consider eternity as another possibility,

and I think of each life as a flower, as common
as a field daisy, and as singular,

and each name a comfortable music in the mouth,
tending, as all music does, toward silence,

and each body a lion of courage, and something
precious to the earth.

When it's over, I want to say: all my life
I was a bride married to amazement.
I was the bridegroom, taking the world into my arms.

When it's over, I don't want to wonder
if I have made of my life something particular, and real.
I don't want to find myself sighing and frightened,
or full of argument.

I don't want to end up simply having visited this world.[3]

— *MARY OLIVER*

HONORING THE LIGHT

The fire of the Sun is the light that enables us to live and makes our lives enjoyable. The Light of the Great Central Sun, the source of Light, nurtures all of Creation. That Light lives within and around us as well.

Native American seers, Celtic vision-poets, Hindu *rishis*, and other intuitives see that we have a luminous egg of energy around us. This is our larger Self—our soul essence more truly than what we have thought of as some tiny spark hidden within us. It can enliven us if we consciously draw it within ourselves with our breath.

There is a wonderful exercise that you might like to do to honor sunlight by bringing it in to nurture and feed yourself. On a sunny day, you can do it for a few minutes many different times.

1. Stand facing the Sun but not looking directly at it.
2. Bring your hands up in front of you and close the middle, ring, and little fingers of each hand gently to get them out of the way, leaving thumbs and index fingers extended.
3. Then by touching the tips of your thumbs together and the tips of your index fingers together, make a "triangle."
4. Hold this triangle so that the light of the Sun shines through it right into your heart. Be careful not to look directly into the Sun while you are doing this; pay more attention to your chest where the light shines through your hands.
5. Welcome the sunlight to warm and nurture you. And invite your body to become more and more capable of feeding itself directly from the Sun, just as plants do.

6. With a slight nod of your head or a small bow, give thanks to the Sun for the energy and beauty it brings us.

Another exercise can be done almost anytime or anyplace:

1. Take a few minutes several times day to sit, perhaps with eyes closed.
2. See, with your inner sight, the light softly shining around you.
3. Rather than using your rational mind to examine it, explore it, or pick at it, simply and gently invite it into each cell of your body with your inbreath.
4. With your outbreath, release anything no longer needed or toxic.

We all have an intuitive knowing that the Light of the soul is in the eyes. So use this knowing:

1. Set a large mirror in front of you with two tall candles, one on each side of the mirror. Study your eyes in the mirror, blinking as little as possible, for half an hour. Write down your experience and "who" you saw!
2. Study your own eyes in the mirror (if you combine this exercise with the breathing, look before and after you draw the Light within you). Is there a sparkle in your eyes, a luminosity in your face? What do you think would put them there if they are absent?
3. Look in another person's eyes and ask the same questions. A great group experience is to introduce workshop participants to one another by dividing them into twos and having them spend at least half an hour looking directly into each other's eyes. Although, at first, it will very likely be uncomfortable, stick with it, for what you see and experience there is quite remarkable.
4. At the end, share with each other what you have seen.

Even though it would be quite unusual, I would recommend this exercise before you decide to date someone seriously or to hire someone as your assistant or your baby-sitter. The knowing you gain will serve you very well.

Remember, too, the benefits of looking directly into the heart of the rising or setting Sun. For a few minutes at each of these times, the orange Sun will not hurt your eyes, yet will increase your frequency levels. As well, it helps you nurture yourself at many levels. It also remagnetizes your body, aligning it with the Earth; helps in the creation of much-needed minerals in your body; and inspires you with regard to the infinite energy coming onto Earth for your use. It's an auspicious time to offer prayers or songs of thanksgiving and gratitude. I like to stand awaiting the Sun in the morning and sing to it as it rises. Standing on the pounding ocean shore in Hawaii, I was given a wonderful song, "O Heo," to honor the Sun in this way.[4]

Once we discover that our soul is not some tiny, hidden seed but a large, warm glow all around us, we become less fearful of life. Too often we feel abandoned, left alone by our !$@#$&$!*+@# Spirit, who always seems to be hiding somewhere when we need it most. This belief has made it difficult for us to feel ourselves cradled by Spirit, warmed and held by our soul in a special kind of personal belonging. We must drop these foolish ideas of separation and abandonment, recognizing the nurturance and grace that have always been and will eternally be present. This, too, is an honoring of fire and light, within and around us.

THE LIGHT SHIELD

My inner guidance has recently given me an amazing instruction in light. Although I have only begun to experience the depth and beauty of it for myself, I will share it with you as it was given to me.

As your spiritual practices bring you more and more into unity and harmony with yourself and your true purpose in this lifetime, your uniqueness begins to bring you great benefits. At one moment somewhere down the line, an unusual energy will snap into place, and something unitary/whole/one will emerge. This event will be accompanied by a kind of hum. What will then emerge from your torso is what my guides call a *light shield*. It will look like an embossing in which points of light and dark create a symbol that is projected to stand out slightly in front on your torso. The shield will have the general outer shape of an elongated diamond or egg, reaching from your collarbones to your pubic arch, with its most vibrant "signature" spanning from your heart to just below your ribs across the front of your body.

This symbol, which looks like a soft, radiant shield, is your energetic signature: a signature of light that is absolutely unique to the individual. When this symbol comes forward energetically, it creates a specific receptacle into which Life can plug *exactly* what you personally need in order to be your highest and finest self—to be truly you. It is not just about a narcissistic expressing of your Self; its function is to bring you whatever you need in order to give the gift of yourself to the world.

This connection comes to nurture you with everything you need in order to live out your particular destiny and give the unique gift you came to give. For a metaphorical example: if you are a sail, Life gives you wind. In other words, it gives you that energy, that movement, that exact thing you need in order to express in the world the *function* that you are. Remember, you are not a name; you are not a thing; you are not a body; you are a being with a function. You came here to be a creative process within the larger whole. You are an activity, not an object. To continue the example above, if you are pretending to be a rock instead of knowing yourself as a sail, Life cannot really give you what you need!

In my intensive trainings, we eventually work toward *naming*. Naming, when it is done well, gives you a functional look at yourself as you are *becoming* and thus draws you forward into being more of who you already are. Once the light shield has been created, you are enabled to offer more fully the gift you came to give. This experience and the resultant connection will be incredibly empowering. They will allow you to live with a grace you have not imagined possible.

However, once you begin to perceive the signature of your own shield, *never* tell anyone else what you have seen. If someone else has the ability to see it, fine. But talking about it, especially bragging about it, will shift its energy and blur the signature in your consciousness. Simply celebrate its presence and consciously hold it before you or within you. You will discover over time that you can have the shield projecting outward, or receding to a smaller image held inwardly.

THE LAST GHOST DANCE

My intuition says that the exercise of forming your fingers into a triangle that focuses the Sun on your heart will help awaken and strengthen this shield. There is also another exercise, chakra unification, that could be useful for this practice.

First, let me give you a brief description of the chakras, in case you are not familiar with them. They are energy centers of the body, aligned upward along the spine. Energies coming into our human system are divided into these functions and aspects, often visualized as white light coming through a prism and separating into the spectrum of seven life forces.

1. Coccyx or Base: red; life, strength, power, vitality, security, grounding
2. Sacral: orange; optimism, self-confidence, enthusiasm, courage, passion, sexuality
3. Lumbar or Solar Plexus: yellow; mental or intellectual power, joy
4. Dorsal or Heart: green; love, harmony, balance, growth, healing, unity
5. Cervical or Throat: blue; inspiration, creativity, spiritual understanding, faith, devotion, manifestation
6. Spiritual Eye and Medulla Oblongata: indigo; spiritual perception, intuition
7. Crown or Pineal: violet and white light; divine realization, humility, creative imagination.

Because this exercise allows you to receive vast amounts of energy without any damage to the physical form, it can be very useful in the process of building the Lightbody, as well as awakening the light shield. It also allows you to harmonize your entire body. Practicing it energizes your heart chakra as the center of your being and spirals out from there to connect all your physical and higher chakras. It involves the alpha and omega chakras, which have been latent until recently, but have now been activated. The alpha chakra (eight inches above your head) connects you to your fifth-dimensional Lightbody. The omega chakra (eight inches below your tailbone) connects you to planetary consciousness. It is suggested that you ground yourself from the omega rather than the base chakra.

Tony Stubbs summarizes it this way:

Basically the process involves

1. getting into a comfortable, relaxed position,
2. deepening your breathing, and
3. breathing Light into the heart chakra.
4. On each outbreath, you visualize your heart chakra becoming larger, opening in all directions like a sphere. You expand it to include each succeeding pair of chakras as you breathe in and out:
   a. third and fifth (solar plexus and throat),
   b. second and sixth (sacral and spiritual eye),
   c. first and seventh (base and crown),
   d. alpha and omega,
   e. eighth and your knees,
   f. ninth and your ankles,
   g. tenth and your feet.
   Your unified chakra is now a sphere of golden light, about twenty to fifty feet in diameter, and forms the center of your unified field, which could be several miles in diameter. Your spirit field coexists with this unified field.
5. So now you ask the appropriate level of your own spirit to blend its energy with that of your unified field, starting at the center of the unified chakra.
6. Now you'll respond from your entire being, including Spirit, so you'll throw a heavy dose of love into the energy stew.[5]

My sense is that when each of us gets humming with our own shield and function, it will automatically hook us up with perhaps six others who make up a functional unit—a powerful and empowering team drawn together by our primal signature of energy and by our intent. Working together in this circle of seven will magnify our accomplishments and our joy.

The Great Invocation (revised version)

From the point of Light within the Mind of God
Let light stream forth into human minds.
Let Light descend on Earth.

From the point of Love within the Heart of God
Let love stream forth into human hearts.
May the Coming One return to Earth.

From the centre where the Will of God is known
Let purpose guide all little human wills—
The purpose which the Masters know and serve.

From the centre which we call the human race
Let the Plan of Love and Light work out
And may it seal the door where evil dwells.

Let Light, and Love, and Power restore the Plan on Earth.[6]

HONORING DARKNESS

Light is easy to honor. But what about the darkness? Creator gave us both of them, and nothing Creator gives is inherently negative. We ourselves have given the darkness a bad name, by refusing to acknowledge the kind of spiritual Light that lives within it as well as All Things. Our fear makes us favor the daytime, where we can claim that we see what is happening around us. Yet I find no instance of seeing more powerful and magical than that of spending time in the darkness and watching the light grow around me as my eyes adjust. I asked my Eagle Song campers to walk without flashlights through the quarter mile of darkness from the lodge to their tent area at night. Seeing me zipping by them on my bicycle gave them confidence that they could make it on foot!

The European theologies that spread themselves across our world have pointed our attention to the spire, the sky, the light, the upper world.

And yet primary peoples on every continent understand the deep underground to be filled with Spirit, perhaps more profoundly than even the upper world. They often go deep into the Earth in their kivas (underground ceremonial chambers, used by Pueblo and other Native peoples) to seek Spirit. The riches of the unknown lie there and the mystery of the unknowable.

The Southern Seers' lineages remind me that what we now know is the smallest speck on that which is still unknown. The flower of Life will unfold itself eternally. Rather than spend all our fascination on the outer world, we would do well to open and nourish our curiosity for the dark unknown. Perhaps the soul will never be openly known; it may be like a small creature whose luxurious fur we can stroke by gently reaching into a dark, sheltered burrow where it lives. We might sometimes see the green glint of its eyes, but it will turn away from the glare of our neon searchlights and will not reveal itself soon again, for the harshness hurts its eyes.

John O'Donohue talks about the soul's feeling more welcomed in the hospitality of candlelight, where the darkness is illumined without harsh light. In his lovely manner, he says, "Candles befriend the dark, and don't have a neon kind of glare."[7] An interesting meditation can be done using candlelight or some other soft light—fireplace light, outdoor firelight—for a softening rather than a banishing of the darkness. Allow yourself the soothing joy of subdued light as you seek communion with your deepest Self by a fire you have lighted or in the natural moonlight and starlight.

On one of my pilgrimages to Peru, we were shown a cave from which ran a small, clear stream. We were told that in days of old, young shamans were given a final initiation by following this stream a half mile through the pitch darkness of the cave until it came out the other side. If they panicked or lost their trust in the darkness, they often did not reemerge. This is such a wonderful metaphor for our spiritual search. Often we do well until we must face the darkness; then we panic and lose ourselves. More familiarity will help us befriend it and remove the fear.

I have always loved springs and wells, where water emerges from the dark richness of the Earth. These are holy places to my people. These places, as well as caves, are metaphors for the subterranean resources we can receive from the dark underground. In modern American culture, our way of tapping them, whether for water or for spiritual understanding, has been to dig up the ground and expose them. I have seen ignorant people time and time again ruin a spring by blasting and digging and trying to expose it.

My family made a practice of enshrining those gifts of water from the Earth by making of them wellsprings that nourish all who come to them. Rather than digging, we set around the flow a stone masonry box that filled up with water. From that box, a pipe ran out a few feet from the ground, creating a wonderful sound as the water fell into a trough for the animals. They, too, could then enjoy the water without muddying the earth around them. Usually we hung an old cup inside the box so that people who came by could easily drink, if they chose not to cup their hands under the water flowing from the pipe.

When we would ride for cattle on the mountain, we planned our day so that we made it to one of these wellsprings near noon. We would sit and enjoy its music while eating the lunch we had packed. The horses would drink their fill and begin to graze. The cattle were always easy to find nearby, because they came to the water each day.

I liked to open the lids of these well boxes and look deep into them, yearning to touch the source from which they sprang. I would sometimes take a flashlight and try to see down in, but the light would just bounce back in my eyes. Then one of my elders taught me to lay the bright light down and stand beside the spring where I could just see the "eye" of it—to find exactly where the clear, pure water emerged into the light.

She urged me to pay more attention to keeping that eye clear than to trying to dig into the depths, even with my own eyes. She would say:

Do not stare at this precious one. You do not like to be stared at. Just stand beside her as you would a friend and receive the riches she offers. Let your looking at her be a caress, not a piercing glare. Remember that the riches of soul that you really seek are the same. Keep the eye of your own spring open so that the purity of those gifts that lie beneath your intellect can come forth unhindered and clear.

In the words of English poet William Wordsworth:

> With an eye made quiet by the power
> Of harmony, and the deep power of joy,
> We see into the life of things.[8]

Here is a journey you can take to your creative flow:

1. Lie down comfortably and close your eyes.
2. Imagine going deep, deep into yourself, beneath the hardened surface of your personality, beneath your ideas of yourself, to the ancient and secret resources that lie there.
3. Visualize an image of the wellspring that is actually your own creative flow.
4. See the mouth of the well, where the hidden flow is first touched by the light of your knowing. This is where that flow is least affected by the outer world; it is a most precious place.
5. If it is ever necessary, unclog the flow. It might seem to be plugged with mud or moss. Notice whether these things are metaphors for anything in your life. Then let the spring run full and clear in your vision.
6. Notice that as the creative water runs out, into nature or your own personal world, it is changed. See if you can allow it to remain pure, clear, unedited, and unchanged. I am reminded here of my understanding of the Christ energy that Jesus manifested so powerfully: it means bringing the energy of life gathered from Earth and Spirit, unrestricted and unchanged, through the heart.
7. You may want to practice coming to the well again and again, so that when you say to yourself the word *well*, you can slip immediately into that deeper place and the purity of its flow.

In these deep places, the flower of your possible life is waiting to unfold, and your intent can be seen as the eye of the spring. If it is clear and pure and open to Spirit's flow, magnificent things come forth. If it is clogged or blocked by your limiting ideas and outmoded beliefs, the result will be less useful. Allow your perception to become tuned to the edge, the interface between the seeable and the unseen. Try not to throw light into the places where things want to be hidden. Being receptive to spontaneous gifts is the task, not trying to change the channel.

I think here of the wonderful words of David Whyte, which speak of this in a different and special way:

> Those who will not slip
> beneath the still surface
> on the well of grief,
> turning down through its
> black water to the place
> we cannot breathe,
> will never know
> the source from where we drink
> the secret water, cold and clear,
> nor find in the darkness glimmering
> the small round coins
> thrown by those who wish
> for something else.[9]
>
> —DAVID WHYTE

GOING BEYOND THE PERSONAL FAMILIAR

One of the challenges that the Toltec seers frequently address is that of the habitual and familiar in our world, those things that stand out glaring in the light of day. Why is it we label the darkness and shadowed parts of ourselves as bad, negative, or repressed just because they are traumatic and difficult? The magic, wonder, newness, uniqueness, fun, and adventure that may also lie there under cover of darkness will never emerge if we continue this denigration. These beautiful things are hidden for a reason, like incubating seeds. They will unfold like a lovely flower if we water them with our love and our intent. Yes, there are some negative and repressed things there in the darkness, but they, too, need to be gently uncovered.

Don't let the unrevealed parts of you lie dormant all your life. My old teacher Moshe Feldenkrais used to say that nowadays people are satisfied with their development as soon as they can walk, talk, and "screw." Beyond that, there's little interest or attention. As much as this made us laugh, it also hit a vein of truth, and we were encouraged by his presence to continue developing more and more of ourselves for all the days of our lives.

How often do we live our lives like wearing beautiful shoes that we've slipped into only partway? Walking like this, we break them down; then we're always schlepping around in these broken-down shoes. But we could actually slip our feet all the way in and walk with beauty and security.

A task I give my students is to find something new or strange or unexpressed about themselves and to act that out for a day. These things that we do not know about ourselves are part of our shadow, which we will never come to know if we don't consciously choose to reveal it to ourselves. Often this part is not even bad or negative; it is simply untouched.

There is a form of education called "complementary education," which suggests that occasionally we should learn something that is not what we would normally choose, that is in a realm far from our daily experience. For example, if you're a writer, take a class in making ceramic pottery. If you're usually sedentary, take horseback-riding lessons. If you usually go to the mountains for your vacation, try rafting a river. This doesn't mean that you must stay with this new enterprise forever and have it become your favorite. But if you approach it with openness, it will inform and enlarge the horizons of your usual ways of being. And interestingly enough, you might just fall in love with it, because those parts of you that have been repressed or unexplored might have ended up that way because of some family or cultural programming that isn't even yours. Explore and enjoy, expecting to find rich and archaic magic in the root cellar of your life. For a wonderful tool to assist you with this kind of growth, I highly recommend Hal and Sidra Stone's *Voice Dialogue* work. Their books, tapes, and workshops can be of enormous benefit.[10]

Here again, I'm also reminded of the practice of *living backward*, which was discussed in Chapter 13. With this approach, each day is new and innocent and bright. You don't have any history with anyone. You're coming from the other side, from the future, so you can allow others and the world to be new in each moment.

Another aspect of the darkness is *not knowing*. One of our greatest challenges is being willing to stay in the unknown, to stay with the questions rather than strive to figure out the answers with our limiting intellect. It will be our greatest strength in these coming times of newness if we can do so, because the answers that come to us through our *logical* mind, based on our old ways of thinking, will no longer serve us. Our concentration must be on clarifying the questions and then holding them with an open faith. If we can move forward only when there is a deep *"Yes!"* we will serve ourselves well. Let us live into our answers, not carve them from the rock of our outmoded past.

Most of us do not have trust and faith in the unfoldment of our soul's purpose. Instead, we scrape and bruise our soul by our negative approaches. But luminosity lies at the heart of our soul. The goodness within us will continue to be unacknowledged if we insist on putting all our energy into work on our negativity. I sometimes wonder whether this comes from the idea of original sin—that some evil taints us and needs to be exorcised. I, personally, think of *sin* as in the Latin, meaning "without." Sin therefore is more likely just our forgetting to include our full selves, Creator, and All Creation in our lives. It is not bad, just stupid, and can be easily corrected as we open up to the truth of the basic goodness that lies at the loving Source of All That Is.

In native ways, there is no devil; there are only parts of life that we have not made a friend of and have not yet transformed. I don't know how many times lately I have heard people talk of what they had once thought were their weaknesses in the end being recognized as their strengths. The wonderful wise woman and healer Rachel Naomi Remen reminds us:

> Reclaiming ourselves usually means coming to recognize and accept that we have in us both sides of everything. We are capable of fear and courage, generosity and selfishness, vulnerability and

strength. These things do not cancel each other out but offer us a full range of power and response to life. Life is as complex as we are. Sometimes our vulnerability is our strength, our fear develops our courage, and our woundedness is the road to our integrity.[11]

We must get over thinking of ourselves as flawed and of Creator as having set things up poorly. The challenges we have given ourselves are those we chose in order to learn the lessons most important to us in this lifetime.

So often we resist and conceal and struggle with parts of ourselves we see as negative, when an embrace, a kind exploration, would lead to transfiguration. This unification, or welcoming all parts of self, is an incredible empowerment: I sense that it's not possible to see our Light Shield until we have done this. There are wonderful gifts in every part of ourselves, waiting for us to discover their power and beauty. If they are consigned to the dank and isolated basement of our lives, they will only rot and poison us, never coming to flower.

EVIL

It's not within the scope of this book to do a lengthy treatise on the intentionally destructive actions of our human family that are called evil. Yet I can say a few simple things. First, I'll share the definition of evil Dawn Star gives:

> Evil is not innate to existence . . . but a denial of God's love as the power of the universe, and denial of the love that you are! When a person has denied the love that he is, he loses the power to command the affairs of his life. In its place he will use force or deception.[12]

Greed, coming from a deep sense of scarcity and fear, is the root of all evil.

There *are* horrible things that humans do to one another (often under the guise of some high principle or assumed knowledge of what is right and just). In response to these things, only a few categories of reaction are possible. One is to allow hate and revenge to rule, which only adds to the negativity and malevolence in the world; we become the same kind of people we are judging. Another is to turn our backs on these things, pretending they have nothing to do with us; this is a denial of our connectedness with everything in the Circle of Life.

A "middle" way makes most sense to me. It is important not to intellectualize or rationalize about the reasons an event happened. With innocent and clear perception, let yourself experience the appropriate heartful feeling of hurt, dismay, grief, sadness, and so forth, for without this, we lose our humanity in a zombielike numbing or indifference. Then, as the waves of that pass, send uplifting energy to all concerned, the perpetrators included. Trying to "kill" or stop depraved behavior never works, for it struggles and strengthens itself through that process. The only way to transform the energy is for those practicing evil ways to be awakened to another, more workable and beneficial way of being, for themselves and others. So send a blessing of love and light to all concerned, that this kind of thing might happen no more. Do this without judgment, for you do not really understand fully what deep lessons those involved are working out.

A next step is the release of forgiveness. Forgiveness is difficult in many situations, yet when you feel ready to forgive, it will lift a load off your spirit to release all concerned to the fruits of their actions and not carry this in your mind and heart like a malevolent seed.

Another concern is always how to avoid evil in your own life. One way is to look deeply into yourself for the lessons you are wanting to learn, the patterns you wish to change, and the "buttons" that life can push in you. Do your homework in any of the ways mentioned earlier in the chapter, especially mirroring, to move through these lessons with grace and a minimum of suffering. When you ignore or resist your lessons is often when your deeper self calls in the "big guns" and creates a very painful experience. If you have done all your homework and these things still come your way, know that some part of you is trying to learn a lesson that only this can teach you. Open your heart to the gifts it brings you.

I'll give one quick story about this. I recently heard of a friend of mine being injured badly by a suicidal person who had called for help. He was shot several times in the torso, and a close friend who accompanied him was killed as they walked through the door. During his hospitalization, when it was often thought he would die, he can remember that his spirit called upon all the healing teachings he had received over many years. Using them helped him to live and be fully functional again. Before this, he had been around many high teachings and, like a lot of us, had been having a difficult time really living them in his life. This seemingly terrible experience helped him choose to use them, choose to live, and live his life with gratitude and zest thereafter. It also pulled together a community of people around him who had been not speaking and/or had been fighting for years. No one is glad this happened, yet all can see the remarkable gifts that came from it.

The best general advice I can give you about this works very well in all arenas *and* is very potent in abolishing evil from your life. *Love Creation—all* of Creation. When you walk in that harmonious connection with All That Is, evil will not touch you.

EMBRACING DUALITY

Native and primary peoples did not hold duality in the same way we do—as a separating and divisive force. They understood that darkness must exist for light to be recognized, that death must exist so that birth can come to be, that there must be a "down" so that "up" can be enjoyed. They embraced and communed with all kinds of energies in order to live well.

We must learn to embrace contradictions: move above right and wrong—round and round to another level where we can create real solutions to our challenges without the designations of bad and good, right and wrong. This reminds me of the saying in Japanese Mahikari, "Everything serves." So how does this challenge serve us? How is it inviting us to empower ourselves to move further into the sweet territories of self?

The following is a journey to embrace both parts of yourself:

1. Let yourself go into an altered state, possibly by listening to music that reminds you of a forest.

2. Be not only the one who will walk into the forest but also one who is watching—the witness part of yourself.

3. Pay special attention to who/what this one is who walks into the forest. How are you represented in this journey—as an elf, your normal self, an animal, a warrior, a white pig? What clothing is this being wearing?

4. As you move down the trail, it forks. As your one inner self moves into this fork, that one divides into two beings: one, the light, seen, outward self; and the other, the dark, shadowy, unseen, shy, elusive self. They are *both* shy, in fact.

5. Your task as the watcher is to call them forward with sweet things, gifts, shiny objects, or whatever each one might like—and get to know them. Be gentle with them. Coax them as you would a shy child.

6. Talk with them, interact, play, ask them to show you themselves in a new way. Get to know this light and this dark one—these twins that are two parts of you.

7. When you return, write about it in your journal or share with someone about it. Explore the images for their meaning to you.

8. Once you have become acquainted with these two aspects of yourself in this way, take a subsequent inner journey. Another part of the continued exploration of these twin aspects of self is dichotomous words: light/dark, seen/unseen, Sun/moon, day/night, awake/asleep, body/spirit, outward/hidden, known/yet to be known, and so on. Assign these as two different parts of yourself and get to know them in the same way.

9. There may also be interesting unities between them: perhaps they both feel unseen in certain ways! Explore any of these you find.

The important part of these exercises is to encourage yourself to remember that perhaps the most wonderful treasures are hidden in the dark—fabulous things yet to be known and explored about yourself.

After you have explored to your satisfaction, do a completion initiation with the intent to consciously join these twin parts in a friendly dance:

1. A fun thing I found for one of these was an M. C. Escher print on a scarf, in which white birds complemented and meshed with black fish. More simply, you can buy a couple of one-yard squares of cloth or long scarves—one white and one black. Light a candle and call these parts of yourself forward.

2. Acknowledge your understanding of their unity and see them together in joyful cooperation.

3. Then reward yourself with a ritual reminder. Remember that it can be very simple, as long as it has meaning for you. In the example of the scarves: women can wear these as an apron, a head scarf, or a small shawl; men, as a neck scarf or a wide belt. You may find something more appropriate for your experience.

4. The most important part is the acknowledgment of the complementarity that lives within you.

In the end, we come to understand that duality is only an aspect of the wholeness. The unity and complementarity of the Oneness are a much better focus of our attention.

As we move forward on this pathway to our higher and lighter selves and to a new and radiant day on Earth, we must remember what all shamans know and practice—that Spirit is alive in both the light and dark, the visible and invisible, in both air and earth. This sacred body we inhabit is not only clay and bone; it is star and stone.

If this meandering path is a way that beckons you, then begin. It is my way; it is a shaman's way; it is the way of the Earth Mage. It will unfold before you in your own particular pattern, and in the end, we will arrive at the same place—expressing our own special uniqueness in harmony with the ultimate Oneness of All That Is, which is our deepest desire and our joy.

CHAPTER 15

SEEDING THE DREAM

We are the generation that will make the dreams and visions
of our ancestors come true—
a renewed Earth in touch with the Sky.

"I keep thinking about seeding this great dream," I told Sparrow when I next opened to his presence. "Being at the bottom of the ninth hell makes it hard to imagine what amazing possibilities lie before us as we ascend through thirteen Heavens. The most difficult part of this is that we are being asked to plant seeds for a new garden without really knowing what the flowers will look like when they grow and blossom. This requires us to be much more willing to tune in sensitively at all levels: body, mind, emotions, and spirit. All our circuitry and awareness must be open, precisely *because* we don't have many instructions!"

"It's quite an adventure, isn't it? A really long hike for which few people have a map or compass. Or that's what you think," said Sparrow, trying to tease me out of my seriousness. "But you've already got most of the information, and even the support, for what you need to do. You just haven't yet opened to fully receiving the amazing and wonderful news—and celebrating it!"

"I think I'll be able to dance in celebration and joy a little better once I have my feet on the ground of this new territory," I replied. "How about giving me a little more help?"

"Well, there are some quite clear things that you will be guided to find, some steps to help ground this Light in your consciousness and in your body. They comprise another level of creating awareness, of clearing the old and practicing the new."

First of all, let's look at some other metaphors for this ascension that we are experiencing. The prophets in our deep history gave us one way of seeing it. Now as it is actually unfolding, we have newer images perceived by our contemporaries, which are worthwhile to review and may be quite useful in awakening us to our magnificent possibilities. In doing so, however, remember that I give them to you as stimulation for your own imagination and creative visioning. All the potential that we will make real has already been given us by Creator. Yet in our process of free choice, we must open ourselves to our own indwelling magnificence in order to awaken the amazing possibilities lying within.

Beginning in the 1870s, when Mme. Helena Petrovna Blavatsky founded the Theosophical Society, and continuing on into the 1930s with Alice Bailey's channeling of Djwhal Khul, information began to come to sensitives and mystics about the nature of this tremendous change coming to Earth. Since then, esoteric circles in the Western world have paid attention to this coming phenomenon, while for the ordinary person on the street, this all seemed like so much nonsense. Now, more and more of us are feeling the momentous changes and can begin to make use of what others before us have brought through for our elucidation.

It makes sense to me that each of the images we explore provides an interesting perspective. None of them is the exact truth. Only when these stages of change actually come to be will we know how they will affect us, and even then, our experiences will be individually unique. So each of us must take what fits at the time and make use of it. Because things are changing so rapidly both outside and within, it is appropriate to check in with the available information frequently, because more and more of it may become pertinent. Yet personal discernment is of utmost importance in this and any of our learning.

We two-leggeds have taken millennia to explore our freedom to experience the illusion of separation, differentiation, and density, and we explored those things magnificently. However, our swing in that direction on the great pendulum of time has come to an end. We are in the process of understanding at a deep soul level that the game is over and we can return Home—to our home in Oneness, wholeness, and Light. What makes it easier to choose this is our growing awareness that we can have it all, in a sense. Never will our uniqueness and individual soul be taken away from us. That is an eternal covenant with our Creator. Now, we can live in a state of total self-expression that is also one of harmony and Oneness with All That Is.

This is one way of looking at it. Until now, we have been living in the third dimension, which is material, and the fourth dimension, which is primarily emotional: the realms in which the illusion of separation is possible. We are now raising our frequency so that eventually this whole separation concept can be folded up like a game that children grow tired of. Then we will move up into a realm of radiant wholeness. Although the old game may be played out on some other plane, the renewed Earth into which Lady Gaia is evolving is no longer willing to host it.

FUNCTIONAL BODIES

One way to look at this transformation is through our functional bodies: physical, emotional, mental, and spiritual. We are quite aware of our physical and emotional bodies. Our mental body is our tool for determining what is "real" for us and therefore what manifests in our daily life. Until now, we've focused essentially on these three bodies and their interactions. Now, as we return Home, we must fully integrate our *spiritual* body into the whole.

Tremendous energy has been used to screen our input from our spirit self; yet now we have the joy of reconnecting to it and, through it, to All That Is. This is where transcendent practices like "becoming a hollow bone" are so useful and important. Once we allow the integration of all these bodies, we will have access to our full capacity. We will be connected to the larger circle of power and will find it much easier to live well and fully.

This process is one of bringing Spirit into our denser bodies and then becoming less and less dense as we fill ourselves with Light. I believe we have all the latent encoding we need for becoming a Lightbody. As the pillar of celestial fire fills us, it is triggering transformational possibilities that already live within us.

One of the ways we have experienced this incoming energy is through flulike symptoms, which are offering us the opportunity to clean and clear our systems of what we no longer need—or to leave our physical bodies if we choose not to take part in the process at this time. However, if we remain physical, we will be part of this awakening process, no matter what rate we choose for that movement.

LEVELS OF LIGHTBODY

This is an eye-opening look at twelve levels of becoming our Lightbody.[1] These levels are measured by the capacity of our cells to metabolize light, much as photovoltaic cells gather solar energy. My sense is that our movement through levels such as these is partly determined by great changes at cosmic levels, yet comes into our own consciousness more readily as we become aware of the changes that are possible. And my experience is that they may not occur in this linear manner: we awaken in ways appropriate to our own development. Yet these suggestions may help you begin seeding a larger dream for yourself and allowing it to unfold in your own unique way.

1. In early 1988, level 1 was activated with instructions to the cells to recognize light as a new source of energy. Old traumas, toxins, and outdated patterns began to leave the physical body. Brain chemistry began to produce new synapses.

2. Light begins to bathe the sixth-dimensional etheric blueprint, which starts the release of fourth-dimensional structures that tie us to karmic experiences across lifetimes.

3. Each cell of the body is receiving light directly. The body begins to decode and work with higher energies and transmit them to the planet. Our latent systems begin to fully open, so they can eventually give us access to infinite energy and infinite information.

4. Massive changes in brain chemistry and electromagnetic energy in the body create an entirely different kind of functioning. Because we are now open to vaster pictures of reality, we may begin to have our first taste of truly nonlinear thinking. Here, the prime directive is to follow our spirit without hesitation. Because we will begin to experience ourselves as so much more connected with everything, we may have flashes of telepathy or clairvoyance.

5. We become clear that we are much more than we used to think we were, and it dawns on us that many of our pictures of reality aren't really ours: they come from family history or consensus reality. This brings on a mental sorting process, so that we can begin to own the larger truths.

6. Our entire sense of identity begins to restructure. Many people who are not appropriate to where we are now begin to leave our lives, as part of our learning to be unafraid of change. New people, with whom we will do the work we came to Earth to do, will come into our lives. We become a delightful dance of Spirit, and a deeper level of Light shines out of our eyes. Fully present, we know that we are Spirit in action on our sweet Earth. This is when we begin to acknowledge ourselves as Earth Mages and accept our part in the unfoldment.

7. Here we begin to enter the emotional stages of Lightbody, focusing on deeper and deeper levels of opening the heart chakra as both a center and a gateway. A feeling of connection with Mother Earth opens—a sense of falling in love with our home here. Playfulness returns, and we become more childlike in the way we function. At this point, if we have emotional blocks, they come up intensely. As we move toward expressing our divinity and vastness, blockages must be released. We begin to operate in the *now* far more than ever, and ecstasy becomes a real part of our experience. Being fully present feels wonderful. At this time, we begin our movement into Spirit-based relationships. Pituitary and pineal glands begin to open up and function more optimally, which means we may begin to look and feel very young. We're beginning to operate from Spirit in our everyday lives.

8. We learn what we really enjoy—what makes our heart sing. These things are directly related to our Divine purpose on the planet, and we have a deepening sense of purpose and service. Structures activate that

receive information from the upper dimensions and from the vast amounts of information the soul has gathered over many incarnational cycles in many realms. It is common here for people to feel they have Alzheimer's disease. This happens because many of the pathways in our brain that we are accustomed to using may become nonaccessible while entirely new pathways are being created. We are hooking up to our multidimensional mind. We are communicating with people on a transpersonal level. When 95 percent of the Lightworkers reach this level, they will have access to group mind, which creates opportunities for entirely new programs of service to the planet. We are already playing with this one, as we use the World Wide Web to share information almost instantaneously.

9. We are beginning to embody Divinity. We begin to understand a whole new level of language—tonal language of Light. Body shifts and changes may occur: we may get taller, thinner, bigger, or grow wings! We begin to sense ourselves as the masters we are. We realize ourselves as Spirit in action, as the ego-self dissolves. We must follow our Spirit with every breath and every step. If we can be that vastness here, we'll be exactly where we need to be, with whom we need to be, doing what we need to do in every now-moment.

10. Here is where we begin to manifest avatar ability. Teleportation and direct manifestation become possible, because we are fully conscious of being one with the Source and being everything. A crystalline light structure, called a *Merkabah*, forms, which allows us to pass through space, time, and dimensions, completely in our totality. Drunvalo Melchizedek's organization gives workshops called Flower of Life, the purpose of which is to awaken your *Merkabah*. These are very powerful and useful.[2]

11. Time is now functioning simultaneously. We can see how our choices affect All That Is across all time and space. What we love to do more than anything is our key to manifesting our part in the Divine plan. We are manifesting our vision of Heaven on Earth and expressing the ecstasy of our Spirit.

12. We are reweaving the planet, and Mother Earth lifts into total Lightbody as Lady Gaia. Everyone is in Lightbody and follows their Spirit in total sovereignty and total mastery.

I'm personally excited about the Spirit-based relationships of level 7 and the possibility of using my Spirit wings more fully in the ninth!! (I'm sure this is what I wanted as a tiny child, attempting to fly off those old cars!) Manifesting avatar abilities such as teleportation and direct manifestation will be wonderful, too. Then the joy of the twelfth level— in which everyone is in Lightbody and follows their Spirit in total sovereignty and mastery, at one with Source!

All these things may seem totally impossible to you at this point, but remind yourself of the magical advances we have made in the last hundred years and allow yourself to open to the possibilities. Your other choice is to stay with the fish of the metaphor presented in Chapter 9, holding thoughts of catastrophe for Lady Gaia and humankind and thus choosing to be washed over the falls. I, personally, am pleased to have these images to help me direct my intention forward on an uplifting path of Light, like the bird in the vision.

You might think of the whole spectrum of reality as a piano keyboard. Our senses are tuned to some of the lower octaves, and so we think that's all there is. Our brain screens out the higher octaves so we can remain focused in the physical. Yet songs are being sung in these octaves, even though we can't yet hear them. Occasionally, nonordinary reality is perceived by shamans and others, but if it intrudes upon most people's consciousness, they explain it away. Now we're opening to our capacity to listen and act on more and more levels in the broader realms of experience. We are beginning to hear the octaves that have gone unperceived by us until recently.

RAYS

Another way to look at what is happening is through the phenomenon of rays.

"Ray" is a metaphysical term for the current of electromagnetic energy that enters the human form through the pineal gland and then distributes throughout the body. There have classically been seven of these: seven different energies that combine and permutate to make up not only our experience, but as well everything on Earth.[3]

There are many different approaches to the qualities of the seven rays that make up the energy available on this planet. I'll give you the basic ones, as healer Jack Schwarz has taught them, to provide a basis for looking at a model of new rays that may begin to come now. It is thought that most people come in to express one ray in a lifetime, although some express several. The order in which they are given here does not denote any hierarchy of importance.[4]

First ray—electric blue, white, and vermilion red: The goal of the first ray is to merge the individual's will with God's will, to transmute the human ego with the Divine ego and then express it.

Second ray—azure blue and golden yellow: This is called the messenger ray, and those who carry it combine universal love with the ability to express that love, and thus they are deeply compassionate.

Third ray—emerald green: These persons feel most at home in a green, natural environment. Their main potentials are creative ideation, innovation, and inventiveness, yet they rarely implement their ideas.

Fourth ray—tawny bronze orange: More than any other type, these people want to create harmony. To sum it up in one word, they are catalysts.

Fifth ray—lemon yellow: This is the ray of the intellectual function in its purest expression. Individuals with a yellow ray love facts.

Sixth ray—rose pink: This ray produces evangelical people. They serve others. In doing so, they are actually serving themselves and fulfilling their primary goal of teaching people to raise their consciousness.

Seventh ray—violet and purple: Individuals who have the purple ray are distinguished by their noble bearing. They love ceremony and ritual and power.

Shakura Rei suggests that the new energies now coming to us on Earth originate in five new cosmic rays, in addition to the seven rays with which Creator traditionally energized Earth.[5] I like to use these during my morning meditation, bringing each one into my head and down through my body, asking it do the work she suggests it can do.

Eighth ray—green-violet: Excellent for cleansing and balancing the emotional body.

Ninth ray—blue-green: Shifts limiting attitudes and initiates the process of breaking the bonds of the physical plane by establishing better contact with the soul; also initiates association with the Lightbody.

Tenth ray—pearl white: Actually builds and encodes the Lightbody, integrates all levels of Self, and speeds us through our initiations.

Eleventh ray—orange-pink: Helps remove remnants of third-dimensional energies that are no longer useful.

Twelfth ray—golden opalescent combination of all rays: Brings energies from the Source level; it is the highest form of energy presently available on Earth and will raise the vibration of anything toward which it is directed.

The eleventh and twelfth rays can be brought in as radiant tornadoes that penetrate us and the entire Earth as well.[6]

Other possibilities are these:

- You can use the seventh ray of violet energy as a pool into which you can throw negative or low energy of any form. The violet ray will alter that energy and raise it to a higher frequency.
- To this you can add visualizing yourself sitting in an immense violet flame that permeates you and extends out about six feet. Do this ten minutes a day, and it will effectively cleanse your aura (radiating light energy around the human body).

As you can see, some preliminary work must be done in order to activate the Lightbody. First, one must have the *intention* to expand beyond one's limiting belief systems, while removing the bars that imprison the personality/ego and thus hold one in a state of separation. Then one must have the *will* or *determination* to follow through on whatever healing techniques are necessary to release non-serving attitudes and stored memory of pain. As these are removed, more space is available for Light to anchor within the bodies, reducing the traumatic effects of healing crises, while also speeding the integration of the Self and building the Lightbody.... After being cleared, the cells can hold more Light, resonate higher and assist in building a Lightbody.[7]

EDUCATING YOUR BODY CONSCIOUSNESS

Educating our body consciousness is something we seldom think of, since modern medicine tells us we have no influence over our bodies—that only an outside expert can help us. When we take a deep look at this, it is very foolish thinking, and in the end, it does us a great disservice. It is time to remember ourselves as whole and take respectful command of our bodies and experience. Our physical body is where all the action is as this process begins, and it is important to be in communication with all levels of it.

You can speak directly to your glands, your organs, your meridian systems, your DNA, and so forth with a message about what is now possible and what you desire. The basic message should cover several points:

- The time of separation and death is over.
- Healing, rejuvenation, and perfection are the order of the day.
- It is now time to release from every level of beingness all pain, dysfunction, and anything less than Divine perfection.
- Ask each part or organ to remember its perfect form and function and return to that state, now!

Take a moment to practice this now so that it becomes familiar to you. Then perhaps you will want to begin your daily meditations with these wonderful reminders to your body.

To encourage you, I'll include a story shared by David and Bruce McArthur, who now work with the HeartMath folks you will read about in Chapter 16. They related it as an example of their research into how the intentions of one who is centered in love can alter the body. Myrtle was in the final stages of terminal tuberculosis when she received an intuitive understanding that she could consciously direct the cells of her body and that they would respond in that direction. She addressed her body organs, apologizing for her limiting thoughts and acknowledging the new understanding she had gained that they were perfect channels of God-life expressing. She did this daily for more than two years, resulting in the total elimination of all disease from her physical body.[8]

I find that working with ourselves in a ceremonial way is helpful. It is very powerful to create a ritual that makes the actions we take more real to our psyche (which loves and learns through metaphor). For example, we can find pieces of bark to represent the things we are releasing and throw them into a rushing stream or cast them into a ceremonial fire lit for their transformation.

Something I especially recommend is to create an altar that represents your new way of being and is dedicated to the building of your Lightbody:

1. Find a place in your own personal space rather than a "public" area.
2. If you do not have a small table or separate place for it, use a small space on a bureau or table.
3. Cover the space with a beautiful cloth, scarf, or woven piece. Remember that the quality of what you place there is a metaphor for what you are calling in.
4. Put on your altar objects that represent the building of your Lightbody and an uplifted life for you.
5. Keep it covered with a silken or gauzy cloth except when you are focusing on it.
6. Take a few minutes a day to honor this developing part of your life.

CREATING A NURTURING HOME

In addition, be sure to nurture your spirit with beauty and light around you in your home and workplace. Keep reminders of the kind of life you want in front of you. A good way to do this comes from my Feng Shui practice. In a consultation, I would suggest changes specific to each room and energetic area of your home;[9] however, I can give you a couple of general suggestions to help you begin using "Feng Shui eyes."

COMING HOME

When you come home, what is the first thing that greets you? Is it a flowering and friendly walkway, leading to a beautiful, welcoming door? Is it a cluttered back entrance, filled with shoes and boots to stumble over? Or do you drive into a messy garage and open the door into a dark hallway?

Take a look at just this one small aspect of your home and determine what this first impression says to you, even though it may be less than conscious. Know that this affects you profoundly at an energy level.

Decide how you can make it feel great!

- It may mean working on your garage—removing what you don't truly love or need and organizing the rest in neat, well-labeled boxes on sturdy shelves.
- Some people who live in warm climates (without the mess of mud and snow) even carpet their garage!
- At least create a small corner display where you put something attractive, bright, happy, or peaceful to welcome you.
- Light up that dark hallway with art or family photos that please you.
- Organize the mail, shoes, and other clutter in appropriate storage units.

In whatever way you need to, make this a happy entrance.

SEEING THROUGH GUEST EYES

If your formal or guest door is not the same as your own daily entrance, take some time to walk into your home as though you were a new friend coming to visit. See your space through fresh eyes. This is the great part of having new friends over: we suddenly look at our home from a more conscious perspective.

What would these guests see as they walk up (especially those things you usually ignore)? How does it feel? What will you want to make excuses for? Realize that these things affect you, because even without guests present, this is where good energy is (or is not) welcoming those who come into your home.

Upon opening the door, what is before your guests? Is it unconscious or ugly? Or is it a beautiful, calming, inviting scene?

Make this place an inviting statement of who you are as a family and of how you would like your friends to feel in your home.

Now use this entrance more often yourself, and enjoy!

No matter what else you do or how you do it, be sure to make your home a place to nurture yourself and step out of your usual daily busyness—to call a sweeter, more graceful life to yourself.

This reminds me that there is, in fact, a very high and wonderful energy called *grace*, which helps erase our old ways of thinking and being. Whenever we need help in releasing our old patterns, we can call upon grace to come into our life and assist us. Grace is a gift from a loving and supportive Creator to help us in this amazing process of transformation.

PERSONAL COMMAND

We can also command to leave our bodies and energy field anything that does not belong to us or serve us. The first step is to connect with it from a loving heart and give thanks for whatever lessons it brought to us. Once we have unified our consciousness with it without reservation, then we can command it to move to its next higher level of evolution.

Do this to help release unwanted physical things such as toxins, tumors, or disease. Use it to remove old programs or ideas from the past, any limitations, negative thoughts that have formed into many kinds of monsters—from the ghoul under your bed as a child to the good-looking woman you fear might someday steal your husband away. Also use this method for discarnate entities who have not gone on to the Light, undesirable or parasitic energies, or dark forces of any kind.

Sometimes these energies are hanging around and living off our energy just because we have not been educated that we have command over our personal space. We may also have deeper issues that must be resolved so that we can disengage from them. This is when we need to call on those with more expertise to help us.

We should be conscious of another aspect of our command as well. We can call positive, healing energy into all our interactions, including our food. It is part of the process of transforming our bodies to bless our food before we eat. Ask that your body accept and retain everything that nourishes and serves you and that all else leave your body.

I have found that personifying some of the beings and energies we're working with is very useful. This helps us become aware of exactly what and whom we're working with. It makes us feel that we can communicate with this part of ourselves.

For example, in meditation, allow an image for fear to emerge (perhaps it could be a young bully who is really scared inside). Call up an image of your masterful self, a radiant, gentle you whose heart is shining with light and love, or call upon an angelic being or a wise one who can help you bring forward your highest knowing.

I often call these images to come into a safe and beautiful inner place I have conceived in which to do my work. You can do this, too, by:

1. Sitting quietly.
2. Forming the image of a place that makes you feel absolutely safe, nurtured, at home, happy, and energetic—anything from a forest glade to a magical castle.
3. Providing it with everything you need to take care of yourself. It can have everything—a warm sheepskin to wrap up in and rest; a turquoise pool in which to do your cleansing; a beautiful room of violet flame for transmuting energies; a resident wise person to advise you; a magical laser beam for cutting away any limitations; a beautiful, flower-filled, restful space for your meditative work.

One of the characteristics of the new work we need to do is that it is much more about releasing and allowing than it is about any kind of processing and working through the lower energies. We have accumulated so much karma and negativity in our separation experimentation that we could be processing forever and ever if we choose that route.

What we need to do instead is to realize that the old game is over. We are no longer playing at that level. We must adopt the rules of the new game and move forward with them. It's like playing tug-of-war until we're exhausted because it's the only game we know to play with a big, long rope. We get injured, pulled through the mud, and angry at the other team. It takes opening our eyes to the larger possibilities and then a leap of consciousness to realize that everyone could work together on the rope and pull open the massive gate to an enormous, magical playground. Tony Stubbs suggests some new "rules" for a game that could be called "Whatever Makes Your Heart Sing!"

1. Does it bring joy?
2. Is it fun?
3. Does it serve the Light?[10]

This game has a wonderful winning conclusion for everyone involved. It is the ecstasy of returning Home to Source—of being in Oneness and harmony. Joseph Campbell has invited us for years to "follow our bliss." Barbara Sher has written several books that walk us gently and easily into what we have always wanted to do but didn't believe we could.[11]

SPINNING YOUR ENERGY FIELDS

You can also spin your energy fields. Remember that energy loves to flow and change, so put it to work to get things moving for yourself! I do it frequently. Begin with my way and then find your own most effective way to do it.

1. Think of your physical energy as a sparkling ball of whatever color feels right to you. I sometimes use a beautiful brown or green here. This ball is sitting still and gathering dust from what moves around it.
2. Now imagine that ball spinning and spinning, faster and faster,

until every bit of dust flies off it and all that is left is that radiant brown or green ball. The dust can fly off into a violet flame, which transmutes it.

3. Now think of your emotional energy as another ball. I sometimes see it as any shade of red. Spin it faster and faster in the same manner to dust it off and send the "dust" to the violet flame to become higher energy.

4. Do the same with mental energy, which I sometimes see as yellow.

5. Then do this with spiritual energy, which may be a deep blue or purple.

6. You can add an extra spin or two to all of them at once, so they become a blended rainbow of color, spinning together in harmony. Let this ball of vibrant color form a semipermeable membrane around you, to keep out all that is not beneficial or appropriate at this time yet allow in all that is beneficial.

When our physical, emotional, mental, and spiritual bodies are harmonized and in service of our wholeness, then we can move forward and evolve.

Actually standing up and doing physical spinning can also be very helpful:

1. Spin left to right, or clockwise, with your arms extended straight out from your shoulders, wrists relaxed.

2. You can make it easier to spin by moving up to the ball of your left foot, keeping it turning in place, while using your right foot to spin yourself around.

3. Start with seven spins and work up from there.

4. To keep from being bothered by the dizziness you may experience when you finish spinning, stand flat on both feet with knees bent and cross your hands in an X over your heart, breathing deeply.

You may want to put an image of yourself at the center within the four balls as you spin them. My sister Heron Wind, in *Spiraling into the Center*, puts it this way:

When we step out or, as is more often the case, fall out of our Center, we are swept away in the illusion of life. The Center is a point of balance, the meeting place of duality. The good and the bad dissolve into acceptance of and value for what is. The black and the white, hot and cold, light and dark all become important parts of the whole.

The Center is a balanced stance from which we can choose our next movement. The spiral path into this Center leads us from the experience of the outer world to the depths of our inner world. We spin inward toward the doorway of the universe, gaining wisdom as we move through an ever-deepening awareness of how expansive we really are. From the Center, we can move to the fourth dimension and beyond. From the Center, we are able to weave our lives in a conscious way and dream our greatest dreams into being.[12]

SEEING FROM THE PERSPECTIVE OF YOUR ESSENCE COLOR

Heron gave me another exercise of color and light one day. We were sharing about the challenges in our lives that so easily seem to pull us out of our higher functioning. We both agreed that to have the magic and power of a new way of being, each of us needs to be truly present in our lives. How often thoughts about the past or future pull us away from this, but a broader perspective can sometimes help. Heron offered this remedy:

1. Sit quietly and imagine that your essence has a color. Don't think about this or try to figure it out; just go deep within and see what color is there. It may or may not be a favorite color or one you would usually pick. Most people find it without too much trouble.

2. Then open to understanding that your essence *is* a color and that you can look out at your world from the perspective of this amazing color being. From this point of view, let your gaze move through your physical eyes with interest in and wonder at the denser reality of your physical body and the world around you. What does this new way of seeing show you? What kind of understanding does it bring you?

3. Remember to lift up into looking through the eyes of your essence color whenever you feel caught in a smaller, less useful perspective.

The attitude we hold when we are doing any of this clearing and releasing is very important. It's time to leave behind the judgmental categories of bad, terrible, and horrible as well as the attitude of hating anything we label this way. It's important to honor each energy that has contributed to our lives, even though it may be outdated, uninteresting, lacking in usefulness, and inappropriate for us at this point.

Everything in the universe has life and consciousness and, as such, is also in a process of moving back toward the Light and Oneness. Always honor the energies you are releasing by sending them into the violet light to be transmuted into higher energy. This assists them and makes sure that negative energies are not left around to hook up to us or others.

"Give them to God," a silver-haired teacher of mine used to remind me. If we try to destroy or repress or imprison any negative energies, they fight for their lives, just as we would. So make it easy on yourself and them by giving them a boost toward the Light.

Remember to use your smudges when doing this work. Lighting a stick of sage can help cleanse your aura of anything that does not belong to you at this time. Cedar has the quality of assisting with forgiveness and letting go of those things that drain your energy. Then it's wonderful to burn sweet grass to fill the cleansed space with positive, sweet, uplifting energy. Native American peoples and many others have used incense in their spiritual work in this way for centuries.

As you work with yourself in this amazing upliftment process, remind yourself often that *the means you use and the attitudes you carry are of utmost importance.* The key instruction, if you will remember, is that you cannot get to a particular place by behaving in the opposite way. You are moving toward lightness, joy, fulfillment of Creator's design, and a beautiful life. It is good to bring these kinds of energies into your practices.

As I mentioned in Chapter 11, most of us forget to use the laughter Creator gave us as an especially wonderful attitudinal tool for clearing ourselves of old patterns. It is remarkably helpful in that it causes our nervous system to release old patterns; then we can use that open space to program in the new and beautiful ways we choose to look at the world.

And remember, too, the powerful attitude of gratitude and appreciation.

"These are some of the things I can do and practice to get my feet on the ground of this new way of being!" I told Sparrow Hawk. "And I know I will find more as I set my intent to move into this new time gracefully."

"That's true," he said. "But don't forget to also ground yourself through your loving connections to Mother Earth. This will help stabilize you to walk comfortably in these new patterns."

"What strikes me most strongly," I reflected, "is all the help we do have available if we simply look within and around us. Although this transformation may have its challenging moments, it is a *natural movement* into a different level of being, as surely as adolescence and its accompanying turbulence move us into our adult lives. It is nothing to fear. And even the fears we may feel can be seen as natural emotions, urging us to wake up to what is happening and to begin to act consciously in the presence of the moment."

"Yes, it's amazing to think that we're the ones here to experience this great transformation—not only of ourselves but the whole of Earth and all Her children, not only for present Earthly realms but for All Our Relations through all of time," said Sparrow.

We are the rainbow children who will make the dreams and visions of our ancestors come true—a renewed Earth in touch with the Sky!

PART IV

BECOMING AN EARTH MAGE

The time has come for us to step into our role as Earth Mages. Mage is a word that conveys the magic that is possible for us now as we put our intention toward the ascendant renewal of our world.

In the past, magic was something done by only a special few, perhaps even in secret. The time has now come for each of us in the rainbow of humanity to become Earth magicians. Grounded in our love of Earth and one another, we must gather in committed circles and use our powerful spiritual technologies to become the new human beings.

This is the task we alive on Earth came to do. And it's time for us to do it. Our hearts will lead the way.

CHAPTER 16

LIFTING
OUR WINGS

We can deny the amazing possibilities that are before us
only by keeping ourselves ignorant of them.

It's obviously time to lift our wings and let the winds of Spirit lift us
into another and more beautiful level of life. Yet even the simple act of
lifting our wings may sometimes seem difficult. We may be frightened or
resistant, despairing or stubbornly angry, and feel like sitting cowed on
the ground. We may want to look only at the past and say, "None of
this ever got off the ground before, so why bother?"

Why bother? Because we have an opportunity to create something radiantly beautiful for ourselves and the children of generations to come,
for All Our Relations—a New Earth. And because, if we open our eyes
and hearts, evidence points directly toward the amazing possibilities before us and *our need to participate for their unfoldment.* We need to leave behind
our outmoded rationalism, our skepticism, our cynicism, and our feelings of defeat and step into an active involvement in the process. "Energy is neutral and travels the path of least resistance. Understanding
this brings to light the importance of the individual's power to shape
destiny and the future for not only the one, but also the many."[1]

Perhaps a few reminders of where we are in time and consciousness will
help. A beginning is to remember that demographic studies show that
nearly 40 percent of Americans today have ideas and values similar to

those this book espouses. We are not alone if we step out and make ourselves known. We have many inspiring examples toward which to look.

The scientific research on the full functioning of the heart tells us
that coming into a place of openness and appreciation in our hearts is
not some odd, esoteric practice. It's actually a sensible practice that plays
a major part in keeping us healthy, preventing heart disease, and harmonizing and strengthening our entire system.

It's not just some weirdo who possesses psychic or prophetic vision.
Even the CIA has been conducting experiments for years that are now
being made public under the name *remote viewing*. Normal people can
and do see in a psychic and visionary way, and this ability grows with
practice.

The use of sound, color, and light in healing is not just something
the leftover hippies down the block play around with. The profound usefulness of such alternative therapies is being documented in "legitimate"
studies by medical doctors.

Regeneration of lost limbs is no longer a fantasy. Simple changes in
the electrical charge around the stub, learned from lizards who regrow
their tails, seems to allow certain levels of regrowth.[2]

Modern companies are starting to understand the fabulous healing
power of herbs. Recently Saint-John's-wort preparations seem to be replacing some of the Prosac prescriptions, for one example.

Having a healthy and rewarding life at more than a hundred years old
is not unknown. People in many parts of the world have been doing it
all along. Even living to be several hundred years old is not unusual
among masters in India.[3] Now, modern science is catching up with the
mystical masters in the area of longevity and many other seemingly miraculous developments. Ben Bova gives us an extraordinary fifty-year time
line that shows how fast and furious technological developments have
come—including advances that would have been deemed impossible mere
months before they happened.[4]

Reports from those who have literally medically died and then been
resuscitated are giving a completely different sense of death than the
dark and terrible happening that had been a prevalent image of it. Most
of those who decided to return were aware that they had to make a difficult choice to come back. Their words tell of a world of light and

LIFTING OUR WINGS

beauty, peace and joy, in which they could happily have remained had it not been for things they needed to finish in their Earth bodies.

People with multiple personality disorders often show amazing ability to heal themselves in seconds. They may require glasses in one personality, have a serious health condition in another. Yet when they switch personalities, these symptoms disappear in an instant, only to reappear immediately when the personality in which they were originally experienced manifests again. This tells us something about inner abilities that we have not yet discovered in ourselves under normal circumstances.

Communication around the globe in seconds is not just some science fiction fantasy. It happens every second on the Internet. And prayer has been shown to help with healing at no matter what distance, even when the one praying is sealed in a Faraday cage to shield for electromagnetic energy.[5]

Warring and conflict have not always been the human way. Documentation of egalitarian groups that lived in peace and harmony are now easy to find in anthropological and archaeological research.[6]

Paul Stamets, one of the new Earth Mages called Bioneers (biological pioneers), has discovered that regular oyster mushrooms love oil and will clean up oil spills very quickly. They happily multiply all over the area, cleaning it up with remarkable precision, even under rocks and in hidden places. And the amazing thing is that they transmute this pollutant into edible mushrooms![7] I love this example because it reminds us of how many gifts Creator gave us that we have not yet discovered and begun to use. Too often we think we have to invent something new when we haven't tapped what is right in front of us.

In the same vein, another Bioneer, John Todd, designs living machines that purify waste by mimicking natural ecologies, understanding that in nature, there is no waste. Janine Benyus wrote a fantastic book called *Biomimicry*,[8] about wondrous inventions that mimic nature's profound wisdom. Anne Edey lives in Martha's Vineyard at Solviva farm and has designed a solar greenhouse that produces food all year round, by heating it with chickens and rabbits.[9]

People from every level of life are making a difference. Superstars are turning their attention to others. From the NFL football stars who work with United Way to Oprah Winfrey and the inspirational programs she

273

is spearheading through her television show, all of us are being invited to participate. Ocean Robbins, son of activist John Robbins, the renegade heir to the Baskin-Robbins ice cream fortune who renounced the family business to work for the environment, spent his early childhood in a one-room cabin on an island off British Columbia. At fourteen, he facilitated international youth summits on the environment in Moscow and Washington, D.C. At sixteen, he founded Yes!, an organization that leads a powerful new generation to environmental awareness.

Maharishi and his students have been practicing group meditation for several decades now. Studies show that when the percentage of Transcendental meditators reaches more than 1 percent in any city, crime, accidents, and violence fall by huge percentages, even when those numbers had previously been been rising rapidly.[10]

Drunvalo Melchizedek is working in a similar way with his students. They create energetic configurations over cities like Phoenix, and the pollution immediately drops.[11]

Recently I received other marvelous news from Drunvalo. He had attended a closed meeting in which the effects of something called "sacred water" were demonstrated.[12] It was brought by a Sufi master, representing a group of Sufis who had created it through sacred chanting. This unusual water miraculously cleaned up both chemical sludge and organic pollutants, and the resulting water was reported to be as pure as it was ten thousand years ago! The beauty of this is that it was created by spiritual practice, by vibratory "science." It gives us support for our own spiritual practice and the actual, real-world results that can come from it. These Sufi masters are Earth Mages par excellence![13]

These are just a few things I pull out of my immediate memory. Yet they encourage us to expand our minds about our possibilities and even our probabilities. Or perhaps I should say, they encourage us to reawaken to the truth of our magnificence and thus invite us to look at our intent and our priorities.

The universe in which you reside is magical and powerful. . . .
The key to tapping the wonders of your power and happiness

lies only in your ability to open your minds to the possibilities around you. When you choose to do this, you open the doors to endless opportunities and become the true co-creators with the Divine.[14]

Many of these examples reflect an Earth Mage level of working in the world. The individuals involved are all human beings, just like us. The difference is the focus of their attention and their empowered attitude. This is what it takes to lift our wings for the flight we are being invited to make.

OUR OWN HEART

I believe that the simplest and most profound place to begin is with our own heart. Transformation here not only leads to more courageous and powerful work in the world; it also supports the baseline of our own health, well-being, and energy level. Working with our heart is vitally important because the heart is not only an organ but a chakra as well and is included as a higher aspect in the functioning unit we have thought of as only our brain. Our heart has a kind of loving wholeness that invites us to function with love and connectedness rather than separation and divisiveness, whereas the brain tends toward a polarized mode in its function of sorting, categorizing, and storing experience. The Sacred Heart is not only our sacred center; it is the center of our power in the world.

The pivotal power of the heart is connecting directly to Source. This obviously goes beyond our normal perception of the heart as only an organ. Remember what Dawn Star teaches us about the location of our own Sacred Heart (see page 151) and the enormous power of this sacred center. Take time each day to focus your attention on this actual physical area as you quiet and ask for connection with Source. This will make a tremendous difference in how well your life works.

In the philosophy of the true Indian people,
Indian is an attitude, a state of mind.

Indian is a state of being, the place of the heart.
Allow your heart to be the distributor of energy on this planet;
allow your heart to bring in energy from Earth and Sky,
and send it out from your heart,
the very center of your being.[15]

In one of his workshops, Joseph Chilton Pearce shared about how the heart is part of the loop of decision making: the heart exhorts, and the brain informs.[16] As long as we two-leggeds were working in the arena of separation, we could disregard this invitation to wholeness. Yet as Spirit awakens within us and we choose to function at a higher level, we will more and more often listen to the heart's sweet calling.

Researchers at an organization called HeartMath[17] have given us a more specific sense of how to work with our hearts. They speak of the varying rate at which our hearts can beat—called heart rate variability (HRV). For instance, in a heart rate of seventy beats per minute, each beat will not necessarily be at the same rate (although there is a regular, minute variance with each breath). Lack of some variance means a stressed heart, and this stress echoes into every other organ and system in the body, because the heart is such a constant magnetic influence. Research shows HRV to be a better predictor of disease and illness than any other variable studied, such as overweight, smoking, and diet. Calming and regulating the heart balances the nervous system, reduces stress and disease potential, and boosts the immune system.

Here is a profoundly healing heart exercise that I have been doing and sharing with my students. First, you want to simply find your heart and your heartbeat; then we will work with the heart to calm and nurture it.

1. Place your open right hand directly over your heart. Do you know exactly where that most vital organ actually is? Touching your sternum, it lies under and slightly to the left of center, a couple of inches below the notch of your clavicles. Keep your hand there throughout the exercise.
2. Find the rhythm of your heartbeat. You will likely not feel it just with your hand resting over it, so you can do several other things. Try

gently pressing your left hand on the side of your neck up against your chin; when you feel the beat, put your more sensitive fingertips directly over the artery that beats there. You'll want to hold your breath as well, for as long as it is comfortable. This also emphasizes the heartbeat as you listen internally.

3. Stay with your heartbeat. Just "feeling your heart" in this way has a profoundly centering and balancing effect.

Here begins the most healing and transformative part:

4. Now that you have found your heart, close your eyes and imagine swirling the energy of gratitude and appreciation through it. Take a moment to think of a time in your life when you had absolute appreciation for something. It could be when you held your baby for the first time, when a particularly beautiful sunset inspired you, in a moment of numinous vision, or an especially lovely spring morning in your garden. Keep this grateful energy full and flowing around and around in your heart. It's good to do this where you can occasionally check a clock, because you can get the most benefit out of this by keeping it going for at least five minutes. In five minutes, the calming effect not only helps your heart but also begins to "tune in" the rest of your body.

5. This energy of loving appreciation and upliftment is, for me, the vital energy of life, and we seldom receive enough of it from those around us. Nurture yourself with this wonderful energy; bathe yourself in its warmth and richness.

6. As you fill your heart with this energy, recognize that this is the kind of energy that comes from Creator to give us life. Recognize this as the most beautiful energy from Source and one that we seldom acknowledge. As you continue swirling the energy, realize that Creator is sending floods of it to join what you have created by your own intention. You might imagine it as a never-ending bath of warm, wonderful energy streaming in . . . and flowing over!

7. Now, realizing that you have more than you can ever use, send this wonderful, supportive, uplifting energy streaming out to all that is around you. Give loving support and appreciation to everyone and everything, from the clothes on your body to your family, friends, and community and out to the farthest star!

8. Doing this for five minutes changes your internal environment for

six to seven hours. If you were to do this when you awaken, at noon, after dinner, and as you go to sleep, it would keep your heart in wonderful energy *all* day! And it would uplift all that is around you as well.

The master Jesus confirms and extends this heart practice:

> Nurture the heart. Strengthen the positive impulses of the heart through admiration and gratitude. Then begin each day by canceling the negative impulses of your body, your existence, and your surroundings through expressions of forgiveness. . . . Another practice to strengthen the heart is innocent perception [childlike, truthful, unedited]. Don't be obsessed with figuring out life before you live it.[18]

As you do these practices and time passes, you'll find that more and more people are choosing to live from this new level of being, and it is wonderful to connect with them. Their presence helps you disconnect from the old reality, which still has a strong hold. Yet you cannot escape the consensus reality by running away to a cave with a few of your friends. You are meant to be, as Jesus said, in the world but not of it— using your intent to transform your reality, which allows you to become a vibratory beacon for others. Whenever you sense that you are being dragged down into that old, outmoded way of thinking and being, use the telephone switchboard exercise I presented in Chapter 9 to unplug from the past and get reconnected to the new way of being.

CHILDREN OF THE COMPASSIONATE HEART

One of the most exciting and uplifting moments I have had lately has been in finding the following information about some very special children. Information about the new possibilities brought in by children born after 1986 comes together with the high masters' invitation to become as little children in order to step into the new world. Let me tell you about them.

Drunvalo Melchizedek, in another interview,[19] speaks of his excitement about the amazing children from around the world whom he is investigating. First, he reports about a group that has an unusual DNA pattern that makes them immune to *every* disease researchers have tested. The first boy who exhibited this new pattern was noticed because he was born with AIDS yet, by six years of age, showed no sign of it. Normal human DNA has sixty-four different patterns called codons, and in humans all over the world, twenty of these codons are turned on, and the rest of them are turned off (except for three that are the stop and start codes, much like a computer). They found out that this boy had *twenty-four* codons turned on. Researchers tested his cells with AIDS, cancer, and many other things: he was immune to them all. Now, UCLA, by watching worldwide DNA testing, estimates that 1 percent of the world's population (many of whom have had AIDS) have this new DNA pattern. This means that approximately 60 million people are a new kind of human by the old standards!

The elegance of it is that these children are simply making use of what is already there, previously unused. Scientists used to think that the extra codons were from an outlived past, but now they are seeing that they were very likely given to us for use in our future.

And here's the really incredible part. It is a specific emotional, mental body response—a waveform coming off the body—that is causing the DNA to mutate. People other than children are exhibiting the pattern! Drunvalo and Gregg Braden believe that the wave phenomenon has three parts:

1. The mind sees unity. It sees everything interconnected in all ways—nothing separate.
2. These people's being is centered in the heart—in the energy of Love.
3. They step out of judgment, polarity, and duality. These people seem to be in a state in which they see everything as One and are immersed in Love.

This means that a heart truly centered in Oneness transforms the human body. These children, lacking the extended life experience that programs normal humans into a belief in separation and dualism, find it easier to manifest some of our latent, magnificent possibilities. As I said in Chapter 10, a secure future may have more to do with our inner ability to resonate with the larger life around us than with bank accounts and material goods. The masters have long told us that the new bodies we will create will be under the direction of Love.

The other interesting thing is that many very aware people feel that AIDS and other challenging diseases have been created by humans to lower the population. A small number of people control more wealth and resources than many nations, and they too often use them in ways that reflect their greed and fear. In the early 1990s, the Rio de Janeiro Conference on Environment and Development (sometimes referred to as the Earth Summit) put out its report that we humans must pay primary attention to population control and to taking care of the environment or face planetary death within a decade or so. Our press in the United States was not even allowed to print the dire warning. Evidently those in power did not want to stop their companies' environmental damage for fear of losing money. Rather than cooperate and join with others, it seems some of these greedy and powerful people began campaigns to decimate the population with biological "warfare" and other means. If this is so, it is very interesting that Creator is now using AIDS as a bridge to total immunity in these children. It's very hopeful to think that these evil actions are backfiring!

Second, hundreds of children have been found in China who are super-psychic. These kids are 100 percent correct *every* time. For instance, researchers put one hundred of them in a room. Taking out a book and randomly pulling out a page, researchers would crumple the page up and stick it under a child's arm. These kids could read every word on the page. The response was flawless, test after test. The phenomenon didn't stop in China: now these children are being found in many places around the world!

Those being referred to in the United States as "indigo or blue children" may be from the same group: at least they have extraordinary abilities from birth. The sad part is that in America, we find these children wanting and often drug them in hopes of making them fit the norm. Instead, we should be investigating their amazing capacities and honoring their abilities with special support. Here is an important place for you educators and parents to do some powerful Earth Mage transformative work!

A fascinating part of the story, with profound implications globally, is that some of these children can either touch or simply think their way "into a computer" and retrieve information from any other computer in the world! The United States has had an ongoing and very angry investigation into how China and Russia have had agents "steal" some of our secret information. It turns out that in both countries, psychics have just picked up the information. The power of this is that *the time of secrets is over*. What one country has, all will have. It makes our global humanity and our Oneness real in a way that we may never have considered.

Many of the children in this group can read everything about any other human being, even from a photograph. One Mexican girl can look at even part of a person's body shown on a fragment torn from a picture and tell you everything about not only the person shown but also the person who took the photo—name, age, address, personal information, emotional issues, and so forth. We are becoming much like the dolphins, who, by sonar, know everything about the other dolphins. Now a dedicated teacher in Mexico is finding that he can train children who do not initially exhibit these abilities to develop them in a matter of weeks.

Others of these kids have varied extraordinary abilities. Several are reported to have levitated their toys over their crib as babies, enjoying playing with them in the air. One of these girls can even levitate other people now!

This group, like the immune children, must be centered in God-realized Oneness. For them, there is no separation, no Time and Space as we normally think of them. They are the unfoldment of prophecies about our stepping out of an old sense of Time and opening to the magnificent possibilities Creator has set within our very cells.

The implications for each of us are very profound. As more and more people on Earth exhibit these characteristics, we will eventually reach a critical mass, after which, it is very likely the phenomenon will spread instantaneously to all two-leggeds. In the meantime, it pays to do our own homework to hold compassion and appreciation in our hearts.

Another useful viewpoint about these events is the prophecy from many religious and spiritual traditions that the high masters will come again at this time. What I have come to understand is that these high masters will come again, truly, but not in the outer form we might have thought. They will come through us. *The masters will return as us,* through our learning to manifest in our own individual lives the principles they have offered us down through time. We will find and awaken this new "force" within us by discovering our own deepest truth and living it into the world rather than by watching someone else use it. The children are a demonstration of this.

HEALING WITH LOVE

This is a reminder of one of the principles by which we keep ourselves in total health. Since the heart commands the basic particles of which our physical body is built, then loving ourselves deeply is a real key to living long and well. I'm reminded of medical herbalist Richard Schulze's telling of a time when he had third-degree burns on his hand. When he showed a doctor this hand, which now looked like a mummified claw, the doctor wanted to do major surgery immediately. Richard protested that he felt he could heal the hand. He had healed himself and others of major injuries in the past—in his own body, he had rebuilt genetically faulty heart valves and healed a mangled knee. Based on this, he felt that a baseline of radiant health in the rest of his body, plus actively loving his hand, would work. To help him see the futility of this, the doctor simply picked the flesh off one of his fingers down to the bone, and pulled everything but the bone off his thumb. Yet Richard persisted in his faith. Hard work on his health and immunity, plus kissing and caressing and lovingly caring for his hand, brought it back almost 100 percent!![20] It was a miracle, yet a miracle attainable by us all if we can faithfully do the practices Richard did. His love commanded his body to rebuild the hand, and his body was healthy enough to support that process. Love can heal anything!

Amazing things *are* possible. As we Earth Mages open our hearts and minds to the larger possibilities, we open the way for even more miraculous things to manifest in our reality. Loving ourselves is a healthful way of living in more ways than one and certainly has to do with the quality of our lives as well as perhaps the "quantity."

You might like to read an interesting guidebook about people whose contemporary lives are lived in a kind of perfection that stimulated author John Randolph Price to call them the "Super Beings":

When your subconscious mind believes that you are all that God is *in expression*, it has no choice but to stop believing everything to be the contrary. The inner chambers of your mind will then be filled with the light of truth, and your whole outer world—beginning with your body—will become a perfect reflection of the light. Health, wealth, success, achievement, love and companionship, protection, strength and vitality, joy and order, guidance, individual freedom, and wonderful service to others will be yours.[21]

I hear many heartwarming stories about living at new levels. They are simple stories, yet powerful as examples of our changing ways of relating to ourselves and the world. Here are just a few, mostly in the words of those who shared them. Names and other details have been changed to protect the privacy of the individuals involved.

"Grace's Grief," from Jaimie

Almost five weeks ago, a dear friend of mine, Grace, returned from an out-of-town trip to find her husband of thirty years, Roy, dead in the basement. He had been killed accidentally from a head injury while working in his wood shop. He was only in his early fifties, and their two children are in their early twenties. This was an absolute shock that sent waves of agony across our whole community. Roy was a very quiet, peaceful, loving man who dedicated endless hours of volunteer time to the local Habitat for Humanity organization (he hadn't missed one day as shift supervisor on Saturdays for the past eleven years). He also ran the wood shop at a university arts department and had created many deep and warm relationships with his students there.

Grace was overwhelmed by grief, guilt, and loss. She was surrounded by her friends, family, and community, who offered her constant support that first week or two. Grace did everything that a person "should" do in a time like this: she mourned and grieved; she meditated and practiced yoga and relaxation; she wrote tirelessly in her journal; she revisited the spot where she had discovered her husband's body and burned sage to purify the basement, then rearranged and painted it. She cried and reached out to friends, and her sons were enormously supportive. She spoke eloquently and movingly at Roy's memorial service, which was the most incredible service I have ever attended. She then elected to go away for several days to heal and to return to her home to look at what should come next.

Grace and I meditate together every Monday, and she said this past week that something very odd was happening. She said that although it's been only a month, she has felt a persistent sense of peace coming over her surrounding the loss of her husband. She had begun to look at all the things that had transpired between her and Roy before his accident and also between him and all his primary relationships. There were many instances of completion and of love's being expressed when it might not normally have been verbalized. Their younger son "just happened" to walk by (at the university) as Roy said aloud to a friend how very proud he was of both his sons and how much he loved them. Coincidence? About one week before the accident, Grace told Roy how much she loved him and how much she appreciated his endless support over their thirty years together for her peace and justice work and how special was his love for the family. This sentiment was then reciprocated.

She also said they had spent the past month rearranging the house over and over again because she just had this "sense" that they either needed a change or that change was in the air. (Little did she know just how big a change was in the air!) She told me that as she's thought about it, she's realized that on a subconscious level, Roy was ready to go: he was expressing love and completion with everyone he needed to.

Grace's sense of physical loss is still very real for her, and she says that this sense of peace doesn't fit with her pictures of where a widow should be in the first month after her husband's accidental death. She said she is afraid people will think she didn't love him if her grief-stricken days are so limited. A very interesting addition to this story is that Roy's sister lives in a spiritual community in California. She arranged for the entire ashram to do a two-day ceremony of chanting, designed to allow Roy's spirit to let go of this existence and go to the next, and also to heal the family's grief. After the two days of chanting, one of the women in the ashram told Roy's sister that she had walked to the stairway and there stood a being of light directly in front of her that simply said, "Thank you," and then disappeared. This story was not related to Grace until she had already been receiving the feelings of peace and acceptance throughout the week.

I told Grace to quit worrying about other people's judgment about her grief process. After all her spiritual and therapeutic work over so many years and years, I said that we should *hope* that our work comes to our aid in times of overwhelming change and personal tragedy. It seems to me that her dedication to a spiritual life is showing the fruits of her labor as she gains a sense of peace surrounding such an incredible loss.

"GRANDDAD'S GIFT," FROM ROSS

Speaking of death, here is a personal anecdote from my friend Ross about the power of ritual and prayer in life:

My spiritual mentor was my grandfather Paul. He was a very simple man who spent most of his life behind a team of horses and was the only "grown" man in my life who would hold my boyish hand. He taught me that a good Christian not only tithes 10 percent of his or her money but also 10 percent of his or her land. He always left hedgerows and fallow fields for "God's creatures." I wish more Christians felt this way.

Shortly after my family moved to California in 1983, I fell asleep on the couch and had a lucid dream. In the dream, Granddad came to me on the couch and told me that he had to go but that he would always be there to help me when I needed it. I was awakened from the dream by a phone call from my uncle telling us that Granddad had passed away half an hour ago. This changed my life! Granddad's final and most overwhelming gift was that direct connection of spirit, and he still visits me from time to time to give me counsel. Yet the loss of Granddad was tremendous—a pain that I was never able to get over as the years passed.

In 1995, shortly after my wife and I were married, I decided that I needed to deal with this lingering, twelve-year grief. Every time I thought of Granddad, it brought a pain that choked me up and affected my ability to function as a healthy adult. I felt that a ritual needed to be performed, so we packed some sage and headed down to Granddad's farm, so we could visit Grandma and I could purge myself.

After hiking to a particular spot along the creek where I remembered going with Granddad on several occasions, I made my sacred circle, sat in the middle, and began to pray. After giving thanks to the Four Directions and to the Great Spirit, I began to give thanks for Granddad and all he had shown me about being a "true" human being. I remembered the good things and made an oath to honor his spirit by honoring the land that he loved and taught me so much about.

Then I brought the grief to the surface and let out a great cry. At that exact moment, a violent windstorm swept over us, and an owl flew out of a nearby tree and headed west away from our position. I vowed to let go of the pain and blew the pain from my lungs and into the sacred sage that I was burning. When I had finished letting the pain out, I released the ashes of the sage into the nearby stream to float down the River of Time. My wife was witness to the ritual and can verify its truth.

Since that day, I have had only good thoughts of my granddad, not painful; and I know that he is always with me, giving me guidance as I need it. I plan on doing a similar ritual about my father on the first anniversary of his death this August.

> Ritual doesn't make mystery happen. It helps us see and experience something which is already real. It does not create the sacred, it only describes what is there and has always been there, deeply hidden in the obvious.[22]

"Spirit Communion," from Kathy

I'm glad to share this story about Grandpa; it is a wonderful tribute to him. I loved him very much, and his support was very important in those early days when the Spirit world was opening its doors to me. I am a Dreamer, able to sense the world of dream, vision, and Spirit easily. This moment in my life was a very important part of my learning.

My grandpa died twelve years ago today. At the moment of his death, I was reading a book in bed. I suddenly threw the book to the floor and began to have a deep, intimate conversation with him. All the images of our times together resurfaced, and we shared the most lovely poignant moments. As soon as these inner memories ended, the phone rang. After a few minutes, my dad called to me, saying that Grandpa had died. It had happened at the very moment when his spirit began communicating.

"He Walks!," from Norma

I was conducting a small choir that had just completed an overly long church service. One of the members had a touchy lower back, and as he moved to stand up, it was clear that he was in great pain. He froze, half standing, leaning over the chair in front of him. "I can't move," he muttered, and simply lowered himself back into his chair.

Instinctively I asked another singer who had been sharing Attunements[23] with me as a client to help out. After asking permission from all of the spiritual Higher Selves involved, a small group of singers familiar with, or at least supportive of, spiritual healing gathered around. I let myself be led by those healing spirits working through me. They directed me to hold my hands near the base of the man's spine and to have another person hold her hands at his knees. We remained there for about fifteen minutes, with energies clearly flowing among us, through him, and also in a circular, encompassing motion through all of those gathered around. Suddenly the energetic current changed and then stopped.

"How is that?" I asked him.

He responded somewhat incredulously, having never before "felt" energy without anyone's physically touching him: "There was energy in my spine, but you weren't touching me, were you?"

"No," I replied, "none of us was actually touching you. How do you feel now?"

He slowly stood up, testing the result for a few moments by standing and then moving his legs and walking around. With his sense of humor intact, he called out *"He walks!"* and looked as thrilled as he was dumbfounded by the results.

Although he claims not to understand it all, he continues to comment on this event as a miracle, often joking about it in tones used by TV evangelists. The story passed through the choir, and those trained in Attunement were often called upon by others in times of emotional or physical need.

Do you have an inspiring story like this? If you do, sit down and write it out or tell it to friends. We all need the support of such inspiration. You might also want to submit it to the Earth Mages section of my Web site, which will be used to gather and share stories of the magic we are doing and seeing around us.[24]

These stories remind me of a talk I recently heard about the changes in science in the recent past. When Albert Einstein's theory of relativity was brought forward, many resisted it, feeling that it would invalidate everything that had come before it. This didn't prove to be so. We still use more common science in the usual realms in which most of us work. Yet his theory expanded the parameters of our knowing and gave us new ways of thinking about many fields beyond mathematics. Now there are many new theories that extend beyond what he has offered. These do not invalidate what he gave; they simply extend it into other levels. And the physicists and others who are doing cutting-edge research are becoming some of our most articulate mystics. These same kinds of amazing leaps in our ability to be fully human are now taking place.

We can deny the amazing possibilities that are before us only by keeping ourselves ignorant of them.

———

Awakening to a new level of being human, ascending the vibratory scale, embodying Spirit fully doesn't mean that we have to fly off and sit on a cloud somewhere. It means bringing the true power and gifts of our humanity into action right where we stand, right now. It's about uncovering new abilities that naturally move us forward more than about leaving something behind. As with the toys of our babyhood, which we abandon as we grow into new levels of play, we will surely leave some things behind. Yet I sense that in the joy of our present moment's expanded experience, we will hardly think of that loss as sacrifice. Or perhaps we will learn to think of sacrifice as an elder taught me: *sacrifice* is the leaving behind of that which you no longer need in order to awaken something new and timely in your life.

An elegant example is a woman high up on the corporate ladder who wanted a family but "didn't have time." She "accidentally" got pregnant and realized that there was no way she could put her precious baby in a day-care center at six weeks old in order to get back to work after her maternity leave. She left her corporate life in the big city and moved to a small rural town upstate. Following her heart, she began to make baby food to take the place of the awful stuff she found on the market. She used fresh organic products and made it with loving care. Soon people around her were asking her to make some for them, and she eventually ended up with a tremendously successful and lucrative cottage industry making this healthful baby food. And all the while, she spent her days with her daughter at home. It was not totally easy. She faced challenges for sure. Yet she let her heart set her priorities, and what opened before her was very beautiful.

CHANGE OF HEART

Such changes are not made with the intellect. They are not made through "shoulds" and "musts." They are not initiated by external action. They are begun and supported by a true change of heart. Dawn Star speaks to us so clearly about this. In *Love without End*, we are told about the minute particles that represent the convergence of the Invisible and the visible, the Unmanifest and the manifest. *These most fundamental particles, the building blocks of what becomes real in our world, are at the command of the sacred aspect of our hearts, the higher Love.* These particles respond to a magnetic field, and the heart is our magnetic center.

This makes it obvious why it is so important to truly know the desires and intent of your heart. Those intentions are the ones that unfold as the reality of your life. So look within yourself and see what is there. Perhaps old programs, traumas, or outmoded beliefs are setting the patterns. Choose something different and your life will unfold in accordance with it. Be sure, as well, to honor and affirm the intentions that are working!

It is our challenge to ourselves to learn this new, magical, graceful, and easy way of doing things—by being in a different way. And the key—the basic skill—is *silence* within the heart, whose magnetic energy attracts what we need without force or effort. When we attune ourselves to our heart center and thus connect to the wisdom of Source and our own higher selves, then we will receive almost unbelievable rewards. "When one is attuned to that power ... life will be filled with great blessings, broader understanding, and conscious immortality."[25]

ETERNAL LIFE

This just happens to bring us to consideration of what perhaps seems an extreme possibility—immortality. Leonard Orr says something about immortality that is important to me as a baseline for this discussion:

> The goal of eternal life is not perpetual longevity, but the present time quality of personal existence in spirit, mind and body. Aliveness produces more aliveness.... To the extent that people realize their personal divine energy and love, everlasting life becomes more attractive than personal extinction.[26]

Jesus, in Glenda Green's book, reminds us that death is necessary only as a clearing of false identities and outmoded programs in our lives.[27]

You might notice in yourself any resistance to thinking about this subject. When I first felt stimulated by my experience with brother Sparrow Hawk to begin considering it and reading more about it, I felt an odd but considerable discomfort with the idea or even the need for the idea. Given my more enlightened understanding of the passage we call death, I was no longer fearful of it and felt it was natural and right. My only question was about the quality of our lives before we leave this body and whether we need all this sickness and deterioration before we do.

Yet something in me kept wanting to connect the experience of the Ghost Dancers lifting up into communion with those who had gone Beyond to the idea of immortality. After much contemplation, I've come to this sense of it: *When we become truly and fully human, which to me means balanced and totally functioning in both body and spirit, then we step out of Time.* Access to all Time and Space is the reward of that advancement. It may be a natural evolution that will lead to what is termed *transfiguration,* the ability to dematerialize and rematerialize the human body consciously without the process of dying (and thus needing to be reborn). When we learn to love, forgive, and allow, we may find the lightness that permits this outcome. This may be a wonderful result of creating our Lightbodies. For more information, several interesting books are now available: *Why Die? A Beginner's Guide to Living Forever,* by Herb Bowie;[28] *Immortality: How Science Is Extending Your Life Span and Changing the World,* by Ben Bova;[29] and *The Complete Ascension Manual,* by Joshua David Stone.[30]

Consideration of these possibilities unshackles our imaginations and may open enormous reserves of energy and creativity. It certainly seems worthy of our attention. It makes sense to me that the only way to immortality and transfiguration is total clarity and purity, radiant health and well-being, as well as an identification with our spiritual beingness rather than the aspect of us that is a fragile and time-bound structure.

> When you know you are immortal, you simply are too free to control, and can jump any fence the agendas of man may erect. Therefore, the true understanding of immortal life has been greatly suppressed. . . . You have only one life, and it is forever. How your eternal life unfolds is entirely according to your love. Where your love is, there you will be also. As your love is, so will you be.[31]

AGELESSNESS

These thoughts certainly lead us to consider an experience of agelessness and youthing, and the self-caring that helps create them. Even if we consciously choose to leave our body (or to transfigure it) to transition into another plane of existence, it seems that living fully and well, as long as we choose, is a valuable enough goal to be well worth seeking. We often shy away from this because it may not be "spiritual" or "graceful." To me, this youthfulness is much like the concept of beauty: if it is sought in outward ways—with fad diets, makeup, surgical enlargements and tucks—then it is a kind of denial. Yet we all know those who radiate beauty of a different sort—a beauty that comes from within. This true beauty is certainly worth attaining and a natural goal that every person seeks by the very truth of his or her highest nature; it is what each of us deserves. Similarly, if we wish to be "young again" to avoid maturing and keep from revealing our deterioration outwardly, we are kidding ourselves. But to do our homework—the purification and practice that lead to life radiant and everlasting—that is a different thing. And in the same way as beauty, it is a worthwhile and natural yearning to come home to the truth of ourselves and our magnificence.

PROSPERING

I also want to briefly address prosperity and thriving. Too often people get confused and think that being poor is the way to be spiritual and pure. Most of us who have been poor know it doesn't have much to do with anything, except a lot of stress and deprivation. Voluntary simplicity and moderation are a different story.

It is my sense that when we bring ourselves into harmony, when we practice and use the deep principles our spirituality places before us, we will have very abundant lives; we will truly prosper and thrive.[32] Our lives will be, by our own choices, simpler, yet much happier and more fulfilling. Rather than being destructively addicted to ever greater consumption, we will learn to take only that which we can love; otherwise, things own us. What truly nurtures us will be given priority through our loving intent. We will rediscover the richness of health and family and community, of being together and caring about each other.

When we learn to live in balance, we will become the inheritors of the New Earth. It is my goal, and I consider it my new level of work, to devote myself to the prospering and thriving of All My Relations. When that is fully manifest, we will be living on the New Earth.

A NEW EARTH

Think of waking up on a spring morning, when a warm wind has come in overnight that caresses you gently as you step outside to draw in the fragrance of blossoming flowers. Birds are singing an ecstatic song in the sacred groves nearby and in the burgeoning green around you. It has rained in the night, and everything glistens. Your heart is light and filled with gratefulness. You know that this is a day when you will continue with a project that you absolutely love—maybe even solving one of its more interesting challenges. As you walk across a pure and rushing stream to begin your day, you know something beautiful is coming.

Although it may not necessarily look like this everywhere, every day, this is the feeling of upliftment and joyful aliveness and purity that I call the New Earth. We will live in flowering green, with life singing and thriving around us. Healthy and fully alive, we will dance our way through our days, offering our individual gifts and being together in harmony. Our challenges will not mean suffering and deprivation but stimulation and excitement. And our victories will be shared with a circle of loving friends. New technologies that are clean, quiet, and sustainable will allow our days to be quieter. Our hearts will be at peace.

Dawn Star speaks of it in more amazing terms, regarding a city in Mexico:

Walk with me through this age of the future. The city shines in all its glory, but the metals are of types we know not. Loving hands have rebuilt the parkways, have paved the streets, have rebuilt the temples[;] ... once more the city is filled with fountains, and parkways are wire-netted for the birds of rare plumage and those who sing to enchant the listener[;] . . . here are buildings unlike those we fashion, yet they have a breathless beauty. Here people dress in materials we know not, travel in manners beyond our knowledge, but more important than all this difference are the faces of the people. Gone is the shadow of fear and suffering, for man no longer sacrifices, and he has outgrown the wars of his childhood. Now he walks full-statured toward his destiny—into the golden age of learning.[33]

Holding a strong, clear, and loving picture of your sense of the New Earth will help bring it about. Stepping into your power and taking spiritual action for yourself and All Your Relations is the only game in town.

This time, the journey is OUR journey. It is up to us now. We must learn the truths and live by them. We are being held accountable now for the knowledge that has been delivered to us, and we must integrate these truths into every aspect of our lives. We are the Ascended Masters of tomorrow.[34]

We are the ones who will re-member/embody the grace and magnificence and wholeness that are our birthright—radiant health rather than dis-ease, resonant aliveness rather than deterioration, abundant supply rather than want, prosperity and thriving rather than fearful competition and conflict, and transfiguration/upliftment of our bodies to a new, resonant level of being human.

It's time to lift our wings . . .

CHAPTER 17

TOGETHER, WE FLY

Lifting ourselves to the level of Spirit and wholeness, we come to our conflicts and challenges with a much different energy.

It is how we are living Spirit into the world that counts.

I was meditating about my sense that every one of our challenges on Earth today are challenges of relationships, when Sparrow Hawk came through to dialogue with me.

"Yes," he said, "the most intensely burning edge of spirituality we face today concerns relationships. They are, in a word, dysfunctional—at almost every level I can perceive—and they affect our quality of life so acutely."

"In order to awaken ourselves fully, to *embody* Spirit at the level that I've been discussing in this book, we must shift this aspect of our lives, and shift it radically," I said. "It is easy to see how basic it is to everything, from our families to our environment."

"Let's look at a primary principle regarding all this," Sparrow Hawk suggested. "The One Spirit lives in, through, and as everything in the universe. That obviously includes our two-legged family and creates a Oneness among us. Too often we judge and separate ourselves from others rather than joining with them to work things out. In personal relationships, we often withdraw to separate rooms and live with cold distance. A more productive solution would be sitting down at the living room table to join in working toward the highest intention for everyone concerned."

"Yes, and in business, we make lawyers rich through litigation rather than working through mediation for mutually useful outcomes. Among cultural and racial groups, we often make the ignorant mistake of assuming that Spirit and goodness live in us but not the other. Among nations, we spend more money on fighting and warring than we do on caring for people."

Sparrow nodded in agreement and went on to say, "It's vital for us to heed the hard lesson learned by the Ghost Dancers before us: *that hatred and divisiveness cancel the magic, and we stay in the old world of conflict.* It has been so easy for us to point the finger at the other person, the other race, the other nation, the corporate giants, ad infinitum. Yet that never solves the problem."

"That's why it is so important to practice, in every aspect of our lives, taking unified action to meet our enormous challenges and to hold everyone concerned in the Light," I offered.

Sparrow Hawk deepened my understanding by saying, "Each of us on Earth shares in the history and karma that two-leggeds have created over time. Each person, according to his or her needs for learning and his or her own development, takes on a part of the problem to transform. The people who seem to be doing the most damage are those who can make the most difference as they see an illumined way of being in the world. Therefore, we must hold them in our hearts, pray for them, and send them uplifting energy more than anyone else. We cannot divide ourselves, even from those we judge as the problem. If we do, we lose the incredible power that Oneness helps us magnetize. We hurt and limit *ourselves.*

"And we surely must drop both our prejudice and the reverse prejudice it generates. Our clan, race, color, or creed can no longer be primarily important. For unless we all walk over the Rainbow Bridge together, none of us will walk over it!"

"And it's certainly not about 'becoming' Native American or Hindu or Tibetan; or about going to the Black Hills, the Ganges, or the high temples in the Himalayas," I rejoined. "Although these peoples have

much to offer in ancient wisdom and their lands are wonderfully inspiring, merely having a different skin or culture has little significance
at this point. There are wise and kind and loving people in every tribe,
race, or cultural group. *It is how we are living Spirit into the world that counts,*
not the color of our skin or the location of our homeland. We must begin to honor, rather than deny, the power and beauty and love in our
hearts."

"You are so right," Sparrow said. "It's not about being someone else
or going to a 'spiritual' place on Earth. It's about each individual's standing grounded in Earth and Spirit right where he or she is—becoming a
hollow bone, joining together in Oneness, and offering the gifts Creator
continually gives us."

It's good to understand some of our Native history in relation to this.
Native peoples in this country still face the same challenge as when the
Europeans first began to gain power on this land: that of unity rather
than fighting among themselves. Unity of tribes on the Eastern Coast
would have changed the face of history. Later, had the tribes been able to
gather around Tecumseh and create a unified stand in the Appalachians,
the new nation in America would have had to deal with them differently,
eventually making them a part of the union rather than being able to
take their lands and subjugate them. Had the Pueblos been able to keep
from fighting among themselves after Popé's rebellion, they could have
kept a territory and perhaps created a powerful yet peaceful nation.

During the time of the Ghost Dance, several opportunities arose to
create more unity among tribal and white people alike. A young Sioux
woman who escaped the horrible murder of her people at Washita was
given a vision of creating a dance to unify enemy tribes and even include
whites. This girl, who hid in the water and breathed through a reed to escape the sabers and guns of those who murdered all her people, had the
courage and spirit to walk away from the bloody bodies of her family
and begin what came to be called Drum Dream Dance. The dance was
designed to be given away from one tribe to the next, each inviting its rival or enemy to come and learn the new way. Even whites were eventually

invited and were impressed with the power of this visionary dance. The drum she was shown to make and use has come down through the evolution of that original dance as the modern powwow drum, around which intertribal groups gather in every part of the land.

John Wilson, who began the formal Native American Church, learned of the medicine plant peyote at a Ghost Dance in Oklahoma. One of the basic tenets of this church is that at these gatherings, all attendees are brother and sister. Peyote's spirit continues to this day doing more to unify tribal peoples in the Americas than any other thing I know. Omer Stewart, in his historical look at peyote religion, concurs:

> Peyotism has been a unifying influence in American Indian life, providing the basis for Indian friendships, ritual, social gatherings, travel, marriage, and more. It has been a source of comfort and healing and a means of expression.... [A]nd it has resulted in one of the strongest pan-Indian movements in the United States.[1]

Today, even though the casinos seem a bit odd to some, reservation gambling is like the return of the buffalo to the native peoples in the prosperity it is bringing. Tribal people have faced prejudice and corruption since the early reservation days as they attempted to make a thriving life for themselves. Now they have found something that is working for them. Yet these nations' rights to gambling are being challenged, so that once again, natives face the test of coming into solidarity. My hope is that we can work together and share with one another in a way that creates prosperity for all.

In all our lives, the issues of race and cultural prejudice, as well as reverse prejudice, must be faced. They are an ugly blot upon our land. Red, white, black, yellow, and métis[2]—the challenge is to unify and support one another, without making that solidarity an angry barrier against yet another group.

———

White Buffalo Woman encourages us to enlarge our lives to include all levels of Life, because we are here to live in many worlds, although most of us are conscious of only one: the physical, the external. Our holy Elder Sister calls us, over and over again, to awaken ourselves into the fullness of who we truly are—the richness of our total being, inclusive of and yet far greater than the simply physical. Hers is the same clarion call that has come to us down through the ages and for which we now receive enormously supportive Light and energy.

In sharing the lighting and smoking of the Sacred Pipe, she tells us:

This, your individual human life, like the single flame that burns this twig, is sufficient to light a great fire. As long as the love that burns within you is turned toward self-centered pursuits, it will remain tiny like this flame. Remaining tiny, it will bring you no joy. Eventually, in the swirling winds of spirit, it will be extinguished. But when you are in harmony with the Great Spirit, your flame of love is fanned by those same spirit winds. You are in love with the very purpose of life! You light the fire of love in all you meet. You know the purpose of your walk through this world, and you know why the Great One gave you a life flame: not so that you could keep your tiny flame to yourself, loving what you need only, but so that you could give it away, and with the fire of your love, bring consciousness to Earth.[3]

In thinking of all we meet, it is easy to slip into thinking only of human people, when all around us are the other nations we tend to take for granted, ignore, or feel separate from—four-leggeds, wingeds, green-growing ones, and so on. These beings are clearly both God's creation and also our intended partners in life; it was not a mistake of Creation that we are in this order of life. Creator gave us these animals and others as well as the lessons going on all around us. We need to face the issue of genetic engineering and the haughty, ignorant stance it takes about the rest of our family on Earth. We are standing on a precipitous and dangerous edge when we judge that we can "correct" what we assume to be God's mistakes, in others or in ourselves.

UNITED WE STAND

We need to touch one another—physically, emotionally, and spiritually. The communion, the Oneness, the transformation we seek on this Earth plane will not be found in separation. Yes, we will certainly seek our own connection with Source through immersion in silent time and do our homework on our own personal issues. Yet we cannot experience the fullness of our daily lives in isolation. That must be found in common union—in community.

I'm reminded here of some of the things my colleagues Tim and Josie report seeing in Brazil. People there donate their time to two-year apprenticeships of hands-on healing, guided by spirits of the ancestors. Once they are certified, they give away their touch for the healing of their community. And miraculous things are occurring! Miracles abound— from the healing of simple illness by "presence" to the work of those who become surgeons without anesthesia. It is the kind of thing most people here can't even fathom, yet the openness and passion, the loving hearts and willing hands of the people there are doing miracles for one another. Spirit and love are waking up in the churches there, and members are actively doing work to alleviate the suffering of those less fortunate than they are, providing a real safety net for those who live on the edge of survival.[4]

This makes me think of the Hindu symbol for those who are healers: a hand with a compassionate human eye in its palm. I believe that much of the actual healing we need will occur as we place our hands upon each other and ask Creator to bring Oneness, and thus wholeness, healing,[5] and in the end, holiness into our bodies and our lives. The medicine we need will never lie in getting smaller or more exclusive; it lies in the direction of unity, expansion, inclusiveness, and caring. By reaching out through our arms and hands, we have the ability to bring the energy of our hearts to bear in a manner that restores wholeness.

Too often here in the United States, we assume that someone else will take care of anyone in need. After all, don't we pay enormous taxes to do just that? Won't insurance take care of those who are sick? Can't Medicare or Social Security take care of my aged parents? Doesn't the government handle the homeless and the Salvation Army the needy? Shouldn't the Department of Agriculture make sure that our soil is healthy so we have enough to eat? Won't religious leaders bring us all the enlightenment we need? Well, the answer that is becoming unavoidable is, "No, *they* won't handle it."

The problems of our people, whether homeless, cold, and hungry on the streets or middle-class people with kids killing one another in schools, are not being solved the way we are trying to go about it—by hoping someone else will take care of it. Social Security, even if it is still around in a few years, doesn't keep up with inflation. Insurance is getting so expensive, no one can afford it; this is partly due to our depending more and more on someone else to "fix" us when we are sick rather than using the nutrition, lifestyle changes, and love we have available. We must open our eyes, unveil our hearts, roll up our sleeves, take a stand, and commit ourselves to the kind of spiritual action that makes a difference.

Part of the lesson of the Brazilian healers is exactly this: they didn't wait for their government or the new age or some new material or spiritual technology to bring healing into their lives. They honored the visions of their hearts and gave their time and energy to develop the gifts Creator has provided. Had more of us in the seventies been willing to take a stand on clean energy and real nurturance for our children, on organic produce and our own health practices, life would be very different today. As much as I have spoken of extraordinary means for our awakening, we can't assume that is where the action is. Almost anything extraordinary that comes to us will do so because of who we are and what we do today, and the power we generate and magnify by working together.

Sometimes the loving connection can be about simply listening—about being what I call a "fair witness." This means coming fully into present time and heartfelt openness to be with another person—to let that person be seen in his or her process without judgment. In the words of the wise medical doctor/healer Rachel Naomi Remen, "When we are seen by the heart we are seen for who we are."[6] It might be thought of as "quality time." Often we feel too busy to give another person this kind of time, or we are distracted when we do offer to listen. Remen has a beautiful way of speaking about this, which she has developed from years of counseling cancer patients:

> Listening creates a holy silence. When you listen generously to people, they can hear truth in themselves, often for the first time. And in the silence of listening, you can know yourself in everyone. Eventually you may be able to hear, in everyone and beyond everyone, the unseen singing softly to itself and you.[7]

JUDGMENT SEPARATES

Each of our souls has come to Earth for experience. That experience is the basis of our human foibles. None of us knows the soul world of another; none of us can see the full working out of all the challenges we face, the falls we take, or the suffering we encounter or engender in our eternal unfoldment. We often forget to respect the power of the lessons we learn in this process and instead judge ourselves and others.

Judgment is the mental act of separating ourselves from our deeper selves or from others and then assuming we can see what is correct for them, what is right for the world. It is not only a very arrogant, foolish, and negative way of thinking and behaving; it is also hurtful to the one who judges as well as to the one judged. Kindness and forgiveness, on the other hand, bring rewards for both parties.

We can certainly be discerning. Discernment, based in a heartfelt sense of what is appropriate for us personally, is a momentary experience that changes with the changing situations in which we find ourselves. Listening deeply within helps us discern the meandering path with heart that leads us to our fulfillment.

Too often these days, we find numerous and seemingly sufficient reasons not to share our love, and thus we lose opportunities to bring more consciousness into our daily lives. Whether it be race or color or tribe or class or locale—we find ourselves excluding others. The cycle of victimization and violence has become too much a part of us, and having been victimized ourselves, we, in turn, seek to victimize others. Tribal and other subjugated peoples have major challenges in this area. A woman named Nancie, in focusing on the white buffalo calf, Miracle, a few years ago, brought through these thoughts:

> She [Miracle] is concerned about healing the spiritual wounds of Native Americans. She talks about the spirit of hopelessness that is among today's natives who are living on the reservations, and says it's a time for a very cellular, generational, ancestral type of healing ... going all the way back to when the vision of White Buffalo Calf Woman's presence first became manifest. Her suggestion is that there is a real need to let go of all the repression and all the belief systems about being repressed. It's not about going into denial about those things, but to acknowledge the pain, to release it, and to begin to move forward. She says these people have tremendous gifts they're not in touch with. They need to be part of what's going on here. She says she comes to remind them of their part in this sacred circle. And it's time to return now.... Native Americans need to understand the strength of their belief systems and to begin working in a co-creative way with that aspect of themselves, because they can create a new way of being; they have a way that needs to be incorporated in the world.[8]

What would work is for all of us to stop criticizing and separating ourselves from one another and, instead, pray fervently for one another's full potential and beauty to be expressed. Yet continually running through all our other challenges is devilish judgment. For some reason, we humans feel we are wise enough to judge others. We use our small-minded standards and haughtily decide the worth or goodness of another person or group. How very foolish! What heavy and unnecessary burdens we are shouldering by doing this. Rachel Naomi Remen puts it this way: "The life in us is diminished by judgment far more frequently than by disease. Our own self judgment or the judgment of other people can stifle our life force, its spontaneity and natural expression."[9]

Great teachings throughout history tell us that whatever we send out, we receive back at the very same time. We make war on others through conflict, anger, judgment, negative energy, and exclusion yet think we will find peace even though we're living in a war zone of our own making. Such a strange way to proceed! How harshly judgment comes back upon us when we presume to judge others.

The energy we extend is immediately perceived, even though this may occur on levels that are less than conscious. Our harsh, angry energy sent to someone who does something foolish or pushy in traffic might be just enough to send him over the edge in his life. We cannot know what events and forces have shaped his life and his day, what challenges and traumas are weighing upon him. Rather than the barbs of anger that we usually sling, we might just say, "Oops, that didn't work very well. That person must need some love and light in his life—to feel better, be more functional, be more courteous, be more awake to what is happening around him. I'll just send him some good energy. And thanks, Great Spirit, for the opportunity to extend and grow my love."

When you are standing in a committed circle of Love, the love bounces right back to you, making your day better. And it is certainly received by the one to whom you sent it. Perhaps, instead of tipping someone over the edge, you might help bring about a lifting of mood and spirit that will make a real and positive difference in her life.

Which would you rather do?

Which way would you rather be treated?

This brings up for me the news stories of children mass-murdering other children in school settings. There are many complexities to these incidents, yet they often involve kids who feel left out or ridiculed. It reminds me of how important it is for everyone to feel included, cared about, and respected. It seems that learning to care about one another is one of the major lessons *not* being taught in our families and schools.

Caroline Myss, in her *Energy Anatomy* series,[10] tells a wonderful teaching story of a woman who is stopped in heavy rush-hour traffic by an accident ahead of her. Several cars down the road, an injured woman is lying on a stretcher. Rather than being angry that she will be late getting home from work, the driver has compassion for this injured woman and sends her the most loving energy she can summon.

At the other end of the exchange, the injured woman is "unconscious," but through an out-of-body experience, she literally sees the warm, golden energy coming from within the other car toward her. Her spirit self moves to see the license plate and the loving face of the woman behind the wheel.

It takes her months to recover her health. But she has brought through into consciousness the license plate number of that one woman who sent her love and light, in the midst of all the other drivers honking, yelling, and cursing the stupidity of those involved in the wreck. Looking up the kind woman's address, she one day rings the doorbell to present her with a bouquet of flowers!

Truly, the energy we send out *is* perceived. Even more than the belated gift of flowers, the kind woman was gifted at the very moment of her sending love, by feeling her own heart full of love. What a wonderful gift to give oneself!

DIVIDED WE FALL

I mentioned in Chapter 8 that as we awakened in the sixties and early seventies, we were beginning to form an invincible coalition for unity, peace, and taking care of one another and our Mother Earth. People from all walks of life, all races, all countries became deeply involved, and our unity was incredibly powerful. I sense that we understood our own power at only a small level. But the ones who recognized it more fully were those who maneuvered to stay in power by creating fear and division and unconsciousness. Big international cartels and powerful moneyed interests saw us more clearly than we saw ourselves and began a campaign of divisiveness. After directly confronting us at Kent State and Wounded Knee and other places that received very negative press and actually *helped* our cause, those in power realized that overt force was not the right tactic. We would obviously not buckle under their direct pressure.

So they got very smart. They went underground, if you will, and began planting seeds of anger, judgment, division, prejudice, and hatred among us. We were not ready to recognize them for what they were. Too many people in the country still bought into the conflict game, and our power was splintered.

I felt it most personally in the anger and scathing attacks directed toward "rainbow" and half-breed teachers who worked across the lines of race and tribe to create awakening. Those in other areas of the country and other walks of life felt it in a backlash by fundamentalist Christians. Foresters and ecologists threw injurious words and actions back and forth.

Wherever their ugly heads arose, judgment and negativity shattered the power we were building. Some forgot that peace was the objective and began to play the games of conflict again. Sad but very true. Disillusionment naturally followed.

STRIVING FOR CREATIVE INCLUSION

So now it is high time to awaken from those games once and for all. Like children fighting and scratching over a toy who then drop it and become friends when offered an ice cream cone apiece, we must literally drop our *attitude* of conflict. Yes, there are things to work out among us. Yes, we have a lot to learn in the area of good relationship. And yes, we can work all this out by practicing unity and peace *in the process of learning*.

A friend of mine shares a wonderful tribal way of keeping humor in our lives by understanding that we are all so very human, that we all have our Achilles' heel, and that no matter what we might do, we are still part of the family. "Oh, oh," we can say. "There goes Jean again. Moving one more time, spending her energy on packing boxes. I wonder if she'll ever get rooted in one place and stop asking us to help her move all that darn heavy stuff!" And laughter ensues, because the speaker recognizes that she herself is getting divorced for the third time—her Achilles' heel. And John is being angry and hateful again—his Achilles' heel. And Pete is wanting to run things and have power over everybody—his weakness. More laughter. Aren't we a deal? Isn't that crazy behavior? And aren't we all so very human? We're obviously here to learn and grow. And isn't it true that we will grow past these things in a loving circle that quiets our fears and lays to rest our need to separate ourselves?

Even when a child is sent out of the circle as a punishment in a Native home, he is not sent outside the circle of love. That love still holds him, saying, "The most loving thing I can do for you is to let you know

now that violence and hurting others are not acceptable. You think about how it feels to be outside of things. Then let's find other ways for you to get what you need and want because you are very much loved."

Inclusiveness, nonjudgment, yes; discernment, for sure. But meanness, conflict, threats, injury, denial—no, no, no. We are a family. White Buffalo Woman reminds us that we are more than family; we are *one* with one another. "Whatever you do to any other thing or being in the Circle of Life," she warns, "you do to yourself, for you are One." When we lift ourselves to the level of Spirit and wholeness, we will come to our conflicts and challenges with a much different energy. But in the meantime, we practice peace, moment by moment.

One simple way we can do this is through dedication. This is the practice of dedicating all good things we do for ourselves to others who might benefit. For instance, when I am using new ways of healing, I dedicate them to those in need of that kind of healing. When I am going through processes that clarify and purify me at any level, I dedicate them to others who could benefit from such clarity. Dedication in this way takes only a moment: close your eyes and offer it to someone if he or she chooses to accept the gift. Then go on with what you are doing.

There has been a terrible history among us two-leggeds in the last few hundred years on this continent. Yet if any of us are to live well, we must listen with all our hearts to White Buffalo Calf Pipe Woman:

Remember always to treat every creature as a sacred being: the people that live beyond the mountains, the winged ones of the air, the four-footed, the fishes that hide beneath the cool rock in silver streams and lakes, all of these are your sisters and your brothers. All are sacred parts of the body of the Great Spirit. Each one is holy.

The most difficult part . . . may be to extend this respect to the people of your neighboring tribes. Remember, like you, they are sacred people, given a specific task to do in the great Being of Wakan Tanka. Their work is not your own, their tasks differ from yours, but the purpose you serve is the same. The sun that shines upon you does not see you as being so very different. In peace you must live side by side with those of a different shade of the color red.

For a people are coming soon who do not share the color of your skin, but are white like the snow that falls in the winter months. With them will also come those of black skin. And those of yellow skin. And those of colors in between.

... The colors [must] blend together like rainbows that arch across the prairie when the storm has passed.... Through peaceful blending with your neighboring tribes, be an inspiration to the wandering peoples. Help lead all races into the harmony of the rainbow.[11]

Métis friends of mine who have worked with fine native elders for many, many years tell a wonderful story. Carl and Jay themselves, as well as many others of us rainbow children and teachers, have suffered derision and attack for many years. Elders' councils (which we later found out were called together and paid by those who wished to create division) had sent out angry and threatening letters warning us of dire consequences to follow upon our "dastardly ways." Without knowing any of us or our work personally, these councils condemned it. They claimed it damaging to all peoples, certainly their own tribes. We were said to be "stealing and selling the sacred ways," even though we supposedly didn't know any sacred ways because the ones with "true spiritual power" had not given us the okay.

Over the years, however, Carl and Jay had studied with the elders, supported them, assisted at Sun Dances and ceremonials, Sun-Danced themselves for many years, and were eventually given some of the traditional dances and altars to carry into their home community.

They laughed when they told me with what trepidation they had begun, during those traditional ceremonials, to sing a few of the "rainbow" songs appropriate to the rituals—the songs that I and many others have written from our hearts and from listening to Spirit's voice. Of course, the elders' heads cocked and they came into rapt attention as these songs were sung. Nothing was said. The ceremonies went on as before, as well they should have.

Finally, after "sneaking" a few modern songs of Spirit and Earth in several different times, they were called by their elders to talk about it. "Where did these songs come from?" they were asked.

"From friends of ours and from other young people across the country who are practicing the ways of Earth wisdom," they replied, almost holding their collective breath. And to their grateful surprise, it was not a "chewing out" they got but interest and encouragement.

"These songs are just like our own," they heard with amazed ears. The elders said, in their own amazement, "They are saying the same thing our songs say, only they are in English! We even like the rhythm of some of them. Could you teach us that one about Earth and Sky?"[12]

It is so heartwarming to hear such a story and to know that the false barriers that have been set up and maintained by our addiction to separation, division, and conflict are melting in the warm Golden Light of our collective Rainbow.

WORKING IN EARTH MAGE CIRCLES OF SEVEN

The Dawn Star tells us that a new pattern has been set in the etheric realms of Earth for our working together. That pattern consists of seven people synchronistically coming together in a circle of commitment on a mutually important issue. Rather than working on it from the usual viewpoint of the physical and manifest realm, and using the normal tools of intellect and emotion, the members of this circle are asked to clear themselves of personal and interpersonal concerns enough to lift themselves into another, more heartful level of functioning.

This is the second aspect of our coming together—becoming one with the greater Life of All Creation through becoming a hollow bone, through lifting our actions up to a higher level. This new, unified level is the Spirit, or Unmanifest, level—the Shimmering Invisible, where energy is yet unformed. Out of the awareness and understanding they find there, a mutual intent can be formed and placed into the Silence, magnified exponentially by the power of seven. Once this focused intent has been sent out and their work completed, the circle can melt into other circles, each person naturally gathering with six other people around a different, but mutual, concern.

Whenever a circle gathers together with this intent to upliftment, Dawn Star indicates that there will be a corresponding pull from above. This pull is especially strong if His energy is seen as a star well above the center of the circle; another personal guide or ancestral helper can be chosen to be seen elevated just above the middle hub. This configuration puts into practice the scientific magic of intent, Silence, and unity. And whatever is placed into the Silence will manifest powerfully in the world, helping us deal with real issues and crises on Earth in a new way.

To help you understand a bit better how this can work, I will illustrate the principle through an example that my friend Pam Montgomery uses in her teaching.[13] Let's say a group of researchers wanted to create a material that would be light, unbreakable, easy to form into many shapes, and waterproof. They came up with something we call plastic.

This material certainly met the criteria they had set, but in the end, it has caused great challenges ecologically and otherwise through the toxicity of its manufacturing process and its very indestructibility. Thus, while a small problem was solved, it brought about larger problems for All Our Relations.

Now picture a different scenario: these researchers came together, set out their criteria, and then added one more thing—the stipulation that it work for All Our Relations down through the generations. They might have gathered together and meditated to lift their energy into Spirit, where all answers are given from Oneness and harmony. The product that would have come from that larger collaboration would have met the initial criteria. But it would also have been in resonance with the larger Life, harmonizing in a good way with the ongoing flow of things without damage, destruction, or harm.

This is a vital key to everything we do, not just what we do in our Circles of Seven. The immersion in holiness we are willing to experience is the essential tool that makes the difference.

James Redfield gives a teaching story about this very kind of uplifted action in *The Tenth Insight*, based on principles of unity he brought through in *The Celestine Prophecy*.[14] Reading these books together and absorbing the principles would be a wonderful beginning for your group. It's useful to understand these fully as you begin your Circle of Seven, and I will highlight the primary ones that apply here.

1. The first principle is about coincidence and how the awareness that something is going on beneath everyday life can serve us well. As we allow ourselves to feel deeply what concerns us, and open our awareness to others with the same concerns, these circles can come together easily and gracefully. The heart rather than the mind will draw these circles together; pay attention to coincidences that might point out others with whom you want to work in this way. In James's example in *The Tenth Insight*, the group gathering finally realized that a member of the circle was one of the "bad guys" who was "causing the problem." The realization that he, too, was attempting to create a solution, and the consequent inclusion of his higher self in the circle, enabled magic to happen.

2. Awareness is one of the principles of physics that is now being accepted; it is one of the powers of the subtle, nonphysical realm. Using our awareness and innocent perception of issues is vital. Realizing that even the physical universe is made up of pure energy that responds to our conscious intent, we can more confidently do our work at nonmaterial levels.

3. In the past, we have felt that the way to get energy for ourselves and our projects is to take it from others by controlling them. We are now waking up to the endless supply of energy that exists in Creation and doing our conscious work of opening to receiving from Source. This is where our skill in entering the Silence, the Sacred Heart pays off. Great dividends come from meditating as a group as you begin your work together. The more "plugged in" to Source you are, the more potent your impact can be.

4. It is also time to recognize how we have tried to control others with the dramas we learned early in life. These usually take one of four forms: intimidator/persecutors and those in the corresponding victim stance, plus aggressive interrogators who probe others in a negatively critical way, and the aloof/passive people who stand back and withhold their energy. The key to ending these control dramas is to recognize our

patterns and realize that true power in an interactive situation is to give energy to others in a supportive, uplifting way. Rather than grabbing control, criticizing, withholding energy, or allowing ourselves to be at the mercy of everyone else, we must be willing to give our support to whoever is speaking, knowing that this will bring forward the highest and best that person has to offer. There are no designated leaders or hierarchy; thus, everyone has an opportunity to speak and the responsibility to do so. Full participation is required. Moving into your heart, where you are able to perceive someone else as "another you," is a key.

5. Remembering the power of a loving place of heartful unity is necessary and beneficial. Realizing that this is the place of power will make your work effective. I like to think of moments when we are "in love"—that joyful, positive, energetic, connected, hopeful, passionate, exalted feeling. Barbara Marx Hubbard[15] calls this loving, impassioned feeling "suprasex," reminding us that sex for procreation is less needed now than the passionate joining of minds and hearts in co-creation of a better world. This kind of upliftment is possible when we are working together in harmony and will make effective what we do.

You will likely be gathering together several times, at least. What follows is an outline of how the Circles of Seven may proceed. The first thing will be to acknowledge the issue that called you together and your intention to make a positive difference. Some of the completion steps will obviously be used in later gatherings rather than in each one.

1. Invoke the help of the ancestors, Dawn Star, devic aspects of the issue, and your own guides and helpers. See yourself as a circle whose hub can be uplifted by these beings, bringing you to an elevated view of the challenge before you and the solutions possible.

2. Lift up into Oneness. The most challenging work is the task of overcoming the urge to control, manipulate, force, push against, exclude, and move from fear or judgment. Becoming a unified hollow bone is a way to express this intent of connection in holiness.

The following is information I was given in a meditation with a Spirit Circle of Seven that included brother Sparrow Hawk:

It is here and now that life must take on new meaning. It is here and now that dying must be resurrected from its dive into nothingness. It is here and now that awakening must happen at all levels of physical and spiritual life.

Oneness is the key—the remembering that we are one with All Things. From this unitary state of consciousness, the energetic patterns needed to unfold yourselves into your full humanity will arise.

To begin your Circle of Seven, sit down with bodies erect and comfortable. Sitting with knees touching will be best, whether in chairs, on the floor, or on the ground. Center yourselves into your bodily being by focusing on your physical center, just below your navel. Next, lift up into the Silence of the Heart and settle in there. Then imagine lines of light coming from each of these points to connect with the center of the circle; here sits a personal guide and Dawn Star. When each and all feel connected to that center hub and higher guidance, then must the inner eye be focused on the intent of the upliftment—the purpose of the circle—and upliftment to the Spirit plane allowed.

At this point, the silencing technique offered in Chapter 11 can well be used. Then the center hub where all your intent is focused will be seen as a heart. This small heart will then be drawn up and up, becoming larger and larger all the time, until that heart contains the whole group. At this point, some sound must be made—a vibration set in the ethers through prayer or song or chant. Perhaps one person will say the "prayer" of your mutual vision. My song of gratitude and thankfulness, "Pila Maya,"[16] is one that was given specifically for this purpose. At the simplest, a group "om" chant will work.

Whatever you use, it must be felt as a serenade of beauty and ecstasy, which echoes out across Time. It is a vibrational intent being sent to everyone involved in this human issue, whether or not they have ears to hear. This certainly pertains to those who are seen as the players in the drama holding the "problem" in place.

There will be a glow that begins to steal over everything. When all in the circle perceive that glow, each says "Ho" or "Amen" or "So be it." You are now in the place to begin your work.

3. As you move forward, get very clear about the issue that brings you together. If necessary, write it down and give everyone a copy. Allow it to change and deepen as you progress.

4. Notice any relationship issues that come up and concentrate on giving energy to each person in his or her turn. Let insights come about past personal issues that may have drawn you to this circle.

5. The next step is to image the highest possible outcome, including even the "bad guys" in the situation. The loving intent for everyone to be uplifted and enlightened through the process is vital. Remember to add the dedication to All Our Relations, which is a way of expressing the wish for the solution to work for everyone, when you send out your prayer image.

6. Always close your circle with gratitude to all who participated on all levels of being. Release the star configuration with a couple of minutes of meditation.

These steps may take several meetings. Only when you feel ready to complete this Circle of Seven process with this group, go to the final step.

7. From a place of unity, move into silence, and from the place of the heart, put that intent forward with all the love in your hearts. This can be a prayer, a chant, an energetic release—whatever feels right to you.

After that, the work is complete; the seven are free to go. They will naturally scatter and move into other Circles of Seven, drawn by other issues and the people vitally concerned. This is a new form of leadership, without hierarchy—fluid and incredibly powerful.

This is why I sometimes call the work Leadership Seven. It can work at all levels, from personal to governmental and international. This is the model used in many Native societies. A group comes together to perform a certain task; sometimes they pick a leader or chief whose energy helps them coalesce and move forward. When that task is accomplished, the group disbands. There is no structured hierarchy.

These circles are circles of intent, based on your willingness to find new ways of being more than on a sense of knowing exactly what you are doing. If there is not a specific issue or problem to solve, you can gather a circle simply to explore new and fuller ways of being human. The members can support in one another the intent to become more aware,

TOGETHER, WE FLY

more open, more fluid, and more present. Becoming more fully who you
are in this moment is what will lead you naturally and gracefully into the
expanded states of your golden future.

Be sure to get clear about your intent as a group, so that you can re-
state it each time you gather. Ask for assistance from the higher levels of
knowing within yourselves and the masterful ones on all planes who are
pleased to assist. Begin each session by hooking yourself up to the star
energy above you; connect to the pattern that has already been set in the
ethers for your benefit. Then you can do any or all of the exercises and
practices that I have suggested throughout the book. If appropriate, do
them together. If not, assign one to be done between meetings and report in on your individual experiences.

One thing to try is a "consensus reality fast." Stay away from news-
papers, radio, and TV as much as possible for several weeks. Remember
that ever since the Vietnam era, there has been no free press, so what
you're getting is primarily a marketing campaign from the powers that be
to keep you in line, consuming a lot, thinking little, and being a good
worker. During this time, use your silencing techniques consistently. Stop
the usual world and allow your deeper knowings to emerge.

Being together in an outdoor setting can add an extra dimension to
an occasional gathering. The beauty and harmony there are inspirational
and can awaken you to new levels of energy perception. New levels of
awareness can be enhanced and integrated.

In whatever way you approach your time together as a group, the support you give one another in moving toward this Golden Time with joy
and awareness will benefit you greatly. I invite you to try this form of
working together whenever an issue comes up that calls for attention.
Your willingness to practice it and make it real will draw wonderful energy to you.

Separate and angry, we will fall low to the ground: we will find ourselves
on the path that leads ever downward into a very unpleasant reality. Yet
there is such an exquisite world waiting for us as we choose to lift ourselves, individually and collectively, into a place of cooperation and
Love—the glue that holds the universe together.

315

The good news is that the Rainbow is arching across all our people again. We are finding the power and the sweetness of unity and cooperation, of sharing and honoring. My elders have told me that for each one of us who stands in the Light, ten thousand receive that Light. A modern term for this is *critical mass*. When a small but significant portion of us walk together toward the New Earth, all will be given that opportunity. It is part of learning to be Earth Mages—the power of small and dedicated numbers working together. Whether or not our civilization becomes enlightened is determined by the number of us who choose to make real our dreams.

> What created success during the (past) Ages of Enlightenment was that during those eras, many enlightened souls chose to incarnate for the purpose of initiating change.... The variable is the quantity of humans who come together to provide direction for a particular civilization.... and the nature of reality which each holds in consciousness.[17]

There are great winds of change blowing through our world today. Rather than cowering on the ground or scattering like frightened quail, we must climb to the highest place we can, open our wings, and leap into the air like eagles who use the thermal currents created by great winds to lift higher and closer to Sky Spirit.

The winds may be strong, yet the sun shines brightly above the clouds.

Together, we will fly.

CHAPTER 18

COME TO THE
CIRCLE OF POWER

*It is vitally important for us to come together in circles of power
to create the life we envision for ourselves
and seven generations of our children.*

*There is something deeply human about coming together
in song and ritual movement. We have the opportunity to again
vibrate Mother Earth with our dancing feet,
stepping to the rhythm of an ancient unfolding song
and bringing forth a radiant and renewed Earth.*

It is vitally important for us to come together in circles of power to create the life we envision for ourselves and seven generations of our children. Taking a brief look at our history, we can see how waves of
spiritual gathering and dancing have awakened again and again.

Dawn Boy speaks of it this way:

The spirit of Ghost Dance of the 1880s had many precedents
among native peoples. In fact, there were so many that one would
almost conclude that dancing for salvation or spiritual goals was
the "normal" response to stress, war, alcoholism, and cultural
disintegration.

Often a spiritual leader would call for purification and lead
his or her people in a series of dances drawn from existing forms
but with greater intensity, stronger spiritual commitment, and

specific goals to reunite the community. Sometimes a new dance form would be given in vision, as happened with the Drum Dream Dance religion of the Sioux in the 1870s. This particular form was given to a young woman who miraculously survived a massacre of her people. The specific goal of this dance was to forgive and embrace one's enemies; and it was effective. The Sioux took it to the Ojibwa, their traditional enemies, and to others. This spirit of sharing later flowed into the modern pow-wow dance that is a pan-Indian phenomenon today. The vision of forgiveness and brotherhood lives on through the dancing, while tribal angers and divisiveness often exist outside the dance. That and the resurgence of Sun Dance among native peoples bring us into modern times. We are indeed blessed by the myriad of forms of dance and ritual still in use that have come through vision, dream, and Divine inspiration. We are rich.

The power of these waves of spiritual dancing not only uplifted the tribes in their time of distress but also often brought visions and power to new prophets and leaders. Neolin of the 1760s, Handsome Lake of the 1800–1820 period, and "Open Door" were all heavy drinkers who became teetotaling prophets after various purifying dance waves carried them into personal vision and salvation. These men often met with Jesus in Spirit and got specific advice on how to purify their old ways, how to adjust to contact with whites, and how to keep their dances and other spiritual practices intact in new Christ-oriented settings and paradigms.

All over the Americas, from California to the East Coast, Indians danced for salvation and got hope, power, and new spiritual direction. The spiritual power was contagious, and many spiritual leaders traveled far from their own tribes and territory, like Smohalla from Washington who toured the Apache-Din'e Southwest and Mexico to return with fresh ideas, hope, and insight to reform and reenergize his own peoples. Sioux traveled to Nevada and California specifically to go see Wovoka and his Spirit Dance and to bring it back home if it was worth having. It was, and they did bring it back.

COME TO THE CIRCLE OF POWER

And Jesus himself, called the Master of Life and the Master of Breath, encouraged many of these waves of dance and helped rebuild traditional form into new Christian, but thoroughly Indian, churches. The Indian prophets were so clear about this commissioning from Jesus that they argued theology with various white missionaries and even asked them why they killed "their Lord Jesus." And common to many of these reforms and visions was the promise and hope that one day Indians would be able to live in peace with whites—even with respect in a world that ended war and became Heaven on Earth. The messianic Christ who inspired Wovoka's "ghost-spirit" dance is often blurred by its Indianness and also by white misrepresentation. Likewise, the Dawn Star's inspiration of the modern Native American Church is often overlooked by non-Natives who enjoy thinking of Indians as exotic and even pagan. Yet the overall pattern is clear. Dancing with spiritual goals does work.

We modern folks feel disconnected and threatened at times by change and modern life like the Indians did; our damage to the life of Earth threatens us; often we lack deep spiritual experience as individuals and as communities; and we have substance abuse problems like the Indians had. Creator and Dawn Star still answer our prayers, and we still have feet to dance and ears to hear the drums. It is time to celebrate the fulfillment of Heaven's promise of peace on Earth and to use these Earth-robe bodies of ours to generate Spirit. That's what Creator put us here for . . . so *let's dance!*

Always there was a resurgence of using strong dancing. There is something deeply human about coming together in song and ritual movement. To be healthy, the human body must move, and movement informs the development of our consciousness. Dancing is a way of moving together, of bonding, of enjoyment and ecstasy. Matthew Fox, outspoken Catholic priest, ecotheologist, and founder of Creation Spirituality, speaks about having three generations of people coming to his Techno Cosmic Mass rituals, all of whom find it profoundly moving. It is clear to me that we

Lakota Ghost Dance

have the opportunity to again vibrate Mother Earth with our dancing feet, stepping to the rhythm of an ancient unfolding song and bringing forth a radiant and renewed Earth.

DEDICATION DANCES

A powerful way of coming together, which I have taught for years, is a Dedication Dance. It is the joining together of an entire community of people, hopefully on a regular basis, to create beneficial outcomes through ceremony and celebration.

To illustrate, let me use a Native American group as an example. In this community, people come together for powwows. These are cultural events where everyone wears his or her finest traditional clothing and dances for prizes. I suggested to them that instead of gathering only in this way and for this reason, they come together in their high school gym or ceremonial center once a month. During the weeks previous to the dance, a group of interested persons would meet to decide the theme for the month: perhaps it would center around issues concerning the children, the elders, the school system, nuclear waste dumping on the reservation, or the need for rain during a parched summer. Once the basic issue was decided, then a clear image of the desired outcome would be formed, so that all who came for the dance could hold a similar vision, in harmony with All Our Relations.

Beginning with a prayer or dedication to that vision and All Our Relations, the evening would be spent dancing in one's finest outfit for the outcome that had been set. Every step, every conversation, every exchange, every bit of energy that was put forward in any way for the entire evening would be dedicated. Then, as a completion, all would enter into silence and send forth the vision.

Usually, people contribute to a potluck supper, and the evening concludes with a feast and celebration. All concerned go home with the good feeling of knowing they have put their best energy forward for something important for their community! And besides, they have had a wonderful visit with friends—an enjoyable time for all.

This can easily be translated to your own community. Perhaps a group who are already working together would decide to focalize these events, beginning with calling people together to decide on the theme of the first dance.

1. An important part of this is to create together one positive, unitary image that can be used as a focal point for the evening. For example, a focal image for the time of drought might be that moment after a long, soaking rain when the sun peeks through just enough to create a fabulous rainbow and all life is beginning to sparkle and come alive again. Another dance might focus on an image of the new youth center, with a clear sense of how it will look. If architectural plans have been drawn up, this image might be projected on one wall for the evening. The exact vision is not so important as is the common focus—a specific image for everyone to hold as he or she dances. Thus, the themes need to be something the entire community can support. As the group grows more cohesive and

manifests many of the community desires, then it may be willing to help manifest an objective of a more limited and specific group that is a part of the community.

2. There should be a ceremonial leader or leaders, to conduct the evening.

3. Begin by welcoming people and thanking them for coming. Then the leader or another appointed person can do an invocation prayer, asking that the guides and helpers of the people and the land be present.

4. Then share the exact focal image by talking about the concern of the dance and the shared image you are inviting everyone to hold at the center of the circle. Set the image "in the center" by connecting it to a center drum, a symbolic altar, or something else appropriate to the intent. A prayer can then dedicate all the energy of the evening to the fulfillment of the common vision.

5. The music you use for dancing can certainly be your choice. For many, dancing around a central drum may be the focus. Other music on CD or cassette can be used or included, especially those songs or sounds that enhance the meaning of your dance. In the drought example, you might play some of the pieces called "Rain" that have recorded rain and other ambient sounds. A wild, lively piece might be used to bring the energy up. We often "free-dance" to these, moving out of our distinct circle and dancing our own way around the room in the same general direction. Often, free-dancing to release the regular circling is a great way to conclude.

6. A majority of the dance time can be used to keep everyone's attention focused on the central vision. That is part of the ceremonial leader's job. A way we do this is by circle dancing, stepping sideways around a large drum or group of hand drums and a simple altar at the center that represents the vision. In our drought example, the altar could be a large, beautiful bowl of water with flowers floating in it and in vases around it.

7. Remember as well to give time for individual visions within the larger one. In moments during the dance, attention can be directed to each person's own version of the positive happening. For example, I might love to picture how happy my own garden will be when the cooling, nourishing rain comes. Another man might think of his animals' be-

ing fed again by greening pastures, and so forth. Give time for this individual "dreaming."

To do this, the leader will occasionally call for turning rather than circling. This invites people to turn individually around their own axis rather than as a group around the central altar, spinning whichever way they wish and dancing their own individual steps to focus on their own personal vision. Then they can be called back into the circling, center-focused dance.

8. Other elements can be added as well. Sometimes there are negative emotions that need releasing, and it is good to formalize a way to do this. One way we have used is to allow a smaller circle in the center to dance in the opposite direction. If the circle dance is going left, then an inner circle of those who feel the need to release some negative energies can be formed and danced to the right as long as needed by each person. Be sure, if you use this form, to remind everyone ahead of time that *all* energies expressed will be transformed into positive energy for the manifestation of the vision. The leader can step into that right-moving circle occasionally and repeat this reminder aloud, rededicating these energies in a positive way.

9. Additional dance steps can be used that are symbolic of what you wish to create. You can stop circling and invite individuals to dance into the center to give away their best energy there or to connect with the vision more strongly. We sometimes enjoy a weaving dance in which we step in and out with the leading foot, simultaneously using our hands to reach toward the center (picking up the vision) and pivoting to reach outward (moving the vision into the reality of our daily lives).

10. If your group is unused to dancing for long periods, or includes elders who do not have the stamina to dance continuously, be sure to create periods of sitting in quiet meditation so that people can rest. One quiet time can be used to focus on the central image; another can be used to allow people their own unfolding vision of how it will be for them when the image manifests.

11. It is a great concluding movement to have everyone stop, focus on the vision, then gather energy from "the ground" with low voices and downstretched hands. The sound and arms can then come upward and end with a jumping shout, throwing the energy up and out into your

world. It's a very satisfying ending. Then, as mentioned above, an energetic free dance is a good way to release the energy of the circle.

12. For your final act, always offer a prayer to affirm your vision, give thanks for its unfoldment in your lives, give thanks to your guides and helpers, and focus the energy forward. This can be done by the leader or by someone especially appointed for this honor.

13. Also be sure to announce when the gathering will be to create the vision for the next dance and when/where that dance will be held.

14. Then, if appropriate, snacks or a feast are a great way to replenish energy and allow the space for visiting, talking about the focus of the next dance, and personal sharing.

I have sponsored these dances in many places around the country, hoping to stimulate communities to carry on the dances on their own. We have danced for the children, for rain, for the solving of a community conflict, and many other kinds of things. Some communities are continuing to hold these dances on a regular basis, even though for some it is quarterly rather than monthly. One Dedication Dance a year is better than none.

Dedication Dances help communities to understand that manifesting something wonderful can be enjoyable. The more unity that is felt, the more energy that is generated, the more fun that is had, the more likely the vision will manifest. This cross-generational gathering allows young and old to come together in a good way to create something special and bonds the group more fully each time it is done.

SPIRIT DANCES

Spirit Dance was one of the names given to the Ghost Dance of the past. It is about bringing Spirit fully into our dance of Life to create a renewed Earth. Perhaps as we renew this way of coming together, it will be seen as a part of the new Ghost Dance.

If we think of the amount of power a Circle of Seven or a small community can generate, then larger and larger groups of people who gather in dedicated ceremony over several days can create enormous amounts of positive, catalytic energy and magic. When I was given this vision, I was reminded of the tremendous energy generated through coming together around music in the sixties and seventies. Sometimes a theme or cause was the focus, but too often the crowd expected the performers to generate all the energy. There was very heartful connection and unity, yet without a ceremonial focus, it often dissipated without producing the kind of effects that are possible in that type of gathering.

What have we had for a decade or two that calls us to this kind of aliveness and joy? Very little, in my estimation. But through such large gatherings, we will energize a whole city, an entire region, to live at a different level of wholeness and intent for the world. We will awaken again our hope and our hearts, something we're all very much in need of.

So I am being asked to bring together large groups of people in ceremony and dancing to uplift our energy and do service for All Our Relations.

This is how I see these Spirit Dances:

1. As in Dedication Dances, a central theme will be decided and announced in promotion of the dance. In general, an appropriate universal theme will be chosen. If there is more knowledge of the group/area and its issues, the central image may be more focused on their needs. These large dances will be, in essence, Dedication Dances taken to another level of participation. There will be a high intention for what we can create in our world as we put our energies together.

2. Initially, Earth Mage groups will put on these dances, inviting all who are interested to come. After having an experience of them, others will eventually be encouraged to continue them.

3. These gatherings will have seven leaders to help participants deepen their understanding of the power of the Four Directions, Mother Earth, Father Spirit, and the heartbeat drum at our center (both our own beating heart and the great community drum). This will be the major activity for at least a couple of the days. They will concentrate on creating unity among the members of each group, learning to work together, realizing how their aspect empowers the whole, and so on.

4. During this time, each group will be asked to create an honoring for the aspect with which it is working, and all seven groups will gather

together at the final ceremony to present a pageant of these honorings. This will be a way of calling in the energies so that we can then use them in vivifying our intent and reverberating it into the world as a completion act.

5. Running through the entire gathering will be music we make together. There will be drumming, singing, and dance, both in individual aspects of the pageant and with the entire group. Singing together in harmony will be a vital part of the experience of unity and ecstasy that will lift the gathering to a new level of resonance and power. I hope to enroll some of the well-known musicians from the sixties and seventies to help us with this essential part of things. Many of them began their careers doing concerts to invite an awakening of consciousness around issues of concern in that time. I think they will love to play again with this kind of intention. In the music and in our relationships, we will practice harmony and have a wonderful time doing so. These ceremonies will be an opportunity join in finding unity and joy and high purpose in being together again.

6. There will be a full day for the pageant ceremony that completes the sending forth of our intent. Once we have called in the powers of the seven "directions," we will continue the ceremony by energizing the central intention/image of the gathering. This will include focused meditation, entire-group harmony on songs and dances we have practiced, and prayer. Then the energy we have gathered and magnified will be sent up through group movement and prayer.

7. We will free-dance to release the energy and come to completion.

8. After this, when everyone is very tired, perhaps the special musicians who are participating with us will send us home with a short concert!

9. There will be one more day after pageant day, and this is a very important one. I will use this day to help participants begin the creation of the next Spirit Dance on their own within a specified amount of time, usually six months or a year. I'll call forward from this community those who can take care of all the aspects, from promotion to music to logistics. We will make a list of the volunteers so that we can keep in contact with them about the unfoldment of their own Spirit Dance. Then we may have time to break into smaller groups, where those who organized

and facilitated this dance can work with their counterparts for the next dance, helping them organize the event.

They will be charged with beginning to create their own Spirit Dances, so that they no longer depend on outside leaders. This is one of the most important parts of the dance!

There is something else to consider as we think about these dances. I have spoken of the vibration we carry as being very important. Another vibration that is of utmost importance is the speed of our lives. Mother Earth's frequency is somewhere around 8 megahertz, yet we spend more time at the 120 megahertz of electricity. Our lives are more like intense screeching and pounding on a tin drum, jumping wildly about, than they are listening to the soft beats on a hide drum and dancing rhythmically in circles. Mother Earth feels our energy and the quality of our steps on Her face.

It is time for us to dance in soothing circles upon Her, stepping lightly with joy and life, holding a beautiful vision in our hearts. It is time to dance wildly, with all our joy and aliveness, ready to make a positive difference with our energy. It is time to truly Dance Awake the Dream.[1]

Sparrow Hawk encouraged me to do this. "In your community, this would be easy to create," he said. "Nonprofit events are easily publicized, and often the places for them are donated. Those who care deeply about the focal issue as well as those who simply wish to put forth some positive energy and enjoy the gathering will be called together."

"Yes, it's time for us to practice these ways again," I agreed. "Primary peoples of the past understood that this was the way they created their lives—by gathering in circles of commitment and power to dance awake their dreams—whether the Sun Dance among the northern Plains tribes or the Corn Dance among the Pueblos. We will come to know again the power and joy of this way of co-creating our world. We will vision and walk a path of beauty into a radiant future."

"These ways of coming together are powerful and can be quite ecstatic," Sparrow Hawk said. "As you already sensed, a part of my new level of 'work' is to sit above you in those Circles of Seven, between you and the Dawn Star's light. I will act as a kind of stepping-down station, a transformer or translator in this and many other ways you will discover.

"Many others who have stepped beyond the Earth plane recently are doing this same kind of work. These ones can be our physical or spiritual ancestors. They were beings who sought to be Earth Mages during their lives and hold the intent for a renewed world even more strongly now that they are unlimited by the physical world.[2] None of us could yet hold the ascended state clearly enough to actually manifest it while staying in our Earth robes, so our intention is strengthened in the clarity we find with one another here. For example, there are some you know of and personally know who are doing this: your Cheyenne mom, Ora June; your medicine brother Sun Bear; your Eagle Song sister Jordan Peck; your singing brother John Denver; Earthkeeper Danaan Perry; your Hunkapi sister Norma; plant visionary Terence McKenna; Princess Diana; and of course, Mother Teresa. It is a beautiful service they offer. You can call on them or others you know who are now in the Beyond World who also had a strong intention for a renewed world. It will be part of the Spirit Dances to call upon their energy for upliftment and support."

"I'm thrilled that we will all continue to work together, my brother," I said to him with tears of joy in my eyes. "I know I will learn to see you even better than I do now, and we will wing together on the high winds."

As we completed our communication, I was thrilled to see a pair of bald eagles winging and soaring above the little bay in front of my windows, lifting and dancing on the strong breeze. Sparrow sensed them too, and we were silent in admiration.

Then he spoke, his eyes shining. "You know, it's very difficult for such large winged ones to fly when the days are still and there's no breeze. It's sometimes difficult for two-leggeds without wings to appreciate the intense winds, yet it is those very winds that help lift these eagles up and up in ever-higher spirals—over the storms and toward the Light!"

CHAPTER 19

FLOWERSONG

FlowerSong is the song of our thriving, our prospering.
It is the song of the flowering of life on a New Earth.

"Dawn Star came long ago, leaving powerful and magical teachings in the temples of the South, in Mexico and Central America," Sparrow Hawk said, recounting the old stories. "A lineage of Light was created that passed down through the generations. These teachers went among the people, sharing their wisdom. That wisdom is known as FlowerSong."

"Yes," I said, "and young seekers from all tribes of the Americas journeyed there to be taught. Among my own northern peoples, the high medicine people would find, once every few generations, a young child who exhibited a unique predilection toward Spirit and the ways of wisdom. When this child was recognized, she (or he) was trained intensely until such time as she was able to travel to the temples in the South. Then an elder would chaperon and guide her, journeying on foot the entire way. The child gained much broadening experience and knowledge during their travels, then apprenticed in temples such as Palenque, in the Yucatán, for many years, usually until she had matured through her teens. She was taught basic principles and philosophies that had import for all disciplines, whether human relationships, science, agriculture, government, or spiritual matters. The heartful connection and unity with All Things that she gained gave her access to deep knowledge across the whole spectrum of human life. When she had passed through all required levels of learning and initiation, she wandered homeward, teaching FlowerSong on her way."

"Often these teachers did not reach their own homeland until well into their adult years," Sparrow said. "They became a unique and powerful resource for the prospering of all they touched. Because of their multicultural experience and their heart of Oneness, they were able to help their people remember their spiritual brotherhood/sisterhood with other tribes. Tribes that worked together, rather than fighting one another, thrived."

"When I was drawn to the temples of Palenque and Tikal as a young woman, I had no idea of this tradition," I mused. "Yet I was one called to the same kind of multicultural experience and sense of Oneness with all people as FlowerSong teachers of the past. Spirit has supported and awakened me to the teachings of FlowerSong, and I strive to learn and share them. When I journeyed to Machu Picchu, I was much more aware and sat for hours near the burial caves of the high agricultural priestesses, absorbing their wisdom."

"Aria was on that trip with you," Sparrow reminisced, "and she told me that the more enlightened keepers there were again growing gardens on the terraces."

"Yes, they proudly showed us these after we asked about the old tradition of bountiful gardens there. They remember and want to bring back the beauty of that way."

"It's important, isn't it, Brooke, that we all devote ourselves to the kind of work that brings back a green and burgeoning Earth for the children of tomorrow?"

"Yes, and to me, whatever leads to a true flowering of life on Earth is a part of the teaching."

"Dawn Star and White Buffalo Woman still whisper this wisdom in a quiet yet urgent voice," Sparrow said softly, with a beautiful light in his eyes. "For those who listen, it can be heard."

FlowerSong is the vibrational harmony we must create for our children and ourselves. It is the song of our thriving, our prospering—a song of the flowering of life on a radiant New Earth. We must step forward as Earth Mages, ready and willing to do our part.

Come, O you children of the flowers. Come back into the circle again, you who are now businesspeople and commercial artists, social workers, homemakers, and laborers—those of you who knew in the sixties that something special was happening and then perhaps got disillusioned. Our virginal minds knew the truth of things and acted upon it. Our vision was clear, but we had not yet matured into the ability to bring that vision into reality. And just as with the wave of those who danced the first Ghost Dance, many fell away from that dream. The way we tried to do things did not seem to work. So we let it go and sought other ways of living.

But you must know this! In the sixties and early seventies, we made a profoundly important statement to the entire world. We, like the Ghost Dancers of old, danced into the ground another way of being, moved to the rhythm of a new song whose words spoke of a peaceful, beautiful Earth. That *did* work; it did exactly what it was supposed to do. Just as the prophecy had said—the children of the oppressors took up the accoutrements of the oppressed, the Native, and began awakening to their stewardship of the land and the sweet Earth. It was the fulfilling of a prophecy. Then the wave broke over and spilled the flower children out into all avenues of life.

And come join the circle you who were *not* flower children—those of you who did *not* wear flowers in your hair or become hippies and march in protest decades ago. You were doing what you needed to do. I was one of you—too busy working and going to school to put much attention into the wave of awakening consciousness until it was almost over and I "happened" to move to San Francisco. Whatever we might have been back then, all of us can see that what we are doing today—the modern American life as we have been given it—is not working.

———

You tribal people are being called as well. You have enormous gifts to give. The strains of ancient song, deep knowing, and harmonious relationship with Earth that you carry are needed in this heartful chorus. Native people have always brought a reminder that we are all of the Earth. As the animals retreat and the streams become empty of fish, you are often the first to sound the alarm that awakens us to the harsh, destructive results of our actions. Primary peoples have given us knowledge of herbs and medicines, shared songs and rhythms, and enlightened our lives with myths. You have even given your own images to heal us and lead us into dance. Now, as all people of Earth become one tribe, the global family needs your sense of unity, of belonging to the Earth, of community and connection to All That Is. You are needed! Come, join the larger circle in spirit and understanding as we come together to create Heaven for everyone on this blessed, holy Earth.

Now it is important for all of us to bring the new vision into every walk of life, *making a difference wherever we are.* You men do not have to have your hair long and flowing, you women do not have to wear a certain kind of long dress, to come again to the circle where hope and joy and unity and caring and peace are the dance. This energy needs to pervade everything we do. We can bring heart and sustainable practices into our businesses. We can back schools that work to support the true spiritual nature of our children (as Waldorf[1] and other types of schools do now) and create unions and barter systems to get ourselves out of a banking system that has lost its base in real value. We can choose to live within the means of our planet's resources. We can create value by finding that what we really need is not more stuff in a bigger house with the latest SUV in the driveway but more caring and sharing and fun and joy and clean air and birdsong. We can join together again every weekend, and perhaps on Wednesdays if we want, in a literal Spirit Dance that reawakens the spark of truth wanting to emerge even more fully now. It's high time we awaken to the power we have in the "establishment": We are the adults now. We are the workers who make things happen; we are the managers and the bosses. We must own again our personal power to make a difference in the world.

At a Spirit in Business conference recently, I was inspired by two wonderful men (who, in their speeches, referred to *themselves* as old hippies) doing exactly this. One was Jack Canfield, who, after ten rejections by major publishing houses, put out the Chicken Soup for the Soul series, which is bringing us inspiring stories in many areas of life. He is reawakening the ancient storytelling tradition that has served humanity so well. His seminars teach people a heartful and powerful way of being in the world.

The other speaker was Ben Cohen, of Ben & Jerry's ice cream. Many of you may know of the grassroots, heart-oriented way they have built their business. Ben is spearheading a very powerful movement called Business Leaders for Sensible Priorities, whose members believe that the federal government's spending priorities are undermining our national security. Business and former military leaders are putting their energy together to make the country aware that more than half of our tax money is being foolishly spent on a military budget that is totally overkill. They point out that something as basic as changing our priorities for spending the federal budget would create amazing changes. Currently, approximately 50 percent of every dollar spent by Congress goes to the Pentagon and immensely wealthy defense contractors. We spend about $281 billion on "defense," and our allies spend another $221 billion, whereas the rest of the major world powers *together* spend only about $117 billion. This unbelievable overkill literally robs money from our children and the quality of our lives—from education, health, and every other category.

We can choose to maintain a nuclear arsenal with the explosive power of 150,000 Hiroshima-sized bombs for $35 billion, or we can use that same amount of money to hire 100,000 new teachers *and* provide health care for America's 11 million uninsured kids *and* still keep a nuclear stockpile equivalent to 40,000 Hiroshima bombs. We can buy another nuclear submarine designed to fight the defunct Soviet Navy or completely repair and modernize all 1,555 Iowa public schools. We can buy forty-three F-22 fighters designed to combat Soviet aircraft that were never built, or we could provide Head Start for the 1.7 million eligible kids currently unserved. Simply getting our needs and priorities straight in this area could totally change the face of the world.[2] A goal of this group is to begin by getting Congress to give just $15 billion of the bloated defense budget back to the people, back to the children, investing in programs that strengthen our communities. Ben is using his life to make a tremendous difference for others.

I consider both these men fine examples of Earth Mages. When we look outside ourselves for the answers, it is too easy to avoid taking responsibility for the real choices we have in front of us and for the magnificent possibilities that each of us has within us. Yet, as they demonstrate, when we are willing to come from an empowered place and bring our best into the world, magic often happens. Each of us can make a very special and important difference.

I want to share with you something from my friend James Buchanan:

> It has seemed to me for some time that the real crisis of our age is the threat of hopelessness. We teeter on the brink of that abyss far too often these days.
>
> Hope is excess. It is what we have left when all else abandons us. It is hope that most stubbornly refuses to be subdued or co-opted. It is hope that is the last bastion against being overwhelmed by the flood tides of life.
>
> Hope is the quiet voice of infinity all around us.
>
> It's not optimism. While there's no doubt that hope and optimism are related, they are not the same thing. Hope, real hope, is something that only happens at the end of optimism. It is only in those strained and strange geographies of the soul that you find hope waiting patiently. Hope is what is left when all of your optimism fails you, when you cross the border into that territory where optimism lacks the backbone to follow.
>
> The sixties were my time of greatest hope. In the sixties I actually believed in things—we all did. We believed that the world could change for the better and that we, each of us, could make a difference. We believed in commitment and that there were things worth committing to. There was an urgency to what we learned, what we spoke, what we did. Ideas were alive and the

ability to express them was the one true power in the world. We had an energy that has somehow gone missing since then.

But to have lived through the sixties—and I mean to have been part of the passions of the age—is also to have lived through the destruction of optimism and maybe the destruction of hope, certainly the destruction of belief. It's to watch yourself give up and be slowly, willingly absorbed into the system you hated so desperately. It's to wake up in the nineties and catch yourself fussing over a tie, or a wrinkle in your shirt, or to watch yourself as your eye trails too longingly after a Mercedes which rounds the corner—cool, detached, important. It's to observe yourself as you dash a check off to your favorite environmental or human rights organization, and just for that instant feel involved again. It's to find yourself reminiscing like some spent ancient warrior, claiming you're trying to forget while actually trying to remember, to imagine what it must have been like to be alive back when real change was still a possibility.

When all of that is gone, when your optimism has collapsed in upon you like a tent whose supports have snapped, leaving you lying there struggling against the weight of it at a total loss—your only hope is hope.[3]

We on Lady Gaia at this time have our part to play in changing this—the most vital part, really. Because this awakening is happening on the Earth plane, in the realm of the manifest, we must be the ones who open the door to allow the Light to flood in. We have set ourselves here to do this very thing; it is in our DNA, our ancient memory. Our feet must dance it into the ground, our burgeoning wings must lift us up. Together we will use:

- *Intention:* to build a critical mass of energy
- *Prayer:* to link our heartful intention with a power greater than ourselves
- *Commitment:* to hold the vision steady until the golden dream becomes real on this sweet Earth

EARTH MAGE WISDOM SUMMARY— KEYS TO EMPOWERED LIVING

It is important to remember these things as you walk through the days of your life:

1. Creator made you perfect; use what you have been given to open and grow like a tree reaching for the Sun.
2. You belong here—here and now. You are a part of everything in a holy circle of Oneness.
3. Everything and everyone else also belong and are part of everything, so let go of judgment and exclusion in your own heart. Honor and care for All Life.
4. You are a vital link in the unfoldment of a renewed Earth: follow your heart with courage and give your unique gift.
5. Touch the silence of your heart often for connection both to very personal guidance and to the holy sense of unity, the Source of All.
6. Work together. Be diligent about clearing the way of anything that divides, separates, excludes, limits, or competes.
7. Keep appreciation and gratefulness in your heart; this attitude promotes your total well-being, gives you positive energy to share with those around you, and supports your heart in living its truth into the world.
8. Let go of your mind's need to know. Awaken your trust in life as an exquisite mystery, unfolding like a flower.

WAKANTIA: FLOWERING EARTH TRAININGS FOR EARTH MAGES

I have learned from Spirit that it is time to focus our attention and energy on one personal spiritual path if we are to give our gifts in the most powerful way. The global connections we have fostered by experiencing many paths will serve as a baseline for the rich work we now must do by committing to one. The way we choose must be guided by our heart's

FLOWERSONG

desire, since we are called to a long-term deepening in what we choose. Wakantia will offer gateway trainings to give participants the information and experience to decide whether this is the path they want to choose for committed and continuing work. These trainings will be powerful initiations in themselves.

> As you move into your spiritual adulthood, it is time for each of you to begin to acknowledge and listen to the divine voice of the Creator within that is waiting to answer your every call and supply you with all the knowledge you need to move forward into the New Age and evolution of humankind. It is time for you to determine which path to enlightenment you will follow that rings true for you within your heart. There is only one truth, and that is the eternal Truth of Creator, but it has been fragmented into many energies and thought forms. It is time to follow the nudgings of your Higher Self, as you claim the truth that resonates clearly within, and then follow it unerringly.... You are being given every opportunity to open and clear the pathway to your vaster self so that you may receive clear, concise information critical to your growth and transformation process. But you must begin by listening to the small nudgings you receive during the day or night, and after validating them in your heart center, follow the guidance that feels appropriate.... You will step gracefully into the next level of awareness, and will gradually perfect the skills, integrate the wisdom, accomplish the opportunities and overcome the challenges that are presented to you. You must flex your spiritual muscles and lay claim to your new-found power. That is why we are showing you that you are the student, the teacher, and also the master—that no one else knows better than you what is right and appropriate for you in each and every moment and in every situation.[4]

These Wakantia trainings are meant to create groups of dedicated people who, by bringing our skills together, work toward the next level of being human. As I find those individuals who are willing to commit deeply to the process, we will delve into the truth that lives within us and rise high on the currents of Love and Light that come toward us. We will explore manifestation, music, and magic—becoming masters of a new way of playing the human game.

Wakantia
Flowering Earth Trainings
Come join us in a place of beauty and sacredness.

The purpose of this work is to awaken and challenge
you to the next level of being human on this sweet Earth.
It is to tune and tone you, cleanse and clarify you,
so that new ways of being will become available.
It is to support you and encourage you
so you have the heart and skill
to leap into the unknown.
We seek beauty.
Come along!
Ho!

Earth Mages doing
magic leading to miracles!!

I've even been shown that this will evolve into an "invisible school," through which people will study with fine teachers in many areas. These courses, administered through Earth Mages Unlimited, will be a part of the continuing curriculum that awakens and transforms us. Many of these courses may be required; the reason for this is that we want to develop common rituals, "language," and understandings upon which all of us can build. Certain individuals, especially Brooke's past students, may find one aspect or another deeply meaningful and train (or be ready) to teach this; thus, more and more opportunities to learn, and to create a livelihood for themselves, become available for Wakantia members. My sense is that new ways of teaching, sharing, and dancing our aliveness (rather than making a living) may ensue. Coming together in new configurations of community will very likely arise from our mutual endeavors.

———

I want to share with you some of how this training developed. Some time after I was given the vision of the Flowering Earth Trainings, I was told the name *Wakantia*. Although I sensed that it was a Lakota word, I did not know its meaning. What I learned from Wallace Black Elk is that it is a feminine word meaning, in the old way of saying it, "dog soldiers of the sacred lodge."

This could also be "caretakers of the sacred house or home," which, to me, means our Earthly home on Lady Gaia. That led me to a deeper understanding of the work of this group. *It is to be an elite[5] corps of individuals dedicated to caring for our home, this sweet Earth and All Our Relations, through exploring and sharing ways of bringing Light to our new level of being.* It refers to a kind of Earth-grounded magic that we will learn to perform, which will give us the energy to help bring a renewed world into being. The name *Earth Mage* means "one who is dedicated to learning and practicing this magic for the good of All Our Relations."

I have been told to invite people to pledge themselves as Earth Mages. Those who wish will be on a list available to others and will keep in touch through an Internet connection and in other ways. Posted on that same Web page will be stories of the grounded magic that Earth Mages are doing around the world, as an inspiration and education for others who wish to do such good work.

It seems a tall order, yet I know that those who come together to train will move powerfully forward, making a way for many others. We will work together in star configurations of seven, set our intent for the highest and finest, support one another, and lift into Spirit. It will be an unstoppable combination. We will mount up on the wings of eagles and, from that uplifted place, create a flowering of life—all life on our Lady Gaia.

EARTH MAGE PLEDGE
CREDO:

As an Earth Mage, I, _____ [name], aspire to know
and live these truths in my heart:

I am one with All Things in an eternal unfolding of Life.

I am supported by the loving heart of Creator.

I am a conscious co-creator of beauty and wholeness.

I came to Earth to offer a unique and beautiful gift.

I know that what's right is that which makes things truly better.

I am working magic in unity with others for the good of All My
Relations.

These are the qualities to which I, _____ , aspire:

To be strong without losing gentleness,

To be articulate and expressive without being mouthy or critical,

To be discerning without being judgmental,

To live in moderation, balance, and harmony without stinginess or
squandering (willing to walk lightly on the Earth),

To reuse, recycle, and restore,

To be steady in my spiritual practice without compulsion or
rigidity,

To allow and choose rather than force or manipulate,

To have a deep, abiding faith in the basic goodness of things,

To carry laughter and joy without sarcasm or mocking,

To honor the lineages I carry by bringing forward what is good,
true, and beautiful,

To be open-minded without bitterness or prejudice,

To be nurturing without being overprotective or interfering,

To be willing to find the heartful Source of wisdom for myself,

To be willing to magnify positive energy by joining with others of
like mind through spiritual action,

To honor the essence of what is real without being tied to the past,

To look through the eyes of innocent perception,

To be a hollow bone for the energy of holiness to enter the world,

To be respectful of the heartful intent of others,

To realize universal law and work with it,
To give the rare gem of my uniqueness to the world,
To walk in the shimmering, flowing Invisible, as well as the
    structured, dense, material aspect of life,
[Add your own.] _____

_____

And to practice Earth magic to create FlowerSong, a new and
    radiant Earth.
See Appendix A for a reproduceable version of the Earth Mage Pledge.

It is a holy path we must walk, a holy dance we must create. It is the
path of Oneness and harmony with All Things in all the realms of
Heaven and Earth. Two wondrous helpers walk with us on this journey,
joyful that we have finally reached this point so long awaited in the halls
of eternity. They are our Elder Sister, White Buffalo Calf Pipe Woman,
and our Elder Brother, Dawn Star. Before me, as I write this book, is an
altar I have made specifically for this purpose. Upon it rest the white
buffalo calf pipe, which calls White Buffalo Woman's sacred ways, and
the red star pipe, which brings in Dawn Star's loving energy.

We can think of their help coming to us in the form of the headdress worn by the symbolic last Ghost Dancer on the cover of this book.
The horns are the ancient shamanic representation of the two aspects of
truth that we must wear as we walk forward. Each of us who wishes to be
an Earth Mage must put the headdress on, remembering to bring each of
these aspects into every action we take.

Although each of these helpers carries both of these principles, we
will symbolically give one to each.

On one antler is the energy of White Buffalo Woman, carrying a
banner of the sacredness of Lady Gaia and the Earthly aspect of our
lives. Again and again, she calls us to remember that we are One with
All Things—that inclusion, communion/communication, and good
relationship with everything are vital keys in our moving forward to renew this sweet planet, our home. She reaches down and lovingly touches
Lady Gaia.

On the other antler is the master Dawn Star, the Christ light, carrying the holy banner of the living Creator within us and within All Things, the heavenly aspect of our lives. He stands tall and reminds us to lift our actions up to the level of Spirit, where the highest good for all will result from what we do. He invites us each to become a hollow bone, allowing the energy of Creation to move through our hearts unrestricted into the world. He reaches up and touches the Heavens.

When we are truly embodying those principles, when we are wearing the horns of truth, then the warrior eagle and the dove of peace become one, and radiant beauty descends upon us and what we do. A flowering of Earth follows in our pathway.

The words of Dawn Star, found in *The Gospel of Peace*, an old Slavonic text in the Vatican Museums, remind us, as does White Buffalo Woman, of where to look for the truth that will guide us as Earth Mages:

Seek not the Law in your scriptures, for the Law is Life, whereas the scripture is dead. I tell you truly, Moses received not his laws from God in writing, but through the living Word. The Law is the living Word of the Living God to living prophets for living men. In everything that is Life is the Law written. You find it in the grass, in the tree, in the river, in the mountain, in the birds of heaven, in the fishes of the sea; but seek it chiefly in yourselves. For I tell you truly, all living things are nearer to God than the scripture which is without Life. God so made Life and all living things that they might by the ever-living Word teach the laws of the true God to man. God wrote not the laws in the pages of books, but in your heart and in your spirit. They are your breath, your blood, your bone; in your flesh, your bowels, your eyes, your ears, and in every little part of your body. They are present in the air, in the water, in the earth, in the plants, in the sunbeams, in the depths and in the heights. They all speak to you that you may understand the tongue and the Will of the Living God. But you shut your eyes that you may not see, and you shut your ears that you may not hear. I tell you truly, that the scriptures are the work of man, but Life and all its hosts are the work of our God.

342

————

White Buffalo Woman came among us bringing the Sacred Pipe, which represents wholeness and holiness—the respectful honoring of our unity with All Things. She reminds us through our modern prophet, Ken Carey, of the importance of our gathering in circles of power and spiritual action for the continuance of Life itself:

> Creation does not take place where there is a scattering and dissipation of energies [she explained]. Creation requires a gathering together and focusing of your power within a circle of commitment—like a seed, an egg, a womb, or a marriage. If you would create and not destroy, you must remember always the Sacred Hoop. Consider wisely the ways in which you would use your power and then around those ways draw the sacred circle of commitment. In the warm atmosphere of that circle, the power of love builds and builds like a storm above the wet summer prairie until the circle can hold no more and explodes in the conception of the new.[6]

"This has been an incredible journey, Sparrow Hawk," I said as we communed. "I would never have guessed when we lost you from this sweet Earth that these great teachings would come forward! I still miss you in physical form sometimes, yet I would not trade what I now understand for anything. The inspiration and guidance you give from your current perspective are opening a new pathway before us."

"It has been my honor to journey with you and with your readers," he responded with his usual grace. "This new life that we will create is worth everything we give to its unfoldment. I look forward to continuing to work with all those Earth Mages who are taking spiritual action to create a flowering of Earth for All Our Relations. The exquisite life to come is still less than easy for you on Earth to imagine. From this higher view, I *can* see it, and you must know that it is radiantly beautiful.

"From the ancestors of yesterday and the children of tomorrow, I hear a chorus of voices singing to thank you for what you do."

As I began this book, I was shown in vision that something greater than my words will touch you. It is my prayer that that is true for you personally. My relationship with Sparrow Hawk and our masterful elder brothers and sisters is a gift from Spirit, an invitation from the world of the ancestors. It is a gift of love and hope and inspiration for all of us as we walk forward in the co-creation of a New Earth.

We must remember and celebrate ourselves as the vital link. Our challenge and our joy as Earth Mages is to keep the Golden Dream alive and to dance it into the ground, this time for good.

This book is a clarion call to awaken from our slumber and take our place in the dance of life that will add conscious support to the coming of a new and Golden Time. It is very much worth doing, for our energy can bring about a time of beauty on Earth unprecedented in human history. We individual two-leggeds will pick up the tune being sung at the center of Life, learn to sing it together in exquisite harmony, and then dance it into reality in the material world. We have the remarkable opportunity for transfiguration. We *are* the dancers; we *are* the flowering; we *are* the mystery. Let us bring the Rainbow Bridge forth from our hearts and walk across it into a radiant and joyful life on Lady Gaia.

We are Wakantia,
Earth Mages awakening
to bring about a flowering
of Earth and All Our Relations.

Come, all who can hear this call:
join the ones who have held the Golden Dream
so very long.
Come again to the circle of power
and dance with me for a renewed and flowering Earth
the Spirit Dance, the new Ghost Dance,
the last Ghost Dance.

FLOWERSONG

Let these words,
come to me through Dawn Star's energy,
sink deeply in and
connect to your most profound knowing—
with *intent* to awaken
the Golden Dream on Earth
for All Our Relations.

I have spoken.

Brooke Medicine Eagle

Modern Ghost Dance Shirt by Falcon Von Karls

May harmony live
in the hearts of all people.
May peace be their way.
May we all be kind and gentle,
our paths straight and true.
May Star Beings show the way
and dark clouds never stay.
May life thrive upon the land,
and peace dwell
in the hearts of man.
—*TEN BEARS*
quoted in T. C. McLuhan's Touch the Earth

FLOWERSONG

Let it start right here, right now, with us
—with you and with me—
and with our commitment to breathe into infinity
until infinity alone is the only statement
that the world will recognize.
Let a radical realization shine from our faces,
and roar from our hearts,
and thunder from our brains
—this simple fact, this obvious fact:
that you, in the very immediateness of your present awareness,
are in fact the entire world,
in all its frost and fever, in all its glories and its grace,
in all its triumphs, in all its tears.
You do not see the sun, you are the sun;
you do not hear the rain, you are the rain;
you do not feel the earth, you are the earth.
And in that simple, clear, unmistakable regard,
translation has ceased in all domains,
and you have transformed
into the very Heart of the Kosmos itself
and there, right there, very simply, very quietly,
it is all undone.
—*KEN WILBER*, ONE TASTE

APPENDIX A

RESOURCES

WAKANTIA TRAININGS

The Wakantia trainings are meant to create groups of dedicated people who will work together over time toward the next level of being human. As I find those individuals who are willing to commit deeply to the process, we will delve into the truth that lives within us and rise high on the currents of Love and Light that come toward us. We will explore manifestation, music, and magic—becoming minstrels of a new way of playing the human game.

The training begins in the summer of 2000 in Montana and will be offered in many places around the country on a continuing basis. My spiritual sister Heron Wind and I will offer the first gateway class, Living the Truth—a powerful initiation in itself, which will help you decide whether this is the path you want to choose for committed and continued deepening and service over time.

Once you walk through this gateway to choose this path, many levels of work will open up, through which we put our hearts and minds and intent together to step into a higher level of being human. We will build a common language and ritual base from which to deepen ourselves, our spirits, and our service to the world. This will give my past students an empowering way to deepen and consolidate their studies with me from the past, as well as a way for new students to integrate into the process. Many of my past students will very likely become Wakantia teachers and leaders in a very short time, making this not only a way of living but also a way of creating their livelihood.

For additional information, see my Web site: www.medicine-eagle.com.

This new level of work will initially be sponsored by Feathered Pipe Foundation along with my Earth Mages Unlimited office. For registration information, contact our office (406-883-4686) or E-mail (Wakantia@MedicineEagle.com).

If you would like to be on our Earth Mages mailing list, please fill out the following and put an X in front of any of this contact information that you are willing to have given out to other Earth Mages.

Address:_____

_____

_____

Phone(s): _____

E-mail: _____Web site: www._____

Copy or tear out this form and send it to:
    Earth Mages Unlimited!
    c/o Brooke Medicine Eagle
    PMB C401
    One Second Ave. East
    Polson, MT 59860

Or check out the Earth Mages Unlimited section of my Web site (by going to www.MedicineEagle.com) and fill it out there. While you're at the Web site, you can also contribute well-written Earth magic stories and see what others are doing.

    To be on the active Earth Mages roster, send a check for $10 made out to Brooke Medicine Eagle.

EARTH MAGE PLEDGE

CREDO:

As an Earth Mage, I, _____ [name], aspire to know
and live these truths in my heart:
I am one with All Things in an eternal unfolding of Life.
I am supported by the loving heart of Creator.
I am a conscious co-creator of beauty and wholeness.
I came to Earth to offer a unique and beautiful gift.
I know that what's right is that which makes things truly better.
I am working magic in unity with others for the good of All My
Relations.

These are the qualities to which I, _____, aspire:
To be strong without losing gentleness,
To be articulate and expressive without being mouthy or critical,
To be discerning without being judgmental,
To live in moderation, balance, and harmony without stinginess or
squandering (willing to walk lightly on the Earth),
To reuse, recycle, and restore,
To be steady in my spiritual practice without compulsion or rigidity,
To allow and choose rather than force or manipulate,
To have a deep, abiding faith in the basic goodness of things,
To carry laughter and joy without sarcasm or mocking,
To honor the lineages I carry by bringing forward what is good,
true, and beautiful,
To be open-minded without bitterness or prejudice,
To be nurturing without being overprotective or interfering,
To be willing to find the heartful Source of wisdom for myself,
To be willing to magnify positive energy by joining with others of
like mind through spiritual action,
To honor the essence of what is real without being tied to the past,
To look through the eyes of innocent perception,
To be a hollow bone for the energy of holiness to enter the world,
To be respectful of the heartful intent of others,

351

To realize universal law and work with it,
To give the rare gem of my uniqueness to the world,
To walk in the shimmering, flowing Invisible, as well as the
    structured, dense, material aspect of life,
[Add your own.] _____

_____

And to practice Earth magic to create FlowerSong, a new and
    radiant Earth.

Raise your left hand and make these pledges aloud in front of a fair witness. Sign and
keep, or choose one of the alternatives below.*

By my hand on this day _____ [date],
signed _____
Please also print your name:

_____

Fair witness: _____

_____

RAINBOW TRADING POST

Products available from the Rainbow Trading Post include my cassette tapes and CD, selected videos and books, and artwork by Vera Louise Drysdale. Any of the items listed in this section can be ordered by calling our office (406-883-4686) or by clicking the "Rainbow Trading Post" link at my Web site (www.MedicineEagle.com).

CASSETTE TAPES
SINGING

In addition to the tapes and CD listed here, I expect to have several more CDs of beautiful songs out soon, including one with the song of gratefulness, "Pila Maya."

For My People: If you know yourself to be one of my people, this album is dedicated to you! This popular singing tape features songs written by me and special friends—lengthened for you to sing along! It includes the title song, "For My People" (written to honor all life around my home in Montana), "Ancient Altar Song," "White Buffalo Woman," "Dawn Star," "Children of the Earth and Sun," "River Song," "Hey Ney Ya Na," "Giveaway," "Vision," "Thankfulness," and other chants.

A Gift of Song: This moving collection of international songs, recorded with my friend Ani Williams, is full of depth, joy, and poetry. These songs are giveaways: to us from Spirit singing within us. This album features the all-time favorite song of fans of my music (including many children): "Wishi Ta." Other beautiful songs and chants are "Cedar Song," "Neesa Neesa" (greeting the moon), "Blood of Life" (moontime song), "Spirit of the Wind," "Secret One," "Morning Song," "Whirlwind," "O Shoo Wa," "Traveling Song," "Ama Terra," "Hey La Shey La," and more. Also available on CD.

Shaman's Cave: The echoing sounds of these lovely songs were recorded "live" in a shaman's cave, known to have been used by two-leggeds for at least six thousand years. I stood deep in a vaulted, dripping chamber near where the stone altar still remains. When the altar was found, a huge, ancient buffalo skull lay upon it, together with a stone simply and elegantly carved on one side with a bear and on the other side with a buffalo. A new tone for this coming age of Oneness has been set at the center of the Earth. From this ancient place of ceremony, I sent my voice deep into Mother Earth to draw forth these healing vibrations and send them out to you with a prayer for harmony and peace among All Our Relations. Now it is for you to sing them and keep the healing vibrations radiating! Inside the cover photograph of me in a traditional bear shaman's outfit, you will find the words to these beautiful songs: "Hanta Yo!," "Welcome to Great Spirit," "Secret One," "Brothers and Sisters," "Altar Song," "We Are Ceremony," "Vision Wise," "Calling Love," "Women's Healing Song," "Hey Ney Ya Na," and "Blessing the Land."

Drumming the Heartbeat: The heartbeat of the drum is one of the first and most powerful sounds made by two-leggeds; it calls us to the circle, to the dance of life, to Oneness, to heartful sharing. Today, many people want this sound in places where drums are not present. This first drumming tape is meant for use in meditation, ceremony, and dancing as well as drumming practice for those beginning their drum journey. Included are a basic heartbeat drumming, excellent for meditation, and two dance rhythms that can be used in your circles and ceremonies.

Singing Joy to the Earth: It's not about singing perfectly; it's about singing joyfully! This classic album features both contemporary and traditional Native American songs and chants and teaches about the use of sound and harmony in this new age. We are in the time of the nine-pointed star, which relates to our throat chakra, the place of making the golden dream of peace, abundance, and beauty real on this Earth. You'll learn about singing, sound, and song in relationship to our ability to manifest what we need at this time. On the cassette, you will find "Chant to Call Spirit," "Women's Healing Chant," "Waiting Song," "Arapaho Ghost Dance Song," "Kate Wolf's Medicine Wheel Song," "May We All Fly Like Eagles," "Ancient Mother," and other songs, including several peyote songs.

RESOURCES

Visions Speaking: We two-leggeds are realizing that we cannot move forward into a new and workable way of being until we stop and listen to the great voices speaking around us. We must come into harmony with All Our Relations—recognizing that the Great Spirit lives in each and every thing and that the entire web of life is interconnected and interdependent—before we can be given the quality of vision that will truly guide us. The title of this cassette was inspired by the many questers from our Eagle Song camps who sat upon sacred land calling vision and returned to gift these songs. Let us open ourselves to allow the great visions to speak through us. I invite you to learn them with your family and circles: "Over the Horizon," "Pine Needles and Earth," "Send Me a Voice," "Sacred Ground," "Willow Song," "FlowerSong," "Kiowa Round Dance," "Vision Beauty Song," "Chant to Call the Moon," "Circle Round the Wheel," "Path of Beauty," and "Pomo Bear Chant."

WOMEN'S WISDOM

Moontime: This powerful tape brings women information on the spiritual aspects of moon (menstrual) time and how to use this special time each month to call vision, benefit our own health, and receive information about women's part in the new life two-leggeds are helping to create on Mother Earth. It is about honoring the lost ways of women's unique power—addressing menopause, the Grandmother Lodge, and other related issues.

Moon Lodge: Learn about the creation of the Moon Lodge (the women's place of retreat and visioning) and its special use during the menstrual cycle. You'll find practical suggestions for creation of the room itself, your group as it comes together, ceremonies for girls entering and elders leaving it, plus song, dance, and spiritual action to help you begin your own lodge.

Maiden: Lessons of Menarche: In this time, a great change is required of us two-leggeds in order to live well upon our beautiful Mother Earth. Part of this transformation will be a renewal of ritual and ceremony that

355

honors the cycles and passages of our lives and those of Earth and Sky. This teaching offers lessons and rituals for a most important and sacred passage in a woman's life: menarche. This is a time when a woman becomes like her Mother Earth—able to nurture and renew life. Especially useful for the family of a girl approaching menarche, this information will help a young woman begin her life in a good, healthful, spiritual way. The cover photo of an Apache maiden ceremony is a beautiful inspiration for all of us.

Grandmother Wisdom: In many tribal ways, the wisdom women, those initiated into the Grandmother Lodge, were the most powerful leaders of the people. This new tape of lessons of the Moon-Pause Lodge honors all "moon-pause" (menopausal) women. The charge of the Grandmother Lodge is to commit to the nurturing and renewal of All Life through the feminine principle, so imperative in these changing times. All women will come to this time eventually, and this tape shares the empowerment, health, vitality, and service that can come through dedication to serving the children of All Things.

We must reawaken this way of being for moon-pause women, so that the great wisdom, life experience, and resources they have built over their lives are not denigrated and wasted as they grow older. This elder time must again become a stage of life revered and honored by others and used powerfully in service by the women themselves.

TEACHING

Visioning: This two-tape set is a definitive explanation of the process of visioning questing, which includes principles, practices, and stories of my experience. Anytime you are planning to go on retreat or on a formal vision quest, these tapes will be a helpful and supportive guide. And there is much here to learn, whether or not you ever participate in a formal quest!

Empowering the Spiritual Warrior: Our challenge in this time is to make real the beautiful dreams we each carry of an abundant, radiant, and peaceful world. This tape is an elder sister's teaching of simple, yet profound, techniques and practices for empowering yourself as a spiritual warrior walking and creating a beauty path. You will find that the exercises given are useful and empowering in your everyday life as a practical spirituality.

Healing through Ritual Action: Exceptionally useful for personal growth and therapeutic work, this tape will help you learn to use physical actions to reprogram your nervous system and become free of habits and barriers in your daily life. Offered are not only principles of healing but also amazing examples of healing self and others through these methods. By creating and acting out these powerful healing metaphors, you can build processes of clearing and growth into your everyday actions as well as share their simple power with others.

VIDEOS

Dancing Awake the Drum (third in the series Quest of the Earthkeepers): Join me in this extraordinary journey into the magical transformation created through dancing and drumming. In this sixty-minute program, I share wisdom of the coming Earth changes, my insight into survival, and prayers of hope for the next seven generations. Also join in a women's Moon Circle and discover this unique healing ritual.

Awaken to the ancient spiritual practices shared with the power and understanding of Earth medicine. Dance awake the dream of a radiant new time and celebrate wholeness as you step into a global circle of harmony set to the heartbeat of a gentle drum.

Living with Prophecy: It is said to be one of the most important times in the planet's history, a time when the ancient prophecies of war, disease, and environmental chaos are being fulfilled each day. We look back to find the wisdom of the ancestors who walked before us. We listen to their wise words to find solutions as we create personal and planetary healing. In this newly released video, I share prophecies that illuminate this present critical time of Earth and provide solutions for our edification. This tape brings messages from the ancients for practical use in these challenging modern times.

Featuring interviews with Sun Bear, Wallace Black Elk, Gilbert Walking Bull, Tarwater, Brant Secunda, and many more modern-day wisdom keepers.

Moontime: Menarche to Menopause: Follow your Grandmother Moon and you will begin a process of learning about the feminine mystery teachings. The moon's illuminating cycles will transform your spirit as you awaken them within your body.

These teachings about a woman's sacred cycles have been lost to several generations of women in many native cultures and to many more generations from European traditions. Now this wisdom is coming back into our consciousness from the few remaining elders who carry it, from our inner questing, and from our practice of the teachings themselves. These wise ways have tremendous import not only for our spiritual practice as a human family but also for our full health and well-being as women.

Vital information is offered for women experiencing their moontime and instructions on creating a Moon Lodge—a place dedicated to the honoring of these sacred ways. I give counsel to the moon-pause (menopause) woman, who can enter her wisdom years in a new and powerful way, dedicating herself in service to the children of All Things. Also included are teachings for the young girl just becoming a woman— lessons and rituals that will help start the young woman on a beautiful path for her life and the lives of those she touches.

The Story of White Buffalo Woman: You are invited to share in the timely magic of this ancient story of the mysterious, powerful woman who brought the gift of the Sacred Peace Pipe to the western Native nations, along with the gift of healing and rituals to provide health and happiness in the hardest of times. My intention is to keep this story alive in the hearts and minds of a new generation of Rainbow Earthkeepers, Earth Mages.

White Buffalo Woman, our Elder Sister, brought us a message whose truth has carried down through time and is now vitally important as we are faced with critical issues about our human survival on Earth. Her so-

lutions to these problems are simple and profound. We must begin now to put them into effect and make an important, positive difference for the coming seven generations.

ARTWORK BY VERA LOUISE DRYSDALE

RAINBOW SUNDANCER
(COVER ART)

Of this beautiful and inspirational painting, its creator, Vera Louise Drysdale, says:

This visionary work is a commemorative symbol of the Harmonic Convergence celebration, August 17, 1987, the year of emerging and gathering 144,000 Rainbow Sundancers in cultures all over the world. It heralds a new level of awareness for an awakening humanity.

Vera Louise went to the Beyond Country in January of 1994, having produced over her lifetime a body of work portraying the beauty and spirit of the Native American peoples, most especially the Lakota. I'm sure that from her larger perspective, Vera can see how perfectly *Rainbow Sundancer* presaged what I have written in *The Last Ghost Dance*.

The following reproductions of the *Rainbow Sundancer* cover art are available:

- Full-color poster (20″ × 30″), either unsigned or signed by me
- Set of greeting cards (5″ × 7″), blank inside for your message

NATIVE PORTRAITS IN PENCIL

White Buffalo Calf Pipe Woman—Carrying Her Pipe of Oneness.

Sacred Pipe Keepers:
- Black Elk, great holy man of the Oglala Sioux, as an old man on

Harney Peak for the last time to voice his plea to the Six Grand-fathers, "Oh, make my people live." In the clouds, eagles come to honor him.

- Martha Bad Warrior, first woman keeper of the pipe, at eighty sitting in the hot summer sun of a drought, holding the pipe in a fervent prayer for rain. In the clouds, White Buffalo Woman and a herd of buffalo listen to her prayers. Her sacrifice was honored by the rain that followed, but soon afterward she died.

Indian Madonnas: Two different pencil drawings of Lakota women holding their babies, one in a cradleboard and one wrapped in fur.

Many other portraits of men, women, and children.

(These and more will be displayed on my Web page.)

In 1980, *The Gift of the Sacred Pipe*, a stunning portrayal of White Buffalo Calf Pipe Woman's coming, edited and illustrated by Vera Louise, was given to the world, and it has recently been rereleased (University of Oklahoma Press, 1995). It is an absolute treasure for those of us to whose hearts White Buffalo Woman speaks. Vera conversed with this sacred woman's spirit over the many years she worked on the book's drawings and paintings, and that contact shines through the pages of her magnificent book.

Vera Louise produced a wide variety of exquisite oil paintings and charcoal drawings of Native people, as well as posters and greeting cards of *Rainbow Sundancer*. Her daughter, Linda Victoria, is continuing to make them available to the public. If you would like to explore adding some of her fine work to your collection, contact us through our Web site or the Singing Eagle–Earth Mages office, as indicated in Appendix A.

BOOKS

Buffalo Woman Comes Singing, by Brooke Medicine Eagle. My spiritual autobiography.

Cooking with Brooke, by Melane Lohmann. Healthy, ecological weight-loss recipes from our Eagle Song camps.

Love without End ... Jesus Speaks, by Glenda Green. I've recommended this book so many times that we now have it available through our office, which you can call for a free tape. *Love without End* is also available as a series of twelve audiocassettes, which can help you absorb the teachings more deeply.

Songs of Earth, Songs of Spirit. Lyrics booklet containing the words of all the songs on all my music tapes.

AUDIOCASSETTE INTERVIEWS

FROM NEW DIMENSIONS TAPES

The following cassettes are available. Order from New Dimensions Radio, Rose Holland, P.O. Box 569, Ukiah, CA 95482; 800-935-8273; www.newdimensions.org; ndradio@pacific.net. Please indicate the number and title of each tape you want, as well as my name. The tapes cost $9.95 each. For the first tape ordered, add $2.00 packaging and handling for domestic shipment or $6.00 packaging and handling for shipment to foreign destinations, including Canada. For each additional tape ordered, add $1.00 for domestic and foreign shipment. (Please *double* the packaging and handling amounts for first-class domestic shipment or foreign airmail shipment.) California residents, add 7.25 percent sales tax; residents of BART counties, add 7.75 percent. Make checks payable to New Dimensions Tapes. If you use MasterCard or VISA, give the account number and expiration date.

Earth Is Our Mother: I discuss the power of honesty in our relationships with one another and with Mother Earth and share insights gained from those who taught me to revere our planet as we would our own parents. (Tape 1633, 1 hour)

The Indian Medicine Way: This is a wonderful and natural look at Native American ways of healing ourselves and the planet. Traditional values and centuries-old cultural forms are still relevant to modern times, especially if we're open to new vistas. (Tape 1485, 1 hour)

Native Visions: Healing the Heart: Here I speak to the challenge of the times in which we live. I share my love of Mother Earth, suggest that we notice what is at center in our lives, and offer new ways to bring healing energies into all aspects of living. (Tape 1978, 1 hour)

The Rainbow Warrior: With guidance from medicine woman Stands by the Fire (known to her people as The Woman Who Knows Everything), I have embarked upon the Rainbow Warrior's way. This is not the way of war but the call of one who heals, who makes whole—the vision-giver-and-receiver: a way of knowing we may all need to experience if we are to regain our rightful relationship with Mother Earth. (Tape 1714, 1 hour)

Spirit Dance: In the sacred tradition of the medicine way, I weave a tapestry of the Spirit within and the Great Circle. I create an energy connection between Father Sky and Mother Earth to move you forward on your path, opening doors to the wonder-filled unknown. Using my rainbow medicine nature, and integrating Western academic knowledge with the wisdom of tribal elders, I present the essential spirit and principles of living a fully human life. Going beyond forms, breaking old barriers, and transforming tradition all are part of the spirit dance as we deepen contact with our true self. (Tape 1936, 1 hour)

Tales of White Buffalo Woman: We are all one with All Things is the greatest teaching now available to two-leggeds, according to the message of the mythic White Buffalo Woman, which I recount here. White Buffalo Woman speaks of "the holy work," the work of wholeness, so vitally important to restoring the balance of nature and life, and of how our essence is one of relatedness to All. I stress the importance of ritual, prayer, drumming, listening, lightening up, and much more. (Tape 2105, 1 hour)

FROM BAT OUT OF HELL PRODUCTIONS

The following cassette is from Bat Out of Hell Productions, 3912 N. Military Rd., Arlington, VA 22207 (888-741-GODS). The tape costs $15.00 plus $1.50 shipping.

Astrologer Caroline Casey interviews Brooke on the *Visionary Activist Show* (station KPFA in Berkeley, California; February 27, 1997). Topics include setting intent, trusting Spirit, loosening the grip of Time, connecting with each person you meet as family, and paying exquisite attention to the intelligence of the natural world. Caroline and Brooke perform healing over the airwaves on frazzled call-in listeners.

BROOKE MEDICINE EAGLE
CONTACT AND ORDERING
INFORMATION

For information about
Brooke's seminars, retreats,
distant learning/home study programs
Leadership Seven work,
Spirit Dances,
Feng Shui consultations,
private sessions and vision quests,
Wakantia trainings,
and other Earth Mages work:

brooke@MedicineEagle.com
www.MedicineEagle.com

Singing Eagle & Earth Mages, Unlimited
PMB C401
One 2nd Avenue East
Polson, MT 59860
406-883-4686

To order teaching and singing cassettes, teaching videos, or Vera Louise
Drysdale art, contact our office, or see Rainbow Trading Post at www.
MedicineEagle.com.

NOTES

PREFACE

1. Ken Carey, *Return of the Bird Tribes* (New York: HarperCollins, 1988), 133.

2. See Appendix A for more information on Vera Louise Drysdale and her beautiful artwork.

CHAPTER I: THE FALL

1. See Joseph Eppes Brown, *The Sacred Pipe* (Baltimore: Penguin Books, 1953; reprint, 1989), for a full explanation of the coming of White Buffalo Calf Pipe Woman and the ceremonies she brought the people. These stories were shared by a Lakota holy man, Black Elk, to keep the traditions alive in a time when they were in danger of being lost because no one could legally practice them. This event is also spoken of in the prologue of my book *Buffalo Woman Comes Singing* (New York: Ballantine Books, 1991).

2. Brown, *Sacred Pipe*, 115.

3. To learn about the books, classes, herbal essences, and information by Machaelle Small Wright that they used as a basis for this work, call the Perelandra Center for Nature Research in Warrenton, Va. (800-960-8806) or visit its Web site (www.perelandra-ltd.com). Also very useful is Pam Montgomery's book *Partner Earth: A Spiritual Ecology* (Rochester, Vt.: Destiny Books, 1997).

CHAPTER 2: SPRINGTIME

1. See Appendix B for other similar words and writings appropriate in times of losing a loved one.

2. Mary Oliver, "White Owl Flies Into and Out of the Field," *House of Light* (Boston: Beacon Press, 1990), 99–100.

3. Chief Sealth (Seattle), Squamish chieftain (1786?–1866), from his famous speech in 1854 at a territorial governor's council.

CHAPTER 4: LISTENING TO THE GREAT VOICES

1. David Abram, *The Spell of the Sensuous* (New York: Random House, Pantheon Books, 1997), ix.

2. All the selections in this chapter are excerpted from "When the Wolf Howls (Mother Earth Answers)," a manuscript of my nature writings, which I hope soon to publish.

3. A Sufi designation for a spiritual teacher.

4. Paraphrased from a crop-circle report by Mary and David Dohrman, *Access Magazine* (Ashland, Oreg.), November 1996, 3. The Khan quotation is from Hazrat Inayat Khan, *Nature Meditations* (Lebanon Springs, N.Y.: Sufi Order Publications, 1980), 186.

5. It was November, and there were already five feet of dense, wet snow (much more in the elks' mountain homes). The temperature hovered right around thirty-two degrees—freezing and thawing and refreezing in such a way that it made everything slick under the surface covering of challengingly deep snow. After the winter of 1997, enormous herds of elk were found dead in the high country. They had been unable to find enough to eat in the shoulder-high snow.

6. A small weasel whose winter coat is prized for its beautiful, thick whiteness and often used in making or decorating fur garments.

7. For a full explanation of this coming time of increasing Light pouring into Earth and its implications, see Chapter 7, "The Drinking Gourd." You may also want to listen to my teaching cassette *Awakening in the Golden Age*, available through the Singing Eagle office (406-883-4686) or the Rainbow Trading Post at www.MedicineEagle.com.

8. A phrase from Mary Oliver's exquisite poem "White Owl Flies Into and Out of the Field," *House of Light* (Boston: Beacon Press, 1990), 99–100.

9. See Chapter 7, "The Drinking Gourd."

10. For a complete discussion of partnering with Earth, see Pam Montgomery's wonderful book *Partner Earth: A Spiritual Ecology* (Rochester, Vt.: Destiny Books, 1997).

CHAPTER 5: RENEWING THE VISION

1. I am thinking here of *Embraced by the Light,* by Betty J. Eadie and Curtis Taylor (New York: Bantam Books, 1992).

2. More on this in Chapter 7, "The Drinking Gourd."

3. Yuwipi is a powerful Native American ceremony in which the central shamanic figure, who is ritually bound and tied at the beginning, manifests extraordinary things and is miraculously untied by the end of the ceremony.

4. For further information, see Teisha Abelar, *The Sorcerer's Crossing* (New York: Viking Arcana, 1992); Florinda Donner, *Being in Dreaming* (San Francisco: HarperSanFrancisco, 1991); the works of Carlos Castaneda; and Victor Sanchez, *The Teachings of Don Carlos* (Santa Fe, N.M.: Bear and Company, 1995).

5. Ascended Masters are high masters who assist with the upliftment of all. See Baird Spalding, *Life and Teachings of the Masters of the Far East,* vols. 1 and 2 (Santa Monica, Calif.: DeVorss & Company, 1944, 1983). These books are vitally important for this new step in our human evolution!

6. You will notice that it is difficult in English to speak of these things, because our language is bound by time and space, yet you can get the basic idea.

7. Highly evolved spiritual leader among his Lakota people, who died in his thirties in 1877.

8. Lakota man who was one of the first Ghost Dance "priests," bringing the dance to his people in the 1890s. See Chapter 6, "Spirit Dancing," as well as James Mooney, *The Ghost-Dance Religion and the Sioux Outbreak of 1890* (1896; reprint, Lincoln: University of Nebraska, Bison Press, 1991).

9. This is also the name by which I know Him and the name I use in *Buffalo Woman Comes Singing* (New York: Ballantine Books, 1991) as well as in the remainder of this book. Much of Chapter 8, "We Stand in the Dawn Star's Light," is devoted to His story and its relationship to the awakening in our present time.

10. For more information on the Christ light of the Americas, refer to *Buffalo Woman Comes Singing*, Chapter 12, 235–56; Spalding, *Life and Teachings*; Levi H. Dowling, *The Aquarian Gospel of Jesus, the Christ of the Piscean Age* (Santa Monica, Calif.: Unity, 1954); and Ken Carey, *Return of the Bird Tribes* (New York: Talman Company, 1988).

11. In Chapter 8, you will find a full explanation of the Harmonic Convergence and its historical antecedents.

CHAPTER 6: SPIRIT DANCING

1. James Mooney, *The Ghost-Dance Religion and the Sioux Outbreak of 1890* (1896; reprint, Lincoln: University of Nebraska, Bison Press, 1991).

2. *Encyclopedia of North American Indians,* edited by Frederick E. Hoxie (Boston: Houghton Mifflin, 1996), 427.

3. Mooney, *Last Ghost Dance,* 664.

4. Ibid., 665.

5. Quoted in Mooney, *Last Ghost Dance,* 693.

6. Mooney, *Last Ghost Dance,* 711.

7. Ibid., 771–72.

8. Robert M. Utley, *The Last Days of the Sioux Nation* (New Haven, Conn.: Yale University Press, 1963), 86–89.

9. Quoted in Mooney, *Last Ghost Dance,* 977.

10. Utley, *Last Days of the Sioux Nation,* 69–70.

11. Ibid., 90.

12. For the full story, see Mooney, *Last Ghost Dance,* Chapters 12 and 13, 816–86.

13. Mooney, *Last Ghost Dance,* frontispiece.

14. Ibid., 698.

15. Ibid., 778.

CHAPTER 7: THE DRINKING GOURD

1. If you wish to read about the subjects in this chapter in more detail, I highly recommend Robert Cox's *The Pillar of Celestial Fire: Lost Science of the Ancient Seers* (Fairfield, Iowa: Sunstar Publishing, 1997).

2. See "Carrying Her Pipe of Oneness," in my book *Buffalo Woman Comes Singing*, 429–45 (New York: Ballantine Books, 1991).

3. Norma Milanovich and Shirley McCune, *The Light Shall Set You Free* (Albuquerque, N.M.: Athena Publishing, 1996), xii.

4. A good, simple explanation of this phenomenon can be found in the "Quantized Vortices" entry, *McGraw-Hill Encyclopedia of Physics*, 2d ed. (New York: McGraw-Hill, 1991), 1092.

5. Cooling helium to below 2.17 degrees Kelvin causes it to assume a superfluid state. It can still be held in an ordinary glass or metal vessel.

6. Milanovich and McCune, *The Light Shall Set You Free*, 16.

7. Cox, *Pillar of Celestial Fire*, 15.

8. Some who pay attention to these cycles think that this incoming energy is the same as the photon belt—a band of intense light energy that is upcoming in the path of Earth. This belt was first discovered in 1961 near the vicinity of the Pleiades by scientist Paul Otto Hesse using satellite instrumentation. For more information on this view, check the Web site www.salemctr.com/photon.html and Virginia Essene and Sheldon Nidle's book *You Are Becoming a Galactic Human* (Santa Clara, Calif.: Spiritual Education Endeavors Publishing, 1994).

9. I highly recommend reading Rob's book if these concepts interest you.

10. A wonderful reference that fully addresses these powerful internal technologies is Gregg Braden's *Walking between the Worlds: The Science of Compassion* (Bellevue, Wash.: Radio Bookstore Press, 1997).

11. Cox, *Pillar of Celestial Fire*, 132.

NOTES

CHAPTER 8: WE STAND IN THE DAWN STAR'S LIGHT

1. One who is masterful or totally proficient—in this case, spiritually masterful, not to be confused with the degraded use of the word *master* as the owner of slaves.

2. For a powerful modern explanation similar to this, refer to *Energy Anatomy*, a set of cassette tapes by Caroline Myss, available from Sounds True, Boulder, Colo. (800-333-9185).

3. For a deeper look at these names and the information supporting them, see L. Taylor Hansen, *He Walked the Americas* (Amherst, Wis.: Amherst Press, 1963).

4. Kandis Blakely has brought forward what she calls New Decision Therapy, which works directly with the transformative power of forgiveness. For information on her work, practitioners of NDT, certification courses, and her book *New Decision Therapy: Your Body Remembers*, contact New Decision Therapy, Intl., P.O. Box 1834, Vallejo, CA 94590, 212-252-4734 or newdecisiontherapy.com.

5. This aged cypress, or American cedar, in the Grove of Tule in the state of Oaxaca (wah-HA-ca), Mexico, is still living. It may be the largest living thing in the Americas and probably the world. It is also perhaps the oldest and soars to great heights. At a distance of ten feet above the ground, its trunk has a circumference of more than ninety feet, which takes twenty-six people holding hands to circle it.

6. For further information, see Hansen, *He Walked the Americas*.

7. This stone is now in the National Museum in Mexico City, after having been used and partly desecrated by the Chichimecas and the Aztecs.

8. Ken Carey, *Return of the Bird Tribes* (New York: HarperCollins, 1988), 70.

9. From the 1880s until the Indian Freedom of Religion Act was passed in 1978, this was not guaranteed.

10. The movie *Thunderheart*, though fictional, portrays the kinds of things that happened during that time.

11. See José Argüelles's work in *The Mayan Factor: Path beyond Technology* (Santa Fe, N.M.: Bear and Company, 1987), *Earth Ascending: An Illustrated*

Treatise on the Law Governing Whole Systems (Boulder, Colo., and London: Shambhala Publications, 1984), and other books.

12. Solara, *How to Live Large on a Small Planet* (Eureka, Mont.: Star-Borne Unlimited, 1996), 30–31.

13. James Redfield, *The Celestine Prophecy* (Hoover, Ala.: Satori Publishing, 1993).

14. From Ernesto Sedillo and Hubert H. Bancroft, "Song of Quetzalcoatl," in *Five Volumes of Antiquities, Native Dances, Etc.*, edited by Hubert H. Bancroft (Appleton, 1875), 167; and from Maya legends.

15. Other ancient Hebrew and Aramaic writings have been found in the Americas—in the mounds of the Southeast and other places. For a summary of this research, see Hansen, *He Walked the Americas*; and recent archaeological reports.

16. James Redfield, *The Tenth Insight* (New York: Warner Books, 1996).

17. Hansen, *He Walked the Americas*, 93.

18. Glenda Green, *Love without End: Jesus Speaks . . .* (Fort Worth, Tex.: Heartwings Publishing, 1992).

CHAPTER 9: THE END OF TIME

1. L. Taylor Hansen, *He Walked the Americas* (Amherst, Wis.: Amherst Press, 1963), 25.

2. If you are interested, you may want to investigate the work of Michael Harner and Sandy Ingerman by contacting the Foundation for Shamanic Studies, P.O. Box 1939, Mill Valley, CA 94942.

3. See "An Old Samurai Moves Me," in my book *Buffalo Woman Comes Singing*, 189–214 (New York: Ballantine Books, 1991); and Feldenkrais's own books, beginning with *Awareness through Movement* (New York: Harper and Row, 1977).

4. Rabindranath Tagore, *Fireflies* (New York: Macmillan, 1928), 17.

5. Read Chapter 11, "The Heaviest Sword and the Sharpest Razor," *Buffalo Woman Comes Singing*, (New York: Ballantine Books, 1991), for a more complete look at my work with Master Kaskafayet.

6. A number of Barry Neil Kaufman's books might be of interest in

NOTES

this context. In particular, his *Happiness Is a Choice* (New York: Fawcett, 1994) will give you a greater understanding of exactly what I'm talking about here. For workshops, contact the Option Institute, P.O. Box 1180, Sheffield, MA 01257; 413-229-2100.

7. Tony Stubbs, *An Ascension Handbook* (Livermore, Calif.: Oughten House Publications, 1991), 89.

8. For more fascinating and useful information on the basic principles of Permaculture, a way of designing for sustainable living, see *Introduction to Permaculture* (Tyalguin, Australia: Tagari Publications, 1995) by Bill Mollison with Rena Mia Slay. Tagari Publications can be contacted at P.O. Box 1, Tyalguin, NSW 2484, Australia. And/or see *The Permaculture Activist* magazine (P.O. Box 1209, Black Mountain, NC 28711; 828-298-2812) for many articles, books, and other resources.

9. For more on this fascinating story, see "White Powder Gold," *Nexus*, August and October 1996. Transcripts of Hudson's talks can be found on the Internet at monatomic.earth.com. (Note that this particular Internet address is *not* preceded by "www.")

10. Although Hudson's Science of the Spirit Foundation is focused on research rather than dispensing information about his story, it does have a newsletter, which can be obtained by writing to P.O. Box 25709, Tempe, AZ 85285.

11. Robert Cox, *The Pillar of Celestial Fire: Lost Science of the Ancient Seers* (Fairfield, Iowa: Sunstar Publishing, 1997), 135–36.

12. Norma Milanovich and Shirley McCune, *The Light Shall Set You Free* (Albuquerque, N.M.: Athena Publishing, 1996), 3–5.

CHAPTER 10: READY OR NOT!

1. From the tape *Conversations with Jesus*, by Glenda Green (Fort Worth, Tex.: Heartwings Publishing, 1997). I highly recommend this series, available through my office.

2. The Great Spirit and all the high helpers, including the Earth.

3. Thomas Mails, *Fools Crow: Wisdom and Power* (Tulsa, Okla.: Council Oaks Books, 1991), 55.

374

4. Gregg Braden, *Walking between the Worlds: The Science of Compassion* (Bellevue, Wash.: Radio Bookstore Press, 1997), 184.

5. Lee Carroll, *Kryon—The End Times: New Information for Personal Peace* (Bellevue, Wash.: Kryon Writings, 1997), 13.

6. Glenda Green, *Love without End: Jesus Speaks . . .* (Fort Worth, Tex.: Heartwings Publishing, 1992), 212.

7. See E. Golden, *Waves and Photons* (Danbury, Conn.: Grolier Electronic Publishing, 1992).

8. Contact the International Society for the Study of Subtle Energies and Energy Medicine (ISSSEEM), 356 Goldco Circle, Golden, CO 80401.

9. Walter Russell's institute in Swannanoa, Virginia.

10. The Tiananmen Square incident happened shortly thereafter, and I've not been in contact with them since to learn how this development progressed in China.

11. James Redfield, *The Celestine Prophecy* (New York: Warner Books, 1996), 209–10.

12. Paraphrased from James Redfield and Carol Adrienne, *The Celestine Prophecy: An Experiential Guide* (New York: Warner Books, 1995), 244–45.

13. Rabindranath Tagore, *Fireflies* (New York: Macmillan, 1928), 12.

14. Braden, *Walking between the Worlds*, 82.

15. Perceiving from an innocent perspective—without editing from intellect, social norms, conventions, or old habits.

16. For information on these personal healing regimens, write to the American Botanical Pharmacy, P.O. Box 3027, Santa Monica, CA 90408, or call 310-453-1987 for customer service.

17. Rachel Naomi Remen, M.D., *Kitchen Table Wisdom: Stories That Heal* (New York: Riverhead Books, 1996), 274.

18. If you haven't looked into this, I suggest you do so. The challenges of eating meat are well documented in John Robbins's *Diet for a New America: How Your Food Choices Affect Your Health, Happiness, and the Future of Life on Earth* (Walpole, N.H.: Stillpoint Publishing, 1987) and Howard Lyman's *Mad Cowboy: Plain Truth from the Cattle Rancher Who Won't Eat Meat* (New York: Scribner, 1998).

19. Available through your local health-food store or by contacting Apple a Day Press, 102 Westlake Dr., Austin, TX 78746; 512-328-3996.

19. Available through your local health-food store or by contacting Apple a Day Press, 102 Westlake Dr., Austin, TX 78746; 512-328-3996.

20. Peter D'Adamo, *Eat Right for Your Type* (New York: Putnam Publishing, 1997).

21. James Redfield, *The Celestine Prophecy* (Hoover, Ala.: Satori Publishing, 1993), 55–56.

22. Growing food based on Rudolf Steiner's principles. For information on his principles applied to gardening, Waldorf education, and so forth, contact Rudolf Steiner College, 9200 Fair Oaks Blvd., Fair Oaks, CA 95628.

23. Write to Pure Synergy Company, P.O. Box 2901, Moab, UT 84532, or call 800-723-0277.

24. Write to Four Plus Food Plan, 1965 Freeman Ave., Long Beach, CA 90804-1211, or call 800-333-0751.

25. Write to The Ultimate Life, P.O. Box 4308, Santa Barbara, CA 93140; call 800-843-6325; or visit its Web site (www.ultimatelife.com).

26. "FDA Ignores Safety Warnings," *Small Farmers Journal* (winter 2000): 18.

27. Contact the Alliance for Bio-Integrity in Fairfield, Iowa (515-472-5554).

28. Green, *Love without End*, 125.

29. For a brief description, see "An Old Samurai Moves Me," in my book *Buffalo Woman Comes Singing* (New York: Ballantine Books, 1991). For full information on the process and to find a practitioner near you, contact the Feldenkrais Guild, P.O. Box 489, Albany, NY 97321-0143.

30. For more information and to find practitioners in your area, write to the Uplinger Institute, 1121 Prosperity Farms Rd., Palm Beach Gardens, FL 33410-3487, or call 561-622-4334 for administration or 561-622-4706 for Healthplex Clinical Services.

31. See Kristin Linklater, *Freeing the Natural Voice* (New York: Drama Book Specialists, 1976), and ask voice teachers in your community for this kind of work.

32. From a 1998 Continuum brochure. For information, write to Continuum, 1629 18th St., no. 7, Santa Monica, CA 90404; contact Continuum by phone (310-453-4402) or E-mail (office@continuum movement.com); or visit its Web site (www.continuummovement.com).

33. For more information, see Budwig's *Flax Oil as a True Aid against Arthritis, Heart Infarction, Cancer and Other Diseases,* English ed. (Richmond, B.C., Canada: Apple Publishing, 1992), and *The Oil Protein Diet Cookbook* (Canada: Apple Publishing, 1994).

34. One excellent supplier is Omega Nutrition in Bellingham, Wash. (800-661-3529).

35. Supplement and information can be obtained by writing to JoAnn and David Health Products, 1698 Marguerite Ave., Corona Del Mar, CA 92625, or calling 800-700-5402.

36. See information on this substance in the work of David Hudson and Rob Cox, discussed in Chapter 9. Also see "White Powder Gold," *Nexus* (August and October 1996).

37. Because we two-leggeds have unfortunately poisoned much of our water, this means that you should always use a water filter. Call health-food stores and health products dealers in your area to learn about good-quality ones before you invest.

38. Thomas Mails, *Fools Crow: Wisdom and Power* (Tulsa, Okla.: Council Oaks Books, 1991), 32–33.

39. For more information on this meditative practice, see Green, *Love without End,* 160.

40. To obtain information or place an order, call Centerpointe Research Institute in Beaverton, Oreg. (800-945-2741; ask for operator 32).

41. For information on Drunvalo's work, visit the Web site at www.drunvalo.net.

42. Ruby Nelson, *The Door of Everything* (Marina del Rey, Calif.: De Vorss and Company, 1979), 33.

43. "How Spiritual Are You?" *Self,* December 1997, 135.

44. Ken Carey, *The Third Millennium* (San Francisco: HarperSanFrancisco, 1996). Cassette tapes are also available of Ken reading this book. Listening to these tapes can be very lovely and empowering. Ask your bookstore to order them for you if it doesn't carry them.

CHAPTER II: SINGING A SONG OF BEAUTY

1. An ancient Chinese book that describes a system of divination through the observation of natural cycles of change.

2. See *Emmanuel's Book* (1987), *Emmanuel's Book II* (1989), and *Emmanuel's Book III* (1994), all of which were compiled by Pat Rodegast and Judith Stanton (New York: Bantam).

3. Glenda Green, *Love without End: Jesus Speaks ...* (Fort Worth, Tex.: Heartwings Publishing, 1992), 136.

4. Through my Essential Harmony business, I am available for Feng Shui consultations for home and office, plus "divine designs" for homes and housing developments. For information and my travel schedule, contact my office via phone (406-883-4686) or E-mail (brooke@ MedicineEagle.com).

5. James Redfield, *The Tenth Insight* (New York: Warner Books, 1996). Read it and use it!!

6. There is fabulous, practical, beneficial information in *The Celestine Prophecy: An Experiential Guide*, by James Redfield and Carol Adrienne (New York: Warner Books, 1995); *Conversations with God*, by Neale Donald Walsch (Norfolk, Va.: Hampton Roads Publishing, 1995); and *The Teachings of Don Carlos*, by Victor Sanchez (Santa Fe, N.M.: Bear and Company, 1995).

7. For more information on Feldenkrais, see note 3 for Chapter 9.

8. Gregg Braden, *Walking between the Worlds: The Science of Compassion* (Bellevue, Wash.: Radio Bookstore Press, 1997), 9.

9. For practitioners in your area and other information, contact the EMDR Institute by mail (EMDR Institute, Inc., P.O. Box 51010, Pacific Grove, CA 93950-6010), phone (831-372-3900), or E-mail (inst@emdr.com) or visit its Web site (www.emdr.com).

10. This method can be used with humans, plants, animals, and so forth. See Machaelle Small Wright's Perelandra workbooks; to order or obtain information, write to the Perelandra Center for Nature Research, P.O. Box 3603, Warrenton, VA 20188, or call Perelandra's Question Hot Line (540-937-3679).

11. See *Brain Gym* and *Brain Gym*, Teacher's Edition, by Dr. Paul Denison and Gail Dennison (founders of the Educational Kinesiology

NOTES

Foundation); and *Smart Moves* (1995) and *The Dominance Factor* (1997), by Carla Hannaford. To order these books, get more information about Educational Kinesiology, or learn about practitioners in your area, contact the Educational Kinesiology Foundation in Ventura, Calif., by phone (800-356-2109) or E-mail (edukfd@earthlink.net) or visit its Web site (www.braingym.org).

12. For private sessions and for classes to learn the work, contact Jyoti (406-883-1105) at Living in Balance, in Polson, Mont.

13. Carlos Castaneda, *Magical Passes: Practical Wisdom of the Shamans of Ancient Mexico* (New York: HarperCollins, 1998). For information on this and other Castaneda books, classes, and videos, contact Cleargreen in Los Angeles (310-264-6126 or 800-490-3020).

14. Taisha Abelar, *The Sorcerer's Crossing* (New York: Viking Arcana, 1992).

15. Florinda Donner, *Being in Dreaming* (San Francisco: HarperSanFrancisco, 1991).

16. Victor Sanchez, *The Teachings of Don Carlos* (Santa Fe, N.M.: Bear and Company, 1995). For information on his work in Mexico and around the world, contact Victor Sanchez at Apartado Postal 12-762, Mexico, D.F., Mexico.

17. This series and many other teaching cassettes are available from Sounds True in Boulder, Colo. (800-333-9185). Also available from your local bookstore is Caroline Myss's *Anatomy of the Spirit: The Seven Stages of Power and Healing* (New York: Random House, 1997). For further information on Caroline Myss and her workshops, write to her at 1210 Hirsch St., Melrose Park, IL 60160; or call 708-338-9128.

18. Gregg Braden, *Walking between the Worlds: The Science of Compassion* (Bellevue, Wash.: Radio Bookstore Press, 1997), 98–146.

19. See Wallace Black Elk's book *Black Elk: The Sacred Ways of a Lakota* (San Francisco: HarperSanFrancisco, 1991).

20. A complete explanation of vision questing is provided in my cassette tape entitled *Visioning*. (See Appendix A, "Resources.")

21. Glenda Green's *Love without End* is a wonderful book that fully explains entering the spiritual heart to touch into Source and our indigenous intelligence.

22. Rabindranath Tagore, *Fireflies* (New York: Macmillan, 1928), 32.

23. Ibid., 34.

24. From a personal conversation, also documented in an exquisite gathering of Native wisdom entitled *Simply Living: The Spirit of the Indigenous People*, edited by Shirley Jones (Novato, Calif.: New World Library, 1999).

25. Tagore, *Fireflies*, 23.

26. From John O'Donohue's 1996 set of audiocassettes *Anam Cara: Wisdom from the Celtic World*, Sounds True Productions (800-333-9185); see also O'Donohue's *Anam Cara: A Book of Celtic Wisdom* (New York: Harper-Collins, 1997).

27. Norma Milanovich and Shirley McCune, *The Light Shall Set You Free* (Albuquerque, N.M.: Athena Publishing, 1996), 7.

28. Caroline Casey, *Making the Gods Work for You* (New York: Harmony Books, 1998). Caroline's seasonal celebration cassettes can be obtained by calling 301-320-0373. Ask also about the tape of her 1997 radio interview with me.

CHAPTER 12: A SHAMAN'S WAY

1. David Whyte, "What to Remember When Waking," *House of Belonging* (Langely, Wash.: Many Rivers Press, 1997), 26.

2. For a full explanation of this way of working with yourself and others, listen to my teaching tape *Healing through Ritual Action* (see Appendix A, "Resources").

3. For a full exploration of ritual and metaphorical action, see "Healing through Ritual Action," in my book *Buffalo Woman Comes Singing*, 307–26 (New York: Ballantine Books, 1991), or listen to my cassette teaching tape with the same title, mentioned in the preceding note.

4. Eugene Gendlin, *Focusing* (New York: Bantam Books, 1981).

5. Mary Oliver, "Wild Geese," *Dream Work* (New York: Grove/Atlantic, 1986).

6. Robert Ghost Wolf, *Last Cry* (Spokane, Wash.: Mistyc House Publishing, 1994), 35.

7. Eligio Stephen Gallegos, *Animals of the Four Windows* (Santa Fe, N.M.: Moon Bear Publishing, 1992), 20, 63.

8. Two of many resources are the Dream Network (call 801-

259-5936 or E-mail DreamKey@lasal.net) and Sun Bear, Wabun Wind, and Shawnodese, *Dreaming with the Wheel* (New York: Simon and Schuster, Fireside, 1994).

9. These teachings came in person, so I want you to know of their informative books: Malidoma Patrice Somé, *Of Water and the Spirit* (New York: Penguin, 2000) and *The Healing Wisdom of Africa* (New York: Tarcher, 1998); and Sobonfu Somé, *The Spirit of Intimacy* (New York: Morrow, 1999) and *Welcoming Spirit Home* (Novato, Calif.: New World Library, 2000).

10. Caitlin Matthews and John Matthews, *The Encyclopedia of Celtic Wisdom* (Rockport, Mass.: Element Books, 1994), 92.

11. For an in-depth look at this research, see Barry Fell's *Saga America* (New York: Random House, 1980), *America B.C.* (New York: Random House, 1976), and *Bronze Age America* (Boston: Little, Brown, 1982), plus his annual magazine *ESOP* 13 (1985), 134, for an article on Chinese Mongolians in Canada. Also see Frank Joseph, *Lost Pyramids of Rock Lake* (Lakeville, Minn.: Galde Press, 1992).

12. Jamie Sams and David Carson, *Medicine Cards: The Discovery of Power through the Ways of Animals* (New York: St. Martin's Press, 1999).

13. Gallegos, *Animals of the Four Windows*, 85.

14. Available from JoAnn and David Health Products, 1698 Marguerite Ave., Corona Del Mar, CA 92625; 800-700-5402.

15. *Amicus Journal*, from the Natural Resources Defense Council (winter 2000): 28.

16. Gail Faith Edwards, *Opening Our Wild Hearts to the Healing Herbs* (Woodstock, N.Y.: Ash Tree Publishing, 2000).

17. Rosemary Gladstar, Sage Mountain Herbs, P.O. Box 420, East Barre, VT 05649.

18. Pam Montgomery, 1525 Danby Mountain Road, Danby, VT 05739.

19. One such book is *Celtic Tree Mysteries: Secrets of the Ogham*, by Stephen Blamires (St. Paul, Minn.: Llewellyn Publications, 1997). A cross-cultural perspective is given in *Man, Myth, and Magic*, vol. 19, edited by Marshall Cavendish and Bryan Innes (New York: Marshall Cavendish, 1997), 2654.

20. Eliot Cowan, *Plant Spirit Medicine* (Newburg, Oreg.: Swan Raven, 1995).

21. Ralph Metzner, Ph.D., "Ayahuasca and the Greening of Human Consciousness," *Shaman's Drum*, no. 53 (fall 1999): 18, from Metzner's book *Ayahuasca: Hallucinogens, Consciousness, and the Spirit of Nature* (New York: Thunder's Mouth Press, 1999).

22. Ibid., 26–27.

23. The Bioneers can be contacted at 877-BIONEERS, www.bioneers.org, or E-mail to chisf@bioneers.org.

24. David Wagoner, quoted in the introduction of David Whyte's *House of Belonging* (Langely, Wash.: Many Rivers Press, 1997). From David Wagoner, *Who Shall Be The Sun?* (Bloomington: Indiana University Press, 1978), 5.

CHAPTER 13: HONORING EARTH AND SPIRIT

1. T. C. McLuhan, *Touch the Earth* (New York: Outerbridge and Dienstfrey, 1972), 136.

2. Cindy Watlington, *Crystal Deva Cards* (Boulder, Colo.: Inner Quest Publishing, 1996), 22–23.

3. For an exercise similar to this one, plus many other spiritual exercises, see Josie RavenWing's book *The Return of Spirit* (Deerfield Beach, Fla.: Health Communications, 1996).

4. *The Four Seasons: Japanese Haiku* (Mount Vernon, N.Y.: Peter Pauper Press, 1958).

5. Neva Howell, from her newsletter *Moon Lodge Visions*, 1997 (A Place of the Heart Spiritual Center, 255 Terry Creek Lane, Pioneer, TN 37847), 3, italics added.

6. Olof Alexandersson, *Living Water*, 6th ed. (Dublin, Ireland: Gill and Macmillan, 1990).

7. For information on Steiner's principles, contact Rudolf Steiner College, 9200 Fair Oaks Blvd., Fair Oaks, CA 95628.

8. For a full recounting of this experience, read my spiritual autobiography, *Buffalo Woman Comes Singing* (New York: Ballantine Books, 1991).

9. Eagle Song camps were spiritual wilderness camps that I held in a

sacred valley in Montana. Experiences from these camps and information about them are also contained in *Buffalo Woman Comes Singing*.

10. I recorded both these lovely songs on the cassette *Visions Speaking* (see Appendix A, "Resources") and will soon include them in a special collection on CD.

11. You might be interested in Brad Blanton's *Radical Honesty: How to Transform Your Life by Telling the Truth* (New York: Dell, 1996).

12. For inspiring help with these celebrations, see Cait Johnson and Maura D. Shaw, *Celebrating the Great Mother* (Rochester, Vt.: Destiny Books, 1995), and Starhawk, Diane Baker, and Anne Hill, *Circle Round: Raising Children in Goddess Traditions* (New York: Bantam Books, 1998).

13. Gregg Braden, *Awakening to Zero Point* (Bellevue, Wash.: Radio Bookstore Press, 1997).

CHAPTER 14: LIGHT IN THE DARKNESS

1. T. C. McLuhan, *Touch the Earth* (New York: Outerbridge and Dienstfrey, 1972), 18.

2. For full information on the ritual, see Vasant V. Paranjpe, *Light towards Divine Path* (Randallstown, Md.: Agnihotra Press, 1976).

3. Mary Oliver, "When Death Comes," *New and Selected Poems* (Boston: Beacon Press, 1992), 10–11.

4. This song can be found on my cassette *A Gift of Song* (see Appendix A, "Resources").

5. Tony Stubbs, *An Ascension Handbook* (Livermore, Calif.: Oughten House Publications, 1996), 87–88.

6. Adapted version of the Great Invocation. Lucis Trust, 2000.

7. From John O'Donohue's 1996 set of audiocassettes *Anam Cara: Wisdom from the Celtic World*, Sounds True Productions (800-333-9185).

8. William Wordsworth, "Lines Written a Few Miles above Tintern Abbey, on Revisiting the Banks of the Wye during a Tour. July 13, 1798."

9. David Whyte, "The Wall of Grief," *Where Many Rivers Meet* (Langely, Wash.: Many Rivers Press, 1996), 35.

10. Hal and Sidra Stone, *Voice Dialogue* (Delos, Inc., P.O. Box 605, Albion, Calif., 95410, 707-937-2424, www.delos-inc.com).

11. Rachel Naomi Remen, M.D., *Kitchen Table Wisdom: Stories That Heal* (New York: Riverhead Books, 1996), 38.

12. Glenda Green, *Love without End: Jesus Speaks* . . . (Fort Worth, Tex.: Heartwings Publishing, 1999), 145–46.

CHAPTER 15: SEEDING THE DREAM

1. Tashira Tachi-ren, *What Is Lightbody?* (Livermore, Calif.: Oughten House Publications, 1995), 38–70.

2. Flower of Life Research, 1618 E. Bell Rd., #106, Phoenix, AZ 85022, 602-996-0900 or merkaba@floweroflife.org.

3. Jack Schwarz, *Human Energy Systems* (New York: E. P. Dutton, 1980), 23–24.

4. Ibid.

5. Shakura Rei, *The Spiritual Warrior: An Interdimensional Technique Manual* (Fairfield, Iowa: Sunstar Publishing, 1997), 57–63.

6. Also see "Twelve Rays of the Great Bow," in *Last Cry*, by Robert Ghost Wolf (Spokane, Wash.: Mistyc House Publishing, 1994), 96–99.

7. Rei, *Spiritual Warrior*, 61, 97.

8. David and Bruce McArthur, *The Intelligent Heart* (Virginia Beach, Va.: A.R.E. Press, 1997), 172–73.

9. For consultations on divine design in your home, business, or development, contact Essential Harmony Feng Shui through my office, either by phone (406-883-4686) or E-mail (brooke@MedicineEagle.com).

10. Tony Stubbs, *An Ascension Handbook* (Livermore, Calif.: Oughten House Publications, 1996), 77.

11. See Barbara Sher's books, including *Wishcraft*, written with Annie Gottlieb (New York: Ballantine, 1986), and *I Could Do Anything, If I Only Knew What It Was*, written with Barbara Smith (New York: Bantam Doubleday Dell, 1995).

12. Linda Heron Wind, *Spiraling into the Center* (Rochester, N.Y.:

Heron Press, 2000), 13. Contact Heron Wind (716-924-5620) or LH Wind@aol.com.

CHAPTER 16: LIFTING OUR WINGS

1. Norma Milanovich and Shirley McCune, *The Light Shall Set You Free* (Albuquerque, N.M.: Athena Publishing, 1996), 14.

2. A. W. Wood, "Health Effects of Electric and Magnetic Fields," *Australasian Physical Engineering and Sciences in Medicine* 16, no. 1 (March 1993): 1–21.

3. Thomas Perk, M.D., and Margery Hutter Silver, M.D., *Living to 100* (New York: Basic Books, 1999).

4. Ben Bova, *Immortality: How Science Is Extending Your Life Span and Changing the World* (New York: Avon Books, 2000).

5. Dr. Larry Dossey (author of *Space, Time, and Medicine* and *Healing Words*), "The Power of Healing Prayer," interview by Russell E. DiCarlo, *The Quest,* spring 1999, 78–79.

6. See Riane Eisler, *The Chalice and the Blade* (San Francisco: Harper-SanFrancisco, 1988).

7. Paul's company is Fungi Perfecti. You can find more information by visiting its Web site at www.fungi.com or E-mailing mycomedia@aol.com.

8. Janine Benyus, *Biomimicry: Innovation Inspired by Nature* (New York: Morrow, 1997).

9. She and other Bioneers are profiled in Kenny Ausubel's book *Restoring the Earth: Visionary Solutions from the Bioneers* (Tiburon, Calif.: H. J. Kramer, 1997).

10. Forty studies of what is called the Maharishi Effect are available at www.kosovopeace.org or through Maharishi University of Management, Fairfield, Iowa 52557 (www.mum.edu).

11. For further information, contact AllLife, L.L.C., P.O. Box 1958, Payson, AZ 85547-1958 (520-474-0314), or visit the Flower of Life Research Web site at www.floweroflife.org.

12. You can read the interview on the Internet at www.drunvalo.net/livingwater.html.

13. A weird twist of events is that some group is now making what it claims to be a similar water for humans, charging a huge price for it, and adding something that makes it very addictive. I wouldn't recommend drinking anything like this until you know exactly what is in it.

14. Milanovich and McCune, *Light Shall Set You Free*, 11.

15. Brooke Medicine Eagle, *Buffalo Woman Comes Singing* (New York: Ballantine Books, 1991).

16. He has written a book to address this issue: *Evolution's End* (New York: Harper and Row, 1993).

17. For information on the organization's books and seminars, contact HeartMath L.L.C., 14700 West Park Ave., Boulder Creek, CA 95006 (831-338-8700) or visit its Web site at www.heartmath.com.

18. Glenda Green, *Love without End: Jesus Speaks . . .* (Fort Worth, Tex.: Heartwings Publishing, 1999), 94.

19. "Children of the New Dream," *Wolf Report* 1, no. 4 (autumn 1999): 9, 22. This article can be found by going to the www.wolf report.com Web site and clicking the "Archives" link or by calling 877-267-5973 (toll-free).

20. See *Create Your Own Healing Miracle: The Dr. Richard Schulze Story*, a 1997 video produced by Dr. Schulze's School of Natural Healing. It can be obtained by writing to Natural Healing Publications, P.O. Box 3628, Santa Monica, CA 90408, or calling 877-832-2463 (toll-free).

21. John Randolph Price, *The Super Beings* (Austin, Tex.: Quartus Foundation, 1981), 118.

22. Rachel Naomi Remen, M.D., *Kitchen Table Wisdom: Stories That Heal* (New York: Riverhead Books, 1996), 284.

23. As practiced by Norma Gentile, Attunement is a hands-off process of energy and sound healing that clears and invigorates the aura and thus supports the physical body.

24. See the "Earth Mages Unlimited" section of my Web site by going to www.MedicineEagle.com and clicking the "Wakantia" link.

25. Green, *Love without End*, 105, 120.

26. Leonard Orr, *Physical Immortality and Transfiguration* (Sierraville, Calif.: Inspiration University Press, 1986), 30. This material and more is now out in a newer version: Leonard Orr and Kathy Glass, *Breaking the Death Habit* (Berkeley, Calif.: North Atlantic Books, 1998).

27. Green, *Love without End*, 102.

28. Herb Bowie, *Why Die? A Beginner's Guide to Living Forever* (Scottsdale, Ariz.: PowerSurge Publishing, 1998).

29. See note 4 for this chapter.

30. Joshua David Stone, *The Complete Ascension Manual* (Santa Monica, Calif.: Light Technology Books, 1996).

31. Green, *Love without End*, 246.

32. There are many books about prosperity these days, but I like Arnold M. Patent's *You Can Have It All* (Piermont, N.Y.: Money Master Publishing, 1987).

33. L. Taylor Hansen, *He Walked the Americas* (Amherst, Wis.: Amherst Press, 1963), 171–72.

34. Milanovich and McCune, *Light Shall Set You Free*, 25.

CHAPTER 17: TOGETHER, WE FLY

1. Omer C. Stewart, *Peyote Religion* (Norman: University of Oklahoma Press, 1987), xiii.

2. *Métis* (pronounced "may-TEE") comes from the French word for "half "—meaning mixed-blood, half-breed, rainbow person.

3. Ken Carey, *Return of the Bird Tribes* (New York: HarperCollins, 1988), 60.

4. Contact Josie RavenWing about trips to Brazil to witness and learn about this kind of healing. She can be reached at 7990 N.W. 37th Street, Ankeny, Iowa 50021 or JRavenWing@aol.com.

5. The words *whole, health, heal,* and *holy* come from the same Latin root and have the same sense of the inclusion of All.

6. Rachel Naomi Remen, M.D., *Kitchen Table Wisdom: Stories That Heal* (New York: Riverhead Books, 1996), 149.

7. Ibid., 220.

8. From a manuscript by Dawn Baumann Brunke, "Remembering All That Is: Human-Animal Awakenings."

9. Remen, *Kitchen Table Wisdom*, 35.

10. A set of cassette tapes available from Sounds True, Boulder, Colo. (800-333-9185).

11. Ken Carey, *Return of the Bird Tribes*, 61–62.

12. To understand these important issues more fully, see Loren Cruden, *Coyote's Council Fire: Contemporary Shamans on Race, Gender, and Community* (Rochester, Vt.: Destiny Books, 1995), and Stephen Buhner's magnificent work *One Spirit, Many Peoples* (Niwot, Colo.: Roberts Rinehart Publishers, 1997).

13. See Pam Montgomery's book, *Partner Earth* (Rochester, Vt.: Destiny Books, 1997) for a complete look at partnering with Spirit and Earth.

14. James Redfield, *The Celestine Prophecy* (Hoover, Ala.: Satori Publishing, 1993) and *The Tenth Insight* (New York: Warner Books, 1996).

15. Barbara Marx Hubbard is a noted visionary, author, futurist, speaker, and social innovator/architect. See her interview by Christine Rock, "Conscious Evolution: Awakening the Power of Our Social Potential": www.newvisionsmagazine.com/hubbard599.htm and her work at www.peaceroom.com.

16. See Appendix A, "Resources."

17. Norma Milanovich and Shirley McCune, *The Light Shall Set You Free* (Albuquerque, N.M.: Athena Publishing, 1996), 10.

CHAPTER 18: COME TO THE CIRCLE OF POWER

1. "Dance Awake the Dream" was the name I gave to our Harmonic Convergence gathering in 1987.

2. As discussed in Chapter 12, Malidoma and Sobonfu Somé remind us, through their African tradition, that *all* our ancestors actually wish to help in this way, and it serves us well to call upon them.

CHAPTER 19: FLOWERSONG

1. For information on Waldorf schools, contact Rudolf Steiner College, 9200 Fair Oaks Blvd., Fair Oaks, CA 95628 (916-961-8727).

2. For more information, contact Business Leaders for Sensible Priorities, 1090 Vermont Ave. NW, Suite 1200, Washington, D.C. 20005 (202-216-1893), or visit the organization's Web sites at www.business leaders.org and www.moveourmoney.org. I urge everyone to get information from this group and share it with others.

3. From James Buchanan's forthcoming novel *Riding the Dragon's Tail*, bk. 1, *Talisman.*

4. Message from Archangel Michael, through Ronna Herman. See her Web site at www.spiritweb.org/Spirit/ronna-herman.html.

5. *E* = outward, *lite* = light; therefore, "those who shine their light outward."

6. Ken Carey, *Return of the Bird Tribes* (New York: HarperCollins, 1988), 56–57.

CHRONOLOGICAL BIBLIOGRAPHY

WORKS BY BROOKE MEDICINE EAGLE

1979. "The Quest for Vision." In *Shamanic Voices: A Survey of Visionary Narratives*, edited by Joan Halifax, 86–92. New York: Dutton.

1980. "The Rainbow Bridge." *Many Smokes* 14, no. 1 (spring/summer): 3.

1983. "The Grandmothers." *Many Smokes* 17, no. 3: 14-1. Elders' Issue.

1985. "The Lineage of the Sun." *American Theosophist* (fall): 350–53.

1985. "Opening the Wings of Spirit." *Shaman's Drum*, no. 1 (summer): 11–12.

1986. "Sacred Time, Sacred Way." *Shaman's Drum*, no. 5 (summer): 4–7.

1986. "Women's Moontime: A Call to Power." *Shaman's Drum*, no. 4 (spring): 2. Women in Shamanism Issue.

1987. "Becoming the Healed Healer: Models for a New Time." *Self Discovery: Arizona Magazine for Mind, Body and Spirit* (fall): 5–6. Premier Edition.

1987. "The Lineage of the Sun." In *Shamanism*, compiled by Shirley Nicholson, 280–85. Wheaton, Ill.: Theosophical Publishing House, Quest Books.

1987. "Singing Buffalo Woman's Song." *Wildfire Magazine* 2, nos. 3–4: 98–99.

1987. "The Way of Healing." In *Shape Shifters: Shaman Women in Contemporary Society*, edited by Michele Jamal, 159–70. London: Arkana Publishing.

1988. "Grandmother Lodge." In *Red Flower: Rethinking Menstruation*, edited by Dena Taylor, 101–3. Freedom, Calif.: Crossing Press.

1988. "The Grandmother Lodge: Postmenopausal Power." *Wildfire Magazine* 3, no. 4 (summer): 19.

1988. "Singing Buffalo Woman's Song: Eulogy for a Nature Activist." *Woman of Power,* no. 9 (spring): 58–59. Nature Issue.

1988. "To Paint Ourselves Red." In *Shaman's Path: Healing, Personal Growth, and Empowerment,* edited by Gary Doore, 209–16. Boston: Shambhala Publications.

1989. "Brooke Medicine Eagle." In *Childlessness Transformed: Stories of Alternative Parenting,* edited by Jane English, 25–38. Mount Shasta: Earth Heart.

1989. "The Circle of Healing." In *Healers on Healing,* edited by Richard Carlson and Benjamin Shield, 58–62. Los Angeles: Tarcher.

1989. "Eagle Song Camps, with Brooke Medicine Eagle." *Wildfire Magazine* 4, no. 1 (winter): 37.

1989. "Grandmother Lodge," "Sacred Time, Sacred Way," and "Women's Moontime: A Call to Power." *Health Consciousness* (October): 18–23.

1990. "Open to the Great Mystery." In *For the Love of God: New Writings by Spiritual and Psychological Leaders,* edited by Benjamin Shield and Richard Carlson, 73–77. Novato: New World Library.

1991. *Buffalo Woman Comes Singing.* New York: Ballantine Books.

1991. "Grandmother Lodge." In *Women of the 14th Moon: Writings on Menopause,* edited by Dena Taylor and Amber Coverdale Sumrall, 260–62. Freedom, Calif.: Crossing Press.

1991. "The Rainbow Bridge." In *Sisters of the Earth: Women's Prose and Poetry about Nature,* edited by Lorraine Anderson, 330–35. New York: Random House, Vintage Books.

1991. "Dancing the Dream Awake." In *The Ceremonial Circle: Practice, Ritual and Renewal for Personal and Community Healing,* edited by Sedonia Cahill and Joshua Halpern, 125–32. London: Mandala.

1992. "The Legend of the Rainbow Warriors." In *Ancient Voices, Current Affairs: The Legend of the Rainbow Warriors,* by Steve McFadden, 7–12. Santa Fe, N.M.: Bear and Company.

1992. "Nature and Spirituality: Time of the New Dawning." In *The Spiral Path,* edited by Theresa King O'Brien, 56–75. St. Paul: Yes Intl. Publishers.

1992. "On My Way to the Sacred Mountain" (excerpted from *Buffalo Woman Comes Singing*). *Wildfire Magazine* 6, no. 1: 40–47.

1992. "The Quickest Zipper on the Reservation." *Shaman's Drum*, no. 26 (winter): 21–25.

1992. "The Rainbow Bridge." *Earth Ethics* 3, no. 3 (spring): 9–10.

1992. "Toning the Belly." In *As Above, So Below: Paths to Spiritual Renewal in Daily Life*, edited by Ronald S. Miller, 83–84. Los Angeles: Tarcher.

1993. "Drumming the Heartbeat" (excerpted from *Buffalo Woman Comes Singing*). *Tantra*, no. 6: 58–59.

1993. "Giving Back the Gifts of Earth." In *Voices on the Threshold of Tomorrow*, edited by George Feuerstein and Trisha Feuerstein, 283–84. Wheaton, Ill.: Quest Books.

1994. "Brooke Medicine Eagle's Vision." In *Through the Eye of the Feather*, edited by Gail Tuchman, 26–36. Layton, Utah: Gibbs Smith.

1994. "Dreamtime—Moontime: On the Visionary Functions of Dreaming." *Dream Network* 13, no. 2: 12–13.

1994. "Paying Attention." In *The Little Book of Native American Wisdom*, by Steve McFadden, 21. Rockport, Mass.: Element.

1994. "Sacred Ecology: On Walking the Good Road and Not Taking the Car." *Wolf Lodge Journal* 1, no. 1: 7–9.

1994. "Singing in the Time of the Nine-Pointed Star." *Encore* 2, no. 4: 22–23.

1995. "Brooke Medicine Eagle Joins the Montana Woman Show." *Montana Woman*, 22d ed. (May): 1, 3.

1995. "Passing the Talking Stick." In *Coyote's Council Fire: Contemporary Shamans on Race, Gender, and Community*, edited by Loren Cruden, 49–51. Rochester, Vt.: Inner Traditions International.

1995. "The White Buffalo's Message: Recognize the Circle of Life." *Gaea* 3, no. 1 (spring): 3–4.

1997. "The Path of Sacred Ecology." *Sacred Hoop*, no. 16 (spring): 13–16.

1997. "The Rainbow Bridge." In *Storming Heaven's Gate: An Anthology of Spiritual Writings by Women*, edited by Amber Coverdale Sumrall and Patrice Vecchione, 8–13. New York: Plume.

1997. Chapter 2. In *When the Drummers Were Women: A Spiritual History of Rhythm*, by Layne Redmond, 17. New York: Crown.

1997. In *The Right Side of Forty: Celebrating Timeless Women*, edited by Patricia

Martin, photographs by Leif Zurmuhlen. Emeryville, Calif.: Conari Press.

1998. In *Human Behavior and the Social Environment: Shifting Paradigms in Essential Knowledge for Social Work Practice*, by Joe M. Schriver, 353–63. Needham Heights, Mass.: Allyn and Bacon.

1998. In *Fabric of the Future: Women Visionaries of Today Illuminate the Path to Tomorrow*, edited by M. J. Ryan, 342. Berkeley, Calif.: Conari Press.

1999. In *Women of Courage: The Courage to Challenge*, edited by Katherine Martin, 241. Novato, Calif.: New World Library.

2000. *Voices of Truth: Conversations with Scientists, Thinkers, and Healers*, edited by Nina L. Diamond, 233–55. Twin Lakes, Wisc.: Lotus Press.

WORKS ABOUT BROOKE MEDICINE EAGLE

1978. "Brooke Medicine Eagle: Messenger of the Heart," by Karen Meadows. *Colorado Daily* 27, no. 42 (November 3): 1, 3.

1979. "Changing the World through the Body: Brooke Medicine Eagle's Aim," by Valerie Moses. *Fort Collins Coloradoan, Sunday Focus* (January 21): 1.

1979. "Holistic Indian Healer," by Greg Luft. *Fort Collins Journal* 88, no. 90 (January 25): 1.

1979. "Journey to Feathered Pipe Ranch," by Alex Jack. *East West Journal* (January): 42–59. (*55).

1981. "Visions of the Rainbow Woman: Brooke Medicine Eagle's Healing Power," by Anne Fawcett. *East West Journal* 11, no. 11 (November): 31–37. Cover article.

1982. "Montana Medicine Woman," by Anne Fawcett. *East West Journal* (January): 24–33.

1983. "Highlights," by Anne Fawcett. *New Age Journal* (May): 17.

1986. "Dancing toward the Light," by Jeff Kaikara. *Wind Circle, An Herbal Monthly* 1, no. 8 (June): 1, 7–8.

1987. "The Goddess Interviews," by Lisa Gentz. *L.A. Resources for Healing, Growth and Transformation* (summer): 3, 36, 38.

1987. "New Age: Inner Power Holds Key to New Era," by Don Baty. *Great Falls Tribune: Montana Parade* (November 15): 1–2.

1988. "Listening to the Great Voices," by Morning Star. *Wildfire Magazine* 4, no. 1: 32–36.

1988. "Native Arts and Spirituality," by Jane Fritz. *Idaho Arts Journal* 5, no. 3 (spring): 12.

1991. "Brooke Medicine Eagle: Intertribal Indian Metis," by Sheila Belanger. *(Seattle) New Times* (April): 15.

1996. "What Is a Shaman?" by Cathy Richards. *Catalist* (November): 35–36.

1999. "The Plains Peoples," by Suzanne Harding, Ph.D. *Alternative Complementary Therapies* (August): 230–37.

INDEX

INDEX